DEDICATION.

TO THE COLONISTS OF AUSTRALIA AND NFW ZEALAND.

GENTLEMEN:

IN dedicating to you my "Reminiscences" I feel called upon to offer the following explanation:

From the year 1843 to 1853, as is well known to many of our Australian community, I was earnestly engaged in what Lord Bacon describes as "the heroic work of colonization," and many of my happiest days were spent in friendly intercourse with those who have made Australia and New Zealand the lands of their adoption, either for themselves or for members of their families, and with some of whom I still keep up a warm friendship and an interesting correspondence.

One very hot day last summer, while seeking shade under a tree in Oatlands Park, Surrey, an esteemed friend came to me with a book in his hand.

He is an Englishman, with strong, very strong national predilections, always ready for a tilting-match with me or any other Scotchman who may venture to maintain that

"haggis" and oatmeal "parritch" are preferable to roast beef and plum-pudding. But on this occasion, an entirely exceptional one, he was complimentary to my nation, and addressing my wife, who is English, asked her "if she had ever read Dean Ramsay's Reminiscences of Scottish Life and Character?" I will not undertake to say what would have been her answer, had I been absent. However, her reply was simply that she had not read the work. "Then, Madam, you will find it most entertaining. Here it is: I have just finished its perusal for the third time. Desire your husband to read some of it daily to you, and I vouch for it making you laugh as heartily as I have done. Moreover, you will discover that it possesses wonderful sedative and soothing qualities, which, while being administered, will allay those neuralgic pains from which you and myself suffer so severely."

Another friend—one of the most estimable men I ever knew throughout a period of forty years, nearly twenty of which we sat together as co-directors at the London Board of a wealthy and successful Scotch Insurance Company—was the late Mr. Isaac Sewell of Gresham House, Old Broad Street, and Wanstead, Essex, a man whose humor and point in relating an anecdote, or in giving effect to an amusing speech, at all times charmed our social circle. He often said to me: "You cannot only relate your Scotch anecdotes in the vernacular, but be a glossary at the same time to your English hearers; why not then sketch out some of your Anglo-Scotch reminiscences, as *you* can say 'Shibboleth' on both banks of the Jordan?" Be that as it may, although born near the Thames, in the county of Surrey, I spent my earliest years near the Cree, in the county of Wigton. There was no man whose advice I more frequently sought and followed than Mr. Sewell's; still, I must here observe that until I read the Very Reverend Dean's work I had as much intention of making a collection of my own reminiscences, much less of publishing them, as I have at present of commencing the study of Arabic. My *olla podrida* is composed of anecdotes which I have heard, among others from my late father, who came to London when William IV. was a "jolly luff" in the Royal Navy, and when Rodney had but just achieved his memorable victory in the West Indies over the French fleet commanded by Comte de Grasse. He recollected Erskine a midshipman, and knew him as Lord Chancellor. He had witnessed the national incense rise over Rodney, Howe, St. Vincent, Hotham, Bridport, and Duncan, and had witnessed the tomb close over Nelson in St. Paul's. He had the honor of being known to Mr. Pitt, with whom he was in frequent personal intercourse from 1790 until the death of that illustrious statesman in 1806; and I may here add that until my father's death in 1844, he possessed one of the most retentive and vigorous memories I almost ever met with. From this and other sources, and from the fact that I have resided in London for upward of forty years, I have been able to throw together a miscellaneous collection of anecdotes which I hope may entertain the reader.

I have given my authorities, where necessary; and I hope that I may be considered entitled to say, with reference to them, "nothing extenuate, nor set down aught in malice." My aim has been to keep closely before me the advice of the poet:

"A story to please should at least be true,
Be *à propos*, concise and new;
Whene'er it differs from these rules,
The wise will sleep, and leave applause to fools."

I have now only to express a sanguine hope that the advice of Mr. Pitt to his private secretary given in my first anecdote, which Earl Stanhope did me the honor to include in his "Pittiana," may be followed by my readers. "Never lose your temper, if possible, at any time, and NEVER during the hours of business," or—while perusing the anecdotes and reminiscences of, Gentlemen,

Your Faithful Servant,

MARK BOYD.

OATLANDS, WALTON ON THAMES, SURREY,
January, 1871.

THE

REMINISCENCES OF FIFTY YEARS.

---

1. *Mr. Pitt and his Private Secretary.*

THE following circumstance was told me by the late Mr. Christmas, who for many years held an important official situation in the Bank of England. He was, I believe, in early life a clerk in the Treasury, or one of the government offices, and for some time acted for Mr. Pitt as his confidential clerk, or temporary private secretary. Christmas was one of the most obliging men I ever knew, and, from the position he occupied, was constantly exposed to interruptions, yet I never saw his temper the least ruffled. One day I found him more than usually engaged, having a mass of accounts to prepare for one of the law courts: still his equanimity was unruffled, and I could not resist the opportunity of asking the old gentleman to give me the secret. "Well, Mr. Boyd, you shall know it. Mr. Pitt gave it to me:—Not to lose my temper, if possible, at any time, and NEVER during the hours of business. My labors here (the Bank of England) commence at nine and end at three; and, acting on the advice of the illustrious statesman, I never lose my temper during these hours."

He also related to me an instance which came under his own observation of Mr. Pitt's extraordinary powers of mental and physical endurance. Mr. Pitt had been immersed all day in intricate accounts with Mr. Christmas (I assume preparing for the conflict of a War Budget), when, looking at the hour, he said, "I must now go to the House, but shall return as early as I can, although I fear we shall have a late sitting." It proved so, as he did not rejoin his secretary until six in the morning. He had something kind to say to Christmas for still keeping at his work, adding, "I must now have a wash," and going to the end of the room, threw off his coat and neckcloth, and applied a wet towel to his head and face.

When this improvised ablution was over, he declared to his *fidus Achates* that he was quite fresh and ready for business, and for four hours he was hard at work in going through the accounts which Mr. Christmas had prepared during the night.

Although Mr. Pitt rarely lost his temper, it is said that on one occasion he was seriously angry with Sheridan, whom he told to his face that he would be much better occupied at home correcting his plays. "Probably I should," said Richard Brinsley, "and the first I shall endeavor to correct will be the 'Angry Schoolboy.'"

2. *The Duke of Wellington at the Highland Society.*

It used to be said by the members of the Highland Society of London, some twenty-five years ago, especially by those who knew him in private life, that the Duke had never been seen to laugh so heartily as at one of our meetings. If my memory serves me, the late Duke of Cambridge was in the chair, supported on the right by the Duke of Wellington, next to whom sat the head of his clan, General Sir Fitzroy Maclean. His royal highness called for a toast to be drunk with Highland honors, but the Duke always shunned that portion of a Scotchman's toast. Sir Fitzroy should have followed the Duke's example, for he was the same age as his grace, if not his senior by one or two years. To my English friends who have not witnessed Highland honors, I must explain, that whenever the proposer of the toast has concluded his speech, adding Highland honors, every one, unless incapacitated from age, is expected to mount his chair, with his glass in hand—a bumper—and put his right foot on the table, supporting himself on his left, which is on the chair. The first round of cheers had been given, when Sir Fitzroy's foot slipped from the edge of the table, and the gallant old Highland chieftain fell at full length across it. As a natural consequence, all decanters, glasses, fruit-dishes, fruit-plates, were smashed; but this was not all, for in his struggle to recover himself he swept the table with his arms to the right and left, so that the area of damage was very extensive. Much anxiety was at first felt for the worthy old veteran, but fortunately he escaped without injury.

The Duke laughed most heartily, and during the rest of the evening he more than once turned round to Sir Fitzroy and returned to the subject. "Ah, Maclean," said the Duke, "I have been content with English honors, and I should advise you henceforth to dispense with Scotch ones, after dinner at least! For myself," said the Duke, "I always thought Scotch honors after a good dinner were more honored in the breach than in the observance."

3. *The Last Time I saw the Duke.*

One day in September, 1852, I was inside an omnibus in the Haymarket, going to Piccadilly, Pall Mall being closed at the time. There was a stoppage, but never were passengers in a public conveyance less inclined to move on. We were blocked up; so was the Duke of Wellington, who was riding behind us. His horse's head was at the door of our omnibus, and there, for more than five minutes, did we study the universally familiar features of the great man. He was looking remarkably well. Two ladies in the cmnibus, when told that the Duke was there, congratulated themselves, on their first visit to London, in being so fortunate as to see the long observed of all the wide world's observers. His dress was a blue surtout, white waistcoat and trousers. We all agreed that, from his appearance, he had several years to live.

How erroneous the anticipation! Within a week from that day, a sorrowing empire heard the news of the Duke's sudden death at Walmer.

This anecdote I related at the time to a Liverpool gentleman, who inserted it in one of the local papers.

4. *The Duke's Penetration of Character.*

When any officer of rank joined the Duke in the Peninsula, on his arrival from England he was asked to dine at headquarters, and sat at the Duke's right hand. On such occasions military subjects were dispensed with; but the Duke was at the same time sifting the qualities of the newcomer through the common topics of the day. One unhappy wight, however, a major-general, a rollicking, free-and-easy son of Mars, launched into military matters with the Duke, in preference to continuing the chit-chat about England. The Duke parried his remarks for some time; but as he persevered, his grace so far gratified him as to ask his opinion. The officer expressed himself as deeply anxious at the critical position in which the army then was. The Duke allowed him to proceed. "If," said the enlightened major-general (the Duke requesting him to explain his movements on the tablecloth), "the French moved there, and then did this, and then did that, which they would inevitably try, what would your grace do?" "*Give them the most infernal thrashing they have had for some time,*" replied the Duke; whereupon the electrified commentator on hypothetical disasters said—nothing. The above anecdote was told me by General Sir John Waters, K. C. B.

5. *The Duke teaching a Colleague Manners.*

The Duke's reception of the Elder Brethren of the Trinity House was usually most gracious; still there was once an exception. Standing with his back to the fireplace, he was receiving the members as they came up to make their bow, and shaking hands with each. But one member for a moment forgetting the august personage he was approaching, bustled up to the hero of a hundred fights, and extending his hand, at the same time enunciating, "How do, Duke?" to the fearful dismay of the spectators. The Duke drew himself up, and placing his hands behind his back, made a solemn bow to his free-and-easy Brother. At the moment, Admiral Sir T. Byam Martin approached, and knowing his grace better than the Brother who had preceded him, received a most hearty shake of the hand. I am indebted to Captain William Pixley, an Elder Brother of the Trinity House, for this anecdote.

6. *The Duke's Last Note.*

It is believed at the Trinity House that the last note or letter written by the Duke was addressed to their Board the day before his death; and the autograph of the Great Master is carefully preserved in the archives of the Corporation.

It appears that an election of an Elder Brother in succession to the late Deputy-Master, Sir John Pelly, was to have taken place at the end of the week in which the Duke died; and a letter was addressed to his grace at Walmer Castle on the subject. He had misconceived the nature of the election, and wrote to say that, as he could not be in town for a few weeks, he would like the matter to stand over until his return. In consequence of this communication, Captain Shepherd, an East India Director, and an Elder Brother of the Trinity House, proceeded on the Monday to Walmer, hoping to explain the case to the Duke; but the Duke had gone to Dover, and Captain Shepherd was obliged to return to London without seeing him. Next day the Duke had gone to that bourn from which no traveller returns.

Captain Pixley also related to me the foregoing incident.

7. *So like the Duke.*

Every trait of the late Duke's personal character possesses a special interest, and I recollect being much struck with the following anecdote told me by the late Mr. Charles Downes, the army agent, of Warwick Street, Charing Cross, who was requested by the authorities at the Horse Guards to ascertain the truth of the application.

In the winter of 1847, the wife of an industrious blacksmith in Essex resolved to knit a pair of mittens for the Duke of Wellington, as she had to ask his grace a favor, to which the gift was to be introductory.

The mittens were received at Apsley House, and the Duke wore them the same day at the Horse Guards, showing them, with a smile, to his military colleagues there, and desiring that the honest dame's request might be immediately attended to. She stated that her husband had been one of his grace's soldiers, and that he had had the misfortune of losing his Waterloo medal, which he had always worn on the anniversary of his marriage. She stated that this anniversary was again approaching, and that she would ever feel deeply grateful if the Duke would allow another medal to be issued, as the loss had seriously affected her husband's spirits. She would only further trespass on his grace so far as to solicit that the medal should be sent to her privately, as she wrote without her husband's knowledge, and wished to give her partner an agreeable surprise on the arrival of the wedding-day.

This was speedily approaching. The Duke had ordered that her request should be attended to, but the poor wife had received no medal. She accordingly ventured to address a second letter to the Duke: this was soon known at the Horse Guards. His grace arrived there one morning in a towering passion, dashed the letter down on the table, and demanded to know why his orders had been neglected. The matter had been overlooked. An instant reference was made to a gentleman in Essex, who inquired if the claim was a correct one; this proving to be the case, the medal was dispatched without delay, but whether in time for the nuptial day is uncertain. This story I told some years ago in a letter to the editor of the *Gentleman's Magazine.*

8. *What the Duke could go through in a Single Day* (1852).

The last anniversary meeting of the Elder Brethren of the Trinity House before the Duke's death was an extremely wet day, still it did not prevent the illustrious Master joining his colleagues at Tower Hill, and accompanying them to Deptford as usual. There, as it continued to rain heavily, a carriage had been provided to convey his grace to the Trinity Almshouses, instead of being exposed to the inclemency of the weather by heading, as he had done for many years past, the walking procession. But the Deputy-Master could not persuade his grace to enter the carriage. "I prefer walking," said the Duke; and accordingly he marched at the head of the Brethren, first taking out of his pocket a mackintosh cape, which he threw over his shoulders, and during his progress to the Almshouses, which occupied nearly an hour, he was amused with the remarks of the crowd, and to many of the young folks he gave biscuits, with which his pockets must have been pretty well filled before starting.

At the Almshouses each of the Brethren is presented with a bouquet; and it was always a struggle among the girls to get that of the Duke, as the lucky recipient was sure of very soon getting a husband. Such, at all events, was the belief among the fair residents of Deptford some quarter of a century ago.

The inspection of the Almshouses being over, all eyes were directed to the Duke and his bouquet. The girls crowded round the great warrior, each in the front rank feeling confident that she was to be the possessor. The Duke enjoyed their suspense very much, but all the time was carefully spying out the prettiest face, when at last seeing a charming girl in the second or third rank, he pushed through the crowd, no easy task, and passed the bouquet into the hands of her whose face had attracted his attention.

The Duke returned with the party to the banquet at the Trinity House, and on sitting down he appeared in excellent spirits, and said to the deputy-chairman, "I have to be at the Queen's juvenile party at Windsor to-night, so you must let me away early." He carried out his wish, and returning to Apsley House to change his dress, he obeyed Her Majesty's commands at Windsor the same evening. For this anecdote, again, I am indebted to Captain Pixley.

9. *The Duke's Hospitality.*

The worthy member of the Trinity Board to whom I was at the time indebted for these memorabilia of the great Duke made me laugh at his description of the perturbation of mind into which he was himself thrown for a brief period. He was residing with his family for a few weeks at Walmer, and was brought to account by one of the Brethren for not having called at the castle to ask for their illustrious Master. He had not forgotten it, but was diffident, or "blate," as we would say in my part of Scotland. However, he at last mustered courage to call and ask how his grace was. The servant, seeing that it was the card of an Elder Brother of the Trinity Board, said, "The Duke will be glad to see you, sir;" but the modest Brother, muttering out an apology, that he would not on that occasion intrude upon his grace, made good his retreat from the battlements of Walmer. Yet he had hardly reached his domicile, when a messenger arrived from the Duke with an invitation to dinner that day. The Duke's invitation was a command: and a very pleasant evening the Elder Brother spent with the conqueror of Napoleon.

10. *The Duke and the Late Lieutenant-General Sir John Waters, K. C. B.*

I was on intimate terms with different members of General Waters's family, and often met that brave man in the domestic circle. Of course on such occasions I had my ears open when the great Duke and the Peninsular War, etc., came on the *tapis.*

The Duke held Waters in high appreciation, and during the Peninsular campaigns, whenever any important information as to the movements of the French was required, the services of the gallant Waters were always called for. It was his report of the movements of the French army that led to the battle of Busaço. It was Waters whom the Duke asked, when on the opposite side of the Douro, if he thought he could cross the river and see how matters stood with the French then in possession of Oporto. No sooner said than done. Waters got a boat, worked himself across the Douro, and returned with an additional boat; and aided by this small beginning, the Duke, at a lower part of the river, got over a sufficient force to drive the French out of the city. On another occasion it was reported at headquarters that Waters was captured, on which the Duke remarked, "Never fear! Waters will rejoin us; I know him too well. Bring on his baggage." The Duke was right; for the same afternoon Waters galloped into camp bareheaded, and resumed his seat at the Duke's dinner-table. His grace laughed heartily, remarking to Waters, "I knew you would manage to be back to dinner."

Another anecdote of Waters will show the esteem in which he was always held by the Duke. At the end of May, 1815, a letter was received at the Horse Guards by one of the officials from his grace at Brussels, in which he said, "Send me Waters;" and in a postscript to the same letter, "Be sure to send me Waters." Accordingly, a messenger was dispatched to the club, to ask for Colonel Waters's address. The only information that could be obtained was, that the colonel was gone fishing somewhere in Wales; but the whereabouts unknown. The messenger was then dispatched to the residence of his brother, the late Mr. Edmund Waters. The same answer, "Fishing in Wales;" but no address was to be had.

Application was next made to his brother-in-law, the late Mr. Bainbridge, the banker; but it brought only a similar reply. Fortunately, the weather in Wales became unpropitious for the disciples of Izaac Walton, and the truant officer wended his way slowly back to London, where he found note upon note awaiting his arrival, desiring him to go down immediately to the Horse Guards. The precise day I have not got, but it was in June, a few days only before Waterloo. The Duke's note was skimmed over by Waters; and that night saw him off to his illustrious chief. He arrived in time to act as deputy adjutant-general of the army, and to sign the returns of the killed and wounded at Waterloo, being himself one of the latter.

These anecdotes in connection with the Duke I sketched out several years ago, and gave them to a friend, who inserted them in the *Liverpool Albion*, and the historian of the Peninsular War, General Sir William Napier, himself a reader of the *Albion*, wrote to the editor confirming from his own personal knowledge those which related to General Waters, and the editor courteously forwarded General Napier's note to me.

11. *Colonel the Hon. Sir Arthur Wellesley.*

I knew the late Captain Prescott, the East India Director, who in early life commanded one of the Honorable East India Company's ships, in which he had Colonel Wellesley as a passenger to Calcutta. The future hero of Assaye and Prescott did not harmonize during the voyage. At its close, and when Captain Prescott and his officers were assembled on deck, to see the brother of the Governor-General leave the ship, Colonel Wellesley walked up to the third-officer and shook him cordially by the hand, saying, "Good-by, Abercrombie, many thanks for your kind attentions," bowed to the ship's company, but took no notice whatever of Captain Prescott, nor of any of the other officers. Prescott used to say, "I never could account for it." I dare say Colonel Wellesley could. Mr. Abercrombie afterward became a merchant in the City, and I have understood that he usually, once a year, called at Apsley House to ask for his grace, and was always cordially received.

12. *Lord Nelson at Antigua.*

His lordship arrived at Antigua, in 1805, with his ships in full pursuit of the combined fleets of France and Spain;

and as he had to take in water and supplies, the island was all excitement.

The late Mr. Robert Coates (better known in London as Mr. Romeo Coates) mentioned to me an interesting circumstance that took place on the occasion, having accompanied his father, with the authorities of the island, on board the flag-ship, to pay their respects to Lord Nelson. Captain Channel (the father of Mr. Justice Channel), who had either retired from the navy or was on half-pay, was one of the visitors to the "Victory." It was he who placed Nelson's ship, the "Vanguard," in her position at the battle of the Nile.

The moment the members of the deputation reached the quarter-deck of the "Victory," Lord Nelson observed Captain Channel, and, apparently forgetting the gentlemen of Antigua who had come to greet him to their island, rushed forward to him, exclaiming, in a rapture of delight, "Channel, my boy, how are you?" After the two Nile heroes had exchanged some kind expressions, his lordship rejoined his visitors, who had come to invite him to a public banquet. "Gentlemen," said Lord Nelson, "I thank you sincerely; but it is impossible for me to accept your hospitality; I am in pursuit of the enemy, and I have not been out of this ship for two years. I am sure that the enemy has returned to Europe, and I, gentlemen, must also *return* without the loss of a day."

The deputation retired much gratified with their reception, but greatly disappointed that they were not to have the honor of entertaining the great Admiral.

Every luxury which the island possessed kept pouring into the fleet during the day; and Nelson kept Captain Channel to spend the afternoon with him.

What occurred within a few weeks from that day is best told in the words of the poet, which Mr. Coates repeated with much pathos:

"Nelson had sought, but long had sought in vain
The still retreating fleets of France and Spain;
When found at last, he crushed them in the flood,
And sealed the awful conquest with his blood."

13. *Lord Nelson, dining with the Highland Society of London, and Commander Keith Maxwell, R. N.*

His lordship had been invited to dine in London with the Highland Society of Scotland. The Duke of Montrose was in the chair. In the absence of a member of the royal family who was expected, but unable to attend, Lord Nelson was the chief guest.

My father, as a member of the committee, had asked his young friend and countryman, Commander Keith Maxwell, R. N., elder brother of the late Sir Murray Maxwell, to accompany him to the dinner; and both sat at the cross-table immediately opposite the noble chairman and Lord Nelson. His lordship had accidentally heard that the young man opposite to him was Keith Maxwell, the gallant cutter-out of "La Chevrette," in Camaret Bay, for which service he had just been promoted to the rank of commander. He introduced himself to Maxwell by asking him to drink wine. The young sailor felt the honor immensely, but was quite unprepared for what was to follow, on the cloth being removed. The usual loyal toasts having been disposed of, with those of the distinguished visitors, "The Highland Society and its Objects," etc., Lord Nelson rose to propose a bumper toast. To his utter amazement and dismay, poor young Maxwell found that his health was to be brought before the company by the great Nelson. Never before had his courage and presence of mind deserted him, but on this occasion both had fled, or nearly so. Lord Nelson described to his grace and the company, in detail, the cutting-out of "La Chevrette," and said that it would stand recorded in the annals of the naval history of this country as one of the most brilliant exploits ever performed.

The young commander thought and hoped that a simple bow was sufficient, but my father whispered to him that he must say something in reply. His speech was short, but it was natural, and consequently effective, and was received with a burst of applause. It was as follows: "My Lord Duke, I am overwhelmed with the compliment that has been paid me. How happy, my Lord Duke, I should at this moment have been had my mother been spared to hear that her son Keith had his health proposed, and his conduct as a seaman approved, by Lord Nelson. I can say no more, my Lord Duke; a grateful heart deprives me of utterance."

The young sailor's maiden speech brought tears from all those who sat near him and heard it.

As the reader may wish to know a little more of the cutting-out of "La Chevrette," I may state that he was early promoted to his post rank, and hoisted his pennant as a commodore on the African station. After this came the peace, and he went on half-pay, and returned to the land of the Maxwells, where my father fitted up a comfortable residence for him on his own property (Drumtarlie Lodge), the future residence of another hero, General the Hon. Sir William Stewart, G. C. B., and where he ended his days. His next brother was Captain Sir Murray Maxwell, R. N., and one of his other officers was Captain John Maxwell, R. N., an excellent officer, who was promoted at the age of twenty to his post rank. This early promotion some illiberal people ascribed to the fact of his being a near relation of Jane, the celebrated Duchess of Gordon, who was by birth the second daughter of Sir William Maxwell of Monreith, the third baronet.

14. *Commodore Sir Henry Trollope and General the Right Hon. John Burgoyne.*

My father used to relate an amusing scene which he witnessed, seventy-five years ago, at the house of a friend in London, who had asked him to dinner to meet the distinguished commodore, Sir Henry Trollope, whose action, when in command of the "Glatton," with the French frigates—for which he received knighthood and a piece of plate from the merchants of London—made him the lion of the day. One of the guests invited was General Burgoyne, who commanded the British army in America as far back as 1777. After the cloth was removed and a bumper (or more) had been drunk to the distinguished sailor, the commodore availed himself of a temporary lull in the conversation to say across the table to the aged general who sat on the left of the chair, "General, do you recollect a youngster who served in the — regiment under you in America, and who gave you from time to time infinite trouble, until you were compelled to dismiss him from his regiment and send him to England—he went by the name of 'Blackguard Trollope?'" The old general brightened up. "Well do I recollect 'Blackguard Trollope,' as did every one connected with my force." "I was in hopes, General, you had forgotten him, for I am 'Blackguard Trollope.'" "What!" exclaimed the general, amid roars of laughter, "do you mean to say, Sir Henry, that you are 'Blackguard Trollope?'" "I am, indeed, 'Blackguard Trollope.'" "Well," said the general, "wonders will never cease. We must shake each other again by the hand; and although I was happy to get rid of 'Ensign' Trollope, I am indeed proud to meet 'Commodore' Trollope, and am well rewarded for having sent him home to enter a service in which he has become one of its brightest ornaments."

15. *Mr. Pitt hearing of the Death of Robespierre.**

I often heard my father relate the following among many anecdotes of Mr. Pitt. For ten years of the last century, and down to the period of Mr. Pitt's death, my father was extensively connected as a merchant with America and the West Indies, and in this capacity was frequently sent for and consulted by Mr. Pitt. He was the first to communicate to him the death of Robespierre, under the following circumstances: My father was at his residence in Surrey, when late at night a clerk in his employ (an American citizen by birth) arrived from Paris, having got across the Channel in a fishing-boat, and announced the fact of Robespierre having been guillotined the day he left Paris. Government intelligence from France being very difficult to obtain, my father considered it important that Mr. Pitt should know the fact without delay; but as he had a good many miles to drive, it was between 12 and 1 when he reached Downing Street. The servant told my father that Mr. Pitt had just retired, but that, of course, he would take up his name. Mr. Pitt at once said: "I know Mr. Boyd has something of importance to tell me; ask him to walk up-stairs." On hearing the news he immediately left his bed, saying: "I must instantly apprise my colleagues; Boyd, many thanks; good-night, good-night." And off he went instanter to tell the news to the other members of his Cabinet.

* This anecdote I sent to Earl Stanhope some years ago, and he did me the honor to say, in acknowledging it: "I return you many thanks for your obliging communication. The anecdote as to the news of the fall of Robespierre, as it arrived in Downing Street, is curious, and I am glad to be able to add it to my 'Pittiana.'"

16. *The Right Rev. Thomas Lewis O'Bierne, D. D., Lord Bishop of Meath.*

When I was a boy I recollect this distinguished prelate very well. With Mrs. O'Bierne and his two daughters, he was in the habit of occasionally paying my father and mother a few days' visit at our residence in Scotland, on his way to or from London. My father prided himself much on his four-year-old black-faced mutton; and for no joint had the right reverend prelate a higher esteem or relish than a leg of mutton, as borne out in the following little narrative:

Dr. O'Bierne belonged to a respectable Roman Catholic family, and he was educated in France for the Irish priesthood. He had arrived in London from the Continent, on his return to Ireland; but having a few weeks at command, he wished to make a walking-tour through the metropolitan counties. One day he found himself likely to be caught in a drenching rain somewhere in mid-Surrey, and sought shelter in a small road-side country inn. He asked the landlord what he could have for dinner, and learned to his satisfaction that there was a solitary leg of mutton in the house. The joint was being cooked for him when three gentlemen galloped up to the door in hunting-costume, drenched and hungry. The landlord was able to give the old gentleman of the party a dry suit of clothes, by which time the leg of mutton was ready to be served up for Mr. O'Bierne. He, however, requested the landlord to take it first to the hungry sportsmen, who were equally strangers to the landlord as to the young divine. This they declined, unless the young gentleman would join them. He did so, and the leg of mutton had ample justice done to it. About 7 or 8 o'clock in the evening a carriage drove up, and a powdered footman, looking in at the door, said, "Your grace, the carriage is here." Two of the gentlemen left for their own residences in the country, but his grace was to return to London. He asked the young stranger who had so considerately insisted upon the leg of mutton being sent to him and his friends what were his plans. Mr. O'Bierne replied that he meant to return to London to-morrow. "Why not to-night," said the duke, "and take a seat in my carriage?" He thanked his grace for his kind offer, paid his bill, and in a few minutes found himself alongside the Duke of Portland, the Prime Minister. His grace had been much struck during the dinner with the young Irishman's general intelligence, and this was further enhanced in the drive to London. The duke put O'Bierne down at his hotel or lodgings, wishing him good-night, and extracting from him a strict promise to breakfast in Cavendish Square next morning. He was introduced to the duchess and her two eldest sons, the Marquis of Titchfield (the late duke) and Lord William Bentinck (the future Governor-General of India).

Before starting for Downing Street, the duke desired his sons to "lionize" their young friend about the metropolis, and to bring him back to dinner without fail. The sequel was, that before the week had ended, Lord Titchfield and his brother were much attached to young O'Bierne. His popularity with the duke and duchess likewise increased; and within a fortnight of the accidental introduction through the medium of the leg of mutton, the duke made a suggestion, followed by a proposal to O'Bierne. His grace told him that he found him exactly the person he would like to superintend the education of his sons, having discovered that he was an excellent classical scholar, in addition to which (a rare requisition in those days), he had a perfect knowledge of the French language. He added that he wished to place his sons under his tuition, and that as he (O'Bierne) had not yet entered the priesthood, he wished him to return to Ireland and consult his family, whether he could not make up his mind to take orders in the Church of England, in which case he would place his sons under his charge at either Oxford or Cambridge, and that he might assure his family from him (the duke) he should have the earliest church preferment after completing his university course. His family acceded to the duke's proposal, and Mr. O'Bierne entered the Bentinck family, having given him *pari passu* with his duties to his pupils the opportunity of preparing himself for those of a clergyman of the English Episcopal Church, and which duties he afterward so conscientiously and ably fulfilled. The Premier had early discovered that his sons' tutor possessed varied and eminent talents, and the result of that appreciation was Mr. O'Bierne subsequently accompanying Lord Malmesbury as chaplain and interpreter in his diplomatic mission to France. The chaplain's private correspondence in his new character in connection with foreign affairs evinced, I have heard my father say, in the opinion of those competent to judge, high powers; so much so, that my relative one day at his own table facetiously remarked to the ex-chaplain of Legation, then become Bishop of Meath, that had he not raised himself to a mitre, nothing could have prevented him becoming an ambassador extraordinary and minister plenipotentiary.

The Bishop married the only daughter of the Hon. Francis Stuart, third son of the sixth Earl of Moray, and had two daughters.

My father visited the bishop at his episcopal residence in Ireland, and the first morning after breakfast his lordship said, "I wish to introduce you to my elder brother, who lives over there," pointing to the house. This brother, to whom the bishop was greatly attached, was the Roman Catholic priest of the district.

17. *Pride of Ancestry.*

My father related an instance of this which, he said, always brought a smile from the noble earl by whom the concession was made to a certain noble applicant, who anxiously desired to be allowed to matriculate himself on the noble earl's family and heraldic tree. My father had gone to pay his respects to the lord-lieutenant of his county, at his residence in London, and, as he entered, he met a noble lord and eminent statesman who was leaving the house. He found the earl in his library, and the first observation he made was, "Do you know whom you met just now?" "Of course, my lord, I do; such great men are always known by sight!" "Sit down, and I shall make you laugh. On the chair you now occupy," said his lordship, "that distinguished man has been sitting for two hours studying the peerage, or rather that portion of it referring to my family, so that I might point out to him (which, *entre nous*, I could not do) or help him to fix where his grandfather or great-grandfather branched off from my family. He acknowledged to me," continued the earl, "that when his progenitor arrived in Ireland and settled, he had understood that he appeared to know little or nothing of *his* family in Scotland. Very little indeed, I should think," said the noble earl—"or at least wished to have known"—a remark in which my father fully concurred. The ancestor was a pedler in a very small way in our county, carrying his little wares on his back, but in his humble avocation was very respectable. His patronymic was certainly that of the noble family with which his distinguished descendant now coveted an hereditary alliance. "Ah!" said the noble earl, a clear-headed and wise man, "is it not surprising? Does it not show the weakness of human nature to find a man, with the vast responsibilities of office on his shoulders, whose name carries such weight in every Cabinet of Europe, with a great Continental war raging, in which the best interests of this country are involved, and who has achieved for himself so high and prominent a position in the councils of his sovereign, laying himself open and betraying such weakness, instead of being proud at the height he has attained by his own consummate talents? His lineage from the honest pedler was of too recent a date to have been unknown to him," said the earl, "for whatever is wrong in the family escutcheon, be it the bar sinister, or humble origin, never fails to be disseminated by a jealous and illiberal world."

"It cannot now be helped," said his lordship; "I have admitted the fiction, and I have this day consented to the matriculation; and now let me take a Scotchman's view of the matter from the point of expediency, political or otherwise, and the conclusion I arrive at is this, that, after all, as the father of a large family, and moreover being frequently called upon and expected, as the lord-lieutenant, to promote as far as in my power the advancement in the world of the young men connected with the two counties in which I hold property, I cannot suppose that my countrymen will find much fault with me for allowing so illustrious an individual to look up to me as the head of his house." I have no doubt my father, as another Scotchman, considered the noble earl's premises and conclusions sound.

18. *The Right Hon. Anthony R. Blake.*

I had the pleasure of knowing the right honorable gentleman during the latter years of his life, which were passed either in London or Brighton. He had the same apartments in the "Albany," Piccadilly, that had been previously occupied for years by Lord Althorp, until he removed to Spencer House. Mr. Blake was a younger son of the ancient family of Blake, of Holly Park, in the county of Galway, and was called to the bar at Lincoln's Inn in 1813, being proposed by Sir Thomas Plumer, Master of the Rolls. He subsequently held the position of Chief Remembrancer for Ireland, and, I believe, was the first Roman Catholic in those days of exclusion (1823) who was nominated to a legal office by the Government. The chivalrous and popular Marquis of Anglesey was then Viceroy of Ireland. He was a man of most engaging manners, and his conversation was not more finished and delightful than instructive. He was old enough to remember many of the chief incidents of the Irish rebellion, but he never allowed himself to be led away by his feelings as a Catholic into the expression of opinions at which even John Earl of Eldon, the most fastidious of Tory chancellors, could have taken umbrage. He possessed humorous powers of a high description; and I can only look back with feelings of unfeigned regret that I neglected the opportunity of recording many anecdotes that would have been highly interesting for me now to rehearse, as coming from so valued a source.

During Mr. Blake's residence in London he was asked by the Government to allow himself to be nominated a commissioner to represent the Catholic party in conducting, with two colleagues, an educational inquiry in Ireland. He amused me much with many of his anecdotes connected with this commission; among them was some evidence which he noted down from a provincial schoolmaster, which, he told me, occupied about three hours, and was really most laughable. It appeared that on one occasion, the day being favorable for fishing, his brother commissioners resolved to indulge their piscatory tastes, and Mr. Blake, not being inclined to join them, to save time sent for the schoolmaster of the district, to take his evidence. The teacher of youth arrived soon after breakfast, pulled his most prominent lock, made his profoundest bow, and confidentially intimated to the commissioner that he was right glad to find his lordship, his worship, his honor—for during his examination he gave the right honorable gentleman the full advantage of the three titles—"altogether alone." Mr. Blake, knowing his countrymen well, soon took his visitor's dimensions; and his own accent being "altogether" English, without a tinge of brogue, he said to his new acquaintance, "I can at once see you have much valuable information to impart to me." "Indade, my lord, I have; and I assure your worship in all raality how entirely glad I am to have your honor all alone this very day." "But," said Mr. Blake, "before we begin, as I have finished my own breakfast, and as you may have breakfasted early—" "That I did, sor, your honor." "I think some bread and cheese, and a glass of whiskey, this damp day will do you good." "A little sup of whiskey, your honor, would do me a dale of good." Accordingly the bread, cheese, and whiskey, were summoned to his aid, when the commissioner's examination of the learned schoolmaster commenced. Every answer he received was usually accompanied with some remark that was to induce the commissioner to consider that it was valuable and exclusive information.

After Mr. Blake, whose difficulty throughout was to maintain an unruffled sedateness, had filled up two sheets of closely-written foolscap, he put down his pen, and thus addressed his voluble witness: "Well, Mr. Flanigan," holding up the two sheets of paper, "you have given me a large amount of very valuable matter to be added to the report my brother commissioners and myself are preparing to submit for the information of Government and of both Houses of Parliament." "Yes, my lord, it is all for yourself." "And, Mr. Flanigan, I cannot express to you the surprise and amazement I feel, as a Roman Catholic and an Irishman, at listening to what you have told me." On hearing this, up started the Irish schoolmaster to his legs, exclaiming, "Oh! murther, murther! My lord, are you the Right Honorable Mr. Blake?" "I am." Then striking his thigh violently, he called out, "Bad luck to me! Oh, murther! I thought all the time your honor was the English commissioner."

19. *The Emperor Alexander of Russia and Admiral Mingye.*

If it be true that our greatest statesmen have usually been noted for speaking the English language with propriety, it is equally certain that there is no rule without its exception. The late Admiral Mingye, when a lieutenant, had the honor of steering the royal barge, with the Prince Regent, the Emperor Alexander, the King of Prussia, and other European crowned heads, from Whitehall to Greenwich.

Mingye's eminent tact and ready wit, in replying in the vernacular to the chaff of the watermen and bargemen who ran athwart him in his progress down the river, was described to me by a distinguished flag-officer who was present as standing unrivalled and unsurpassed in the marine vocabulary of that day. None of his messmates had ever conceived that Mingye had reached any thing like so high a point of excellence; but he proved on this occasion, to their thorough conviction, that he had studied assiduously and successfully in the schools of Billingsgate and Wapping, as well as of Deptford and Portsmouth Point. The Czar of Russia, an accomplished English scholar, was kept in a continuous roar of laughter; and it was alleged that he paid infinitely more attention to the steersman and his utterances than to the stately warehouses, crowded wharves, and forest of masts through which he was passing on the royal excursion to Greenwich.

Mingye was imperturbable throughout. His diction was as pure, as extensive, and varied, and as much at command in Deptford Reach, as it had been between Whitehall and Blackfriars.

His fine handsome appearance and magnificent voice added, no doubt, much to the fascinations which had attracted the almost undivided attention of the emperor. At the Whitebait feast that followed, Mingye was especially noticed by the different royal personages, but by none so much as by the Emperor of all the Russias.

The events of this day were important in Mingye's professional career, as it secured him his promotion, and his further advancement was soon followed by the command of the king's yacht.

In later years he became an ardent admirer and supporter of Don Carlos, and accepted the command of that prince's fleet—yet to be built.

He always had the commission of King Carlos of Spain, as admiral, sewn under the sleeve of his coat; and when he dined at our house, which at one period he frequently did, and if he appeared in low spirits—for which there was, unfortunately, a cause—I used to rally him, and raise a smile by telling him that the responsibility and anxiety attending the charge of the Spanish Carlist fleet were too much for him, and that I should advise him to strike his flag and retire, as his duties were far too onerous!

Mingye was a good-tempered man, to whom the praise from Gil Blas did not apply, "n'entendent pas raillerie," for no one more enjoyed a joke.

20. *How poor Sir John Ross lost his Dinner in the neighborhood of London, although he may have been no stranger to such a casualty in the neighborhood of the North Pole.*

We who lived thirty-five or forty years ago remember that poor Ross and his gallant party were given over as lost in the polar regions for more than three years. I believe his name had even been removed from the navy list, and his goods and chattels sold and divided among his heirs. An immense sensation was created in London one afternoon in October, 1833, when he was reported to have reached Hull, people rushing about on 'Change and elsewhere, exclaiming, "Have you heard the news? Ross is safe, after all!" etc.

His arrival at the Admiralty was looked for with intense interest, and by no one more eagerly than our sailor king, William IV., who immediately asked Ross to dine with him at Windsor. In fact, Ross at that moment was the nation's lion; and he considered himself a lucky man, whether peer or commoner, who could secure Ross to partake his hospitality. He kept himself disengaged, however, to dine with his own Scotch county friends in London—the Dumfriesshire and Galloway Club—and my brother and myself had the satisfaction of meeting our old friend on the occasion. There was a member of the club present who had been Ross's school companion—a successful British merchant, and a most hospitable man—who said across the table, as our convivial meeting was about to close, "I presume John Ross is too great a man now to dine with the friend of his boyhood?" "Try him," said Ross. "Well, my good fellow, will next Saturday suit you?" "It will," said Ross. "Our dinner hour is half-past six" (a fashionable hour in those days). "Oh! my dear Ross, I take it exceedingly kind, and it will make my wife so happy to be introduced to one of whom she has heard from her husband so much." "But, my good friend," said Ross, "you have told me you live in the country, without saying where." "Ah, ah! Ross, that's very good; but all, my dear fellow, you have to do, is to find your way to Gracechurch Street, at ten minutes before five, and tell the coachman you are going to dine with me." Accordingly, Sir John was punctually in Gracechurch Street at the appointed time, found himself among a bevy of coaches and coachmen, informing one of the latter that he was going to dine with Mr. ——. "All right, sir; jump in, sir; off in two minutes; put you down, sir, at Mr. ——'s door." Clapham Common was the point for which the polar navigator had been informed by his host that he should steer; but unfortunately there was a city man of the same name, who hailed from a different quarter—Sydenham. This sexagenarian of Sydenham had married a second time (I mention this fact as it is an important feature in my little narrative), and the young lady was some thirty or forty years his junior. I may also add, *en passant*, another important piece of information, that she possessed great personal attractions.

The coachman landed Sir John at his supposed friend's door; but instead of the charming young bride having to meet the embrace of her *carissimo sposo*, she heard announced the name of Sir John Ross, or rather, as he told us afterward, that the footman styled him Sir Jonathan Ross. There can be no doubt that, after the usual courtesies had passed, the young lady who had so recently taken upon her the cares of a household, finding a visitor arrive to dinner *en grande tenue*, and one with whose name every newspaper of the day had familiarized her, must have been in a dilemma. Still she knew that the dear kind soul with whom she had so recently commenced the journey of life would shortly arrive, bringing down with him the fish, etc. from Leadenhall Market, and the soup, *entrées*, and jellies from Birch's; so that the only orders she had quietly to give were that the cook should go on with her duties in the vegetable department, and the footman with his table arrangements.

Sir John was quite unprepared to meet so young a wife; but as he had been nearly four years absent among the snow and ice of the Northern regions, where the Supplement of the *Times* is not always to be met with, he said to himself, "Ah, my friend has lost one wife and married another since I left England. I must therefore avoid asking questions, and limit myself to one, namely—'Pray, has Mr. —— arrived from London?'" "Oh, no, Sir John," looking at the clock on the mantel-piece; "I do not expect him for half an hour." That being so, he opened his budget of anecdotes "by flood and field," to which the young and charming Mrs. —— listened with the deepest interest. All this Sir John afterward told my brother and myself, in a very dry and humorous way. Rap, tap, tap, and the lord of the mansion arrived at his own threshold. "I am so glad, Sir John, that Mr. —— has at last arrived; he will be quite distressed to hear that you have had so long to wait."

Before I proceed, I must here explain that the events of this afternoon became somewhat historical in the neighborhood of Sydenham: the footman, who was resolved that his own course of action should be clearly understood, informed a friend of his master's, to whom I was indebted for the underground or down-stairs details. The footman opened the coach-door for his master, then at once looked up at the coachman, and said, "Now, Bill, gie me down the fish and t'other parcels sharp; *has* we *hain't* got a morsel o' time and cook's *hin* such a stew." "Vy, sir, you *ave* put missus sadly hout this day; you *ave* hindeed, sir, in *hasking hof* Sir Jonathan Ross to dinner vithout *hever* a telling er hor hus, hand cook hand hall hon us har hin a regular fix, hand no mistake heether." The passengers by the stage had the advantage of hearing Davis, the footman, lecture his master; and they, as well as the coachman, being rather curious to know what it all meant, and Sydenham coaches generally not being in a hurry, they had now to listen to the master opening upon his domestic. "*I* ask Sir Jonathan Ross to dinner! what the deuce do you mean?" "Vell, sir, hall hi know his, Sir Jonathan has been ha sitting hin the drawing-room vith missus for more than han our." This intimation made the master hurry into his house and up-stairs to the presence of his wife with all dispatch, when the first words that met his ears were, "Why, my dear, we were afraid of some accident, as Sir John has been here for almost an hour." Mr. —— of course knew Sir John Ross—at least by name and fame—although the distinguished sailor until that afternoon in Gracechurch Street was not in the least aware that such a person existed as Mr. —— of Sydenham. The explanation or *dénouement* on Sir John's part was speedy, and its *sequitur* equally so, delivered very gruffly. "Oh, Mr. ——; he lives on the borders of Clapham Common, some miles from this, and quite another road." Sir John declared this to have been uttered in a very *icy* tone, for which he was quite unprepared in his Fatherland, having calculated that as he had lost one dinner owing to this man having unfortunately a similar patronymic to his friend, he reasonably might expect, as being rather hungry, to be asked to take pot-luck as a partial set-off. It proved otherwise; for the only civility that Mr. —— offered was to desire his footman to stop the next coach for London, into which Sir John Ross was hurried dinnerless. Oddly enough, at the "Elephant and Castle," my brother, then on his way home, saw poor Sir John Ross. "Hallo!" exclaimed my brother, "I thought you had discussed your turtle an hour ago with our friend." "I must get out of the coach to tell you all about it." "Then you have had no dinner?" said my brother. "None," emphatically, and at the same time pathetically, answered Sir John. "Nor have I," said my brother, "although it is so late; so come along."

Accordingly Sir John's third trial for a dinner was successful. Under our mahogany the brave old sailor soon found restored that appetite which he had lost in his visit to Sydenham. It would have been unpardonable to allow the gentleman from Sydenham to escape scot-free; and on the following Monday the affair became known to some old friends of the party on Change.

Never was a man more unmercifully quizzed; and he deserved it. "Here comes the most hospitable man in England." "How did Sir John Ross relish that old port?" etc. Others spoke in plainer language, and it was only out of a good feeling for the youthful bride that proceedings were stayed.

If a feast at the Albion or Freemasons' Tavern to a hundred guests could have saved the sexagenarian of Sydenham from the criticism which his want of hospitality had brought down upon him, he would have been only too happy to have provided such an entertainment.

In respect to Sir John's old schoolfellow, it is reasonable to conclude that when he next invited the K. C. B. to dinner, he gave him a somewhat more defined address than simply "Gracechurch Street."

21. *Saying Farewell to Sir John Franklin.*

I never pass the Athenæum Club without stopping to contemplate the statue of Franklin, which vividly recalls the following incident:

My friend Tom Bushby, the rear-admiral, with his wife, who had come down to see us in Kent, and next morning (Sunday) he received a note from a naval friend in town to say that Franklin and Crosier were adjusting or swinging compasses at Greenhithe, and would proceed on their voyage that night or the following morning. Accordingly, after church and lunch we drove across the country to Greenhithe, and went on board Sir John Franklin's ship. I had never previously seen the distinguished sailor (a survivor of Trafalgar), who, after receiving the ladies of our party, took me by the hand, saying, "Bushby, you need not introduce me in this quarter; I know him from his likeness to his brother." My brother had visited Sir John Franklin when Governor of Van Diemen's Land, or as it is now more generally called, Tasmania, and had received great kindness and attention from himself and Lady Franklin at Government House. We went to the saloon, where Lady Franklin with a few relatives were just finishing the last Sunday's dinner she was ever to partake with that husband whose sad fate she subsequently devoted years of firm and determined resolution to elucidate. A similarly distressing task I had five years afterward to engage in for the same brother to whom Sir John Franklin declared I bore a striking resemblance. To the solution of that brother's fate my family and myself stand indebted to another gallant sailor, Admiral Sir Henry Mangles Denham, F. R. S. Sir John appeared in buoyant spirits, for in passing to the cabin where the ladies were, he said, "Bushby, don't mention Mr. Boyd's name, as I wish to see whether my wife detects the likeness.—My dear, do you know who this gentleman is?" "Why, it is Mr. Boyd's brother." I well remember, in a bumper of port, accompanied by a few remarks, drinking Sir John Franklin's health, and all success to the expedition. After this, Sir John, leading the way, showed us over his ship, explaining to us many of those arrangements which, as may be conceived, were as multifarious as they were minute, for braving the winters of the Northern regions. As the period of our visit was drawing to a close, he asked me if I should like to see Captain Crosier's ship. I said, "Very much indeed;" on which he took his speaking-trumpet, and called to him to show us his lions.

We then bade adieu to Sir John and his officers, with a parting salutation to as fine a ship's company as I ever beheld.

After spending an hour with Captain Crosier, who, like Sir John, spared himself no trouble to point out what he thought would interest us, we returned home highly pleased with our visit.

With the exception of Lady Franklin and her own party, Admiral and Mrs. Bushby with my wife and myself were the last to say farewell to Sir John Franklin.

22. *The Late Earl of Cardigan.*

No military man "in the piping times of peace" ever attracted more criticism than this noble Earl, *ci-devant* Lord Brudenell. There was his high social position, his large fortune, his rapid promotion under the system of purchase, his martinet manners with his officers, his popularity with his men, his love of the profession, his readiness at all times, if the necessity arose, to fight a duel. But he had other good points, which fully equalled his dashing bravery in the Crimea.

When the late General Sir De Lacy Evans was preparing the expeditionary force to Spain (1835–'36), a youngster, the son of an old and meritorious Peninsular officer, whom Lord Cardigan (then Lord Brudenell) had known when he first joined the service, was appointed to a cornetcy in one of the two cavalry regiments then being raised. But the youth was without any means whatever. Lord Brudenell accidentally heard of the fact, and immediately came to his relief, had him fully equipped at his own expense, and, in addition to this, lined the young cornet's purse with an ample sum to make the ways and means run easy until he had reached his destination. I only knew Lord Cardigan by sight; but the above fact was given to me by one of the most promising officers and estimable men in the army, the late Colonel Lauderdale Maule, 79th Highlanders.

23. *Field-Marshal Lord Clyde.*

While many a man has risen to a lieutenant-colonel's commission without having seen a shot fired in earnest, the gallant Colin Campbell, the volunteer in two or more "forlorn hopes" during the Peninsular War, in one of which he was twice severely wounded, although recommended for his bravery for promotion at the Horse Guards by Lord Wellington himself, came out of the great Peninsular struggle a captain. At the present time, not only would he have received his step of promotion, but it would have been accompanied with the Victoria cross.

I confidently believe that without the friendship, and something more, of one kind and generous man—a West India merchant whom I have met in society—the gallant Campbell would never have borne a field-marshal's baton, won a peerage, or been laid to rest in Westminster Abbey Years after the war, Campbell, still a captain in the 21st Regiment, was with a detachment at Demerara or Berbice. He had received a letter from his agent in London, mentioning an approaching vacancy in his regiment by the early retirement of a field officer. Campbell, who read the paragraph in the house of a friend, remarked, "There again, the old story; that youngster"—indicating the party—"who has the cash will obtain the step; a majority." His friend inquired, apparently without any other object than curiosity, what sum he, the "youngster," would have to pay. Campbell replied so-and-so. The conversation dropped; but his good and warm-hearted friend, by the return of the packet, instructed his correspondent in London instantly to pay the sum required to the army agents for the purchase of the majority in the 21st Regiment of Foot for Captain Colin Campbell.

In a couple or three months—there being no mail steamers in those days—a Gazette arrived, and to Campbell's astonishment he saw his promotion. He declared to his friend that it was a painful and provoking mistake, which would, as a matter of course, be rectified in the following Gazette. His friend felt convinced it was no mistake, and told him so; but to keep the gallant Highlander no longer in suspense, gave him some insight into the cause of the promotion which had been gazetted.

24. *Lord Clyde in Private Life.*

In private society no one was a more welcome guest than Colonel Colin Campbell. He was naturally of a warm and joyous disposition. In another relation of life he was a good son and brother. To no friends in London did he more cordially attach himself than to those whose kindness and hospitality he had formerly experienced in the West Indies. I had the pleasure of seeing him a guest at my brother's table and my own, and elsewhere in society, especially at one friend's house, where for many years previous to his accompanying Lord Saltoun's expedition to China I always met him on New-Year's Day. Nothing short of the commands of her Majesty to dine at Windsor Castle or Buckingham Palace would have prevented Colin Campbell from fulfilling his standing engagement to dine with his kind and hospitable friend in Park Crescent. The party generally numbered twenty, and if once on the New-Year's Day list of our friend, were you married or single, you were expected, if in London, to dine with him.

I enjoyed that privilege for twenty-five years, never having missed a single anniversary; but as may be conceived, in so long a period I saw many chairs to be filled up in succession to such men as General Lord Keane, General Lord O'Neill, the Honorable Admiral Best, General Sir Charles Smith, and many others; for, in fact, I believe, if not always on January 1st—as my friend's dinners during the year numbered legion—I have met in that most hospitable of mansions almost every governor or commander-in-chief who had held office or hoisted his flag in the West Indies during the present century down to 1853–'54.

An evening party usually followed, when our host never failed to make Colin Campbell master of the ceremonies. If a quadrille required a couple to make it up, the Colonel was ready; and it rarely happened that any young lady remained without a partner, for if the future hero of Lucknow could not find one for her, he danced with her himself.

Lord Clyde, or rather Colin Campbell, at these happy reunions frequently indulged in sly caustic humor, and could bring out the recital of an amusing grievance as well as any man I ever knew. One of our party, who like myself lived to complete his twenty-fifth anniversary dinner in Park Crescent, was that excellent man who has lately passed away at the age of ninety, the late Mr. Edward Marshall, Chief Examiner of Accounts at the War Office, where he had served for half a century, not reckoning two years he passed in Ireland, where he acted as private secretary to Sir Arthur Wellesley when Secretary for Ireland. Mr. Marshall was an encyclopædia of knowledge in regard to military details, and, in fact, in all things appertaining to the military, naval, and civil services generally; and as the guests were chiefly military or naval men, he was constantly referred to.

It would seem that the office of the Secretary-at-War, which department superintended and guided wars on a large scale, was not itself exempt at times from little wars within its own walls.

Lord Palmerston and Mr. Marshall did not always ride their horses together. The former, one day, directed Mr. Marshall to prepare for transmission abroad an important document, which instruction the latter had most carefully carried out, sending the paper by a clerk or messenger to his lordship, then in his own room. In its perusal, Lord Palmerston came to the word "waggon," which his amanuensis had spelt with one "g." Not taking the same view of orthography, his lordship said to the messenger, "Take that back to Mr. Marshall" (of course unsigned by his lordship). In a few minutes the messenger returned with two dictionaries, one or both of which authorized the word being spelt either with one "g" or two. "Carry back these books to Mr. Marshall, and assure him I do not require to be told how to spell waggon;" and he dashed the books on the floor.

On another occasion Lord Palmerston came into his room and said, "Here, Marshall, is a very long affair, and I know you will give it your immediate and undivided attention, as I wish to have it back either to-night or early to-morrow forenoon." Mr. Marshall, seeing his lordship's anxiety for dispatch, assured him that it should be forthwith attended to. "But what," said our friend, "*do you think* of Lord Palmerston, on leaving my room, quietly locking my door, putting the key in his pocket, and all this without my knowing it? When lunch-time arrived I found myself locked in. I rang the bell, and only obtained my freedom by having the lock picked." Of course we agreed that the noble Secretary-at-War took this precaution to prevent the future Chief Examiner of Accounts from being interrupted; but that view of the case we never could persuade the latter to admit.

An hour or two afterward Lord Palmerston returned and found Mr. Marshall's door open and his official hard at work. The incensed gentleman took the initiative with his chief. "My lord I am now no longer a school-boy; I am as old, if not older, than your lordship, and I must beg your lordship in future not to lock my door." Although we had often heard the story, it was incumbent upon us to ask how his lordship took this sharp rebuke. "Oh, he smiled, and made the *amende.*" "Ah! Marshall," said Colin Campbell, or some one else, "I have no doubt Lord Palmerston, although you won't confess it, assured you, in his own happy manner, that what he had done was to prevent intruders." That view of the matter never satisfied our friend, for thirty years afterward his feelings appeared to be as little assuaged as on the day of the occurrence.

We had another good joke against our amiable friend, to which he smiled acquiescence when it was alluded to. He was about to be married, and had promised to breakfast with his best man on the morning of the ceremony. He arrived at his friend's house in a full suit of newly-built black. His friend scanned him over. "Why, Marshall, good gracious! we are going to a marriage, and that marriage your own; my good fellow, we are not going to a funeral. Do you understand that?" "I assure you," said the bridegroom-elect, "they are fresh from my tailor's. Will they not answer?" "Not at all." "But I never wear any thing else than black. What do you advise me to do?" "Why, finish your breakfast and come up to my room, where I shall redress you in a more *fitting color* for a marriage, although possibly in a less *fitting suit* for you." Accordingly he was married in the garments furnished from his friend's wardrobe.

Marshall knew Sam Rogers the poet; and one of his recollections of the poet-banker was his dread and horror of practical jokers, arising from the following circumstance, which, although it may be well known in connection with the history of the author of the "Pleasures of Memory," I never heard until my friend related it. Rogers was hanging on the arm of a friend in St. James Street, a notorious practical joker. They had reached Piccadilly at the moment a coach from the West of England was setting down its passengers, one of whom, on alighting, discovering that one of his shoestrings was loose, had stooped to tie it, and had accidentally thrown up his coat over his shoulder, leaving the lower part of his back denuded of its legitimate covering. The practical joker could not resist the tempting opportunity for distinguishing himself, and, dropping the poet's arm, gave the unhappy traveller a tremendous slap with the palm of his hand. Pain and indignation—I conclude both—brought the sufferer instantly to his legs. "What do you mean, sir? I was only tying my shoe." "Tying your shoe, sir; you are always tying your shoe!" Then walking coolly away he put his arm into Rogers's, who was almost prostrate with terror at what he had witnessed, and left the unfortunate and insulted traveller to turn over in his mind whether his assailant was not a madman, or whether he himself, by the accidental turning up of his coat, had not offended against some recent police regulation of which he was not cognizant. Be that as it may, never was a man happier than Sam Rogers to find that he and his companion were not pursued by the aggrieved party; and when relieved from that source of anxiety, never was anyone more thoroughly resolved than the poet for the future to avoid the society of practical jokers.

There was a standing joke against the Chief Examiner of Army Accounts, which, I am told, lasted during the war, and indeed more or less to the day of his death. "Ah, Marshall, you know it was you who selected Sir Arthur Wellesley to command the army of the Peninsula." I had accompanied my friend to his club, the Union, after a dinner-party, at which he had been congratulated by Campbell or some one else for his foresight in selecting so good a general to meet the legions of the great Napoleon on the Iberian Peninsula, and later on the plains of Waterloo. The conversation generally wound up by a severe attack upon the advisers of the Crown for neglecting to recommend Edward Marshall to be the recipient of an hereditary distinction. Marshall was an extremely sensible man, and I never saw him ruffled in the least with all this banter, to which he always submitted in great good humor. I was anxious to know the precise origin of a joke I had heard so often, and he told me the whole story, with much more of a highly-interesting nature in reference to the "Iron Duke," during the period through which he was associated with him in Ireland. He said: "I was in the habit of keeping up a close correspondence from Dublin with an esteemed colleague of mine in one of the Government offices at Whitehall, and much of that correspondence related to the illustrious statesman and general under whom I was then serving; for he was, even at that time, 'illustrious' as the hero of Assaye. I described Sir Arthur to my friend as the most remarkable public man with whom I had ever been thrown into communication, for there was nothing, however abstruse, in public affairs which he could not at once master. For instance, on one occasion the Government wrote to him to ask his opinion on the Tithe Commutation Act for Ireland. Almost simultaneously with this was a dispatch from Downing Street requiring his views on the defences of the kingdom. 'Here,' I said, 'is a question for the distinguished soldier to be at home in;' and his reply to the authorities proved that such was the case." He instantly set to work and wrote an elaborate minute on Tithe Commutation (which Marshall transcribed), and although the question was shelved for a period, when Earl Grey's Government came into power, the very paper which Sir Arthur Wellesley had furnished to his own Government a quarter of a century before was the one which Lord Grey and the members of his Cabinet mainly applied to and acted upon. "I presume," continued my friend, "when a general was wanted to meet the great Napoleon in Spain I must have expatiated on the qualifications of my own chief as better suited than any other, in my humble opinion. It appeared, of which I was entirely unaware, that my letters, with which I had taken some pains for the information of one whom I very much esteemed, but never contemplating they were to be seen beyond himself and his own immediate circle, were regularly perused by Lord Castlereagh, Sir Arthur Wellesley's earliest patron and stanchest supporter in the Cabinet; and he, I conclude, was not displeased to hear even the opinion of a young Treasury official who had presumed to write so much *ad libitum* regarding his chief the Secretary of State for Ireland; for occasionally, on the receipt of the news of some victory in Spain, if I accidentally met Lord Castlereagh, he would stop and say: 'Ah, Marshall, you formed a correct estimate of Lord Wellington in Ireland,' adding, as he pointed his finger to his head, 'I knew it was here.'"

"That, my dear friend," addressing me, "is the full extent of my share in the appointment of Sir Arthur Wellesley to command that army whose achievements culminated on the plains of Waterloo."

Mr. Marshall stated further in regard to Sir Arthur Wellesley, that he never witnessed the business of a public department better looked after than that of the gallant Irish Secretary. He was up very early, and had his official duties cleared off by mid-day, so that in the afternoon he would be seen on horseback in the gayest throngs of the Irish fashionable world, impressing the mind of the spectator that Sir Arthur belonged to the *dolce far niente* class, rather than that he was one who had previously done a good day's work.

25. *The Preston Miller in the Gallery of the House of Commons.*

I once witnessed a laughable occurrence in the House of Commons. A country cousin of mine had asked me to take him to the Gallery of the House of Commons—his first visit to that august region. Mr. O'Connell was expatiating on the wrongs of his country, and charging England with being a heavy drain on unhappy Ireland. A well-dressed man close to us shouted at the top of his voice, "You are a liar!" Down sat the honorable and learned member, up rose the Speaker (Sir C. Manners Sutton) and in his clear, mellifluous voice exclaimed, "Sergeant-at-arms, do your duty." The doors of the gallery flew open, and the noisy offender was in custody. A minute more, and he was in the presence of the House. The Speaker again arose, and in that majestic tone which was so much admired, addressed the delinquent: "Prisoner at the bar, what have you to say in explanation of the grave insult you have offered to the dignity of this House?" The utmost silence prevailed, when the prisoner, in a facile, jaunty style, addressed the head of the Commons of England thus: "Mr. Speaker, when I heard the honorable and learned member for the county of Clare assert"—"Stop," exclaimed the Speaker, "you are adding insult to insult. I ask you what explanation you have to give to the offended dignity of this House for the insult of which you have just been guilty?" The prisoner, who appeared quite at ease, in no ways disconcerted or abashed—rather the reverse—for he seemed to be elevated in his own opinion in regard to the prominent position he had so rapidly attained, again essayed to address the House. "I do assure you, Mr. Speaker, that when I listened"—"Stop, sir!" roared the Speaker, probably in a higher key than he had ever previously reached within the walls of Parliament or out of them.

The House was convulsed; and the laughter was not diminished by a member calling out, "Let the prisoner proceed with his explanation." After the House was partially relieved, and a suppressed conversation had succeeded the other species of entertainment, Mr. O'Connell rose, and appealed to the Speaker, whether it was not the better course to dismiss the *wretched* man (never was a word more misapplied than wretched) at the bar from custody, than to sacrifice any more of the valuable time of the House. Sir Robert Peel opposed this course; but to save any further loss of time—it appearing quite evident to Sir Robert that even if the prisoner intended to make an apology, he would not do so without an introductory speech, having already more than satisfied the House that he possessed, to a large extent, the *cacoëthes loquendi*—he moved that the prisoner be committed to the custody of the sergeant-at-arms, and brought to the bar of the House the following day. The prisoner was taken off in custody; but it was some minutes before the gravity of the House returned. Next day, the prisoner was brought up, his eloquence having subsided in the interval, as he made a full apology, and for his escapade the miller from Lancashire had the satisfaction afforded him, in return for having had the privilege of twice addressing the House, of paying its fees, amounting to £15 or £16.

26. *David Roberts, R. A.*

I had the pleasure of knowing the late Mr. Roberts rather intimately, having been a member of two clubs to which he belonged. He had been invited by a relation of mine to meet a party of friends at dinner, but coming late was well rated for his want of punctuality. He promised to explain the cause on the removal of the cloth. One of the guests was the late eminent Scotch Whig, Mr. James Stuart of Dunearn, through life a warm supporter of artists, and an excellent judge of pictures.

The moment had arrived for Roberts's explanation, when he declared he would at once enter upon it, provided he was allowed to conclude by giving a bumper toast. This we readily conceded. He said, "I have now the sincerest pleasure in meeting for the first time, and seeing for the first time, a gentleman who was my earliest patron thirty years ago" (Mr. Stuart, who was all attention, being quite at a loss to what the Royal Academician referred). "When

I was a poor friendless boy in Edinburgh, I was in the habit of making little sketches; and one of my productions having been praised in my own humble family circle, I was recommended to send it into an exhibition for the productions of young artists, then patronized by the gentry of modern Athens. In a few days the secretary of the institution sent for me to tell me my painting had been purchased, 'And by whom do you think,' said the official?. 'By no one less than Mr. Stuart of Dunearn, and for ten shillings more than you asked—thirty shillings.' I rushed home to inform my poor mother of my good fortune, that my '*wee pictur*' had been bought for two pounds by Mr. Stuart. From that moment my career of success commenced, and this evening on my way here I delivered to Mr. Jones Loyd" (Lord Overstone) "my picture of Edinburgh" (which we had all just seen in the Exhibition in Trafalgar Square), "for which I have received this little piece of paper (throwing down on the table a check for £525—five hundred guineas). "I now propose the health of my earliest patron, Mr. Stuart." This was immediately followed by the health of his latest patron, Mr. Jones Loyd; and both toasts, as may be readily conceived, were received with great enthusiasm.

27. *Lord Brougham.*

I heard Mr. Stuart of Dunearn describe the extraordinary power which this distinguished orator had in quickly mastering a subject. He mentioned an instance of a visit which the rising barrister and future statesman paid him at his seat in Fifeshire. He had placed on his visitor's bedroom table a new work just published, which was causing at the time considerable interest. At breakfast Dunearn said, "Brougham, you must have sat up late last night, as I thought I heard you moving about your room when I was half through my night's rest." "Oh, yes, it is quite true. I wished to read the volume you left for me." The book being somewhat a large one, Dunearn remarked: "You don't mean to say you achieved that?" "Well of course I read rapidly, but I am now quite *au fait* with its contents." Mr. Stuart had read it attentively, and being anxious to hear Mr. Brougham's views, found him at home on every point to which he called his attention.

Dunearn described to me his first visit to London with Harry Brougham. I believe at the time they were youngsters attending the high-school of Edinburgh or the univesity. Among their first lions in the metropolis to visit was the gallery of the House of Commons. An important debate was going on. Brougham became greatly interested in it, and every now and then he whispered, "Oh! Stuart, this is very fine." He had repeated this several times, and just as the gallery was about to be cleared for the division he said: "Stuart, you'll see me here some day."

In 1832, I met Mr. (afterward Sir Francis) Walker Drummond, of Hawthornden, at dinner in London, when he told us with much heartiness: "Well, to-day Stuart and I have been down to the House of Lords to see our old schoolfellow, Harry Brougham, on the woolsack." About Brougham Mr. Stuart mentioned the following anecdote:

There was a rule among the Scotch judges and the senior members of the bar, when on circuit, that *they* only had the privilege of drinking claret; the juniors being restricted to sherry and port. The circuit was at Ayr, and Brougham sat as senior member of the junior bar present, just "under the salt." The claret came down to him, and should then have crossed the table without paying tribute, but each time it came, Brougham filled his glass.

This had been observed by the president. "Do you see," said his lordship to his friends on the right and left, "that impudent *fallow*, Brougham, helping himself to *claret*. If he tries it again, I'll speak to him."

Round came the claret, and Brougham as usual filled a bumper. "Maister Brougham," exclaimed his lordship, *ore rotundo*, "that's claret." "I know it is, my lord, and excellent," was his cool reply.

At the hospitable table of a friend near Harrow, I met a gentleman who had spent one Christmas recess at Brougham Hall in Westmoreland with the Lord Chancellor and his aged mother. The old lady was sitting by the fire in her arm-chair with her illustrious son between herself and her visitors, when Mrs. Brougham, tapping the Chancellor on the arm, said in her purest Scotch, which I believe she never lost: "*Hary*, you should never *hae* left the *Hoose* o' Commons." To which he replied: "I believe, mother, you are quite right."

28. "*No bobbing here, Boyd*" (*Lord Clyde*).

The siege of Antwerp, in 1832, attracted many military and civilian amateurs from London, among the latter my late brother. He was an intimate friend of Colonel Colin Campbell (Lord Clyde), who was then at Antwerp reporting the progress of the siege, as was believed in a semi-official capacity, to the British Government.

On one occasion the colonel and my brother were watching, in rather an exposed position, some heavy firing between one of the Dutch and one of the French batteries. Campbell, observing my brother suddenly make a profound bow to a shell that was passing nearer his head than was agreeable, called out in stentorian voice, at the same time crossing his arms and looking extremely stern: "No bobbing here, Boyd, no bobbing here." Then *sotto voce:* "Don't you see who are close to us?" (a party of French officers.)

My brother, by way of being facetious, supposing the Peninsular hero was no longer at fever heat, remarked:

"But you know it is your profession, not mine." To which the future field-marshal sharply retorted: "Then what the —— brought you here?" It was a standing joke against my relative, which the colonel heartily enjoyed and often told. My brother, however, firmly maintained that he had precedent on his side for bobbing the first time under fire, but Campbell contended that the plea was inadmissible when Frenchmen were so near.

29. *The Grand Duke Constantine of Russia at the Island of Iona.*

Captain Charles G. Robinson, R. N. (now Admiral Robinson), the writer's brother-in-law, who commanded for some years one of her Majesty's steamers in his survey of the west coast of Scotland, used to relate a circumstance showing the strict observance of the "Sabbath" in the western islands. He had instructions from the Lords of the Admiralty to receive on board his ship his Imperial Highness the Grand Duke Constantine of Russia, with directions to escort him to as many points of interest on the west coast, and in as brief period as possible, as the grand duke was on the eve of returning to Russia. It unfortunately happened that Captain Robinson steamed toward the famous little island of Iona, and dropped his anchor in its sacred waters with the Russian flag flying on the "Sabbath" day.

No doubt the subject of this famous island as the retreat of learning during the Gothic ignorance which pervaded Europe after the overthrow of the Roman empire, and as the seat of learning from which issued those pious monks and laymen who were again to revive and propagate Christianity throughout Europe had been ably and extensively discussed in the gallant captain's cabin the previous evening with the illustrious passenger; but great was Captain Robinson's disappointment, in landing for the purpose of acting as the Grand Ducal cicerone, while inspecting the remains of those monastic ruins so interesting to the archæologist and traveller, to discover that the custodian of the keys would be no party to the royal visit on a Sunday. Captain Robinson knew the man, but no persuasion would induce him to resign the keys for even half an hour. The captain then explained how urgent time was, but it was of no avail. He then tried what a great name would do, and asked the obdurate Ionian if he was aware whom he had brought to the island? "O, ay, Captain! I ken that fu' weel [1] by the flag; *he's* the Emperor o' a' [2] the Russias." "No," said the captain, "he is not the emperor, but he is the emperor's second son, and admiral of the Russian navy." "Weel, Captain Robinson, I ken you vera weel, [3] and there's nae officer in her majesty's navy we like better to see at our wee island than yersel, but had it been Queen Victoria her ainsel I wadna' gie up the keys on the 'Lord's Day.'" The captain during this discussion kept the illustrious tourist, with the members of his suite and some of his own officers, at a little distance, pending the negotiation; but seeing it was a hopeless case, brought it to a close by remarking: "I presume you would not be so scrupulous in drinking a glass of whiskey on the Sabbath Day?" "That's a different thing entirely, Captain Robinson." The visit to Iona concluded by the gallant captain persuading his imperial highness to jump and scale walls, and inspect antiquities, and thus make himself, under the circumstances, independent of the holder of the keys.

30. *The Duke of Gloucester and the Mayor of Liverpool.*

His Royal Highness, when general-in-command of the Lancashire district at the end of last or the beginning of

[1] I know that quite well. [2] of all. [3] very well.

the present century, received great attention and hospitality from the corporation of Liverpool. One of the mayors, whose table he frequently honored with his presence, was an especial favorite with the royal Duke, but the worshipful gentleman had not had in early life the advantage of much education. The Duke used to relate two anecdotes of the worthy mayor. He was seated at the chief magistrate's right hand at dinner. It was in the dog days. When the fish was introduced, it was speedily discovered by all whose olfactory organs were in the least sensitive, to be in such a progressive state that his royal highness, with the guests on both sides the table, lost no time in sending away their plates. Still the mayor went on with his fish. "Mayor, Mayor," said the Duke, "do send away your plate — the fish is quite tainted." The mayor, at the moment he was addressed by royalty, was in the act of taking another mouthful. "I thank your Royal Highness, but I have a stomach that will *disgoust* any thing." On another occasion, the mayor was a good deal surprised to observe that his royal highness did not send for a second supply of turtle. "Surely your Royal Highness will take another help of turtle soup?" "No thank you, Mayor." "Do pray, your Royal Highness, fill your royal stomach," was the reply, "for there's plenty more in the kitchen."

31. *Only one Word out of Place.*

Soon after the conclusion of the late war between the Northern and Southern States I was introduced by my friend Mr. Ward, an American citizen who had resided for many years in this country, to General Burnside, since nominated to a seat in the Cabinet at Washington, as Minister of War. This distinguished soldier told me he had entered the war a Captain of Engineers, coming out of it a Major-General. I never passed a few hours more agreeably than I did with the gallant officer. He gave expression to his own views without reserve or any apparent bias; whereas my friend Ward, who has since passed away from us, a very excellent man, who had spent the greater portion of his life in London, where he had acquired a large fortune, was politically as deeply prejudiced against England and English institutions as on the day he first landed on our shores from the United States. In fact, during the five years of my intimacy with him I never heard him praise or applaud any thing English. He was even reticent in regard to the fair sex. Opposite General Burnside and Mr. Ward at dinner sat a countryman of mine, whose affection and admiration for the land o' cakes remained unalloyed and undiminished, but who had never studied that line of Scotia's great poet:

"To see ourselves as others see us."

For there was little or no difference between friend Ward and himself in respect to national predilections, inasmuch as with the one there was nothing perfect out of Scotland, and with the other nothing perfect out of the North American States. Still my countryman "thocht it vera, vera wrang that Maister Ward, who had made all his cash in the ceety o' London, should be forever *rinning doun* and depreciating this country. Die ye think," said he, "that if I had made ma money in London, I would be forever disparaging it? It's a *blote* and a *vera* serious *blote* in Mr. Ward's character; it is vera, vera ungrateful toward that ceety which made him a *laarge* capitalist. Hoo vera different from his distinguished *frien'*, the general, who if he were not a strong-minded and discreet man and *only* coming to this country for a few weeks, he might return to America wi' some of Ward's *wrang* impressions! As it is, he led the general to *mak* a single observation which I'm sure he did not mean offensively, but, nevertheless, it went *recht* through me as a Scotchman." I asked to what he alluded. "Oh, *donnt* you recollect? it happened just after we had dined. Ward was going on as usual, telling us that if we *didna* keep a *calm sough* (civil tongue)—the Alabama claims were under discussion—America would teach our little island a lesson we should long remember; and by way of giving weight to his assertion, he added, 'I'll appeal to the general here.' All the general said was little, but it was deevilish severe, and it went through me like a dagger. 'We have no wish to hurt poor old grandmamma.' *Onnly* fancy the words, 'Puir auld Grandmamma' applied to Great Britain!! It stung me to my vera vitals. It *spok* volumes, just as if we were a *puir* worn-out country that could be subjugated at *onny* time, but it was all Ward's doing, confound him."

I never afterward saw the general, which I much regretted; but he has my best wishes that he may be as distinguished in the cabinet as he was in the field.

32. *A Scotchman's First Visit to Windsor.*

My father used to relate an anecdote of a country friend of his who in 1795 or 1796 arrived in London from Scotland, to spend a week or ten days, being his first appearance in the English metropolis. The first few days he lionized his visitor in town, and Saturday having arrived and about to close, my father asked him where he would like to attend divine service the following day, St. Paul's or Westminster Abbey? "Weel, as I *hae* seen *baith*,[1] I acknowledge if it is *a'*[2] the same to you, that I should greatly like to see King George, Queen Charlotte, with the princes and princesses, at their *ain kirk* in Windsor; besides, it would be killing *sae mony* dogs *wi ae stane* to see the royal family *thegither*;[3] and although it is in my opinion far from recht,[4] still as it is so, I would hae nae

[1] both. [2] all. [3] together. [4] right.

objection to gang on the Terrace at Windsor after the kirk had scaled,[1] and see the royal family walking there—all which I hae read o' in the newspapers, and listen to the band o' music, although for *ma ain* part, I disapprove o' music on the Lord's Day." "Well," said my father, "you must mention all this to my mother, for unless she consents to accompany us, I cannot leave the old lady in London." My grandmother was gained over, and at an early hour next morning the carriage was on its way to Windsor, reaching the castle yard in good time for the service at the Chapel Royal. Our friend from Scotland was highly satisfied with having said his prayers in company with King George, Queen Charlotte, and the larger portion of the royal family. After service lunch at the Castle Hotel followed, and as a preliminary to a stroll down the long walk, dinner had to be ordered. But before this was arranged my father asked his friend if there was any thing he particularly liked. "Na, my good sir, I live very plainly at *hame*, but there is *ae* thing I am vera fond of, and I am told it is better in England than *ony* where else, I allude to *dooks* and green peas." "Ah," said my father, "I find you are no bad judge of what is good, but ducks and green peas are most expensive." "Weel, it is *onnly* once in a way, and I *dar* say I shall never be at Windsor again, and I wish you would just allow me to order the *dooks* and green peas on my own account." "Oh," said my father, "I cannot object to that, but recollect what I have told you." "Ah, never mind that, my kind friend, that part o' the dinner shall be mine." After the long walk had been explored the party repaired to the terrace, where the king, queen, and royal circle, soon afterward appeared, and the worthy Caledonian had to submit to a large infliction of music, which vibrated on his Presbyterian ear on a "Sabbath" perhaps as strangely as a Spanish bull-fight strikes

[1] The congregation had separated.

the eyes of an Englishman who beholds it for the first time.

However, my father considered that his friend and countryman had so far passed through the trying ordeal of the early division of a day at Windsor with wonderful tranquillity and composure without any apparent violent disturbance of conscience, either in listening to the tones of the organ in the Chapel Royal, or to those of the military band on the Terrace.

They now returned to the hotel for dinner, and after the fish, soup, and possibly *entrées*, had justice done to them, the "*dooks* and green peas" came on the table. Personal appearance has much to do with success in this world; and the ducks and green peas secured an instant tribute of praise. He had never seen in the whole *coorse* of his life finer *birdies*, or peas so weel dressed, in fact, every thing he had ever heard of *dooks* and green peas in England was now confirmed. "There is no doubt," said my father, "that you are correct in that, and they should be better than in Scotland or anywhere else if the quality is to be regulated by the price, for the charge they make for this article of food is quite monstrous." "Have you any idea," said my countryman, "what 'dooks' like these will cost, for really they are fine birdies?" The first gleam as to price had evidently at last broke upon him. "I cannot tell you at present," said my father, "but you will hear of it soon enough, so let us proceed with our dinner, and talk of this afterward, and I am in no way to blame, as I intended to have ordered a nice small saddle of Welsh mutton, which I dare say you never met with in Scotland." My father's brother was one of the party, but the difficulty was to keep my grandmother in the dark as to the *ruse* which was being concocted. As the day drew near its close, and a twenty-miles' drive to London lay before them, two orders had to be issued, the bill and the carriage. My father quietly left the room, paid the bill, and enlisted the landlord as *particeps criminis* in the hoax that was to be practised on his Scotch friend.

Dinner, So and so.

	£	s.	d.
Wine, etc., in all	1	18	0
Ducks and green peas for 4, at £3 3s. each .	12	12	0
	£14	10	0

The waiter handed the bill to my father and retired. "Ah, just as I expected, enormous, but my part of the bill is moderate enough, £1 18*s*." "What," inquired his friend, "is the sum tot-al?" "Why here is the bill, and I very much regret to say you are charged £12 12*s*. for the confounded ducks and green peas." Fortunately, my grandmother had retired to prepare for the home journey, as at this juncture my father described the excitement of the visitor to Windsor as something bordering on the terrible, and there was every probability of his Majesty's liege subjects being disturbed in passing, by such exclamations as "Most scandalous charge; villanous imposition; disgraceful robbery," etc. "Why, I verily believe I could buy a' the *dooks* in my part o' Wigtonshire for twelve guineas, and the green peas into the bargain; but," addressing my father, "it's a' *ma ain* fault, for you gave me timely warning *no* to meddle *wi' sic* like food." "Ah," said my father, "you must keep yourself calm, for it will not do for you to speak so loud in Windsor, and what is very unfortunate I brought very little money, not calculating on an expensive dinner, but I can pay the £1 18*s*., and the hostler's charge for the horses. Now, William," addressing his brother, "what money have you?" "Only thirty shillings." Then applying to his friend, whom he adjured to keep cool, "What money have you got in your purse? "*Weel*, here's every penny I *hae* in my pocket, as I *dinna* like carrying much money *aboot* me in the streets of London." The amount proved to be five pounds and a few shillings. "This," said my father, "is very awkward, for it will never do to offer to pay half the bill. The only way I see to meet the difficulty is this, that as my brother and myself have to be in London early to-morrow, and under any circumstances must return to-night with the old lady, who never likes to change her bed, we have no other alternative than leaving you behind in pawn as it may be termed, and my servant shall ride down the first thing in the morning with the cash to redeem you." "Leave me *alane* in a strange country and *amang* a set o' d—d robbers! *Na, na;* I am ready to-morrow (Monday) morning to pay this swindling bill, but if King George himself *cam doon frae* the palace there, and asked me to sleep in this *confoonded* inn, I would refuse. *Na*, I'll speak to the landlord from the inside o' your carriage," which by this time had come round to the door; and, fearing even the bare possibility of detention, he forthwith bolted downstairs, and hurried into the carriage, where my grandmother was seated. The old lady, who was still in the dark as to the trick her sons had been playing their friend, became quite alarmed at the excited manner in which their visitor had bustled into the carriage, where he instantly screwed himself into a corner, squinting out in a direction exactly opposite to landlord and waiters standing outside the door. My father and his brother getting into the carriage and driving from the door soon comforted their friend, whose first inquiry was how they had managed with that "*awfu* shark o' a landlord?" "Why, of course, by telling him that you did not wish to run away without paying the bill, and that it was your first visit to Windsor, and that you were ignorant on the subject of ducks and green peas, but would know better next time." "That is quite true." Then addressing my grandmother, "Why, madam, I shall never *thole* (endure) the *sicht o' dooks* and green peas for the remainder *o'* my life." "I cannot understand you," said the old lady. "Then, madam, you have not seen the bill *o'* the dinner which your son has had so much difficulty in settling." "Do show your mother the disgraceful bill, which I would like to frame and hang over my mantel-piece in my dinner room at *hame.*"

She soon inspected the document, and at once detected the large item of £12 12*s.* for ducks and green peas. The *dénouement* arrived by the old lady handing back the bill, which she designated "a work of fiction, barely suited for a week-day joke, and altogether improper for the Sabbath."

In after-years, in Scotland, my worthy friend, as an old man, often told the Windsor story with great glee, expatiating upon it as being one of the most successful *Hox-es* he ever knew.

33. *A Distinguished Nephew.*

My brother and myself received an invitation to dinner from our friend the late Mr. John Ritchie, father of the late Advocate-General of Bengal, whom Lord Canning subsequently appointed a member of the Supreme Council, and whose premature death at an early age, in the midst of a brilliant professional career, was so deeply mourned by a large circle of private friends and public admirers.

I was unable to dine with my friend; and next day my brother told me I had lost the opportunity of meeting one of the most extraordinary young men he had ever met in society. This was William Makepeace Thackeray. The public had yet to read "Pendennis," "The Virginians," "Vanity Fair," "English Humorists," etc. He was a great favorite with his uncle Ritchie, who, while he was a boy at school, had foretold that such brilliant talents must lead to a conspicuous career. A good many years after this, I was one morning on the railway platform at Brighton, coming to town by the express, when I observed the gifted author passing to and fro, peering into different carriages, unable to find a place. There was one vacant in our carriage, and I brought him back to occupy it. We had been disappointed in our London newspapers, the consequence of which was that before we were almost through the first tunnel an animated conversation was going on, though my distingushed fellow-traveller remained silent.

I began by asking one of the party, a banker of note, some question or other, which I knew would receive an effective reply—probably, the cause of the large shipments of specie at that moment being made to China. A short discussion on Eastern banking ensued, which I did not unnecessarily prolong, as I had to unfold the avocations of three others of the party, so that I had to proceed at once with my process of development, otherwise the express train, by which we were then rapidly approaching Reigate, would, I saw, defeat me. One of our party was connected in commercial affairs with America and the West Indies: no doubt the high price of cotton and miserably low price of sugar, which I, as a matter of course, glanced at, were indices sufficient to show my astute friend the table of contents of traveller No. 2. There were two of our fellow-passengers as to whom and their callings the great *littérateur* was still unenlightened. They were both leading members of the money market; and as I was racing against time, I had to launch out at once into stocks and shares, contango and backwardation, and every other puzzling term I could think of for the edification of my friend, whom I had watched narrowly throughout our journey, and discovered that the *olla podrida* I was serving him with was extremely palatable; so that by the time we were entering the London Bridge station, "I guess we had boxed the financial and commercial compass pretty considerably."

I accompanied my companion into the city, and during

our short drive he said: "What a lot of subjects *we* have been discussing! and my impression is, you brought them on the *tapis* on my account." "Solely," I said, "especially as I could not speak to you at the commencement of the journey *sotto voce*, for I soon perceived you were puzzling your heavily-taxed brain as to the four individuals with whom you were to be imprisoned on our journey." In wishing me good-morning, he said he should not easily forget the trip from Brighton, nor the manner in which I had furnished him with a glossary of the occupants of carriage No. 63, adding: "Why, you compressed within an hour information sufficient to have been spread over a week." "Ah, recollect," I said, "we were travelling by express, and as we do not every day meet a Thackeray, I should let him into a secret—*videlicet*, that I wished to set off my friends as well as myself to the best advantage." "And you succeeded admirably in doing so." "Now pray do not make a Scotchman blush so early in the day. *Au revoir!*"

A friend of mine had been an unsuccessful candidate for parliamentary honors, and resolved to drown his disappointment by treating a party of exhausted M. P.'s, at the end of the parliamentary session, to a whitebait dinner at Greenwich. I found myself unexpectedly asked to officiate as vice-chairman, and was equally unprepared for the unlooked-for pleasure and distinction of having as my right-hand supporter Mr. Thackeray. The latter had never met so many Scotchmen at dinner before, or at least at a Greenwich whitebait party. There was an immense amount of post-prandial oratory, involving much mutual laudation. "Good gracious," said he to me, in a whisper, "do they mean all they say? for, if so, there are some three or four men at this table already—how many more may come to the surface before the evening closes I know not—qualified to be prime ministers; what say you?" I could only tell him that it was pure metal—no alloy whatever, for he must have observed that Scotchmen are averse to waste any thing, even oratory. "So it is not claw me and I'll claw you?" "Oh dear no." "Then," whispered Thackeray, "I have been extremely remiss in not having carefully perused the debates during the past session, so as to have been familiar with the political characteristics of your great Scotch statesmen. Your explanation," he added, "being so perfectly conclusive, and as you make every thing so self-evident, you may be equally able to enlighten me on another point. I am told there are several men of immense wealth at this table." "Quite true." "That being the case, is there one of them, supposing I stood in need of it, that would lend me £1,000?" "A dozen, you may be sure. There would be quite a rush and scramble who to get his check-book out first to fill up the amount." "Thank you very much for the information, and if there are any marines at Greenwich oblige me by telling them this."

34. *A Deputation to the Colonial Minister on Australian Affairs.*

I had been intrusted by the Pastoral Association of New South Wales with a large number of petitions to both Houses of Parliament, embodying the claims of the squatters of Australia to have granted to them leases of their runs, instead of being merely yearly tenants of the Crown, liable to have their licenses withdrawn at the whim or caprice of a Boundary Commissioner, or other official of the Colonial Government. There had occurred some very grievous cases of oppression, to which the "squatters," as the owners of the herds and flocks, and as the pioneers of the increasing prosperity of the huge island-continent of New Holland, felt that they could no longer submit. The petitions having been presented to Parliament, we had next to arrange a deputation to wait upon the Colonial Minister

—at that time Lord Derby, or rather, I should say, Lord Stanley, for as yet he had not succeeded to his father's title. I had the honor of being requested to select the members of the deputation, and the applications to join it were very numerous. We were to be introduced to the Colonial Secretary by a member of the Lower House; but as neither he nor myself had ever been in Australia, I saw that, in approaching Lord Stanley, a serious responsibility devolved upon me in having undertaken the nomination of the individuals who were to head the deputation. I therefore resolved that no point or topic in connection with the Australian wool question, or with the pastoral interests generally of that widely-extending region, should arise, either directly or incidentally, without having some one of our party fully competent, as a practical man, to impart the information the minister might call for. I accordingly looked for representatives of our Yorkshire and West of England cloth manufacturers; next, for one or two squatters who possessed some years' experience of Bush life in Australia, and could recount its hardships, and explain the management of those vast flocks on the extensive area over which they pastured. I was right, for this appeared to interest his lordship much, as well as the answer which one of the squatters gave his lordship to his inquiry who his neighbors were in the Bush. "Why, my lord, my two nearest neighbors I discovered to be old Cambridge Trinity friends." This struck the minister forcibly, as he remarked that it portended the germ and nucleus of an important future population in Australia. I had next to look for support in strengthening our deputation with representatives of the London and Australian merchant and shipowner, as well as the Sydney, Melbourne, and Adelaide merchant. All those interests were represented in the sanctum of Lord Stanley, and we were accompanied, besides, by one or two members of both Houses of Parliament; so that we numbered about twenty-five in all—as many, indeed, as there were chairs to seat. The question was entered upon seriously, and it proved a source of extreme satisfaction to me to find that no point was mooted by the illustrious statesman (and none escaped him) which some member of our deputation could not elucidate and explain. His lordship gave us an attentive hearing, extending over two hours, and, at its conclusion, intimated his willingness to grant leases to the Australian squatters, "but *not* for twenty years, as Mr. Boyd asked—being more than is granted in this country—but on a footing to be subsequently arranged, and which nothing would be wanting on his part to render satisfactory."

As we rose to retire, his lordship very courteously said that he had never received a body of gentlemen from whose extensive and valuable information on matters of importance in connection with our southern possessions he had gained more benefit. Sir William Molesworth, who was a few years afterward Colonial Minister, subsequently complimented me for the judicious manner in which I had culled and selected the members of the party to wait upon Lord Stanley, proving, as it did, from the successful results of that day, that we had approached the minister armed at all points. The honorable baronet gave me a *carte blanche*, which I frequently availed myself of, to call upon him at all times, either to join future deputations to the Government on Australian affairs, or indicate where I might consider that his services in or out of Parliament would be useful.

35. *The Late Major Nolan, 70th Regiment.*

Major Nolan, the father of Captain Nolan, whose name is identified with the charge at Balaclava, was a man of infinite humor, and told his anecdotes in a very quaint style. The following, which he told me, was one of his best; and he shall tell it to the reader in his own words:

"At the time that I was *locum tenens* for the Consul-General at Milan, in 1835–'36, a countryman of yours, by the name of Russell, called upon me to have a *visé* for his passport, at the same time handing me a letter of introduction, and announcing the important fact that he was so much *plaised* with the capital of the Austro-Italian States that he had *sarious* thoughts of remaining some weeks in it. 'All right,' said I, 'and that being the case, you'll dine with us to-day;' and I showed him *jost* the same little attention I should have shown you or any other *dacent* sort of a fellow, and I tell you that but for the *lapsus*, which I shall relate, I had no fault to find with Russell. Their Imperial Highnesses the Grand Duke and Duchess had issued invitations for an afternoon party at the Palace, and I had secured one for my newly-imported Scotch friend, who accompanied Mrs. Nolan and myself. After the presentations to their Imperial Highnesses were concluded, the guests were desired to be seated; but it would appear that the Palace chairs had not been accustomed to receive a full-sized and full-weighted Scotchman, for no sooner had Sawney sat *down* than *down* went the chair, landing him in its *débris* on the *Imparial* floor. He got up as *spadily* as possible, and, to the great astonishment of the proud members of the Austro-Italian Court, commenced instantly to repair the chair, keeping back the royal footmen who had hurried up to remove the wreck. When I witnessed this, I could have wished an opening in the floor into which I could have leaped to get out of sight, for my vice-consular dignity as the representative, at the time, of British majesty was sadly humbled. But, will you *belave* it, your countryman—bad luck to him—continued his operations as carpenter, or cabinet-maker—both if you like—to the broken-backed and broken-legged chair. There was now nothing else left for me to do than to rush forward and call out to him in the broadest and most emphatic Scotch,

'What the deil are you aboot? Will you keep you d——d *hauns aff* the chair, and let the *flunkies* remove the bits?' What do you think he said? 'I assure you, Major, I can repair the chair; I can indeed.' I had now lost all control of my temper, for the eyes of *la crême de la crême* of the society of Northern Italy were upon me and the Scotchman, and I exclaimed in my despair—I fear not in a subdued tone—'D—— you and your repairs!' I was now asked who my friend was, and I thought my best defence would be at once to say that he was a member of the Russell family. This saved me, for it circulated magically through the royal circle that he was a scion of the ducal House of Bedford. This affair, with his supposed connection with Woburn Abbey, made Russell a lion, and the inspection went off right well, as he was a powerfully-built, good-looking man. But such,' said the Major, 'is the dourness (obstinacy) of Scotchmen, that I never could persuade Russell that he was not quite *en règle* in his endeavor to repair on the spot the Emperor of Austria's broken chair.'"

36. *A New Zealand Jury in the Early Days of the Colony.*

I was much amused last summer by meeting with the the son of a well-known and much-respected Yorkshire rector who had spent fifteen years as a stock-holder and squatter in the district of Otago, and hearing him describe some of his colonial experiences. One of these was the non-orthodox, or, at all events, unusual course pursued on one occasion by a jury composed of Scotchmen before they could agree on their verdict.

A midnight row and fight had occurred at a sailor's public-house in Otago, in which one of the earliest colonists, a Scotchman, was killed in an encounter with a foreign sailor. The coroner issued his warrant, and the prisoner was committed for trial. When the case came before the judge, it was seen to be clearly one of manslaughter; but one of the jury took a different view of the matter, contending rather vociferously in the jury-box with his colleagues that it was murder. The judge therefore desired them to retire and fully consider their verdict. The court-house at Otago in those early days was a wooden erection; and the authorities, not calculating on jurymen disagreeing among themselves, had made no provision for an apartment to which they could adjourn. Under these circumstances, a room was ordered for them in Donald Ross's public-house. On his way to the hostelry, one of the jurymen, who resided in the country, called at a shop for a parcel that was lying for him, which, on rejoining his brother-jurymen, he placed in the corner of the room. My informant was staying at the inn, and occupied the apartment adjoining; and as the walls, at this infantine period of the future city of Otago, were similar to those of the court-house, every word was heard by him. The obstinate juryman began by making some slight apology for having given so much trouble in the matter, but they must recollect that the "*puir* murdered man was a Scotchman, and *ane o'* their earliest settlers. *Hooever, ma friens*, you'll *sae* far agree *wi'* me, that it is dry, *drouthy wark*, and I propose that before we begin we *tak* some *whuskey*." This was unanimously assented to; the hand-bell was rung and the floor stamped upon for Donald Ross, the landlord, also a Scotchman, who quickly obeyed the summons. "*Noo*, Ross, let us *hae* some *o' yer vera* best *whuskey*, for we are *a'* terribly *drouthy wi'* that bothering job in the *coort*, and we *canna* settle the matter there, and we are *ganging* to try what we can do here." The whiskey was soon brought, and dispatched, when the foreman reminded them that they must now set to work seriously and settle their verdict. Their obstinate friend confined himself to one point, and admonished them never for a moment to lose *sicht o'* the fact that "the *puir* murdered man was a Scotchman, and *ane o'* their earliest settlers." "But," said the foreman, with the concurrence of the others, "the judge will not *tak* that as a verdict, nor will he mind a bit *aboot* his being a countryman *o'* ours." "Then," said his impervious colleague, "his Honour must be *brocht* to our way *o'* thinking, that I am resolved on." "This is *naething* but nonsense," exclaimed the foreman, and the others fully supported him. "*Weel, weel,* I *canna* help that, the *puir* murdered man was a countryman *o'* our *ain—ye canna* deny that—and *ane o'* our earliest settlers. I *doa'nt* mean to say I should *haud oot* as I am doing had he been an Englishman or an Irishman, but I owe it to *Scoteland,* and *sae* do you, to see justice *doon,* and *naething* short o' hanging the *scoonerel* will ever satisfy me." The foreman and the rest of the enlightened panel were now quite at a loss how to proceed. "*Weel,* as I see," said their refractory friend, "that this affair will occupy a good while yet before we can agree, I move that we *hae* some *mair whuskey,* for never since I *cam* to the colony was I ever *mair* exhausted by *ony thing* than this." The proposal met with no dissenting voice, and Donald soon entered with a fresh supply *o' whuskey.* While this was being discussed, the eye of the obdurate juryman settled upon the parcel in the corner of the room. "What *hae* you got in that *laarge* paper, Mac?" "Oh, that's *ma* fiddle: I *brocht* it into the *toon* last week to be repaired, and I called for it as I was coming here." "Oh, man, it is a long time since I *hard ye* play the reel o' Tulloch." "*Noo,* Mr. Foreman, what *dir* ye say to a little music?" "*Weel,* I *hae nae* particular objection, but we must not forget that we must soon get back to the *coort.*" The reel of Tulloch-gorum was played in Mac's best style; and my narrator ably described my countrymen beating time with their feet so lustily, and accompanying this with such Highland vociferations, to which until that day he was a stranger, that there was some peril of Donald Ross's floor giving way.

The music over, and the second supply of *whuskey* finished, the foreman insisted, notwithstanding the unsettled position of the verdict, of returning to the court, where he took upon himself the responsibility of stating to the judge that they had agreed upon a verdict of manslaughter, for the whiskey had so far a good effect on the pertinacious juryman as to render him nearly altogether tongue-tied, for all he could manage to lisp out was that "the *puir* murdered man was a Scotchman, and *ane o'* their earliest settlers;" but he was utterly incapable, thanks to the *whuskey*, of proceeding with his original view of "wilful murder," as contradistinguished from manslaughter.

37. *Quarter or Half-Margin.*

A letter signed "Victoria Cross" appeared in the *Pall Mall Gazette* on October 20, 1868. "Victoria Cross" was one of the officers of the storming-party at the capture of the quarries, an advanced work of the Russians in front of the Redan. The party ran out of ammunition, and thereupon the officer ("Victoria Cross") sent a sergeant and two men to the rear with orders to bring a supply as fast as possible. They returned with a polite message from the officer in charge of the magazine, that he should have what he required if a proper "requisition" was sent in writing. In the mean time they were driven out of the quarries, and had to recapture the work at the point of the bayonet. On another occasion this officer, after the fall of Sebastopol, had found one of the Russian magazines on fire, and had, on returning to camp, to make a hurried report on the circumstance, but it was returned to him, because it was written on "quarter-margin" instead of "half-margin." On reading

"Victoria Cross's" letter, which was an amusing one on a very serious subject, as the brave survivors of the Redan and the quarries knew to their cost, I sent the following letter to the *Pall Mall Gazette:*

"QUARTER-MARGIN *v.* HALF-MARGIN FOOLSCAP."

"SIR: Which sized foolscap Lord Wellington wrote upon I cannot at this distant day discover; but I am reminded, on reading 'Victoria Cross's' letter, in your impression of the 20th, of an anecdote I heard from the lips of the gallant Peninsular general, the late Honorable Sir William Stewart, G. C. B. An Irish soldier in the General's division had been detected robbing a poor Spanish peasant. Lord Wellington, in consequence of some previous cases of a similar kind, had issued a notice to the troops that the first man discovered robbing or pilfering would be hanged. General Stewart sent a written report of the matter to headquarters by an aide-de-camp, a young officer, who returned with a verbal reply from his lordship ordering the delinquent's instant execution. 'Do you know,' said the General, addressing his youthful aide-de-camp, 'that if you should have made a mistake in delivering this verbal order, and I hang this man, I may be hanged myself when I return to England? Go back and bring me written instructions.' Off rode the aide-de-camp to Lord Wellington, and told his lordship that General Stewart was afraid, if he hanged the prisoner without a written order, he might himself be hanged when he got back to England. 'Quite right,' said his lordship, who issued the written authority; and the execution followed—no doubt without General Stewart scrutinizing whether the commander-in-chief's instructions were written on 'quarter-margin' or 'half-margin.'

"I am, etc.,

"A SUBSCRIBER."

October 22, 1868.

38 *General the Honorable Sir William Stewart, G. C. B.*

When I was a boy, Sir William was a frequent visitor at my father's, and at one period for several months while a villa residence (Drumtarlie Lodge) on our property was being prepared for him. Subsequently, he purchased the estate of Cumloden, and built a residence, from the windows of which he could see the ruins of the old castle of Garlies, in which his ancestors, the Lords of Galloway, had resided. I believe no general officer whose active military career closed in 1814 had been more severely or frequently wounded. If my memory serves me, he had from the period of his entering the service received thirteen wounds. From the one at Ferrol he suffered to the day of his death in 1827. A musket-shot struck him on the breast, and sent part of the glass of a wine flask into his chest, and at times he was subject to intense agony from the glass working out of the wound. I received very great kindness from him, and I used to listen to his recitals of different incidents of the great war with fervent delight. He liked me to sit with him at Drumtarlie Lodge in the forenoon, but, fearing I might be guilty of intrusion, I went on with my shooting at some little distance in front of his residence, when I was pretty sure of being sent for to lunch.

Among the members of his household were Brice, his old valet during the war, and Mrs. Brice, his wife, a Peninsular heroine. The general used to tell many anecdotes of them, and this he did with much quiet humor. One story especially I recollect. General Stewart had been wounded in the early part of the action, and was brought to his tent to have his wound dressed, which being done, he ordered his charger, so that he might again go to the front. Amazed to hear this order given, Brice ran to his wife to tell her, and she instantly appeared before the general, expostulating most loudly against his doing so just as she had dressed and bandaged up his wound. Her expostulation was of no avail; the general mounted and went again into action, but within half an hour he was carried back severely wounded. Mrs. Brice received her wounded master almost in a passion. "Better, sir, you had followed our advice;" adding *sotto voce* as she went to prepare fresh dressings, "it almost serves him right, after what we told him." One of the general's aides-de-camp was his nephew, Lord Charles Churchill, and the following anecdote the general brought out against him while Lord Charles was on a visit to his mother's family in our county. His father, the Duke of Marlborough, had sent his son, as a birthday present, out to the peninsula, a splendid charger, of which the youthful aide-de-camp was immensely proud.

The two armies were lying opposite to each other, and there had been no active fighting for some weeks. Lord Charles, for want of something to do, apportioned a part of each day to showing off his charger, and frequently much closer to the enemy's lines than either prudence or safety warranted. The general had cautioned his nephew frequently: "I tell you, Charles, you will do this once too often; what folly to expose yourself in this way!" Next day the good advice was forgotten and the aide-de-camp as usual was riding at full gallop in front of the French lines, and closer to them than ever. At this moment off went a shot from the French, and over went the Blenheim charger, leaving his owner, who was unhurt, to walk back into camp amid the jeers and laughter of his brethren-in-arms, and to receive from his uncle a reprimand: "It almost serves you right, after what I told you, Charles."

General Stewart's numerous anecdotes of Lord Nelson were deeply interesting and instructive, and I have ever regretted, when passing my forenoons with him at Drumtarlie, that I had not made more notes of them.

I believe no two men were the more intimate and cherished friends of Horatio Nelson than George, ninth Earl of Galloway, who died an Admiral of the Blue, and his brother, Sir William Stewart.

There was no topic in General Stewart's eventful career on land and sea on which he delighted to dwell so much as on his early associations with the hero of Trafalgar. In those days, from having so many ships-of-war afloat, our marine force was insufficient to supply the demands upon this arm of the service, so that several regiments of the line were scattered through our fleets and squadrons to make up for the deficiency. General (then Lieutenant-Colonel) Stewart was directed to embark the 49th regiment, and a portion of the 95th (subsequently the Rifle Brigade) for service in the fleet, ordered to Copenhagen; "and my good fortune (said Sir William) was to be appointed to Lord Nelson's ship (the Elephant, Captain Foley), by whom I was treated as a brother." He was with the illustrious hero at the battle of Copenhagen; and when this event came up in conversation the general always spoke of the additional laurels which Lord Nelson that day gained as a negotiator. He described the instance of his coolness in sending off the well-known reply to the Danish authorities at the moment when his own position in regard to ammunition was so critical. "No; let my letter be sealed, otherwise they will think we are in a hurry." The night previous to the bombardment, Colonel Stewart, to whom Lord Nelson had given a share of his own cabin, mentioned to me that he had never seen the Admiral in higher spirits. He that evening entertained at dinner several of his own, as well as of Colonel Stewart's officers. On such occasions the famous portfolio was in requisition and on the table, containing much that was prized as works of art; but the chief attractions of the collection were the "Guardian Angels," as Nelson termed them, being different likenesses of the celebrated Lady Hamilton. Next day, as we know, Vice-Admiral Lord Nelson "put his blind eye" to Admiral Sir Hyde Parker's signal to retire, and on his own account commenced the bombardment. Colonel Stewart was at his side on the poop or quarter deck, when he said hurriedly to one of the men, "Send my steward to me." The order was obeyed at once. "Steward, see that the 'Guardian Angels' are put away safe below, and out of fire."

I recollect a deeply-interesting passage in Sir William Stewart's home-life, which gave us, as young people, much delight, and which lasted a whole week. The general was paying my father a lengthened visit, and one morning at breakfast the latter saw by the county newspaper that the 92d Highlanders were on their march through Galloway, to embark at Port Patrick for Ireland, and that the first detachment would arrive in our town (Newton Stewart) the following day. This famous regiment had formed part of Sir William Stewart's division in the Peninsula. The tears came down the cheeks of the old warrior when he heard this, for it naturally brought back many incidents and reminiscences of that great war in which those kilted soldiers had born so conspicuous a part. "I tell you, Boyd, I shall give the men a dinner each day as the regiment passes through." "And I," said my father, "shall give the officers a dinner each day to meet their old chief." "Agreed," said the general; and, breakfast over, he mounted his horse, Old Tom, which my father had presented him with, to ride into town and order a course of dinners for the Highlanders, while my mother had at once to commence her preparations for her military dinners to the officers. One of the chief difficulties at that time was to secure fish; for, although salmon was in abundance in our river, and in the estuaries of our coast, the best of it went off to London by mail-coach.

At least one-half of the men still on the strength of the

regiment had been in the Peninsula, and subsequently at Waterloo, but they wore the medal for the latter only. This ate into the vitals of the Peninsular army, that portion of it especially who had not shared in the glories of Quatre Bras and Waterloo. I have often heard General Stewart express himself strongly against this cruel injustice, that the heroic men who composed the victorious army at Salamanca, Vittoria, Albuera, and mounted the walls of St. Sebastian, Badajos, and Cuidad Rodrigo, were not considered entitled to have their breasts decorated with a medal! How that concession was so long withheld, or why the illustrious Duke who led those men in their triumphant career in Spain and Portugal opposed it, is an enigma I have never had explained. But the tomb closed on General Stewart, as it had done on a very large proportion of the survivors of that brave army, ere the late Duke of Richmond, who, as Earl of March, had shared in the glories of the Peninsula and Waterloo, persistently agitated the question, until this act of justice, so long refused in one all-powerful quarter, was at last reluctantly conceded.

I had often been told that no commanding officer during the campaigns of the Peninsula was held in more affection and respect by his men than Sir William Stewart. We had constantly heard this, and the fact was now proved to his countrymen in the march through Galloway of that Island corps which then bore on its colors Egmont-op-zee, Mandora, Corunna, Fuentes d'Onor, Almarez, Orthes, and Waterloo.

Many of the officers had the Waterloo medal, and nearly all who wore it had also been through the Peninsula. Each day, after dinner, while the regiment was *en route*, there was of course a change of military guests. One day General Stewart prefaced a toast—the health of one of the officers present—with some very animated remarks. Addressing my father he said, "No one felt more satisfaction than you did when I received the thanks of Parliament at the end of the war; and how was it that I secured this? Why, owing to the support I had from such men as my gallant friend opposite. He it was whom I placed as a young officer in charge of one hundred and twenty-five Highland soldiers on that now historic rock in the pass of the Pyrenees, desiring him to hold his position *coûte que coûte* and keep back the enemy who would approach him through the valley or defile. The result of that night's brave defence now stands recorded in our military details of the Peninsular War. His efforts were crowned with success; but only twenty-five men of the one hundred and twenty-five descended from the rock, and the officer in command is now your guest." The reply of poor Major Campbell (who had lost an arm) was that of a modest and devoted soldier, and, as far as I can at this distant day recall its purport, that he would rather again ascend the rock in the mountain-pass of the Pyrenees with another detachment of the 92d Highlanders than be called upon to make a speech in the presence of that party and of that distinguished general who had proposed his health, and who had so often led him and his men to victory.

At the termination of the war Sir William Stewart was offered a British peerage along with his brave brothers-in-arms, Lords Lynedoch, Hill, Hopetoun, and the Earl of Dalhousie; but from prudential motives at that period he declined the proffered honor, although, could he have anticipated that his grandson* would so soon inherit, by the death of two heirs of entail, a magnificent Scotch estate, with a palatial mansion, in the land of his sires, irrespective of a large property in Ireland, he most probably would have accepted a coronet.

* Now Mr. Horatio G. Murray Stewart, of Broughton, Wigton.

39. *A Scotch Marriage.*

My mother was always much opposed to my father, as a magistrate, interfering in the connubial affairs of other parties, matters which she considered should exclusively belong to the Kirk; and unless it was *very necessary* he seldom or *never* did so. The request to him was usually made under the seal of confidence by the female herself, and very frequently by her mother. A case of urgency having reached him through a private channel, he sent for the delinquent, a farm-servant, who was in no way anxious to be bound by a matrimonial link, and it was only by severe pressure being brought to bear that he at last consented to come next morning to my father's private room to meet a family group, and to make an honest woman of a girl whom he had wronged. I was a boy at the time, and witnessed the ceremony, which I considered very simple. After a brief exordium from the magistrate, the swain declared his name, and acknowledged the female—pronouncing her name—as his wife; she then, following suit, pronouncing his name as her husband. My father had now, I may say, got the parties into the vestry-room, as he had merely to write out the "lines," as they were termed, on two slips of paper, being a declaration by both, which he signed, his signature being attested by two male witnesses, while a copy of the document, or rather of the "lines," was handed to each. This constituted, as my Scotch friends know, a marriage as valid as if performed with full choral service at Westminster Abbey by his Grace the Archbishop of Canterbury. My father always gave the happy pair and their friends a marriage breakfast in the servants' hall. On this occasion they were all seated prepared to commence their *déjeuner*, when the bridegroom rose, as if he had forgotten something, and said he would return in two minutes;

but the two minutes having reached ten, the young bride was heard to exclaim again and again, "Whatever has become o' Willie?" The others proceeded to discuss a substantial Scotch breakfast, while the poor girl sat crying. A full hour was given Mr. Willie to return to his disconsolate and interesting young spouse. When all hope of his entering an appearance was given up, the poor creature returned in tears, with her father and mother, to their cottage. It turned out that the cruel and worthless Willie betook himself to the woods, where he secreted himself until nightfall, when he crossed to Liverpool in a coasting vessel, thence in an emigrant-ship to New York. The sequel of the story must be told—that before the vessel had reached its destination the family was increased by the appearance of a "little" Willie. My father was sadly mortified he had not received a hint of Willie's intentions, as he would have promptly issued a *ne exeat regno*, for Scotch magistrates in those days were almost omnipotent. His satisfaction in having brought Willie just in the nick of time *in vinculis* was a good deal diminished by finding he had slipped through his fingers in the manner I have explained. I well remember the benedictions my father received for having made *puir* Mary an *honest woman* (a Scotch expression for a marriage under such circumstances), her mother exclaiming, "Wasn't it *raal gude* o' the laird to *mak* Willie marry *ma dochter!*"

40. *The Late Judge Talfourd.*

Doctor Temple, the Bishop of Exeter, in his farewell speech at Rugby (November 30, 1869), stated that "among all the deaths of good men that he had ever read of—though there have been, no doubt, others that express more heroism, that express, in some way or other, loftier characters, that express what may deserve at other times more admiration — the one that had always touched him most was that of Judge Talfourd on the Bench, when he expired with his last words expressing a wish that all classes should have a closer intercourse with one another, and that there should be fewer of those barriers which keep men apart."

Lofty, noble, and generous sentiments so constantly flowed from the lips of that good man and upright judge, that I was quite prepared to find in one in whose breast similar feelings hold sway the panegyric pronounced on the lamented and accomplished Talfourd, clothed in language so chaste, so felicitous, and so appropriate.

Doctor Temple's allusion to the deceased judge calls to my mind a rather singular and striking incident in connection with his assuming the ermine. One Saturday he and Lady Talfourd, or, more correctly speaking on that occasion, Sergeant and Mrs. Talfourd, had come to dine with us at our country residence in Kent, intending to remain until the Monday. On the Sunday afternoon we started together on a walk. The first "lion" I had to show him was all that remained of the garden walls of the ancient Abbey that formerly stood close to the Abbey Wood railway station. I had in my pocket a sketch of the portion of the Abbey that was standing a few years previously. "But what think you, sergeant," said I, "of the trustees of a large educational foundation, dating from the days of Edward VI., the owners of the property, pulling the walls down to erect this farm-house from the *débris?*" "Do you mean to say so? I thought there were no such Goths and Vandals in England; and," continued the learned gentleman, "the garden walls would no doubt have fallen likewise, had not the protection of the cabbages and onions been looked upon in a pound, shillings, and pence point of view." We proceeded on our walk, and among other questions I put to my learned friend was, whether he was fond of the House of Commons.

He said emphatically, "I hate it!" I then told him I had heard his name discussed a few evenings before at the club, and that there was not a dissenting voice as to his having the first seat on the Bench, on a vacancy occurring, as the Liberal party were then in power. He stopped and said, "My dear friend, I have been overlooked by my own party two or three times, and I dare say shall be overlooked again." He conveyed to my mind the impression that he never expected to be made a judge. I changed the conversation as soon as I could, perceiving that I had unfortunately touched on a tender chord. Our friends left us next day, promising to repeat their visit on the following Saturday week. On Tuesday the newspapers announced that one of her Majesty's judges (Sir T. J. Coltman) had been seized with cholera, which carried him off on the Friday. Various surmises appeared in the public prints as to his probable successor, but on the following Tuesday it was announced that Sergeant Talfourd had been chosen to fill the vacancy. On the Saturday afternoon, in accordance with their engagement, the newly-appointed judge and Lady Talfourd arrived at our house early, so as to have a stroll before dinner. We met them as they drove up, and when he had shaken hands with my wife, he seized me by both hands, and before uttering a word, as the tears rolled down his face, addressed me, "Oh, my dear friend, how inscrutable are the ways of Providence; do you recollect our conversation last Sunday week?" "I do, indeed." "I assure you," he added, "the circumstance being so striking, the first observation I made on hearing of my appointment was in reference to what had passed between us on that occasion." I need scarcely add that after dinner, and before the ladies had left us, we drank to the health of our youngest judge in a bumper of our oldest port.

41. "*The World is still deceived with Ornament.*"

This is quite as true now as when Shakespeare wrote his "Merchant of Venice," and I shall here give a practical instance of it.

Some fifty-five or sixty years ago, Tom Reid, as he was familiarly known in the city of London, subsequently Sir Thomas Reid, Bart., was about to announce himself as a candidate for a seat in the Direction of the Honorable East India Company.

To those unacquainted with the preliminary arrangements of a candidate for that coveted distinction—now a thing of the past—the candidate or candidates for future election had to sit or walk about with their hats off in the court-room of the proprietors on the occasion of the election of a director, as a sign of their candidature. On this occasion Mr. Reid asked my father as an intimate friend, "Can't you give me a lift among some of your Scotch grandees at my first appearance as a candidate next week at the India House?" My father promised to see what he could do to serve his friend, and accordingly called upon the Duke of Gordon and told him confidentially that the simple recognition of a few coronets in Leadenhall Street would serve his friend and countryman very much. His Grace took up the matter heartily, and promised that his relation, the Earl of Aboyne, with himself, would do all they could to assist Mr. Reid. The result was that some dozen or more carriages, with coronets outside and a noble lord inside each, drew up at the India House, under the portico of which the Duke of Gordon introduced Mr. Reid for the first time to his noble friends.

When this section of the peerage began to move through the court-room, and were reported to be all the personal friends of Mr. Reid, the mercury instantly rose in his favor;

he was declared to be No. 1 on the list of candidates, and when the following vacancy occurred he gained the Directorship.

42. *The Late Mr. Rothschild.*

Upward of forty years ago my brother said to me, "Put on your hat and come with me, as I wish to introduce you to Mr. Rothschild." I was received by the great European capitalist very kindly on that and all subsequent occasions. I well remember how heartily he made me laugh. He said, "I like your brother, and I dare say I shall like you; and I do, generally speaking, like Scotchmen, but not all of them. Do you know," he said, addressing me, "that Scotchmen and ourselves are just the same? But your brother is a tight hand at a bargain, for when I deal with him in French Rentes I always lose money by him; he is such a screw. I hope to be more fortunate with you."

I may mention an instance where I discovered that he did appreciate a Scotchman. My brother and I met on 'Change a friend, who asked us whether we had written for any of the new English Loan (then contracted for by Messrs. N. M. Rothschild and Co.). "No, I have not," said my brother, "but now you mention it, I will." "Oh, my good sir, you are a day after the fair—the loan is all appropriated, and twice the amount applied for; and, moreover, it will come out at three per cent. premium." "Never mind," said my brother, "I shall apply for some—'Nothing venture nothing have.'" Accordingly, we went across to New Court, where my brother filled up the usual letter of application. "Is Mr. Rothschild in his room?" "He is." "Pray take in our names." He was as usual glad to see us. "Well, my friends, what can I do for you?" "I have come," said my brother, "to ask you for a *small* slice of your *large* loan." "Ah, you Scotchmen, you know what is good, but you have come very late; I hope you don't want much." "Only £10,000." "Well, my good friend, you shall have that amount." "Thank you, Mr. Rothschild," said my brother; "and will you kindly put your initials to my application, in case it may be overlooked in the hurry of appropriation?" He had a hearty laugh at this precautionary measure of my brother's, adding, "Well, as I have often told you, Scotchmen and ourselves are just the same; you shall have your £10,000, and my initials into the bargain."

43. *At Times there may be a Disadvantage in being a Scotchman.*

Provisions being very high in price, and a general discontent prevailing among the laboring classes, a meal mob or famine disturbance arose in our little town in Scotland. My father, finding matters to be so unsatisfactory, availed himself of a troop of the 5th Dragoon Guards, passing through the county from Ireland to the north of England, to call upon the commanding officer, to whom he furnished the requisite magisterial authority for the Horse Guards, and detained the troop, so that the tranquillity of the district might be preserved. Great excitement existed generally throughout the South of Scotland. The men composing the detachment were extremely well conducted, and no cause of offence had been given the inhabitants by the soldiers during the first few months, when one morning a trooper was detected robbing a hen-roost, or committing some act of petty larceny.

The delinquent was brought before my father, who, finding the evidence to be conclusive, was about to sentence him to imprisonment in the county jail. One of the corporals of the troop, who had been watching the case in the justice-room, was in the act of leaving it, when my father heard him muttering to himself in the richest brogue, "Well, and sure we are all ashamed of him in the troop;

but I am truly thankful to say that he is the *ounely* Scotchman in it." "What is that you say, corporal?" exclaimed the magistrate—"the only Scotchman in the troop?"!!! "On my soul and honor, your worship, he is the *ounely* Scotchman in the troop." "You don't say so seriously?" said my father. "On my sacred oath it's the *rale* truth, *sor.* There's Dennis here, who will tell you the same, your worship." "All right, *yer* honor," said Dennis—"it's sure and *sartain* he is the *ounely* countryman of yours, *sor*, we have in the troop." The prisoner did not attempt to deny this part of the impeachment; in fact, he hoped it would have a favorable influence with the magistrate; but it had a contrary effect, for, in addressing him, my father declared that his intention was to have given him a fortnight's imprisonment, but now that he knew that he was the only Scotchman in the troop, he would sentence him to a month. The corporal was delighted, and was heard to exclaim at the top of his voice to some of his brother troopers who were anxiously waiting outside to hear the result. "There's the proper sort of Justice o' the *Pace* for you, for the moment I *tould* his honor that he was the *ounely* Scotchman in the troop, he at once gave him a month instead of a fortnight."

Whether the prisoner, under the circumstances explained from the bench, would not have had a good ground of appeal against the extra fortnight, not being a lawyer, I leave others to decide.

44. *Scotch Funerals.*

I never enjoyed an afternoon more—and it was a very wet one—than one which I spent on the banks of the far-famed Lochinvar some twenty-five years ago. We were living at the keeper's house, and our friend the Laird of —field came to dine and spend the day with us. I had not seen my worthy friend since I was a boy, when he was in the habit of coming over as a guest to my father's. No man was so extensively acquainted with every person and every thing in our district as himself. The rain poured, and all shooting being out of the question, I had with him the longest and most agreeable conversation on Galloway matters I ever had, either before or since.

Among other topics, I got upon the subject of Scotch funerals, and asked the laird if the manner in which they were now conducted had been altered or improved since I left the country. "*Weel*, they *hae impruived* and they *hae* not *impruived;* for they still *gang* on in *mony* places *maist* [1] the same as when ye *wer* a bit o' a lad." I sought for information in regard to the "services."

To those not initiated in the arcana of a Scotch funeral I should explain what the "services" were in my day. The parties invited to the funeral assembled in the dining-room. The servants began their duties by handing round a tray with glasses of port, accompanied by sponge-cake, Scotch currant-bun, short-bread, and biscuits; a few minutes elapsed, when the tray went round again with sherry; a moderate interval ensued, when glasses of brandy circulated—always a favorite, and generally eliciting such remarks as, "here's something that will *haud the grip;*" [2] then followed a round of whiskey, and the last two "services" were usually rum or shrub; I have seen both. Having recounted to the laird my early impressions of Scotch funerals, he said I was nearly as *recht* [3] as possible, and then described to me a disgraceful scene he had witnessed at the funeral of my grandfather, at which a clergyman of the Kirk of Scotland—"Was it not a mercy he did not belong to Galloway?" said the laird—"fell *aff* his horse in the avenue quite *fou*, his horse *rinning awa;* and the minister, unable to move, was dragged to one side of the road,

[1] almost. [2] tickle the throat in passing down. [3] right.

speechless and insensible, while the funeral procession was passing."

"*Weel*," continued the laird, "as we are on this subject, I must just tell you that I was *sairly* put to it *mysel*, and *no* a hundred miles from *whare* we are sitting. *Div* you[1] recollect Mr. ——?" "Yes, I do; he who had so excellent an appetite?" "The *vera* man: what a *gude* memory you must *hae* to *mind*[2] *sae lang* back! I was *lang* connected *wi'* him, and took a' the trouble about the funeral. We *gied* a *gude wheen*[3] o' his *friens* a dinner after we returned *frae* the Kirk-yard, and I was *deevilishly* put *oot* o' temper after it. I had the key o' the cellar, and there was *naething* wanting in the way o' drink, and every thing was *ganging*[4] on discreetly when a *whalp* o' a chap, *withoutyn ance*[5] consulting me, began, that he did, and finished a very *gude* amusing *sang;* for I was *forfoughtened*[6] wi' a' the arrangements o' the funeral that day, and *vera* foolishly *did'na stap* him at first, as it would *hae* prevented a' the *collieshangie*[7] afterward. But the *sang* was *ower*, and there was *nae* use looking back; but it was a *vera* improper proceeding in the house o' mourning. The *de'il* was in the *maist*[8] o' them that afternoon, for they actually *caa'd* on him for *anither sang*. Then I *spok* out, and I *tauld* them distinctly that if there was *anither* verse o' a *sang* in that room not *anither* bottle o' drink should they *hae*. That was the only threat that would *stap* it, for they liked the drink *ower weel*, and we had *nae mair* singing."

Following up the same subject, I remember the late Mr. John MacMillan, formerly of Charleston, South Carolina, and afterward of Liverpool, describing to a large party in London a scene which he witnessed at a funeral in Kirkcudbrightshire, either in the Glenkens district or the Minigaff. He had left Galloway as a youth, never having been

[1] do you. [2] remember. [3] a good many. [4] going. [5] without once. [6] fatigued. [7] quarrelling. [8] most.

at a Scotch country funeral; but on the first visit to his family he was asked to attend the funeral of a gentleman farmer, a friend of his father's.

The party invited had assembled in the house of mourning, a great number arriving on horseback. Then commenced the "services," to which Mr. MacMillan, although a Scotchman, was a stranger. When the hearse came to the door to receive the coffin, a scene of outrageous impropriety presented itself, such as he would never be able to forget, for the spectacle came before him of the wife and daughters of the deceased, overwhelmed in grief, watching from behind their bedroom curtains the departure of the remains of him whose spirit had fled, and in whom their dearest affections centred.

The operation of mounting the horses as a sequence to the "services," was a most difficult one, although it was not yet 11 o'clock A. M. A considerable proportion of the funeral *cortége* had to be lifted into their saddles, amid the jeers and noisy laughter of those who had been asked that day to pay respect to the memory of the deceased. When the procession was about to move, one of the riding party exclaimed in a loud voice, which the poor ladies heard, "We *maun tak* the near cut across the moor, and we shall *bate* the hearse and the corpse by some miles; I *ken* the *roddie* weel." This was unanimously agreed to, and Mr. MacMillan, who was on horseback, was invited to join the equestrian party, which, on leaving the hearse and the procession of carriages and gigs (sometimes very numerous at a Scotch funeral), immediately struck across the moor, when a series of Meltonian feats commenced, leaping ditches, breaking down stone walls, *alias* dikes, and jumping in every variety of style. This was usually followed by some heavy falls, accompanied by plenty of uproarious laughter. Mr. MacMillan described the scenes of that funeral and the funeral ride as something monstrously indecent. Several of the riders never reached the church-yard at all, having indulged in the "services" to such an extent that after being *cowped* from their horses they had to be consigned to the care of a shepherd or some other farm-servant who had been watching the proceedings of the party, until they had recovered from their disgraceful intoxication.

In returning to his father's house, Mr. MacMillan told us that he asked himself, in pondering over the proceedings of that day, "Am I, after ten years' absence in America and other parts of the world, again in moral and intellectual Scotland?"

45. *Charles Dibdin and his Son, Thomas Dibdin.*

One of my earliest recollections in boyhood was listening to my father repeating verses—for sing he could not—from the sea-songs of Charles Dibdin, whom he knew personally, and the impression this left on my then juvenile mind has never since been removed. He almost looked upon Charles Dibdin in his capacity of lyric poet as important to Britannia the ruler of the waves, as he did on William Pitt at the helm steering the vessel of the State. My father had lived constantly in London from 1785 to 1807, and no landsman could be more familiar with the details of the services of Rodney, Howe, Hotham, Bridport, and St. Vincent. He was personally acquainted with Lord Nelson, and had been present in St. Paul's when the tomb closed on the hero of Trafalgar.

As a merchant trading with America, the East and West Indies, as an extensive underwriter and shipowner, my father was thrown much into communication with sailors, from the admiral down to "Poor Jack." He knew well the hardships and grievances of which the man-o'-war's man complained. He felt convinced that this murmuring and fretting must sooner or later culminate in an outbreak.

This was proved by the alarming mutiny at the Nore, when the mutineers gravely threatened to deliver the British fleet to France, and were within twenty-four hours of carrying the menace into execution. There was no rhodomontade in this threat; the Government believed it. The public did the same, and I have heard my relation, an intelligent British merchant, one whom Mr. Pitt, as premier, frequently sent for to Downing Street, say, that the darkest days Great Britain ever saw were those during the mutiny at the Nore, which sent our Three per Cents to their lowest point of depression, namely $47\frac{5}{8}$. Some moderate and reasonable concessions were made, and Jack became again a loyal subject of King George the Third.

Who so much soothed or partially reconciled the sailor to his fate against the horrors of the press-gang as Charles Dibdin, whose verse, while it humanized, incited courage and inspired love of country? What so comforted and soothed the wife, mother, or sister, for the absence of their kidnapped relative as listening to one of Charles Dibdin's soul-stirring songs?

The sailor was unquestionably better off at the end of the eighteenth and the beginning of the nineteenth century than he was in the days of the Spanish Armada, when he was half-starved, as clearly shown by the American historian and diplomatist, Mr. Motley, and other writers. Still in Dibdin's time the instances are too many of the discipline on board the English man-of-war being apt to degenerate into tyranny. How could any thing else be looked for, when youngsters a very few years out of their swaddling-clothes were, through parliamentary influence, placed in command of ships? At this moment I have a distinct recollection of two cases—related to me by a distinguished admiral—of two youngsters, who had barely completed, the one his seventeenth and the other his eighteenth year, being made post-captains. One of them was the son of the admiral in command of the East India station; and when the death-vacancy occurred to which this boy succeeded, the admiral sent for his sailing-master (the late Sir William Bain), who told me the story, and said, "Bain, you must go with the boy, and keep him straight." Bain went with the boy, but could not "keep him straight," and within six months, or at all events a very short period, this youthful despot's pranks as a captain of a man-of-war so disgusted his crew that a mutinous spirit broke out, which ended in some of the poor fellows being hanged at the yard-arm. All this—as much less might—led to that painful charge against poor Jack, which unfortunately was too true, that British seamen who had fought at the Nile and Trafalgar were fighting against us on board of American frigates. But distressing as it is to think that there ever was such a blot to be pointed out in the character of the British seaman—and we hope the instances were not numerous—still no man in his individual capacity did half so much to popularize the British navy, and to invite and encourage loyalty among English seamen, as Charles Dibdin. Under such circumstances one might have expected that the Government of the period, when the necessities of such a man arose, would have carried out in no niggard spirit what would have met with the unanimous support of the nation had it been consulted—the grant of a *liberal* pension. The Government did grant him a pension of £200 per annum, but he was deprived of it by Lord Grenville, though it was afterward restored by another Ministry.

But to come to Charles Dibdin's son, Thomas Dibdin, whom I knew personally. My elder brother accidentally discovered him some thirty-five years ago living in poverty in an obscure part of London, and brought him to our house, where he became a frequent visitor. He was then about seventy-five years of age, and must have been a tall man when young, but he stooped very much. He was very intelligent, and looked a man of talent. There was a playfulness about the mouth and an expression in the eye extremely winning. He usually visited us on a Saturday, which was an important day with him, and lunched. My brother told me he would endeavor to get him on the Pension List, and I was fully persuaded he had succeeded, for shortly after my brother went abroad (1842) Tom Dibdin ceased coming so often on the Saturday. I ascribed the suspension of his visits to a delicacy of feeling, which he seemed to me to possess in a high degree, now that he had become, as I had in error supposed, a pensioner of the Crown; but no doubt death had ended his troubles suddenly.

The following is a copy of a note addressed to my brother by the poor old gentleman in 1839:

"September 17, 1839.

"Dear Sir:—Induced by your frequent kindnesses, I venture to enclose the attempt of an octogenarian to express what he imagined himself inspired with on seeing your pretty little brig the 'Wanderer' come in yesterday, and can only lament my verse lacks the power which, half a century back, gave popularity to my 'Snug little Island,' and, since, recorded the deaths of 'Abercrombie' and 'Wolfe,' form'd an effective Covent Garden 'Cabinet,' commission'd an 'English Fleet,' and composed 'Family Quarrels,' etc. I cou'd *then* boast not only of possessing 'a Friend,' but 'a Bottle to give him;' and altho' industrious, but unfortunate, dramatic speculations have brought my fifth act to a melancholy close, and nearly all my old patrons have gone before me, I trust I may find some left who may aid an unpensioned poet to terminate his lyric career with his once-favored finale of 'All's Well.'

"I am, dear sir, most truly and respectfully,

"Your obliged servant,

"Thomas Dibdin.

"B. Boyd, Esq., R. Y. S. 'Wanderer.'"

THE WANDERER;

WRITTEN BY

T. DIBDIN,

AND RESPECTFULLY INSCRIBED TO

B. BOYD, Esq.

I.

"Come, lads, here's good luck to the purser,
As long as he keeps us in grog,
And, tho' grumblers say times can't be worser,
We'll keep up hilarity's log.
Tho' a rolling stone, cynics may tell us,
Is famed for not gathering moss,
Its absence to *wandering* fellows
Like us can be scarce deem'd a loss.
While thro' each change of scene 'tis our notion
For air, health, and pleasure to roam,
We'll drink or in *port* or in ocean,
The *Wanderer* always at *home.*

II.

"She skims o'er the surge like a fairy,
With wonder while landlubbers gaze,
No lady so lissome and airy,
Looks smarter than *she* does in *stays!*
So ship-shape she graces the water,
Of each tar she's the love, pride, and joy!
And love, too, has boarded *her* quarter,
For she's often *attach'd* to a buoy!
So through each, etc.

III.

"You may talk of the 'Breeze and the Battle,'
For neither has she any fears,
Were great guns to blow, or shot rattle,
She'd greet 'em with so many cheers.
Had the lyrical pride of our navy,
Old *Charles*, seen her scudding along,
His muse he'd have 'dipped in the gravy!'
And made her immortal in *song*.
So through each, etc.

IV.

"She's placid and calm in fair weather,
Or when *storms* seem her hull to o'erwhelm,
She rides o'er the waves like a feather,
And cheerfully answers the helm!
With *idleness* ever untainted,
A huswife from stern to her *bows*,
With *Needles* she's not unacquainted,
And no *dairy* maid knows more of *Cowes!*
So through each, etc.

V.

"As for *female* attractions—she's got 'em,
Her cloth and her seams without flaw,
She's taut in her *tops*, and her *bottom*,
Surpassing all Neptune e'er saw.
She's fast on each point of her sailing,
While rivals wou'd pass her in crowds,
To beat 'em as yet never failing,
And looks quite alive in her *shrouds*.
So through each, etc."

In the manuscript I find that Dibdin had intended to have given more verses, as there is a VI.; but nothing follows. There is also written *in pencil* above "old Charles," "my dear father." At the end of stanza No. II. there is the following *môt à double entente:* "And by good fortune ever Be Buoyd."

Fickle fortune seemed to have decided against Thomas Dibdin receiving a pension from the Civil List, either as the son of Charles Dibdin, or in recognition of his own literary claims, which were varied, extensive, and distinguished, but here at least we find him the author of his "Snug little Island," the "Deaths of Abercrombie and Wolfe," his effective Covent Garden "Cabinet," or having commissioned an "English Fleet," and composed "Family Quarrels." These came from his pen when he had a "Friend and a Bottle to give him," besides much more, entitling him, on his own merits alone—without reference to his distinguished father—to a substantial recognition from the Crown, and the more necessary when he fell into poverty.

Under these circumstances, no one experienced a sincerer satisfaction than my deceased brother that an accidental meeting with this interesting and neglected old man should have enabled him to assure him that he had found "a Friend and a Bottle to give him."

No one could be more grateful for what was done for him than Thomas Dibdin. The giver and the receiver having gone, let us hope "*requiescant in pace.*"

46. *Duelling and Dining.*

The amusing fracas of Lord Robertson (at that time an eminent member of the Scotch Bar, and subsequently Dean of Faculty Mr. Patrick Robertson) with the officers of His late Majesty's — Regiment of Dragoon Guards, then stationed in Edinburgh, created a vast amount of amusement among his friends in the Scottish capital and in London.

I only hope that so good a story—one which Theodore

Hook pronounced to be among the best and most humorous he had ever heard—may not suffer in my narration.

A lady of *ton* in the modern Athens had issued her cards for a large evening party, and among the invited were the officers of the Dragoon Guards. I believe the colonel had allowed his band to attend on that occasion. As supper was about to conclude, a few toasts followed; and the one considered next in importance to that of the lady of the mansion was a bumper dedicated to the colonel and officers of His Majesty's — Regiment of Dragoon Guards. One of Shakespeare's characters in "Twelfth Night" says, "I have heard of some kind of men that put quarrels purposely on others to test their valor." Mr. Robertson had too much of the milk of human kindness to be suspected of any thing bordering on this, and the more unlikely among a class "jealous of honor," if not "sudden and quick in quarrel." But the gallant colonel of His Majesty's — Regiment of Dragoon Guards had himself alone to blame by opening the flood-gate to receive Mr. Robertson's uncontrollable rush of humor, for in a peculiarly mincing, lisping, affected tone he thanked the company for the honor conferred on himself and the officers of His Majesty's — Regiment of Dragoon Guards, and begged to assure the ladies and gentlemen present that the kindness which he and the officers of His Majesty's — Regiment of Dragoon Guards had received ever since the arrival of the regiment in Edinburgh had sensibly affected them: that in whatever portion of the globe His Majesty's — Regiment of Dragoon Guards might be stationed, the recollection of the hospitality they had met with in the metropolis of Scotland could never be effaced; and ever and anon, in a ten minutes' speech, out came "on the part of himself and the officers of His Majesty's — Regiment of Dragoon Guards." Whether the learned Mr. Robertson was carried away with the gallant colonel's grandiloquence, or whether he thought there had been "a wasteful and extravagant excess" of the colonel and officers of His Majesty's — Regiment of Dragoon Guards, was never clearly known; but it was a settled point in the minds of those present, from the peculiar twinkle in the eye of the learned gentleman, that before the evening closed there would be in one shape or other a second edition of the speech of the gallant colonel of His Majesty's — Regiment of Dragoon Guards. The description I heard reminded me of what I had myself once listened to in my own house in an after-dinner speech from an officer belonging to the Bombay army whose oratory lasted from twenty minutes to half an hour, during which time the Bombay army was honored by being mentioned once every two or three minutes. The late Mr. McCulloch, the political economist, who was present, muttered to his neighbor, "I wish to goodness there never had been such an army formed as the Bombay army, for depend upon it until we annihilate the Bombay army we shall not get another glass of claret."

Mr. Robertson being called upon to propose "The Ladies," took his cue in voice, manner, and pronunciation from the gallant colonel of His Majesty's — Regiment of Dragoon Guards. The imitation was perfect, and in a speech eliciting roars of laughter, which could not be controlled or suppressed by either sex, gave his toast. The speech had scarcely commenced when the clang of uneasy armor was heard from both sides of the table—the preliminary adjustment of swords previous to marching was clearly perceptible. The ladies, through their representative, had their thanks returned, when the gallant colonel of His Majesty's — Regiment of Dragoon Guards and his gallant companions at once took formal leave of the hostess, and retired from the gay scene.

Of course considerable excitement ensued, Mr. Robertson protesting with his usual gravity that the whole matter was quite inexplicable; that he had merely taken the gallant colonel's speech as a model for his own, and judging from the support he had met with, especially from the ladies, he naturally felt, as a diffident man, encouraged to proceed, for without their support and countenance he must have broken down. Next morning, at an early hour—duelling being in vogue and fashionable—Mr. Robertson received a message from the colonel of His Majesty's — Regiment of Dragoon Guards by a brother officer, demanding an instant apology, or that satisfaction which one gentleman was expected to give to another whom he had grossly insulted. Mr. Robertson at once said, "I am quite prepared to give Colonel —— the satisfaction he demands, but as he has challenged me, I think it right to inform you, sir, that I shall select my own weapons; for never having fired a pistol in my life, which I have no doubt the colonel has done very frequently, I should not be on an equality with him as an antagonist. I must beg you to convey that answer to him; at the same time assure him that I am at once prepared to afford him the most ample satisfaction, but, as I have already stated, I must name the weapons."

The gallant friend of the offended colonel endeavored to assure the learned and challenged gentleman that the course he proposed was altogether unusual in affairs of honor. "You, sir, may consider it so, but my determination is fixed; and as I must now go to court, I defer all matters until four o'clock, when I shall be found here, and prepared to receive any further communication." With this answer the bearer of the message from the colonel of His Majesty's — Regiment of Dragoon Guards retired.

A consultation of the officers followed on hearing from their *chef de mission* what had passed; and at four o'clock Mr. Robertson was again waited upon by the same officer whom he had seen in the morning, and at once discovered that *la chaleur* of the mess-room was rising precisely as he desired. "Well, sir," asked the learned gentleman, "what answer have you brought me?" He replied that in the opinion of the colonel and all the officers of the regiment only one interpretation could be put upon his (Mr. Robertson's) conduct in alluding to other weapons. "What interpretation, sir, I demand to know?" "That you wish to shuffle out of the responsibility of giving Colonel —— a meeting." "I argue," said Mr. Robertson, "from another point of view *in toto.* Your colonel is at home in the use of pistols; I am not; but in the weapons I shall propose he is equally at home as I am. Let the colonel make the concession—and let me tell you I consider the honor and character of the officers of His Majesty's —— Regiment of Dragoon Guards involved—and I give him instant satisfaction." Away went the officer to report to his colonel and the whole body of officers who were assembled in the mess-room throughout the day on this momentous affair. He told the colonel that Mr. Robertson would not yield a jot, and in fact hinted that he, the colonel, being the party challenging, and refusing to allow him, Mr. Robertson, to select the weapons, laid himself open to the charge, which he would not hesitate to expose, of shuffling and evasion. This being the learned gentleman's ultimatum, after such an innuendo against the commanding officer of His Majesty's — Regiment of Dragoon Guards, there was nothing left than to yield the point, and accordingly the officer was once more dispatched to Mr. Robertson, who had now also assumed the character of belligerent, to communicate the important fact that the question involving the selection of weapons was conceded. In the mean time the colonel thought it prudent to consult an old experienced military friend on the spot, to whom he related all the circumstances, and who, it appears, had more common-sense and acumen than all the officers of His Majesty's — Regiment of Dragoon Guards put together. "Why, colonel, if you don't take precious good care, you will have yourself and your officers made the laughing-stock of the army. Do you not know that Mr. Robertson, one of the most eminent men at the Scottish bar, is also one of the wittiest men in Scotland, and you will all be shown up as a pack of fools. Why, the story of your speech and his speech at the rout on Tuesday night is all through the club already, and will be soon notorious in Edinburgh and everywhere else. Take my advice, and get out of the farce without a moment's delay, otherwise you will find yourself trotted out in a manner not very agreeable to the regiment." On the colonel's return to barracks, no doubt considerably crestfallen, he found his friend had brought a formal letter, addressed to himself by Mr. Robertson, acknowledging his (the colonel's) courtesy in having waived the question of weapons, and that he, Mr. Robertson, had therefore the pleasure to inform Colonel —— that the weapons he would select were knives and forks, to be used in the mess-room of His Majesty's — Regiment of Dragoon Guards to-morrow evening at dinner.

The colonel now found how correct his experienced military friend had been; and the whole affair was pleasantly arranged by Mr. Patrick Robertson finding himself next day the guest of Colonel —— and the officers of His Majesty's — Regiment of Dragoon Guards; and if the learned gentleman was witty and facetious on the previous Tuesday night, he was doubly so on this occasion, as no guest during the stay of the regiment in Edinburgh was a more welcome visitor in its mess-room than the future learned judge, and the hospitality that was afterward mutually exchanged led to warm friendships between the eminent and learned gentleman and the officers of His Majesty's — regiment of Dragoon Guards.

47. *A Young Scotchman's First Introduction to a Lord Mayor of London.*

My father used to relate an amusing incident in connection with his first introduction to a Lord Mayor of London. He was then a youth of seventeen, and was residing with an old friend of his family, Sir William Douglas, of Castle Douglas, N. B., in America Square. The great merchants in those days did not object to live within sound of Bow bells. He was returning from the west end, about twelve o'clock at night, when an old gentleman, who had evidently dined, was, as the sailors say, "backing and filling" in the latitude of Somerset House.

As my father passed him, he said, "Young gentleman, do let me take your arm." The arm was at once tendered, when my father inquired, as he could not discover when he first hove in sight of the distressed pedestrian, and who now solicited him as a convoy, what tack he was upon, whether to the eastward or westward. "Oh, young gentleman, I go east." "Then it is all right, as I go in the same direction." My father was a strong-built lad, otherwise the duty he was undertaking might have proved somewhat difficult. In those days the devotees of Bacchus passed unnoticed and unheeded along the streets, and a Lord Mayor of London without his chain or his state-coach was not different from "other men;" so that the old Charleys, alias watchmen, of that period, allowed the chief magistrate with his youthful protector to proceed uninterrupted. The old gentleman said nothing to his juvenile help or prop of his high position within the region of Temple Bar. The only topic he dwelt upon, and a favorite one usually with Aldermen and Lord Mayors, was the dinner at which he had that day been present, either at the Thatched House or Freemason's, and that he thought a walk into the city afterward would do him good, as, generally speaking, he had very little pedestrian exercise.

At the end of Cheapside, he said, "Young gentleman, you must see me to my door," and to the immense surprise of his youthful escort—who had hitherto in Scotland only read of Lord Mayors as great historical personages, killing a Wat Tyler in Smithfield, or a Sir Richard Whittington possessing a cat, and listening to the chimes when about to leave London forever, which told him to return and be thrice Lord Mayor of London—the door he reached with his unsteady company was the Mansion House. He now discovered that the old gentleman whom he had picked up, or who had picked him up in the Strand, was no other than London's Lord Mayor. The doors flew open, and the state footmen received their master as usual, it being evident to my father from their composure that the Lord Mayor was not in the least more elevated or disguised on this occasion than the head of the corporation in those days generally was, in returning home at half-past twelve from a dinner-party. My father now wished to retire. "No, young gentleman, you now know who I am, and I must know who you are, and you must come in and be introduced to the Lady Mayoress," who, like a good wife, was sitting up for her husband. When he found that his youthful companion from the Strand, and who had answered his signal of distress so promptly, was on a visit to Sir William Douglas, he told him that the worthy baronet was one of his most cherished friends, that he was to dine at the Mansion House on the following Thursday, and that he (my father) would receive his own invitation next day, and must accompany Sir William, "and be sure to tell him what good care you have taken of the Lord Mayor to-night, and kept him out of all mischief." Sir William was immensely amused with his young friend's adventure with the Lord Mayor, and suggested his writing that day to his mother in Wigtonshire a full account of it; but the young Scotchman suggested that he had better delay doing so until he was able to say he had dined at the Mansion House.

This accidental meeting with the chief magistrate of London in the Strand at midnight led to my father being a constant guest at the Mansion House during the remainder of the year, and afforded abundant topics for many long letters to his father and mother.

I recollect my father relating the anecdote at his own house to a party of friends who had not heard it before, when I ventured to remark that this *bon vivant* of a Lord Mayor might have raised himself on a pedestal of imperishable honor for impartiality and ingenuousness through his medium. My father was at a loss to know how this could have been worked out. "Well," I said, "his tender of hospitality to you for bringing him home safe to the Mansion House, was not enough; he should have said: 'My young friend, I wish to see you to-morrow morning in the Justice Room of the Mansion House, as I shall have an important piece of business to transact, in which you can alone assist me.'

"This of course you would have attended to. The Lord Mayor should have stated from the bench that this young gentleman had found him, their chief magistrate, the previous night drunk in the Strand, and that he should now inflict a fine of five shillings on himself. If he had done this, and thus proved that he held the scales of justice with an even and impartial hand, that in his administration of the law it was the same for the rich as for the poor, he would have gone down to posterity as the Lycurgus or rather the Aristides of Lord Mayors, and you, my parent, would have been pointed at through life as the person who had brought such great qualities to the front, whereas your friend may have descended to the tomb, as many Lord Mayors have done, although there are some brilliant exceptions, 'unwept, unhonored, and unsung.'"

48. *The Scotch M. P. with his Companion, McCulloch's Commercial Dictionary, in the House of Commons.*

A member who had sat in Parliament for many years and was held in high respect on the Treasury as well as the Opposition bench, described to me a class of men who came into Parliament, but who neither from education nor from experience of the world and society were qualified to do any thing beyond voting, but who nevertheless fancied themselves statesmen, and occupied the time of the country in hearing themselves talk, so that they might next morning see the report of a speech infinitely better than any they had delivered paraded to the country. He often told me that in his opinion the gentlemen in the Reporters' Gallery were far too indulgent to those parliamentary bores. He described to me such a member, whose only qualification, it was alleged, was giving good dinners. This man fancied himself the successor of Adam Smith and David Ricardo; for if a financial or politico-economical question was to be discussed, the honorable member for —— took his place early in the evening, passing to it along the floor of the House with slow step and grave countenance, looking patronizingly on the Treasury as well as the Opposition bench, so as to convey the impression to the minds of the Commons of the United Kingdom that for this evening "I am Sir Oracle." His companion-in-arms on such occasions was that most valuable of all commercial volumes, "McCulloch's Commercial Dictionary." One memorable evening, when seated with his "trusty and well-beloved" mercantile lexicon at his side ready for instant reference, he found that the debate which he was to illuminate would not come on for another hour, giving him time for dinner. He left his McCulloch behind him on his seat, and a well-known and facetious member, one of the wags of the House, having ascertained that he was snugly seated at dinner, took the *great* absentee's place, to the infinite amusement of his brother M. P.'s. The wag carefully inspected the marked passages of the volume, and looking up at his friends, who were enjoying the scene, exclaimed, "Why, good gracious, if he gives us all McCulloch says on the subject, he must speak for hours. This won't do, I must stop it; the interests of Parliament as well as our own domestic comforts demand it. We shall be regularly bombarded; therefore, in nautical phraseology, I must close the channels by lifting the buoys." He at once proceeded to give an advanced or retrograde position to all the slips of paper which the coming orator had so carefully arranged to lead him unerringly to those lengthened quotations which were to constitute the main staple of his intended speech.

Dinner over, the honorable member returned to his place, where the great fear was that before he commenced his speech he might detect the displacements of his marks; but this event did not occur. A very few introductory remarks sufficed, when his hands were forthwith on his bulky tome; on went the spectacles, up went the volume. "I shall now read to the *Hoose* what Mr. McCulloch says." But alas! the eminent political economist's authority was not forthcoming. Up and down and across did his eyes flit and wander, but as nothing would avail, he made the important announcement that he would save the time of the *Hoose* (hear, hear) and proceed to another branch of the subject. And on this head he would refer also to Mr. McCulloch, but with like success. After floundering and floundering, to the vast relief of the *Hoose* he resumed his seat.

All the consolation or sympathy he got was from his next neighbor, an old and experienced member, who asked him why he always borrowed or attempted to borrow Mr. McCulloch's brains instead of applying to his own; for that he, like many others in that House, had a copy of the work, which he infinitely preferred reading at home, and for the future would advise him to do the same, otherwise another such exhibition in the House of Commons might render the volume unpopular, and make its distinguished author very angry.

One of London's city celebrities, an alderman and ex-lord mayor, who disliked this M. P. very much, was highly pleased at what had occurred the previous night in St. Stephen's, and for two or three days occupied himself chiefly in asking his friends if they had read the account of the absurd exhibition of Mr. —— in the House of Commons. "I always was prepared," said the alderman, "for what happened: for I knew him to be a most pretentious individual. He never," continued the alderman, "rose to any eminence as a tradesman, and because he has had some £60,000 left him by a relation, he imagines he is shortly to become Chancellor of the Exchequer." The alderman usually wound up his criticism—"Well, as long as he continues in Parliament he must be a distinguished member, as he is considered the ugliest man in it."

On another occasion this persevering *statesman* had been endeavoring to carry conviction to his hearers in the *Hoose* on one of his financial crotchets, and had occupied its attention, or rather its time, for some twenty minutes. When he sat down, Sir Robert Peel, who had lost all patience, told him that he had been talking on a subject of which it was evident he knew nothing, and gave him one of the severest castigations ever administered within the walls of Parliament. A member who was not in the House while Sir Robert spoke, asked on his return how the rhinoceros bore it. "Oh, he told us all on our bench, 'Mark my words, if I don't serve that d—— *fellow* Peel *oot* for this.'" "I hope," said an old and shrewd member, "that I may be fortunately present when you are serving out Sir Robert, for if you do it well, I shall expect on the next change of Government to see you in the cabinet."

There was a scene described to me as having happened at this member of Parliament's first election, which must have been highly amusing. He had to address his future constituents for the first time, and the meeting was to come off in the evening; but there being a difficulty in finding a place sufficiently capacious for so important and interesting an object, the clergyman offered to open his kirk for him, in return for the honorable candidate having already opened his purse-strings extensively in the district. Every corner of the sacred building was crammed, when the candidate for senatorial honors was seen mounting the steps of the pulpit with a large volume under his arm. "Ay, *mon, div* ye see that he is *ganging* up into the *pupit wi'* the Bible under his arm?" "*Na, na,* it *canna* be the Bible, *frae* the *binnen* (binding) o' the *buik.*" The mysterious volume was soon opened, and proved to be McCulloch's Commercial Dictionary, from which he read for nearly two hours, instead of attempting a speech of his own. Had he tried the latter plan, he never, it is said, would have graced the House of Commons, at least for that constituency. The author of the dictionary was always quizzed for having sent him to Parliament.

But the greatest of his numerous weaknesses, a rock on which so many self-made people suffer shipwreck, was an unquenchable thirst to have great people at his table. He had got so far as having invited one or two Junior Lords of the Treasury and Admiralty, with now and then a stray Under Secretary of State, but his ambition was to supersede them by one or two cabinet ministers.

In the fulness of his pride, he had confidentially announced to those near him in the *Hoose* what his aspirations and intentions were; still, the precise course of action he intended to pursue to secure his quarry was never exactly known. It was whispered that a member *de l'ancienne noblesse* had arranged the prandial programme for him, and it was fully expected that he would honor the prime minister with an invitation to a Wednesday or a Saturday banquet, but some one wisely advised him not to aim at such high game—placing before him, with a translation, the motto of the noble house of Cavendish, "Cavendo tutus." He therefore contented himself, perforce, with counting among his guests a Chancellor of the Exchequer, Mr. Spring Rice, and another cabinet minister whose name I forget.

49. *The Young Parson and the Duke of Norfolk.*

The late Rev. W. Wright, LL. B., of Brattleby Hall, Lincolnshire, Rector of Healing, whom I was in the habit of meeting occasionally some years back at Brighton, used to relate in a very humorous way how he first became acquainted with Charles, Duke of Norfolk. He was keeping his terms at Cambridge, and had come up to London on the Saturday for the purpose of seeing some famous actor, Kemble or Kean. He went to Joy's in Covent Garden to dine, so as to be in good time for the theatre, and had given his order to the waiter, who had left the coffee-room to see it executed. Wright's eye in the mean time was attracted to an elderly gentleman sitting at a table in the centre of the room, with a much more *recherché* dinner than he had ordered. He muttered something to himself as to his stupidity in not seeing this before. "You cannot do better," said the old gentleman, "than sit down here." "I quite agree with you, sir," said the young Cantab, "and I shall countermand the dinner I ordered." When the waiter returned, he found the young gentleman hail fellow well met, eating his dinner with the duke, concluding that, as he appeared quite at home and at ease with his grace, he must be at least a grand-nephew of the duke.

The Earl Marshal's dinner, which during the theatrical season he took almost daily at Covent Garden, never exceeded, wine included, a guinea, and four shillings to the waiters, or one pound five shillings in all. An extra bottle was ordered on this occasion. Dinner over, Wright had to be off to the theatre, and was about calling to the waiter to bring in his bill, when the old gentleman said, "Oh, no, you are my guest to-day, and next time you come up from Cambridge I shall be yours." Thanking his hospitable entertainer, and extending his hand, and receiving a hearty shake in return, he left the coffee-room, at the same time beckoning to the waiter to follow him. "Who is that nice old gentleman with whom I have been dining?" "Vy, does you mean to say you doesn't know?" "I don't, indeed, I never saw him before in my life. "Who is he?" repeated the young Cantab. "Oo his e," said the waiter, with an expression of countenance which the undergraduate of Cambridge never afterward forgot. "Vy e his the Dook o' Norfolk. Didn't you not know that ven you sat down so cool to dine vid im? Is grace a dines *eere* halmost hevery day, hand ve himagined you vas a relation hof hisn."

The collegian, after this hurried explanation, considered that something still was required from him to England's premier duke, with whom, and at whose expense, he had been dining *tête-à-tête*, and he hastened back to the coffee-room to enunciate if possible something like an apology; but the head of the Howards met this by saying, "Here is my card; I shall always be very glad to see you, either at Joy's or at Norfolk House: give me yours. I think," said the Duke, "we have enjoyed our little dinner together very much. I know *I* have," said his grace. "By this time," said Wright, "I was transformed into a diffident college youth, as the only rejoinder I could make was a profound bow."

50. *Sir Walter Scott.*

Nothing ever occasioned me at the time more surprise or disappointment than the result of an attempt made in the city of London to promote a handsome subscription for the Abbotsford fund, which was raised in order to secure the estate of Abbotsford to the descendants of the illustrious "Author of Waverley." I calculated upon £2,000 as a minimum. I suggested to the then Lord Mayor, who was a Scotchman, that nothing would distinguish his mayoralty more than giving his aid to this object, and his lordship entered at once heartily into the idea. Finding that the chief magistrate of London would give us his influence, we placed ourselves in communication with the present Earl of Stanhope, the late Lord Polwarth, and others, who cordially supported our views. The Lord Mayor requested me to arrange the *dramatis personæ*, and I accordingly suggested that we should make the meeting as attractive as possible, by inviting such personages as the Lord-Lieutenant of Middlesex, the Bishop of London (Bishop Blomfield), Dean Milman, and others alike distinguished by position as by literary and official eminence, to take part in the proceedings. Nothing apparently could be more satisfactory or promising to the well-wishers and promoters of the City of London Scott Abbotsford Testimonial. The Egyptian Hall of the Mansion House had been placed at our disposal by the Lord Mayor, and no sooner were the doors open than the place was filled. The Lord Mayor, the Marquis of Salisbury, the Bishop of London, and the other speakers stated the precise objects for which the money was required in the clearest, most forcible, and convincing manner; but I had "reckoned on the chickens to be handed over to the west-end committee before they were hatched." Lord Salisbury and most of the leaders in the affair had subscribed to that fund, but all that we got in the city, including the Lord Mayor's subscription—and £50 sent us by the late Earl of Aberdeen—was under £150! So much for the metropolitan admirers of Sir Walter Scott. Be that as it may, on this occasion *at least* they had left their check-books, their purses, and their sympathies, at home.

51. *How my Faith in Archæology received a Shock.*

I was escorting a party of friends to see the far-famed grotto in Oatlands Park, Surrey, now the property of Sir William Drake. One of them was a man of high accomplishments, and an archæologist to boot. "By-the-by," said I, "before we enter the grotto, or examine the tombstones of the Duchess of York's dogs and monkeys, let me show you this interesting ivy-covered tower and castellated relic, which is always much admired by visitors." In the mean time, as it was a broiling hot day, I found some shade for the ladies until the learned antiquary and virtuoso had minutely examined the remains to which I had called his attention. I told him I was anxious to hear what date he gave to the erection. His answer was, "I dare say you believe it to be four centuries old, but I assure you it is not more than two." I shook my head and declared such a date would never do, and, as I wished to roast my friend a little longer in the sun and in antiquities, I suggested one more walk round the building. That completed, he held to his original belief, and would not rise a year beyond the two centuries. He then asked me if I knew the date; I said I did, and that it was built by my late friend Mr. Peppercorne, the former proprietor of Oatlands, twenty years ago. We immediately took shelter in the grotto, and I need scarcely add that the subject of archæology was not resumed that day.

52. *His Royal Highness the Duke of Clarence (King William IV.) as a Member of the House of Peers.*

Among those who conscientiously and disinterestedly advocated the cause of the West India planter and proprietor, when the slave-trade was the question of the day, was Prince William Henry, Duke of Clarence, who, as a young officer in the navy, and subsequently as a captain of a man-of-war, knew the West Indies well. He always expressed his opinions firmly and distinctly, that the process entered upon of working out the emancipation of the negro should be gradual, and *pari passu* with the preparation of the negro mind for that freedom which ought not to be thrust upon him when his mental capacity was yet in too infantine a state to receive it. A notice of motion had been given in the House of Lords on the subject of suppressing the slave-trade, and in consequence my father had solicited an interview with the Duke of Clarence, and suggested to His Royal Highness that it would be highly desirable that his clear and sensible views on a question so nearly affecting the commercial interests of the nation should be made known to the country in his place in Parliament. The Duke agreed to take part in the debate, and requested my father to see him occasionally in the interim to talk over the subject. When the day approached for the discussion, His Royal Highness asked my father to be present, and I have heard the latter say that the Duke of Clarence's speech was excellent, well delivered, and commanded great attention.

At the conclusion he came to the bar to see my father, who offered His Royal Highness his congratulations on his success as a debater, at the same time remarking, "Why, your Royal Highness spoke for twenty minutes."

It may not be uninteresting to know the heads of our

future sailor-king's speech. As parliamentary reporting had scarcely come into vogue sixty-six years ago, it is consequently short. Mr. Wilberforce, attended by the Attorney-General and several members, brought up the bill for the abolition of the slave-trade for a limited time. The bill, on the motion of Lord Walsingham, was read a first time.

Thursday, June 28, 1804.—"The Duke of Clarence said he would only trouble their lordships with a few remarks. Since a very early period of his life, when he was in another profession, in which he knew not why he had no longer employment, he had ocular demonstration of the state of slavery, as it was called, in the West Indies, and all that he had seen convinced him that it was not only not deserving of the imputations that had been cast on it, but that the abolition of it would be productive of extreme danger and mischief."

On July 2d, of the same session, His Royal Highness, having now taken up the question, again addressed the House:

"The Duke of Clarence presented two petitions against the Slave Trade Abolition Bill—the first from Liverpool, the second from the merchants and mortgagees in London connected with our British West India colonies, praying that the bill may not pass into law. His Royal Highness said: If the bill be read a second time this session he would then feel it his duty to move their lordships, that the petitioners, pursuant to their prayer, should have leave to be heard by their counsel against the measure."

On the 3d of July, 1804, "The Duke of Clarence expressed himself decidedly in favor of the motion for delay. He adverted pointedly to the injustice of attempting to pass a bill of this nature without hearing at their bar those who had petitioned the House against it. Property to the amount of a hundred millions was embarked in our West India colonies, which returned annually eighteen millions to this country, producing to the revenue four millions a year. Was all this to be hazarded without deliberation, and without hearing those who were so materially concerned? He stated the titles of two Acts of Parliament passed expressly for the encouragement of this trade, which he considered as an additional and very cogent reason why their lordships should hear with attention those who had thus embarked in a trade on the faith of Parliament. He did not consider as any reason for their not now coming to a decision upon the subject, as had been stated, that some of those noble lords who approved the abolition were not present, since it certainly was the duty of every peer to be in his place. He had heard a great number of tales of cruelty exercised toward the slaves by the West India planters, but he was acquainted with many gentlemen of that calling of the highest respectability, whom he did not believe capable of committing or sanctioning any such acts of cruelty, and with whom, if he did, he should be ashamed to associate. He concluded by declaring his intention strenuously to support the motion of the noble Secretary of State for postponing the bill."

The question was then put on Lord Hawkesbury's amendment, which was carried without a division.

Whenever my father met His Royal Highness after this on any public occasion, he usually said, "Ah, Boyd, you brought me out on the West India question."

53. *A Wife's Devotion.*

My late friend Commissary-General Fitzgerald told me that, of all the horrors connected with war, the worst that he had ever witnessed was being called upon by his aunt, the Hon. Mrs. Fitzgerald, to accompany her, on the night of June 18, 1815, to the field of Waterloo, to search for the body of her husband, Colonel Fitzgerald. My friend, then a deputy-assistant, was stationed at Antwerp, and report having reached him that his uncle had been killed, he asked for leave, mounted his horse, and hurried to Brussels, where he found his aunt, with the Colonel's servant, about to start for the field of battle. He begged and prayed that she would leave the melancholy duty to himself and the servant; but neither expostulation from himself nor from some English ladies at Brussels was of the least avail. She insisted upon proceeding on her mission without any delay, fearing she might be too late to secure the much-loved remains. The journey there being accomplished, the widow and nephew, with a hand-lamp each, assisted by the attendant, discovered the body in one place and at a short distance the head, which had been carried off by a round shot. A cart having been procured, the aunt and nephew returned to Brussels during the night, with the remains of him who three evenings before had mixed with the gay throng at the Duchess of Richmond's ball. It may be inferred from this story that Mrs. Fitzgerald was a woman of great determination. She was on terms of intimacy with my father and mother, and I can recollect that a few years after Waterloo she passed a week at our house in Scotland. She was the mother of the late Right Hon. James Alexander Stewart-Mackenzie, many years M. P. for Ross-shire, subsequently Governor of Ceylon, and afterward Lord High Commissioner of the Ionian Isles, who married the eldest daughter and co-heir of Francis, Lord Seaforth. He was a man of high talents, with whom the writer and his late brother long lived on terms of confidence and private friendship. He had known us from boyhood, being a constant visitor, while he resided in Wigtonshire, at our house.

Mrs. Fitzgerald's maiden name was D'Aguilar. Her first husband was the Hon. Admiral Keith Stewart, third son of Alexander, sixth Earl of Galloway. The Admiral died in 1795, and his widow in 1797 married Captain

Richard Fitzgerald, whose career closed as a lieutenant-colonel at Waterloo.

54. *A Recollection of Mr. Secretary Stanley* (*Earl of Derby*).

On February 13, 1834, I witnessed one of those brilliant displays of rhetorical power in the House of Commons for which the late Lord Derby—then Mr. Stanley—was so famous. Connected with the occasion were a novelty and anomaly which greatly enhanced its interest, for Mr. Stanley, then Secretary for Ireland, was supporting Mr. O'Connell, who had moved that a select committee be appointed to inquire into the conduct of one of His Majesty's Barons of Exchequer in Ireland in respect to the exercise of his duties as a judge, and to the introduction of politics in his charge to a grand jury. The speech of Mr. O'Connell introducing his motion was couched in terms of great moderation, as no one listening to the eloquent and learned gentleman could gainsay the fact that circumstances of a very irritating nature had marked the conduct of the judge; and this view the Chief Secretary in his speech confirmed.

Mr. O'Connell declared that the question he had to submit to the consideration of the House was one involving the liberties, property, and lives of the people of Ireland, and that if the members of the House of Commons were resolved to turn a deaf ear to his appeal, then they were unacquainted with the state of Ireland, or grossly ignorant or grossly careless of the feelings of the Irish people. He charged the judge, firstly, with wilful neglect of his duty as a judge; and, secondly, with endeavoring to make up for his deficiency on the bench by acting as a violent political partisan. One of the charges was, that he scarcely ever attended in court before half-past twelve, and that he (Mr. O'Connell) could bring forward instances where fourteen prisoners had been tried between six in the afternoon and six in the morning.

Into the discussion of the gravest matters connected with Ireland I have always observed a tolerable amount of humor imported; and this case was not an exception, for the great Liberator—although expatiating, at times most earnestly and solemnly, on a gigantic social evil where the conduct of one holding the high and sacred office of judge was impugned—could not resist the opportunity of throwing some spice into his remarks, and giving them a flavor which seemed to be extremely palatable on both sides of the House.

If my memory at this distance of time is correct, the honorable and learned member for Clare, Cork, or Kerry—I forget which—told the House, in a vein of racy humor, that it was extremely hard, because this judge of the Exchequer liked to sleep in the daytime, the members of the Irish Bar, the solicitors, the jury, the witnesses, and the prisoners, too, who preferred to sleep at night, were to be prevented from doing so through the eccentricity of one man; the effect of which was—at all events with the gentlemen of the jury—that what they lost in the way of sleep in their beds they endeavored to make up in the jury-box. But then followed another serious evil, for the witnesses coming into court at six o'clock had dined, and, having refreshed themselves copiously, were frequently quite unable to give their evidence.

Mr. O'Connell, from the foregoing specimen, fully succeeded, as Tom Dibdin used to say, in keeping up "hilarity's log." He then quoted an instance of great hardship, where a Liverpool merchant had brought over to Dublin twelve or fourteen witnesses whom he had to maintain at a hotel at a serious expense; but this judge of Exchequer not appearing in court until almost the close of the day, the case never came on, and merchant and witnesses had to return to Liverpool. He then amused the House, and the gallery as well, with a description of one of the judges on circuit, who really was an early riser, coming into court betimes—frequently at eight o'clock—while his colleague complained of not unusually made it half-past three in the afternoon before he appeared on the bench, where he occupied himself writing one or more private letters. "Then," continued Mr. O'Connell, "at the very time when we have the lightest calendar of crime on record, for which the people of Ireland should have been highly praised and congratulated, the Government are allowing their characters to be steeped in the filth of a political disquisition from a judge on the bench." Mr. O'Connell, to use the words of the great dramatist, had now shot "all his shafts into the court (Exchequer) by which to afflict the emperor in his pride." Life-buoys were thrown to the doomed judge by the Right Honorable Frederick Shaw, Sir Robert Peel, Sir Robert Inglis, and Sir James Graham (then a member of the Government), who declared it was the most painful vote he had ever to give in Parliament, as in all probability he was about to sever himself from those friends with whom he had so long acted; but all was of no avail, as the Liberator's speech had placed the judge beyond every means of rescue; he was hopelessly among the breakers. His fate was sealed when Mr. Secretary Stanley rose and supported Mr. O'Connell. His speech, as usual, was most eloquent and piercing, at the same time free from any thing bordering upon acrimony; but the case was lost to the friends of the judge when he reiterated one of Mr. O'Connell's strongest charges against the accused, in having, with a calendar before him that should have elicited from the bench—especially in a country such as Ireland—the highest encomium, most heedlessly and inconsiderately launched into politics in his charge to the grand jury.

Mr. O'Connell carried his motion by a majority of 93—

167 ayes against 67 noes; this vote led to the judge's retirement.

A few months afterward, when I was a guest at a public dinner in Dublin, it fell to the lot of this very ex-judge to return thanks on behalf of the bar and the legal profession. I listened to one of the most classical and charming speeches I ever recollect hearing. He touched, with the brush of a skilful artist, on his own case, his colors being "so blended, softened, and united," there was nothing else left the most fastidious to do than to admire. His peroration was the only passage of his speech that could be questioned, for, like the postscript to a lady's letter, it was important, carrying with it a sting in reference to his retirement from judicial life, at the same time giving Earl Grey's Government a kick. He concluded:

> "When vice prevails and wicked men bear sway,
> The post of honor is the private station."

55. *The Marquis of Lansdowne, K. G.*

One evening, travelling by the 5 o'clock express-train to Brighton, I found myself the only fellow-passenger of the late Marquis of Lansdowne, who had been, as Lord Henry Petty, Chancellor of the Exchequer in the short-lived Government of the Whigs so early in the present century as 1806. I had shortly before this had a meeting on Australian affairs at the Treasury with his son, Lord Shelburne,[1] and having spoken to a friend, as the train was about to start, as to the date of his last letters from Sydney, his lordship made some able allusions to our southern colonies, and, what was satisfactory for me to hear, approved of the wholesome agitation we were following out in the promotion of emigration and steam communication. The conversation changed as we were passing Gatton, near Reigate.

[1] Afterward fourth Marquis of Lansdowne.

"There," said the marquis, "is the place (the gardener's house was all that was left of the ancient borough) that sent two members to Parliament before the Reform Bill of Earl Grey became law." I ventured to ask the marquis what his views were in regard to such boroughs. "Well, under certain limitations they are very useful, without reference to the party in power; for, if the country, through a Parliamentary majority, points to certain men to take charge of the government, some members of which, of high and commanding intellects and acknowledged experience, are of limited pecuniary means, it is a great hardship that such men, who have reached the goal after years of toil and struggle, should be compelled to meet some rich political cipher on the hustings, and there to incur serious liabilities in answering the corrupt demands of a body of venal electors. Some alteration must be devised to correct this, as well as to purify and curb the electoral body generally. The Reform Bill of 1832 achieved much, but there is much yet to be done."

I alluded to his lordship's borough of Calne having given Mr. Macaulay his first seat in Parliament, to which he remarked, that "nothing at a general election could have kept such a man out of the House of Commons, as half a dozen constituencies would have been proud to elect him, although the opening of a seat for him at Calne probably *placed* him in Parliament two or three years sooner. Therefore," continued his lordship, "here was a positive advantage, for to have seen such a man's political advancement retarded, no seat being procurable for him, would have been a national loss greatly to be deplored."

56. *Mr. George Dempster, M. P.*

I have heard my father say that, when he was a young man in London, he was in the habit of meeting in society Mr. Dempster, member for the Burghs of Forfar, Perth,

Dundee, Cupar, and the learned city of St. Andrews, who had entered the House of Commons in 1762, two years after the accession of George III., and did not retire from Parliament until 1790. He was a man much respected in and out of Parliament; and, as little more than half a century had elapsed when he became an M. P., since the Union of Scotland with England, and less than a quarter of a century since the battle of Culloden and the executions on Tower Hill, following the rebellion of 1745, he was peculiarly sensitive and tenacious in respect to the maintenance and vindication of Scottish rights; and his national susceptibilities were well known on both sides of the House.

One evening an English member, in his peroration, in some humorous remarks respecting Scotland, had given sad offence to Mr. Dempster, who was no exception to Sydney Smith's charge against Scotchmen of not understanding a joke, for the moment he concluded, up rose the aggrieved member, and in a loud voice addressed the Speaker, being resolved that his pithy rejoinder should be heard distinctly throughout St. Stephen's: "Sir, I beg to inform the honorable member, in reply to those most illiberal remarks with which he has concluded his speech, that I am proud of having been born a Scotchman and brought up a Presbyterian," and down he sat; when his honorable opponent rose and said, "Mr. Speaker, all I have to say is, that I consider the honorable member very thankful for extremely small mercies."

57. *Foreign Affairs, or rather a Temporary Complication in Home Affairs.*

I have always looked upon the Minister intrusted with the seals of the Foreign Office in this country with interest and respect, whether the holder of them was Lord Palmerston or Lord Russell, Lord Clarendon or Lord Stanley. The statesman who can keep us out of quarrels, or, when in them, get us out of them, must necessarily command a distinct and separate consideration in the eyes of the nation. That consideration was with me largely enhanced more than a quarter of a century since by an *imbroglio* into which I found myself, as the head of a *domestic* cabinet, most innocently thrown with a somewhat too sensitive foreign gentleman.

When —— was Prime Minister to King Louis Philippe, he had for his private secretary a gentleman of considerable powers, who subsequently held positions in diplomacy, both important and responsible. He had come to London on a short visit, and during his stay I asked him to meet some friends at my house at dinner. On such occasions, so as to avoid politics, which at that period ran peculiarly high, if any humorous celebrity were present, it was not unusual to ask for a recitation, song, or impromptu. Alfred Crowquill was one of my guests, and in his usual obliging manner had made an amusing contribution. The wine had again passed round, when my father, addressing Mr. Robert Coates (so well known as Mr. Romeo Coates), asked him to recite Fitzgerald's "Ode on the Death of Nelson," which some of us, with myself, had heard Mr. Coates deliver with such effect a few weeks before at one of Sergeant Talfourd's private theatrical parties, and where the foreign element was not unfrequently to be met with. It never occurred either to myself or any other of my friends that the ode in question was somewhat *mal à propos* for French ears, but it appeared, which I had not observed, that my Continental visitor suffered acutely at the lines—

> "Is there a British breast that does not beat
> At Nelson's triumph and the foe's defeat?"

and the climax, it seems, was reached while Mr. Coates was delivering the following passage:

"Yet as he lived, so did the hero fall:
Crouched at his feet he saw the humble Gaul,
Saw hostile navies into ruins hurled,
And England's trident rule the wat'ry world."

When Mr. Coates concluded, and had received our thanks, up rose our visitor, and *that* moment, and not till *then*, did the horrors of the foreign complication in which I, as the responsible party, had become involved, present themselves before me. A clear *casus belli*—the French flag insulted, every thing *de bello Gallico* flashed before my eyes. In fact, and in accordance with diplomatic usage, I fully expected that the aggrieved French gentleman would forthwith leave the table. Now I said within myself, "Oh, that I were for five minutes endowed with the diplomatic talents and power of a Palmerston, a Russell, a Clarendon, or a Stanley!" for I feared any explanation of mine would be *de pis en pis.* He told us that never before, in English society, had his feelings as a Frenchman been so deeply wounded, and a good deal more in a like strain. All I could say, in reply, was to assure him I very deeply regretted that the recital of the ode or address, written by Fitzgerald, had caused him so much pain, that I knew my regret was shared by all my friends, and by none more than by Mr. Coates; that it was entirely accidental, etc. We soon, however, discovered that Mr. Coates could not only admirably deliver a beautiful ode, but take the responsibility of doing so on his own shoulders. Addressing the offended gentleman, "Why, sir, the author of that ode, Mr. Fitzgerald, was an Irishman, and your father was an Irishman, although you are by birth and by domicile a Frenchman. Now, *that* to some extent should remove a portion of the poison from the case, and with a distinct disavowal on my own part of meaning any thing offensive, I must be permitted to say that I consider it very unfortunate that you had not for *this* evening allowed yourself to be considered an Irishman.

Still, I cannot sit down without begging to tell you, as you have alluded to your royal master, that there is no English gentleman at this table who has received so much marked kindness and attention at the hands of your Sovereign as I have done. Why, sir, King Louis Philippe has allowed me to address him with a freedom seldom accorded to any one by a crowned head. When I had the honor of placing my apartments at the Hotel du Nord, Boulogne-sur-Mer, at His Majesty's disposal; his yacht having been driven into that port by stress of weather in the Channel; at the very moment, let me tell you, sir, when it was feared that His Majesty's Prime Minister, who succeeded the illustrious statesman with whom you were connected, wished to go to war with England—I allude to the complications at that moment in the Mediterranean on the Eastern question, when the French fleet was considered superior to the British—I said, addressing His Majesty at the public reception he gave on that occasion to a body of my countrymen, 'Long live the King of the French; long live the Queen of England, and *peace* with England.' His Majesty's reply was, holding me by the hand, 'Mr. Coates, you shall *have* peace.' Sir, these words, when they reached the London Exchange, raised the funds within the next few days 4 per cent. For the incident to which I allude I refer you to the newspapers of the day."

Matters now assumed, if not a milder, a more promising complexion for the English party, as Mr. Coates had adopted an aggressive rather than a tranquillizing tone, at the same time intimating that he would have no difficulty whatever with the afflicted gentleman's royal master, as, were it requisite, he was quite prepared to proceed to Paris to solicit an interview with His Majesty, to explain, when in all probability he should learn that His Majesty, who in 1805 resided at Twickenham, knew Fitzgerald. Mr. Coates then turned his head to the now astonished Frenchman, and with infinite *naïveté* asked him this question: "Do you think His Royal Highness le Duc d'Orleans, as an illustrious *emigré* in this country in 1805, would have objected to Fitzgerald's ode, or even to the destruction of the Emperor Napoleon's fleet at Trafalgar?" This puzzling question was not answered; and Mr. Coates resumed his seat, when the amicable and convivial relations, which had been suspended for an hour, were restored.

58. *John Gordon, Viscount Kenmure, and Lord Lochinvar.*

I well recollect the agreeable impression made on my mind as a youth, the first visit I paid in company with my father, to Lord Kenmure at his ancient Castle of Kenmure, probably the oldest inhabited residence in Scotland. He had resided in early life for some twenty years on the Continent, and *la belle* France had imbued him deeply with those attractive and courteous manners which, without any reflections on our nationality, both sexes might do well to imitate. In after-years, during various tours which I have made in Europe, I have often had pointed out to me some old member *de l'ancienne noblesse*, the resident of the Faubourg St. Germain, of which class I always looked back upon Lord Kenmure as an unmistakable type. In the plays of Molière we meet with personages whom I carry in my memory as striking portraits of the Lord of Lochinvar. Burke tells us that "manners are of more importance than laws, as upon them in a great measure the laws depend. The law touches us but here and there, now and then; whereas manners are what vex or soothe, corrupt or purify, exalt or debase, barbarize or refine us, by a constant, steady, uniform, insensible operation, like that of the air we breathe. They give their whole form and color to our lives. According to their quality, they aid morals, they supply them, or they totally destroy them."

Had Burke lived after Lord Kenmure, I should have supposed that in writing the above passage the Scottish viscount's portrait was before him. Lord Kenmure likewise acted up to the full character of his countrymen in being most hospitable. He was fond of a joke, and few men could practise one more successfully. One of his jokes I now enjoy as heartily as I did when I first heard it. Most Scotchmen know that his grandfather William, sixth Viscount Kenmure, attached himself to the Stuarts, and fought, in 1715, against George I., at Preston Pans, where he was taken prisoner, and suffered on Tower Hill. One hundred and nine years afterward, George IV. (1824) restored the honors of Kenmure and Lochinvar. The family estates—at least the Kenmure Castle portion of them—when confiscated, were repurchased by the widow of the attainted viscount. Her son, John Gordon of Kenmure, married Frances, only daughter of William, fifth Earl of Seaforth; and she was the mother of the viscount of whom I write. He always spoke of his mother in terms of the deepest affection, and declared that she, and she alone, saved the family from a second calamity in the rebellion of 1745. Being a clever, strong-minded woman, she had discovered, soon after her marriage, that her husband, like his unfortunate father, was a warm supporter of the Stuarts. This discovery caused her the deepest anxiety and uneasiness. She likewise found out that he was keeping up a secret correspondence with the adherents of the Pretender. She had, therefore, to act promptly and decisively. Accordingly, she made a friend of the postmaster, and through a confidential servant had all letters for her husband first handed to herself for inspection, and thus possessed herself of all the secret dispatches coming either by post or by the hands of messengers. The moment for action having arrived, her husband's impatience knew no bounds. He was highly indignant that his letters were unanswered. Those his devoted wife had never allowed to be dispatched, and, by quietly and judiciously hinting to her husband that Prince Charles's party might probably not deem his adherence of value, he had been, in consequence, overlooked or set aside. This view of matters, so admirably put before her husband, succeeded. He became disgusted at being thus slighted, and remained in his old Castle of Kenmure, dispensing his hospitality and discharging his duties as a country gentleman and as head of his family, until the explosion broke forth, the sequel of which was the attainder of Boyd, Earl of Kilmarnock, Fraser, Lord Lovat, and others, followed by their execution on Tower Hill. Lord Kenmure had two English friends on a visit, and, to show them the lower district of the county, had arranged to take them the following morning to a meeting of the landed proprietors at Kirkcudbright. His lordship had sent orders to the landlady of the little inn half-way, where the horses were to be baited, to have a first-rate Scotch breakfast ready for two English gentlemen and himself. He had prepared his friends for seeing an original, on whom he was about to play a trick. During the evening he ordered six eggs to be sent to the drawing-room, at the same time desiring one of the grooms to go to the stable and pull out some long hairs from a horse's tail, a thing very usual on the banks of the Ken, where fishing-lines had frequently to be improvised.

The eggs having arrived through one channel, and the horse-hairs through another, the noble lord had to carry out his first operation, which was, with the aid of a needle, to puncture the shell, through which a horse-hair was introduced in each egg—a simple process. Having arrived at the inn, where breakfast was waiting, Lord Kenmure sent for the landlady, and said, "I hope you have not yet boiled the eggs?" "*Na, na*, my lord, I *hae na* boiled them yet." "Because," said his lordship, "one of my friends is *so* very particular, that he must see the eggs first, after which he will tell you, should he like their appearance, how long he wishes them to be boiled; bring up half a dozen as quickly as you can, as we are very hungry." The landlady went out and came back instantly with half a dozen eggs. The transfer or exchange of the Kenmure Castle eggs for the landlady's having been slyly effected, the former were ordered to be boiled two minutes and three quarters; the landlady promising to watch the boiling herself (*my ain sel*). As soon as the two minutes and three-quarters had expired, the lassie had the eggs on the table, but scarcely had she got down-stairs when the bell rang violently—"*Gang* back, Mary, this moment; *rin*, lassie, *rin*, for there's something *wrang*." "Tell your mistress to come here instantly," said his lordship. Away ran the girl, and her mistress was in the presence of the breakfast-party forthwith. "Why, my good woman," exclaimed Lord Kenmure, "what in the name of wonder, is this? Here is a horse-hair in my egg!" "Good gracious, ma lord, a *lang* horse's hair in the egg! Weel, weel, this is *ayont*[1] *ony* thing I ever *kenned*." The poor woman stood so bewildered at the long hair which had come out of the egg and was now lying on the table-cloth, that Lord Kenmure came to her relief, by telling her that it was at all events no fault of hers, and that they would now try another egg, when out came another horse-hair. His friends were convulsed, while the landlady stood aghast. They each broke the shell of their respective eggs in the presence of the landlady, whose state of mind and amazement at what she was witnessing had now reached a point not easily to be described; and the climax of her distress was reached when the two visitors for whom she had so anxiously prepared a good breakfast had each drawn out as long a hair from his egg as Lord Kenmure had from both of his. "How can you account for this?" said his lordship. "Oh, ma

[1] beyond.

lord, I see exactly *hoo* this comes *aboot:* that *doure*,[1] stubborn man, John, in the yard (the ostler) is forever letting the hens into the stable, and they get into the bunkers and eat the horses' corn, and it is *noo* clear to me that they *hae* swallowed the hair." "Well, never mind, landlady, we have an excellent breakfast here, and I don't think the eggs appear much the worse."

The party drove off, and in the evening returned to rest the horses. The first salutation Lord Kenmure received from the landlady was, "*Weel, ma* lord, they are *a'* killed." "What are killed?" "The heads are cut *aff* every hen I *hae*, as I will not risk *sic* anither thing as happened to your lordship and the gentlemen this morning; the *like* o' *it* never was known in the *hale* o' this *kintra*[2] *afore*." Sure enough, Lord Kenmure and his two visitors saw the poor headless fowls. "Then," said his lordship, addressing the persecuted hostess, "as you are resolved to change the breed, I must do this for you, as my hens at the castle never lay eggs with horse-hair in them," and accordingly his lordship replenished the landlady's poultry-yard on an extensive scale.

There was always some joke springing up with which the excellent Lord of Kenmure was in one way or other connected. My father used to relate one which is worth recording. There was a prisoner of war in Scotland, a distinguished officer of Napoleon's army, who was much esteemed by all who knew him. He was a keen sportsman, as well as a joyous, agreeable man, and no pains were spared either by Lord Kenmure or any of the adjoining proprietors to contribute to his amusement. The party assembled at Kenmure Castle were the following day to shoot across the country to a neighboring proprietor's seat, he being one of them. Early in the forenoon the attention of the general was drawn to a few small black-faced sheep

[1] obstinate. [2] country.

running to the top of a *knowe*,[1] and facing round upon the sportsmen. "Vat, vild?" "Yes," said the wag, at whose house the party were to dine and sleep, "wild sheep." "Vild ships! Ah, I see," said the general, "vild moutons—yase, yase—vild moutons; and are they to shoot?" "Oh, yes, general; go carefully round and go up to them quietly, and you will get an excellent shot." "Veri good, veri good, I vil approach them *doucement*." Accordingly, off he started, and carried out the instructions given him most correctly, which in a few minutes were rewarded by his bagging, at least killing, a "vild mouton." He rejoined the party, greatly delighted at his successful *début* in this new branch of sport.

The shooting proceeded, but the general, who *was* much *more* on the lookout for the "vild moutons" than for grouse or black game, soon espied at a short distance a few more of his woolly friends. "*Voilà, voilà*, vild moutons!" "Now, general, another shot," said his friend who had first directed his tastes to "vild moutons" or "vild ships," "and now you know how to proceed." "Oh yase, oh yase, I vill go *doucement*." He again succeeded in killing another "vild mouton," amid the roars of laughter and congratulations of his brother sportsmen, one of whom was the proprietor of the soil, if not of the sheep. As the day's sport was about to close, and most of the guns had been fired off, they were approaching the house of their friend, who had wickedly made the general a sheep-slayer, and who was famous for his breed of Dorking fowls. The general's attention being called to a flock of them, he immediately asked if they "vere vild?" "Oh, yes, very wild." It was forthwith suggested that the general should have an *innocent* shot on this occasion, and the keeper was desired quietly only to put a charge of powder in the gun. The owner of the Dorkings enjoyed as much as his friends the

[1] a hillock.

general's anxiety to be off for a shot among the feathered tribe, telling him not to wait for the birds being on the wing, but to fire whenever he was within proper distance. One of the party, probably Lord Kenmure, artfully substituted a gun loaded with shot for the one intended for the general, merely charged with powder. They were now quiet spectators of the general's enthusiasm while starting on his mission to the Dorkings, and who soon had four sprawling on the ground, to the utter dismay and amazement of the laird, their owner. All eyes were upon the keeper, who, equally astonished as the laird and the rest, emphatically declared that he had put no shot in the gun he had handed to the general. Napoleon's general gave a cheer of delight at his own prowess and great success. The owner of the sheep and the owner of the Dorkings were left to settle the question, which was pronounced by the neutrals to be one of "diamond cut diamond," and their Gallic friend, who was one of the best-tempered men in the world, when all matters were explained to him after dinner, laughed as heartily as the others did, adding, "Vell, I vill say you Scotch *genteelmon* are *veri, veri* fonny. You tell me to shoot 'vild ships'—I shoot 'vild ships.' You tell me to shoot 'vild ——', vat? "Dorkings."—"Ah, 'vild Dorkings"—I shoot 'vild 'Dorkings.' Ah, raillerie excellent, excellent."

59. *General Sir James Outram, Bart., G. C. B.*

How much my late brother, William Boyd, the resident at Baroda, and Political Commissioner in Guzerat, would have enjoyed to learn of the honors that late in life awaited his dear friend "Jemmy Outram"—le Chevalier Bayard of the East, as he was called, "the knight *sans peur et sans reproche.*"

He had formed a correct estimate of Outram as a lad. He used to rate the young soldier, in his own happy humorous style, among his friends at Poonah and Nassuck. "I can't persuade that fellow Outram of the great talents he possesses. If we live to see it, we shall find him a great diplomatist, as well as a great general." Often did my brother, when assistant commissioner, under Sir Henry Pottinger, in the social circle at Poonah, give out his auguries regarding Outram, in which the future Chinese plenipotentiary heartily concurred. A good anecdote was told by my brother of a rather extraordinary meeting, or almost *rencontre*, he had on one occasion with Outram, while he was one of the secretaries to the Government at Bombay. The circumstance is well known of Outram, who had most chivalrously volunteered to the general (Lord Keane) for the hazardous service, arriving at Bombay with dispatches from the army, having passed through hostile tribes, in the dress of a native; in fact, accomplished a journey of days or weeks, under circumstances of peculiar peril and adventure. He reached Bombay at midnight, and made his way to the residence of my brother, then government secretary in the Persian department. He effected an entrance to his house, but, not wishing to disturb the household, quietly betook himself to the secretary's studio, rolled himself up in tiger-skin, and was soon, as may be conceived, in a state of oblivion, after the passages by "flood and field" he had just gone through. The secretary had work to do at an early hour, and accordingly repaired to his sanctum, when a huge mass presented itself to the astounded secretary. Few men had shot more tigers than my brother, and, as the heap on the floor presented evident proofs of vitality, the dirk, the rifle, the pistol, all flashed across his mind, as he viewed something of which *quoad* the genus tiger there could be no doubt. Fortunately for the future hero of Khooshab and Lucknow, he merely applied his foot, when, to his unspeakable amazement, out rolled the unwashed and unshorn "Jemmy Outram."

60. *A Presentiment.*

I remember in my juvenile days the late Colonel the Honorable James Stewart, C. B., afterward Secretary to the Treasury in the Duke of Wellington's Government, interesting us extremely, during the Christmas holidays in Scotland, with different anecdotes connected with his eventful life as a Peninsular soldier. He was the youngest son of the noble family of Galloway, and the possessor of talents of a high order. He served under the great duke, along with his brother, General the Honorable Sir William Stewart, G. C. B. On the occasion to which I refer, among the topics that were discussed was the amount of faith which might be attached to a presentiment. Colonel Stewart, although disclaiming, as far as I can recollect, any firm reliance upon such matters, yet (as Schiller tells us, that "so often do the spirits of great events stride on before the events") mentioned, in connection with the subject, a singular and painful occurrence previous to the battle either of Salamanca or of Vittoria. The two armies had taken up their position before the fight, when a brother officer, a very dear friend of his, came to him and said, "My dear Stewart, I have had a presentiment that I shall be killed to-day; so take this locket, and give it to my dear wife." Colonel Stewart tried to rally him, but it had no effect. "Something tells me," he said, "I am to be killed, and early in the day." There was no time for more; Colonel Stewart put the locket in his breast, and among the earliest who fell was his friend. After the battle of Toulouse he handed the locket to the widow on his return to England.

We had now to go from grave to gay, and I made the colonel and the circle smile at a case in which my elder brother and myself were made the pitied objects of a presentiment which fortunately for us was not realized. We had taken our boat one very dark night, about nine o'clock, to set our night lines in the middle of a loch, or small lake, in front of our house. The lines were attached to a long thin upright pole. We had with us an old *retired* carriage-lamp; and after we had adjusted our hooks, the idea struck my brother that, if the fish would not rise to our bait, possibly the natives ashore might rise to our candle. We therefore attached the lamp to the supple pole, whose flexibility, aided by a moderate breeze, sent our illumination from one side of the loch to the other, as fantastically as we could possibly desire. It would appear that our cook, like all Scotch cooks at that period, was smoking her pipe, at the conclusion of the day's labor, outside the house, when her eye caught the mysterious light that was flitting so rapidly across the surface of the water. Down went the pipe, and up rushed the cook to the drawing-room to her mistress, exclaiming at the top of her voice, or as near that pitch as she could reach, "Oh, *leddie*, *leddie*, the *deede lichts* (dead lights) are *fleeing* across the loch! We shall *hae* something happen *awfu!* Oh, the *puir* young gentlemen!" In Scotland it is alleged that, three nights before a person is drowned, the dead lights are seen floating over the precise piece of water where the drowning is to take place. After landing from our boat we had a short distance to walk home, during which we heard a Babel of tongues; but this was soon accounted for, on finding on the lawn in front of the house the members of the family, including our tutor, a parson, with all the domestics, assembled, from whom we received hearty congratulations that we were safe. "Ay, ay," cried the cook; "thank *guidness* the young gentlemen are safe *the noo* (at present), but it *winna last lang*." According to the *deede lichts*, the catastrophe that awaited us could not come off for three nights—that was, two after the one then passing. As the cook was the first to discover the mysterious lights, she was the great authority and spokeswoman. She had a long list of cases to enlarge upon in our country, handed down in her own family from father and grandfather, where the *deede lichts* had invariably appeared three nights before the person was drowned. My brother and I offered our reverend tutor to take him in the boat, so as to have a pull after the lights, but, with all his divinity, he declined, and considered such foolhardiness on our part most improper. We pressed the matter upon him, but no persuasion of ours would induce the reverend gentleman to risk his person in the boat that night. In fact, had the cook and the tutor gone up in a competitive examination as to which of the two was the greater alarmist, they must have been "bracketed equal." But no one that eventful night discoursed more eloquently, being on terra firma, upon the extraordinary phenomenon which they were all witnessing, than the parson. During the next three days my brother and I, although contrary to all advice, clerical and lay, were in our boat, night and day, more than usual, and, when the period of suspense was over, we asked the cook to explain the cause of our escaping. "*Na, na*, young gentlemen, it is true you've escaped mercifully this time, but that's *no'* the proper way to *tak* it, for ye *dinna ken* that there's *no'* a drowned man or woman, or *twa* perhaps, lying at the bottom o' the loch at this *verra* moment, for the *deede lichts* are never *wrang*."

When the story had run an extensive course throughout the district, we explained all; and, although I have not any proof of the fact, I yet hope it may have assisted in removing a stupid superstition. This I do know, that our tutor avoided for the future all allusion to *deede lichts* in connection with drowning.

61. *The Rev. Dr. Richardson, of Clonfeacle, in the County of Tyrone.*

My copybook informed me, before I had read "Hamlet," that "brevity is the soul of wit," and I am reminded, in these days of disestablishment and disendowment, of one who observed this eminent qualification beyond any one I ever knew. I have before me, in remembrance, that charming and aged Irish Episcopalian clergyman, the late Rev. Dr. Richardson, of Clonfeacle, in the county of Tyrone. In addition to his divinity, he was a leading and practical agriculturist, and occasionally spent a few weeks with my father in Scotland, when they were arranging their plans to keep the price of wheat at a steady average of 100*s.* to 110*s.* a quarter! At this period, as a youth, I was generally desired by my mother to say grace before and after dinner; but, of course, on the reverend doctor's arrival, I found myself superseded in my office.

As boys, we admired the doctor's grace much, because it was pithy and concise. My mother's usual request, "Doctor, will you say grace?" "With pleasure, *ma'am.*" The words were uttered rapidly, but sonorously—"God bless us and our *mate*, *Amen.*" At the conclusion of dinner, "Doctor, may I ask you?" "Most *sartenly*, *ma'am.* Thank God for what we have *resaived*, *Amen.*' "

On the reverend doctor's departure I was reëstablished as dinner chaplain, and thought I could do nothing better than strictly to adopt my predecessor's grace, being much shorter than my own, and imitated his accent and mode of delivery as closely as I could contrive to do. He was a worthy man, and I considered the nearer I could follow him the better. My first attempt, "God bless us and our *mate*, *Amen,*" was considered by all but my mother very successful, but she administered to me a tolerably good wigging, accompanied by a strict injunction not to do so again. She was at all times the mildest of mothers, and no sooner had she corrected me than it was followed up by, "You know, my dear, I never approved of the doctor's mode of saying grace." Dinner concluded, and called upon as usual, and wishing to finish the grace I had studied so carefully, out came "Thank God for what we have *resaived*, *Amen.*" My disendowment was a simple affair, and my disestablishment instantly followed.

The worthy doctor, as an enthusiast in agriculture, generally arranged his visits to my father so as to accompany him to the agricultural meetings of one of Cumberland's distinguished "worthies," the late Mr. John Christian Curwen, M. P., of Workington Hall. The doctor had discovered, or at least had cultivated, a rare *spacies* of grass called fiorin grass. My father was easily inoculated with any new agricultural doctrine. "*Ounely* try it," said the doctor, "and *yer* cows will give *dobble* the quantity of milk *immadiately;* and what is so beautiful in the *houle* matter is, that fiorin grass grows better on a *mane* soil than any other, *ounely* you must be particular the *forst* year in getting *yer* ground into order." My father accordingly desired his bailiff to prepare a quarter of an acre to test the merits of this wonderful grass, and the following season, when the reverend doctor paid his visit, there was an excellent crop, which he pronounced to be as beautiful as *nade* be *sane.* Our bailiff was from Berwickshire—a district where they drop the letter "r" as universally as the "h" is dropped by so many of Her Majesty's lieges in the neighborhood of Bow Bells. "Well, bailiff," said the doctor, "how do you like my new grass?" "It is a *gand* (grand) *gas* (grass), doctor, but it is too *dea* (dear)." "Och, now, never mind the *dareness*, at all at all." The fact being, that in regard to expense they might as well have been preparing the ground for tulips under a committee of gardeners from the Horticultural and Botanical Societies. But the doctor looked *ounely* to the solution of his own problem, namely, that the bovine race preferred fiorin grass to any other. There was unquestionably an aroma from this grass which was very enticing, and this the doctor wished to demonstrate by *ocular* proof. A party of visitors, the agricultural element prevailing, assembled in front of our house to witness the trial of "grass proper" *versus* "fiorin grass," and the doctor, a septuagenarian, with his Irish valet, Dennis, superintended the arrangements, which were not complicated. Dennis placed a small quantity of the fiorin grass on the ground, and while this was being done one of the spectators remarked how fragrant it was. "It is all, *sor*, fragrancy," remarked the doctor. Over the fiorin grass a thick coating of grass proper was thrown. During these preliminaries Dennis and his master were earnestly colloquial, but the talk was carried on in *ould* Irish. Dennis and another servant were now to be dispatched to the byre, or cow-house, for a cow, but before starting a witty spectator said to him, "Now, Dennis, after all that old Irish your master and you have been talking so quietly, don't you be bringing out an Irish cow that may be in the secret." "Upon my sacred honor, *sor*," said Dennis, "I never exchanged a single word with master about the cow, and *furder*, *sor*, I *doun't belaive* his honor here—and he is not far wrong—has a single Paddy among his cows.—Plaise, *sor*, will you come *wid* me and pick out a cow?" "Oh no, Dennis; be off and bring your own cow?" The animal arrived, and had its attention directed to the little heap of grass, when it at once scented out something, for sure enough it pushed aside with its nose the grass on the top until it reached the fiorin grass, which it lost no time in devouring. The test was a great success, and the veteran divine and agriculturist was in a rapture of delight. "If that *doun't* carry conviction to you Scotchmen, what will? It is as *clare* as daylight that fiorin grass must *suparsade* all other grass." The doctor and my father's bailiff did not fraternize, as the latter looked to the cost of production and not to the aroma. "What's the use," said the doctor, "of *spaking* to a man who won't use all the letters of the alphabet? How can such a man know any thing about fiorin grass!" The bailiff, although he dropped the letter "r" in all words entitled to have it, stuck to his point. "We *a* (are) obleeged, *docto*, in this county to be content with mutton *both* (broth), although we should not object to *tutle* (turtle) soup." The controversy here ended, and with it the future production of fiorin grass as a cheap staple food for my father's cows.

The doctor was full to overflowing with the most interesting details of the Irish rebellion, and as boys we often asked him to recount some of them, and describe scenes of which he had been an eye-witness. He was a man of great determination and personal courage. Never was there a stouter member of the Church—militant shall I say?—than he was. He and his household had once to defend their lives against a midnight attack of a body of rebels, who were effectually beaten off. I remember the first time that he related the circumstances, his asking me to ring the bell for Dennis, as he could correct him if he went astray in his narrative, "And, moreover," added the doctor, "Dennis did a *dale* more of the fighting than myself." It would appear that the reverend doctor had very strong political proclivities, such as would not be tolerated, as exercised by him, in the present day, and private information reached him that his residence would most probably be attacked on an early night. "Well, then," said the doctor, "I thought it *ounely* prudent to provide myself with a few copies of 'Brown Bess,' *alias moskets*, and a fairish quantity of powder and shot. My indoor *sarvants* were all right and faithful—more than I could say for those outside. That being so, I *damed* (deemed) it wise to lay in a good stock of provisions in case we had to stand a bit of a *saige*. It was rather a *starmy* night, but it was full moon, and we were all as near being in our beds as *passible*. Every thing was well barricaded below, when Dennis slipped into the drawing-room, and at once put out the candles, "For *bedad*, *sor*," says he, "the boys (the rebels) are coming over the lawn, and will be firing slog (slug) into this room before they ever ask a question." At this part of the recital the doctor, addressing his man Friday, "Now, Dennis, correct me if I go *blondering*, for I wish to tell the *yong gintilmen* the *houle* story before they go to bed." "You're all right *sor*, yet." "Then I thought the proper order I should give, and I recollect I said to Dennis—now, didn't I, Dennis?" "Yes, *sor*, you did." "'Now, Dennis,' says I, 'you'll just let the boys alone until they try *aither* the front door or the back door.'" "That's the very words you said, *sor*." "Now, Dennis had resolved to place one half of our little force to command *aich* door; and didn't Brown Bess do her work right well! for after the first discharge they all *boulted*. But the *ounely* foolish thing we did that night—and Dennis you *aften ouned* it"—"I did, *sor*"—"was wasting our shot when they were scampering *aff*, and they thought so too, and that we couldn't have much more left, and they were about right, but not altogether. Dennis saw the mistake we had made in wasting our powder, and, although I say it before Dennis himself, it is *ounely* the truth when I do say it, that I never knew him to be at a loss for an *expadient*. 'Now, *sor*,' said Dennis, 'their *blod* is up, and they're right *shure* to be back in an hour, thinking we shall be glad to be looking after some rest in our beds. Well, *sor*, this very afternoon I *cot* off the lead pipe as far as I could *raitch*, to save the boys the *troble* of doing it, and *slog* is never at all of any use without powder; and I'll *jist* tell you what, *sor*, Tim and my own self are going to do *widout* a *marcel* of delay, and that is, to put two pots on the kitchen fire for to boil the lead, and the very moment I see them *comming* I'll put one pot under Tim's care, and the other I'll take mighty good care of myself.' Sure and *sartain* Dennis was right, as it was very little more than over the hour when we saw a larger *nomber* than ever *comming*. They evidently thought we hadn't another shot in the locker—which was not exactly the case, as we had all our Brown Besses loaded—or that we were sound *aslape.* Dennis said we must not fire another shot outside the house, but *kape* them to guard our staircase, for Dennis saw what I did not—that, if they once got in, we should be driven up to our first landing, and then that every shot would tell a good tale for itself."

I so well recollect how deeply my brothers and myself had now become absorbed in the reverend doctor's description. "Now, Dennis, I'm going on all right?" "Every word, *sor*, is the truth, if there never was *annother* word spoken in the *houle* world." "Then, *yong gintilmen*, all I now did was to superintend, for I left all to Dennis." "You did, *sor*." "Well, *jist* as Dennis had *foretould*, a part of the rebels came to *aich* door, and, in less time than I have been now *spaking*, Dennis had a shower of boiling lead over his lot, and Tim the same over his. Never since *ould* Ireland was a *contry* was such a *scraich* heard as that night the moment the hot lead *rached* them. They *boulted*, och, *scraming* in such a manner as I shall never forget, and although I knew right well they came to *morder* me, my heart gave way to hear their cries. Well, then, I called Dennis to ask him what he thought, and all he said was, 'I promise you, *sor*, they'll not be after *trobling* us *agin* this night; and take my advice, *sor*, and go to bed and *slape* at *aise*.' I was never once bothered after this during the *houle* of the rebellion, but I always *tould* the boys when I met them that Dennis and I would be ready to fight it out with them at any time. Their usual remark was, 'Och, bad *lock* to Dennis!'" We asked the doctor if any of the rebels were killed. "That," said he, "I never inquired after, for I was *tould* that they preferred *kaping soch* matters to themselves; and I had no objection. All I know is this, that there were little pools of *blod* all round the house, and, as Dennis will tell you, the *ounely* thing we picked up in the morning was one of their fingers." Dennis, who was a good deal more communicative on this more delicate part of the subject than his master, said that he had "good *raison* to *belaive* that the *kilt* and wounded were *aither* thirteen or fourteen."

62. *A Reason for eschewing Politics.*

A friend of mine, now an octogenarian, gave up politics from a fright he had in early life. He happened to be in Piccadilly when Sir Francis Burdett was being removed to the Tower, and, seeing the mob busily engaged in tearing up the paving-stones to throw at the soldiers, he retreated, and sought refuge in the Gloucester Coffee-house; but there he discovered it was a case of removing from the frying-pan into the fire, for entering the coffee-room he found a gentleman, who proved to be a lieutenant in the navy, telling a person, who was evidently a warm sympathizer of the honorable baronet, that he would not allow him to go on uttering such sedition against the Crown and the Government. But the other retorted that he would say or do what he liked. "Then," replied the son of Neptune, "if you persevere I shall stuff your head up the chimney." This threat proved, in legal phraseology, an effectual estoppel, but it gave my friend ever after a distaste for politics.

The following letter in connection with Sir Francis Burdett, which my esteemed friend, Mr. Richard Galloway, allowed me to see and to have a copy from his valuable collection of autographs, will be read with interest. It is addressed (1837) to his father, then about to leave London for Egypt, by his friend Mr. Hume, M. P., and shows the opinion entertained in France in 1810 of the honorable baronet, *alias* (*then*) Westminster's glory:

"BRYANSTONE SQUARE, *July* 1, 1837.

"MY DEAR SIR: I have read Mr. Backhouse's letter, and your answer to the memorandum to Viscount Palmerston, and you may depend on my attending to any wish you may have respecting the affairs of Egypt. If you have the opportunity of mentioning to the Pacha that I have always retained a sense of obligation for the attention showed me in 1810, when I was in Egypt, he may, perhaps, recollect the circumstance of my being with him when the French Consular Agent read a paper from Paris, in which there was an account of a revolt in England, and that Sir Francis Burdett had been declared king. I mentioned that it was impossible to suppose such an event, but it was possible he might have been arrested on some charge of treason. It was the time he was taken to the Tower. Wishing you a pleasant voyage,

"I remain yours sincerely,

(Signed) "JOSEPH HUME.

"Alexander Galloway, Esq."

Mr. Galloway, whom Jeremy Bentham, in his correspondence, addresses as "My worthy and highly-esteemed old friend," used to relate a good story of two city officials, one Sheriff Parkins, a somewhat eccentric and irascible person, and the other Charles Pearson, afterward the City solicitor, usually styled "Charlie Pearson." (I may mention *en passant* that Pearson may be considered the godfather of the Underground Railway system in London, inasmuch as he foresaw what was coming, and recommended that the Corporation should retain the Fleet Valley property for railway purposes.) Pearson was for two or three years M. P. for Lambeth. When a young man, he and Sheriff Parkins could never agree, and their disputes frequently reached a very dangerous point, the sheriff threatening to give Pearson a thrashing. A member of the Corporation, who felt an interest in Pearson, said one day to him: "If you don't take care that sheriff will give you a precious good licking, for he prides himself on his boxing accomplishments; and were you to take my advice you would follow the fashion, and, like the Marquis of Worcester and other young swells, go to Belasco (the black pugilist) and have some lessons." Pearson took the hint, and lost no time in placing himself either under Aby Belasco, who flourished as a pugilist in 1817, or Israel Belasco, who was equally famous in 1819. Pearson was an apt scholar in this as in every thing else he set his mind to, for within a week of practising with his dark instructor he planted so strong a blow into Belasco's chest or stomach—a little of both—as to make him exclaim, "Vy, my goodness, you 'its has 'ard has Sheriff Parkins!" "What do *you* know of Sheriff Parkins?" "Vat do hi know hof Sheriff Parkins! Vy, hi did teach 'im to box."

This information made Pearson the more assiduous in his studies, and Belasco having pronounced his pupil a most apt and accomplished scholar, it is supposed that the hit Pearson made so successfully into Belasco's "bread-basket," as I believe it is pugilistically termed, must have reached the ears of the sheriff, as he kept himself for the future at a respectful distance from Charlie Pearson.

63. *Lord John Russell and the "Repale" of the Corn Laws.*

Roger Rock—I give his name, as I have nothing to record of him that is not of a satisfactory nature. Rock had his strong political predilections, and to no distinguished member of the political arena did he extend his admiration so fervently as to the above illustrious member of the House of Bedford. Rock was acknowledged by all my friends to be a perfect valet—no boots ever shone more brilliantly, nor clothes ever better brushed than by Rock, and no morning newspaper was earlier or more minutely scanned over than by Roger Rock. When he came to my room in the morning I generally asked him for the news, as he seemed to me to have some means of obtaining the morning journals the moment they were published. He was a walking agenda, and could place before you, in the richest vernacular of the county of Roscommon, a synopsis of the politics of the previous day. "You will find, *sor*," such and such a question "ably *discossed* in the *Times*, *Post*, *Daily News*, and *Chronicle*" (for he had an opportunity of seeing all the morning papers), "and also in the *Herald*, but then, *agin*, *yer* honor, the *Herald* has its own *lanings*." It not unfrequently happened that I could have preferred delaying Rock's political information for another hour so as again to "shrink to that sweet forgetfulness of life." But if Lord John Russell had put an opponent down in debate the previous night in St. Stephen's, Rock could not possibly allow me to read the fact in the paper for myself—he must be the first to communicate it. One morning Rock, after locating the hot water, clothes, and boots, avoided politics entirely, and touched upon horse-racing. "Why, *sor*, the young *gintilmen* are going to Ascot Races to-morrow, and are very anxious that *yer* honor would give me *lave* to attend them, and look after their *lonch*; at same time, *sor*, I would *jost* be taking a bit of care of them." I told him I had no objection to his going to look after the young *gintlemen*. "All right, *sor*." Next day Rock was at Ascot, and when *lonch* was over, and the time fixed, some two hours afterward, to leave the course for London, he told the party "he would like mightily to have a stroll, if it were *ounely* to *saa* (see) what sort of a place Ascot was; although it was a *quare* (queer) thing for him to say, he had never been on Ascot race-course till that day." The permission was given; but my young relatives being most desirous, as their companions were, to see how an Irishman —and that Irishman Rock—conducted himself on a first visit to Ascot, resolved to watch his movements, *vulgo*, to "dodge him." They were close behind him when he entered a large booth filled to a cram, pushing his way into it with great difficulty, when it seems the thought struck him that the talismanic name of Lord John Russell might assist him in making progress. Villiers, Cobden, and Bright, were then riding their corn-law race on all the chief courses of the kingdom. At the top of his voice he called out, "Lord John Russell and a *repale* of the corn laws—*you* understand *that*." And again, in an equally high-pitched key, "Lord John Russell and a *repale* of the corn laws." The astounded Berkshire farmers faced round upon the intruder. "What do you know, Paddy, about the repeal of the corn laws?" "'Paddy,' do you say?"—and down went the Berkshire farmer, more probably two of them, for Rock was six feet in height, and powerfully built. My young friends called in the aid of the police to rescue Rock, without which he would probably never have again mentioned the name of Russell. He was released with a smashed hat, instead of head. The hat was never again seen by Rock, and was no doubt retained as a relic of what a Berkshire farmer had carried off in his fight to retain the corn laws. Next day, having heard of the affair, I asked Rock how it happened. "Och, *sor*, and it is all true, for I had been *aften tould* it, that these *Barksheere* farmers were a very bad lot." "But, Rock, you must have brought it entirely upon yourself, for the Berkshire farmers are a quiet, respectable body of men." "I beg pardon, *sor*, but *yer* honor is entirely mistaken in that, for I was *jost* as *pacably* inclined as any man on Ascot race *haith*. I *ounely* wanted to know how these farmers *trated* the question of corn-law *repale*, and I thought there was no mighty harm, *sor*, in mentioning a respectable and clever *gintilman's* name, and I quietly called out, 'Lord John Russell and a *repale* of the corn laws.' What right, *yer* honor, had they be to be *displazed* at that?—and *thin* to be *comming* on me with their right down *impurtenance:* 'What do you know, Paddy, about the *repale* of the corn laws?' You know, *sor*, no county of Roscommon man could stand *soch* an *insolt*, and I knocked one of them down—it might be two—there and *thin*, and a dirty *mane* advantage they took, by destroying my hat, and *kaping* it too."

64. *The Dean of Faculty (subsequently Lord Robertson) and Rock.*

Mr. Patrick Robertson, afterward the eminent Scotch judge, was very partial to my Irish servant Rock, and Rock in return always described the *larned dane* as the very *cliverest gintilman* that Scotland had ever produced. A friend who was at my house one afternoon, when Mr. Robertson called, and was behind the scenes, described a laughable colloquy between the Dean of Faculty and Rock.

"Is your master at home, Rock?" "He is not, Mr. *dane*, but he is somewhere hard by. I hope I see you well, *sor?*" "Only so so, Rock; the hot weather knocks me up." "I *doun't* wonder, *sor*; it reminds me, *sor*, of the weather in the *Houly* City in the month of August" (Rock was a stanch Roman Catholic.) "It creates thirst, great thirst, Rock." "It does, indeed, *sor*." "Rock." "Yes, *sor*." "What excellent claret that was we had here the other night!" "First-rate, *yer* honor." "If your master had been at home, I would have asked him to allow me to quench my thirst with some." "I can manage that for you, Mr. *dane*, as I have got a nice cool bottle that was left out last time, and master will be right glad to hear that *yer* honor got it." "Then, Rock, I shall walk up-stairs; first, the claret." "Yes, *sor*." "Then a bottle of iced water; I know you can manage that." "All right, *sor;*

and the newspaper?" "After that, you need not disturb your master." "I shall have all with you, *sor*, *immadiately*." The moment after attending to the learned *dane's* wants, Rock returned to the gentleman, who had heard the *tête-à-tête* between them. "*Sor*, do you know who that *gintilman* is?" "Not exactly, Rock." "Why, *sor*, he is the *dane* of all the law in Scotland; and *auch*, *sor*, for an after-dinner *spaich* there never was such a *gintilman*; *ounely*, *sor*, *git* my master to tell you the story about the county of *Pables* (Peebles) and the *dane—ounely doun't* say, *sor*, I *tould* you."

This story, which tickled Rock's fancy, as many others of the learned dean's did, arose out of the following circumstance: Mr. Robertson was in London as counsel on some important appeal case from the Scotch courts to the House of Lords, in which one of our northern counties was interested—Sutherland, I think. The case had been before their lordships one or two days, and Mr. Robertson was to proceed in his argument the following forenoon. At a dinner-party, at which I met the learned gentleman, there was present a baillie, or other magisterial magnate, from the county of Peebles; and, some allusion having been made to the case in which Mr. Robertson was engaged, the baillie remarked, "Ah, Mr. Robertson, there is no fear o' the *coonty* o' Sutherland not being attended to, but our *wee coonty* o' Peebles is just looked upon as a nonentity. You never hear o' the *coonty* o' Peebles *nae mair* than if it *did na belang* to Scotland." "That is very wrang, baillie," said the learned Scotch advocate. "Oh, it's *mair* than *wrang*," said the baillie; "it's *doonright* disgracefu.'" "Well, said Mr. Robertson, "any thing, baillie, I can do to bring the county of Peebles into notice, I beg to assure you, without any particular reference to its excellent trout-fishing, which should never be lost sight of, will afford me great pleasure and satisfaction."

A witty friend at the table asked the learned gentleman how he could bring the county of Peebles into notice. "Why, I shall satisfy you very soon on that head, and the baillie also, by making a beginning to-morrow. After what I have heard to-night, I shall consider it my duty, so long as it does not interfere with those interests which I now represent, to bring the county of Peebles under the especial attention of the Chancellor and the judges, as well as all the peers, lay and spiritual, who may be present. The baillie has made out a very strong case of grievance, and the sooner it is remedied the better."

The baillie was silent, and, if one could judge what was passing through his mind, I think he regretted that, in his patriotic desire to serve his native county, he had ever mentioned the subject. Our witty friend was still pressing to know precisely how our learned friend was to proceed in the Peebles affair next day in the House of Lords. "I shall take my own course in that," said the learned advocate, "but, if you will promise to give me whitebait at Greenwich on Saturday, I in return promise you, as I do my friend the baillie, to mention the county of Peebles twenty times to-morrow before the Lord Chancellor, and, before the week is out, the baillie, with his friends in Peeblesshire, will see by the Scotch newspapers that I fulfilled my promise." The baillie, so far as the claret and other good things permitted, was very grave at this intimation. Accordingly, next morning, when Mr. Robertson was about to resume his argument before the Chancellor, and seeing some of his friends of the previous evening present, he said to one of them, "I hold you responsible to keep a correct account of the number of times I mention the county of Peebles." He then began, and had not proceeded in his speech more than five minutes, when he said: "My lords, I shall now put a hypothetical case. I shall suppose I am arguing this case before your lordships for the county of

Peebles, and your lordships are aware—at least some of your lordships are—that the county of Peebles is in the south of Scotland, within a short distance of Edinburgh, the capital. The county of Peebles, my lords, is therefore differently circumstanced from the county of Sutherland, a northern county." The learned counsel kept constantly looking over his shoulder, and in something more than a whisper expressed a hope that he was taking a correct note of the numbers. At last his friend tapped the learned gentleman on the shoulder, and told him his whitebait for Saturday was safe, as he had mentioned the county of Peebles twenty-four times. "Honor bright?" "Honor bright," was the reply. The learned gentleman now concluded his argument without further reference to the county of Peebles, and on the Saturday enjoyed his whitebait much, telling the party that he had never won a Greenwich dinner so easily.

65. *Lord Robertson dining with Mr. Galt, the Novelist.*

I heard the late Mr. Galt say that one of the most brilliant after-dinner displays of Patrick Robertson's powers took place at his table in London; my late father and elder brother were present. I unfortunately was not invited, and can, therefore, give only an outline.

It may be recollected that, some forty years ago, two Scotch magistrates took upon themselves the responsibility of closing an Orange lodge in the town of Newton-Stewart, Wigtonshire. Both magistrates were strict Conservatives, or rather Tories, and anti-Catholics. The Hon. Montgomery Stewart was one, my father the other. It created much excitement throughout the land, and the magistrates in question were pronounced to be a brace of Justice Shallows in arrogating to themselves such extensive powers. Their plea was expediency. They considered they were acting wisely and prudently in their attempt to prevent a collision in the district between the Catholics—an important section of the local population—and the Orange party. The late Duke of Cumberland and the Earl of Roden thought differently, and a prosecution was commenced in the Scotch courts against the two offending magistrates. Mr. Robertson was retained by the Orange lodge party, and the case was ripe for discussion, when the two magistrates, terrified out of their propriety at the costs which they saw might be thrown upon them, struck their colors to the Orange flag, and the prosecution was quashed. The Earl of Blessington, who that day dined with Mr. Galt, had been for some time absent in Italy, and after dinner made an accidental allusion to the fact of some Scotch magistrates having attempted to close an Orange lodge, unconscious that one of them was present, and equally so that Mr. Robertson, the leading counsel for the prosecution, was also one of Mr. Galt's guests. "Oh!" said Mr. Galt, "Mr. Robertson, can tell you every thing connected with the affair." The learned gentleman at once said it would afford him the greatest pleasure, and, as Lord Blessington was as familiar as himself with the language of Tasso and Ariosto (at that time he knew nothing whatever of Italian), he would state the whole case as it would have been laid before the court in Scotland, in an Italian chant. His voice was *basso*, and as powerful as that of Lablache. Each line ended magistrato or Orange-lodge-o. The unfortunate magistrates—one an attentive listener—were laid out in the richest colors of burlesque. The roars of laughter that accompanied the learned chorister throughout his chant may be well conceived, and Lord Blessington's surprise was extreme, when he discovered that one of the two delinquent magistrates was sitting next to him. My father's health was immediately proposed by Mr. Robertson, and in returning thanks he wisely avoided the main issue, but expressed the great satisfaction he had experienced in finding the Italian language, in which his learned friend appeared so much at home, so simple to understand, as he had not lost a single word. All he would say in reference to the important and exciting question which had been brought up that evening and had convinced him, as a Scotch magistrate, that the learned gentleman's jovial powers were as formidable when clothed in Italian as his legal powers when attired in Scotch, was, that, as it had been the first Orange lodge which either his colleague or himself had attempted to close in their magisterial capacity, his learned friend might rely it should be the last.

66. *The Dean of Faculty (Lord Robertson) at Eglinton Castle.*

The late Earl of Eglinton, who was very partial to the learned lord, on one occasion invited him to pass a few days during the autumnal recess, at Eglinton Castle, where a house full of visitors from the south had assembled. No doubt he had told them whom they would meet—possibly even Mr. Robertson's personal appearance had been canvassed; in fact, in telling the story he said he was satisfied it had, although he well knew that his kind and popular host would make him out as handsome as he dared to do. To those who never saw Lord Robertson, I may mention that his countenance was a most sagacious one and full of bonhommie. He was the possessor of what Montaigne declares to be "the most manifest sign of wisdom, continued cheerfulness." He was of the build of Dr. Johnson, one whom you could not fail to remark and could never forget. As he could not allow the slightest opportunity to escape of having his joke, even at the cost of his own person becoming the subject of it, I must relate how he played himself off against a distinguished visitor at the Castle, on the day of his arrival. He had reached the drawing-room *en grande tenue* before even his noble and popular host or any of the company had arrived.

In a few minutes a very exquisitely-dressed visitor, about twenty-five years of age, sauntered into the room; the Dean was about forty-five, and the disparity in regard to weight and rotundity, between himself and the gentleman whom he was about to address, was even more disproportionate than that of years. The learned Dean argued to himself: "This personage can be nothing less than an hereditary legislator, high, very high, in the upper ten thousand. I wonder," said the wit, "if he ever heard of me in the lofty region in which he floats. It would be surpassingly gratifying to find that Patrick Robertson was a name familiar in that elevated sphere. I can't reasonably expect such a thing, but ascertain it I *will*, and that before Lord Eglinton enters the room." He approached the visitor, and opened thus: "I presume, sir, I have the honor of addressing Mr. Patrick Robertson?" In a reply as rabid as it was rapid, he said, "I am not Mr. Patrick Robertson," turning instantly away to a table covered with prints, and throwing off with electric speed an expression of ineffable disdain and marked displeasure at the bare idea that he was Patrick Robertson, or the possessor of a name so plebeian. While the Dean was ruminating and quite convinced that he had "taken nothing by his motion" of inquiry in regard to himself, the door opened, and Lord Eglinton entered with a large number of his guests. "How do, Dean?" "How do you do, Mr. Robertson?" from half the party. The astonished friend of the noble earl, who had made good his first retreat to a table covered with works of art, now made a further retrograde movement to one end of the room. After the full and usual exchange of civilities had passed—for in those days introductions were the rule —the learned dean heard in modulated soprano, "*Eglinton, Eglinton*, I wish you to explain the subject of this picture to me." Lord Eglinton obeyed the summons. "Why, Eglinton, your friend, that dean whom I found here alone when I came down-stairs, must be an odd man, for he said to me, 'I presume I am addressing Mr. Patrick Robertson.'" "Well, what did you say?" "Why, I told him I was *not* Mr. Patrick Robertson." Lord Eglinton's roar of laughter which followed this explanation affected the risible organs of all, save one.

The story was in excellent hands with the joyous head of the house of Montgomery, who made it the prelude of one of the most joyous evenings of humor and jocularity (and they were many) ever passed in Eglinton Castle.

67. *The Dean of Faculty and Waterloo Bridge.*

Nothing came amiss to the learned Dean, provided it secured a good laugh, and no joke was in his opinion more successful than racing a friend across Waterloo Bridge, which he declared to be superb, though others less learned might have looked upon it as the half-holiday pastime of a pack of school-boys. A friend well known in the Scotch circles of London, who was proud of his gymnastic powers, and especially of his running, was expatiating on this branch of athleticism at his own table, when a facetious guest challenged him, in all apparent earnestness, to run, on any morning he chose to appoint, between the hours of half-past six and half-past seven, from the Surrey to the Middlesex side of Waterloo Bridge. Our host accepted the challenge, and invited the party to breakfast with him afterward. All arrangements being made with the bridge-keepers, at half-past six on the morning fixed, with two companions, our friend appeared in a light overcoat, attired underneath in the costume of a regular athlete. No Greek or Roman competitor could have been more correctly equipped, although the dress was somewhat more absurd than that, if we may believe Thucydides, worn by those who contested at Olympia with mere linen badges round their loins.

The bridge was crossed and recrossed by the subject of the hoax, until the clock struck seven; his opponent and his friends having screened themselves at the Surrey side of the bridge to witness his peripateticism: and among the remarks that reached them was: "That fellow —— is always late. I never asked him to run, it was his own offer; he promised to be here at half-past six, and now it is past seven," etc.

Ten minutes past seven. More people passing by this time than was altogether agreeable. The clock chimes half-past seven, when even the bridge-keepers become uneasy, and politely intimate that they consider it now too late for the race, and recommend it being postponed until next morning. The expectant runner, thoroughly disappointed, hurries with his companions from the bridge and drives home, and just as he arrives, another much larger party headed by the challenger drives up to eat a first-rate Scotch breakfast. The entertainer—the victim in both cases—was complimented on his brilliant appearance on the bridge, and congratulated on the charming hour's walk he had had undisturbed on so brilliant a morning in the charming month of June. He was then assured by the challenger that he must have misunderstood him, "as he never wished to run him out on Waterloo Bridge—his desire was to trot him out."

68. *A Recollection of Tom Campbell.*

The poet was dining with my brother and myself when a witty and humorous friend, whose hospitality in the neighborhood of Harrow for many years is still remembered by a large circle of friends, was of the party, and drew out the Bard of Hope very successfully. The poet had just returned from Algiers, and was full to overflow with anecdotes connected with his residence in Northern Africa. He gave us a most animated description which did not suffer in illustration from his having imbibed a bottle and a half of claret. "Oh," said the poet, "I can never forget my visit to the desert; oh, dear me, no; an impression was made on my mind there, that can never be erased. Yes, it is quite true; her image is before me now—one of Nature's gentlewomen. Oh, that poor and exquisitely beautiful Arab girl! it grieves me to the heart to think what will be her fate. The chisel of Canova never produced any thing to bear a comparison with that angelic young Arab."

His pathos had now reached a serious point, as the tears trickled down his cheeks; but he so far rallied as to be able to tell us, that if he had ever intended to marry a second time, that Arab girl should have been his wife. On hearing this, we reminded him, that there were always two interested in a marriage contract, and that possibly on his popping the question to this captivating and enchanting girl of the desert, she might have replied in the words of "the Shunamite woman," "I dwell among my own people." "That is quite true," said the poet, "and it might have been the answer."

Our friend, the same who plotted and carried out the Waterloo Bridge "trot out," took up the question, and, addressing the poet, said, "Supposing you *had* married this lovely maiden of the desert, what would you have called your eldest son?" "How can I answer such a question? But, on second thoughts, I dare say"—looking round the table—"it is something good—I really do not know what I should have called him." "Well, I shall tell you what, in my opinion, you should have called the boy—'Sandy Campbell.'" "Ah," said Campbell—"good, very good—you will be the death of me. In the mean time, here's to you in a bumper of claret."

69. *Dr. Blomfield, Bishop of London.*

The last time I saw the Bishop was at the Mansion House. The Lord Mayor (Alderman Hunter) and Lady Mayoress had invited my wife and myself to the annual banquet given to the Bench of Bishops in the Egyptian Hall, which is considered, with the usual dinner to the members of the Cabinet and to Her Majesty's judges, among the most attractive of the Lord Mayor's parties. I shall always look back upon the speech of the Bishop of London on that occasion with peculiar interest. The Lord Mayor and the Bishop had been schoolfellows at a school kept by the Bishop's father at Bury St. Edmunds. They had now reached their respective goals—the one the Bishopric and the other the Mayoralty of London, and were there to congratulate each other; and we to congratulate ourselves on having witnessed in their persons what brilliant talents and moral worth in the one, and indomitable industry and high character in the other, can achieve in this country.

The Bishop was not only himself a witty man, but one who could appreciate wit in others. I recollect a much respected friend of mine, a clergyman in Essex, making me laugh at an anecdote which the Bishop used to relate with infinite zest. A new church had been erected in his diocese, and a day was appointed for the consecration. The Bishop having received several letters, some anonymous, attacking the taste of the architect, as they alleged, for introducing gewgaws both externally and internally, resolved to judge for himself, and accordingly drove down two hours previously, having desired the architect to meet him. His lordship could find nothing outside the building to question, and then began his inspection of the interior, with which he was also satisfied; but just as he had reached the pulpit he looked up at four wooden images. "What, Mr. Architect, do *they* represent?" "The four Evangelists, my lord." "They look to me asleep." "Do you think so, my lord?" "I do." The architect, turning round to one of his men working in a pew, called out, "Smith, bring your chisel and open the eyes of the Evangelists."

The Bishop had been a widower and had some children. He married a second time a widow who also had a family. He had asked a country clergyman to dine with him at London House on Christmas-day, telling him, "You will only meet our family party." He found a much larger circle assembled in the drawing-room than he anticipated, and was introduced by the Bishop thus: "These are *mine*, those are *hers*, and those are *ours*."

70. *A Non-elected Scotch Laird taking his Seat in the House of Commons.*

The following anecdote I heard from Mr. Cutlar Fergusson, M. P., as well as from the laird himself the day after the occurrence. I wrote it out at the time, and it appeared shortly afterward in a London magazine. A worthy Scotch proprietor whose estate was in Kirkcudbrightshire, then represented by the Right Hon. R. Cutlar Fergusson, the Judge-Advocate in Lord Melbourne's Government, came up to London for a few weeks shortly after the assembling of a new Parliament. He called upon his Right Hon. friend, who asked him what he could do for him in town; the laird said that nothing he would like so much during his stay as being present at the debates in the House of Commons. "That being the case," said the Judge-Advocate, "I will have your name placed on the Speaker's list." The following evening the laird was early in his attendance at the House, found his name on the list, and was told by the door-keeper to enter. Where the

Speaker's privileged friends sat he knew not, but up the body of the House he walked, and took his seat on the second bench of the opposition close behind Sir Robert Peel. An interesting debate came on, and the laird sat undisturbed until the House adjourned at midnight. Fortunately for him there was no division, and equally fortunately it was a new Parliament. Next day he called upon Mr. Fergusson, whose first inquiry was: "What became of you, as I looked for you in vain?" "Oh," said the laird, "I saw you moving about the House, and tried to catch your eye. I was delighted with the debate, and I shall now be a constant attendant." From the laird's vernacular he was supposed to be a recently-elected Scotch member, and being a tall, portly, gentlemanly-looking man, so far as appearance went, passed muster very well. Next night found the laird occupying his former seat. However, about nine o'clock Lord Granville Somerset, who the previous evening had his doubts as to the genuineness of the reputed Scotch M. P., went to the sergeant-at-arms and asked who was that tall man sitting behind Sir Robert Peel? "Oh, he is a Scotch member, one of yourselves, Lord Granville." "I doubt that exceedingly," said his lordship, "and I doubt his being a member at all."

The sergeant-at-arms, all excitement, flew round behind the opposition benches and gave the laird a sharp tap on the shoulder, desiring him to come to him. The laird so far complied, but not being accustomed to be treated unceremoniously, asked the stern official what he meant? "Why, sir, you were in the House last night?" "I was." "You sat in the same place you have been now occupying?" "Yes, the very same, and what right have you to disturb me?" "You are in my custody." "In your custody; for what? Hands off!" exclaimed the laird in any other tone than a mild one. "Who are you?" asked the sergeant. "Who am I! go and ask Mr. Cutlar Fergusson; he placed my name on the Speaker's list, and if there is any mistake"—the laird being now very angry—"it was your duty, as the servant of the House, to have shown me where to sit." The sergeant-at-arms was so far relieved; but still holding the laird's arm, the latter again exclaimed, "Hands off!" and being a powerful man, soon wrested himself from the official's grasp. "Tell me where my place is." This he was only too happy to do, and the laird now took his fresh seat in St. Stephen's under considerable excitement, muttering to the sergeant-at-arms, that it was a matter of indifference to him where he sat, provided he heard the speeches, but he must beg not to be again disturbed.

This escapade of my countryman in the House of Commons used to amuse a hospitable friend of mine in town beyond measure, the more so from the fact of his coming from his own and my part of Scotland. One day, after dinner, I was asked by my friend to tell the story, and finding myself sitting next to Mr. William Holmes, M. P., the Conservative "whip," I remarked that Mr. Holmes would correct me if I went wrong. The Hon. gentleman was kind enough afterward to say that I had told it *right* well.

Mr. Holmes then proceeded in a vein of dry humor to tell us, that such an occurrence had never before happened in the House of Commons, and that the "actor" could only be a Scotchman. "Ah, you Scotchmen do like to get things *chape*, but it is the first time there was ever *soch* a *chape sate* had in St. *Staven's*. The fact is, your friend and countryman intended to keep his *sate* during the rest of the session, and being a clever fellow had discovered that all he had to do to avoid detection was to slip out of the House a few minutes before a division, and when that was over to come back to his place. I told Lord Granville Somerset that he had made a mistake in sending the sergeant-at-arms to look after your friend, as we were in desperate want of some more Scotchmen on our side of the House." I recollect on this occasion amusing Mr. Holmes by telling him of a young friend of mine going home to his father and mother and in apparent ecstasy exclaiming that Mr. Holmes was certainly the nicest man in England. "He is indeed," said the youngster. "Why do you say so?" asked his father. "Why, this very afternoon I was going down Parliament-street to Westminster, when I saw Mr. Holmes coming toward me with the Duke of Wellington hanging on his arm. Of course, papa, I looked down, not wishing Mr. Holmes to see me while he was walking with so great a man; but what do you think? he put his hand on my shoulder in passing, and said: 'Well, youngster, all well at home?' Fancy how kind that was when walking with the Duke of Wellington. I do say Mr. Holmes is the nicest man in England." It would be well if this youth's estimate of Mr. Holmes's bonhommie were more generally appreciated and followed. A kind word spoken at the right moment often forms an important element in the success of the noble, the politician, the lawyer, the divine, the banker, and the merchant.

71. "*It's* no' *worth while rinnen* (*running*) *the risk*."

I recollect my father doubling the beauty of a very attractive girl—a daughter of a toll-gate keeper in the South of Scotland—by a very simple process: Madame Rachel in her labors to render the fair sex "beautiful forever," was never half so successful.

We were travelling from home to Edinburgh, a distance of a hundred and twenty miles, by easy stages; and on stopping at one of the gates the girl came out of the house to receive the shilling. She had one of the dirtiest faces I ever beheld. She extended her hand for the money. "Oh no, my girl," said my father. "Coachman, drive on." "You've *no payt* (paid) me, sir." The coachman continued to drive on; the girl racing alongside the carriage bawling at the top of her voice: "Stap, *cotchman*, the laird has *no' payt* me." As tears now rolled down the begrimed beauty's cheeks, my father, no doubt recalling the lines of the poet—

> What heart but melts, their force is all divine—

desired the coachman to draw up. When the breathless damsel had partially recovered the use of her respiratory organs, and from her alarm, my father addressed her thus: "Do you not know that by the Act of Parliament any girl coming to ask for the toll with a dirty face, we are not obliged to pay her?—that is the reason I desired the coachman to drive on." "Dear me, sir, I never *kent* (knew) that *afore*, and *ma faither* never *tellt* me I assure you, sir." "How very wrong of your father! I must speak to him very seriously on the subject, as I find you are not so much to blame." "*Na*, sir, *it's no' ma faut* (my fault)." Her alarm was rapidly returning that the toll was not to be paid. "Well," said my father, "there is a shilling for the toll, and there is a shilling for yourself to buy soap with." "Oh sir, *ma* mither has got plenty *o' sape*, I'll *no tak* that shilling, sir." "Well then, keep the shilling for yourself, and tell your mother to give you a piece of soap immediately." "I'm *meikle* (much) *obleeged* to you, sir; and for telling me *aboot* the Act o' Parliament, I'm truly *thankfu*." About a fortnight afterward on our return from Edinburgh, out came the girl to receive the toll, and in regard to her face and its cleanliness no imperfection or omission could be traced, and our arrival was quite unexpected. "Well," said my father, "how do you do?" "*Vera weel*, thank you, sir, for *spiering* (asking)." "I cannot keep you out of the shilling to-day." "*Na, na*, sir," with a dangerously bewitching smile, "I *hae ta'en* (taken) *guid* care o' that. I assure you, sir, ye *hadna* driven *awa* five *meenuts* when I *weeshea ma face*, but I *shoud* tell you, sir, that *ma faither* says, that *hadna yer* honor been a *magistratt* he *woud hae dooted aboot* the Act o' Parliament, but he *thocht* it as *weel no* to be *rinnen ony* risk, and that I had better *weesh ma* face every *morn* (morning)." My father alleged, from not seeing either the toll-house keeper or his wife on this occasion, that the question of the ablutions of their daughter was a somewhat delicate affair; in fact, that their *amour propre* had been wounded, and that in conseqnence they "*were not at home.*" This only encouraged my father the more in his determination to send in the wedge still deeper, by continuing the *tête-à-tête.* "You seem, my girl, although you have washed your face, to have forgotten to comb your hair." "*Weel*, sir, ye'll excuse me, but *ye* never said a word to me about *reddin ma heed* (combing my hair)." "It is quite true, I did not, for I forgot whether combing the hair as well as washing the face is mentioned in the Act of Parliament, and if it is not, it must be inserted without delay; for what is the use of a clean face if there is an untidy head of hair?" "*Weel*, sir, as I *hae noo* (have now) got into the habit of *weeshing mysel*, I'll soon get into the *wey* (way) *o' reddin ma heed.*" "Every morning," said my father. "O, ay, sir, every *mornin* after I *weesh ma* face, and do *ye ken* (know) sir, I begin to like it."

A lady who was in the carriage said, "I am sure you are a very good girl, and go to church regularly." "I never, *ma leddy*, miss *ganging* to the kirk." "Well, you will find, in reading your Bible, that godliness and cleanliness go hand in hand.[1] Good-by."

I shortly afterward left Scotland to be a long absentee; but it is to be hoped that the domestic or household reform intended by my father in his recommendation of a more general use of soap and water, is largely extended in con-

[1] It is often said that a proverb to this effect is to be found in the Bible, but the statement is not correct. It may be found in a sermon of John Wesley on dress.

sequence of his colloquy with the toll-keeper's daughter; and I think it reasonable to expect that such may be the case, especially as his pupil at the end of the first fortnight had said, "I begin to like it."

72. *A Somewhat Extensive View.*

My late esteemed friend, Mr. John Mackie, M. P. for Kirkcudbrightshire, used to describe an extensive view which one of a friend's hills commanded. This he never failed to call to the attention of his English visitors when the weather was clear. Willy, the shepherd, was always the guide on such occasions, as he knew precisely the weather that would suit.

One forenoon an English friend was placed under Willy's charge to mount the hill, in order to enjoy the glorious view. "I am told, shepherd, you are going to show me a wonderful view." "That's quite true, sir."

"What shall I see?" "*Weel*, ye'll see a *feck* (many) o' kingdoms, the best part o' *sax*, sir." "What the deuce do you mean, shepherd?" "*Weel*, sir, I mean what I say." "But tell me all about it." "I'll tell ye *naething mair*, sir, until we're at the *tap* o' the hill." The top reached, Willy found every thing he could desire in regard to a clear atmosphere. "*Noo*, sir, I hope you've got *guid een?*" "Oh, my eyes are excellent." "Then that's *a' recht* (right), sir. Noo, *div ye* see yon hills *awa'* yonder?" "Yes, I do." "Weel, sir, those are the Hills o' Cumberland, and Cumberland's in the kingdom o' England; that's *ae* kingdom. *Noo*, sir, please keep *coont*. Then, sir, I must *noo* trouble you to look *ower* (over) yonder. *Div ye* see what I mean?" "Yes, I do." "That's *a' recht.* That's the Isle o' Man, and that was a kingdom and a sovereignty in the families o' the Earls of Derby and the Dukes o' Athol frae the days o' King David o' Scotland, if ye ken *ony thing* o' Scotch history." "You are quite right, shepherd." "Quite *recht*, *div ye* say; I *woudna hae brocht* ye here, sir, if I *wus* to be wrang. *Weel*, that's *twa* kingdoms. Be sure, sir, to keep *coont*. *Noo*, turn *awee aboot*. *Div ye* see yon land yonder? It's a bit *farder*, but never mind that, *sae lang* as you see it." "I see it distinctly." "*Weel*, that's a' I care *aboot*. *Noo*, sir, keep *coont*, for that's Ireland, and *maks* three kingdoms; but there's nae trouble *aboot* the *niest* (next) for ye're *stannen on't*—I mean *Scoteland*. *Weel*, that *maks* four kingdoms; *div ye* admit that, sir?" "Yes, that makes four, and you have two more to show me." "That's true, sir, but don't be in *sic* (such) a hurry. *Weel*, sir, just look up *aboon* (above) *yer heed*, and this is by far the best of *a'* the kingdoms; that, sir, *aboon* is *Heeven*. That's five; and the *saxth* kingdom is that *doon* below *yer* feet, to which, sir, I hope you'll never *gang;* but that's a point on which I cannot speak with *ony* certainty."

73. *Tom Campbell's Authorship of the "Pleasures of Hope" called into Question.*

Campbell had promised to dine with my brother and myself, to meet a party of friends, and in the afternoon of the same day our much esteemed friend, the late Mr. Hugh Kennedy, of Cultra, in the county of Down, called upon us on his way through town from the Continent to his seat in Ireland. We asked him to dine with us, which he feared he could not do, but on hearing that he would meet the author of the 'Pleasures of Hope,' he exclaimed, "I would wait in London a month of Sundays to dine with *Tam* Campbell" (when the Laird of Cultra became emphatic he had the richest Irish brogue), "for Campbell was my earliest and best college friend at Glasgow, in fact, my college tutor, and I have not seen him for thirty years.

Pray, don't tell him, if I arrive late, whom he is to see." This was promised, but Kennedy arrived first. On the poet's name being announced, his old friend advanced to meet him. "*Tam*, how are you?" "Ay, ay," exclaimed the poet, throwing himself into a tragic attitude, his dark eyes sparkling brilliantly, "I know that voice; don't tell me who you are." By this time, as they were holding each other by both hands, the scene created much interest, and we had closed round the two long-absent friends, Campbell still exclaiming, "Don't tell me who you are, but ay, ay, I know your voice." "*Gar*, *Tam*," said Kennedy, "you should know it, and right well too." He then dropped his hands, and inspected his friend minutely from head to foot. "Just speak once more," asked the poet. "I'll *spake* to you, *Tam*, a *dale aftner* than that before the *avening's* out." "Oh, man," responded the bard of "Hope," "I now find old age, and its too frequent companion, loss of memory, have arrived, for I cannot recognize the man, although I know the voice, as if it were only yesterday. I must give it up." "Well, now, *Tam* Campbell, did you ever hear of Glasgow College?" "Good heavens!" throwing himself into his friend's arms, "Hugh Kennedy, my dear, dear Hugh"—the tears rolling down his cheeks; the ever-joyous Cultra, and the spectators, too, could with difficulty refrain from following the catching example.

They sat opposite each other at dinner, *and were in truth* what we are not always, although fond of adopting the expression of the French, "Les vis-à-vis sont des amis." After dinner, Mr. Kennedy told us he had a bumper toast to give, but would reccommend a preliminary one to be discussed, as he had a good deal to say, and some of it rather of a dry, and all of it of a personal nature. His advice being followed, he again rose and told us that it was somewhat painful for him to make the statement he was about to enter on, as it was nothing more nor less than to announce to the company that "*Tam* Campbell," for more than the third of a century, had been claiming for himself the entire authorship of the 'Pleasures of Hope.' Campbell was now in a roar of laughter, while we were grave as judges. "He very well knows that I am the *rale* author of the 'Pleasures of Hope.'" "Quite true," exclaimed Campbell. "Now, gentlemen, hear that, and hear this *Tam* Campbell, a self-confessed plagiarist before you, and who, but for this blot on his moral and literary escutcheon, was always a wonderfully veracious sort of a fellow—the more the *pozzle* to me that he should have run the risk of shipwrecking himself as he has done in this matter, when I was just the man with whom he could have made the *asiest* imaginable terms. *Tam*, I say—and as old Horace said before me, although I forget the original—'Out on ye imitators, a servile herd!' You know that I am the *fons et origo* of the 'Pleasures of Hope.'" "You are, indeed, Kennedy," said Campbell. "Then, I ask you, *Tam*, why have you kept the fact so long from the world?" "It was very wrong, I confess; but wait, Hugh, for the next edition." "I won't, *indade*, I shall expose you now," 'Magna est veritas, et prævalebit.' There's a bit of Glasgow College Latin for you." Our curiosity having now reached fever-heat, we called upon Kennedy to come to our relief, and explain. "Well, gentlemen, my father thought I should be nothing the worse of a little more learning—and I dare say he was about right; and he sent me to Glasgow University, and there *Tam* Campbell fortunately became acquainted with Hugh Kennedy, and Hugh Kennedy fortunately became acquainted with *Tam* Campbell. My father said to me before he started me *aff*, 'Now, Hugh, my good fellow, while you are at college you shall not want for money'—'Thank you, father,' said I—'nor shall you want for books.' The sequel was quite true. I looked after the money myself, and I let the books look after themselves." "I'll vouch for the truth of that," said the poet. "Thank you, *Tam*, for the remark. My father wrote to his London publishers, telling them, no doubt, that he had a very sharp son at Glasgow University, and that every month they were to send him a box with all the newest publications. My friend *apposite* there *fraquently* breakfasted with me, and one morning he woke me out of a deep *slape*, having been up all night, and a bit of the morning too, at a ball. I said, '*Tam*, just see, like a good fellow, what's in the London box, and let me go on with my rest.' I got up in about two hours, and instead of finding *Tam* devouring his breakfast, he was devouring Rogers's 'Pleasures of Memory,' which came out of the box, and with which he seemed mightily delighted. 'Ah, Hugh,' said he, 'you have given me a great *trate*, and we shall now write the 'Pleasures of Hope.' 'With all my heart,' said I, and I just added, '*Tam*, as you have read the one book, you may as well write the other.' Now, gentlemen, there is my simple tale, and I must wait, I presume, for the next edition, when you and the public will be able to *jodge* correctly of my claim to the authorship of the 'Pleasures of Hope.'" This was followed by a shout of "Clearly established." "Thank you, gentlemen, *moch* for listening so patiently to the recital of my claims to a great literary distinction, and for the verdict you have now given in my favor; but as I have no particular ill-will against the man, will you join me in drinking *aff* this bumper to his health, although it is more than he deserves?"

Campbell, in returning thanks, acknowledged the correctness of the statement; but his friend Kennedy in urging his own claims to the authorship of the 'Pleasures of Hope,' with which the public had been so long deluded (April, 1799), had entirely overlooked the name of one whose claims must take priority: "That name was 'Sam Rogers,' for had there not been the 'Pleasures of Memory,' in Kennedy's box, there might *never* have been the 'Pleasures of Hope;' therefore I beg to propose the health of Sam Rogers." It is almost needless to add that the toast was received with all due honors.

74. *M. Alexandre.*

A friend lately applied to one of his guests, either kindly or satirically, the line *nec tecum possum vivere nec sine te.*

This reminded me of having been in a provincial town in France some forty years ago, and very anxious to get a cup of tea. But I found it a difficult matter, for I was compelled to resort to a chemist's shop for it, so little was tea used at that period in France. My friend's latinity brought up an occurrence at Paris which he used to relate admirably, and which has caused me much merriment. Monsieur Alexandre, a distinguished cook at Paris, who was, I believe, at one time chief-de-cuisine to the late Lord Chesterfield, feeling unwell, called upon an English physician resident in the French capital, to consult him. Our countryman found not much the matter with the distinguished professor of the culinary art. However, he prescribed, and told his patient to follow up the prescription in about two hours by taking some tea and keeping himself quiet, adding that he would call to see him next day. Monsieur Alexandre on reaching home sent for half a pound of tea, and resolved to prepare it himself. He put the whole of the tea into a stew-pan with a small quantity of water, and allowed it to simmer for an hour, when the invalid considered it must be sufficiently cooked. Alexandre then commenced to eat, not to drink, his Chinese repast, and got as much down his throat as he could. Next day the doctor called. "Well, monsieur, did you take your medicine?" "Yase, docteur." "And did you take your tea?" "Yase, docteur, but I found *de* tea *veri, veri toff.*" "Tough?" said the doctor. "Oh yase, docteur, *veri toff*, and I did cook it my ownself, I assure you, docteur, and I have *enoff* of it to last me one month." "Pray let me see it," said the doctor. The stew-pan was produced, and sure enough poor Alexandre astonished the doctor by showing him how much he had swallowed. "Well," said the doctor, "I may ask you to cook for me a *vol au vent*, a *fricandeau*, or a *Charlotte russe*, but certainly I shall go elsewhere for a cup of tea."

75. *The Laird in search of a Wife.*

When I was a boy, the Laird of —— consulted my father on the subject of matrimony, informing him that he was *awfu'* anxious to get married. My father promised to render him his best assistance in what he described to the laird as the most important and delicate matter in life. Addressing my father in an unusually animated manner, the laird said: "I *ken'd fu' weel*[1] what you would say to me, for I always *thocht* it was no common affair marrying, and I candidly tell you, *ma guid* sir, I *hae* been too *blate*[2] to speak to you on the matter, but I at last made up my mind to do so. In fact, I had a bit o' a dream the *ither nicht*, and something *tellt* me in the dream that there was *nae* gentleman in *ower neeborhood* to come up to *yersel* to talk *ower sic* an affair *wi*; for I *hae aften* said to *mysel* when I *hae* been listening to what *ye hae* informed me o' from time to time *aboot* London, and the politics, and the *gangings* on there during the *lang* war, and *a' aboot* the commerce o' the nation, and the *coorts* o' law, and *a'* manner o' information, that I *hae* been made *mair* a man o', and *hae pickt* up *mair counsel*[3] in dining at your house than *frae a'* the *buiks* I *hae* read *sin* I left school." "Well, laird," said

[1] knew quite well. [2] too modest. [3] information.

my father, "would you wish me to consult my wife, as you are a great favorite of hers, and ladies are generally much more useful in arranging such affairs than our sex?" "Oh, no, I *coudna* face the *leddies* in the drawing-room, if I *thocht* they *kenn'd* what I *hae* been talking to you *aboot*. *No* at present, *gin ye*[1] please." "Very well," said my father, "I shall keep it strictly to myself." I must now describe this candidate for the honors of St. Benedict, and then the *modus operandi* suggested by my father. He was well built, about five feet ten or eleven in height, under thirty years of age, with an excellent expression of countenance, *awsomely blate*,[2] good-looking, in blooming health, and, what stood at the top of my father's estimate of respectability in our then *drouthy*[3] part of Scotland, the laird was very sober. He was unquestionably a Simon Pure. It so happened that within a few weeks of this interesting and confidential conversation between my father and the laird, the eyes of the former were directed to a quarter where he considered he had an immediate prospect of securing a prize for the laird in the matrimonial lottery. My mother had received a letter from her aunt in London offering a visit. In those non-railway days the journey to Scotland—travelling with your own horses—was a tedious affair, and could only be made to answer by a corresponding length of visit. The old lady was to be accompanied by a charming young friend whom she had educated and brought up, and to whom her late husband had left a few thousand pounds, rendering her, in case of her kind friend's death, quite independent.

The thought at once struck my father that here was a most suitable wife for the laird, well educated, prudently brought up, and with comfortable means in addition, for his acres were very moderate in extent; but he had always lived within his income, and his sterling qualities as a man more than compensated for any pecuniary shortcomings.

[1] if you. [2] dreadfully bashful. [3] thirsty.

The following Sunday, after service, my father beckoned to the laird, who was at his side in an instant. "You must come and dine with us to-day as I have something important to tell you after dinner." The laird mounted his horse, and returned with our family.

The dinner over, and my father and the laird being alone, the former at once opened the proposed treaty of alliance, telling him that the very wife to suit him would be at his house within the next few weeks. The laird was delighted at the intelligence, but assumed an air of gravity, and exclaimed, "*Noo*, sir, I leave all to you to manage, for I must tell you I am *naething* but a *cuif*[1] at *ony thing* o' this kind." "But now," said my father, "you have to put your best foot forward—look up, instead of looking down; you *must* turn over a new leaf, and have more confidence in yourself among the ladies; otherwise I shall have a difficult matter with you." All this the laird promised strictly to observe. My father made another suggestion, that he should place himself forthwith in his tailor's hands, and have some smart things made without delay. "I can carry out," said the laird, "this part of your instructions, sir, *vera* easily, and if I could *onnly* get *ower ma blateness* by the time I get *ma* new *claes*, it would be a' *recht;* but I *hae ma* doots." "You must have no doubts." "*Weel, weel*, I promise you, *ma* kind sir, to do *ma* best." Next Sunday while the *kirk was skailing*,[2] the laird whispers into my father's ear: "*Ony accoont o'* the young leddy?" "Another fortnight, and she will be here." "That's grand," said the laird; "but I hope, sir, you *hae* said *naething* to your own leddy *aboot* this?" "Not a word," said my father.

This was a proper precaution, as my mother was much too ingenuous, and would have opposed any thing bordering on matrimonial jobbery. The following Sunday-week

[1] blockhead. [2] the congregation separating.

the laird had the young lady from London in full view in the front seat of the gallery belonging to our family in the old parish church, but his *blateness* appeared to my father to have increased rather than diminished, as he had hoped to find it, for he could not detect him casting a single glance toward the gallery where sat that fair occupant who had commanded for the past few weeks so large a share of his thoughts.

At the conclusion of the service, my father resolved to walk home, so that he might have a private conversation with the aspirant for connubial bliss on that action of a man's life which, Selden tells us, "does least concern other people, yet of all actions of our life is the most meddled with by other people." Then for the discussion of such an important subject as that of marriage, and with a novice like the laird, he considered "the better day, the better the deed."

"Well, laird, what became of your eyes to-day? You never once looked up toward our gallery." "Na, na, sir, I *dar na* even *gie a keek*[1] at your party, that's the *recht doon* fact, and I was afraid of catching your *ee*." "Oh," said my father, "I did not wish you to catch *my* eye. Now, laird, as I must get home as soon as possible, I wish you to come and lunch with me to-morrow, and we shall have the course clear, as my wife and her aunt are going off in the forenoon to make a round of visits." "Please, sir, I hope you *hae na* yet spoken to the young leddy aboot me?" "Not a word. Now, laird, make yourself look smart." "*Dinna* fear that; I *hae* got some nice *new claes*, and a pair o' new *tap* boots." "All right," said my father, "and I must now tell you what to do. You will find the young lady most probably at the piano, and I shall be in the room. Of course you must be very fond of music." "Weel, I really am fond o' music." "I am glad to hear

[1] give a glance.

that, laird, as 'music is the food of love,' and 'kindles love.'" "It is strange to say, sir, I never knew that before." "Then, after lunch, I shall go into my room to write one or two short letters, and leave Miss —— and you to chit-chat together." "O, sir, *dinna be lang awa*, as I am *swithering*[2] *aboot* the conversation part o' it." "O, nonsense; recollect 'faint heart never won a fair lady.'" "That's quite true. It's like 'setting a stout heart to a *stae brae* (stiff hill).'"

Next day the laird was punctual, riding up to the house in his new *tap boots* and bran new *claes*, and was all or even more than my father had anticipated in regard to outward appearance. His difficulty with the laird was to induce him to remember the value of first impressions, and to adopt on this occasion at least an air of self-reliance. On being announced, my father saw that his lesson had been partially learned, but not to the extent he could have desired. However, this portion of the educational test was over; the laird had been introduced; and my father remarked to him, "I know you like music." He had just made the observation when to his horror he discovered he had omitted to give the laird a strong caution on one essential point to which he was cruelly addicted in the drawing-room, that of twirling his thumbs round at an immensely rapid rate.

This made my father uneasy, so he at once applied the break by asking Miss —— kindly to play and sing to them till lunch was announced, as Mr. —— was peculiarly fond of music. What the laird's thoughts were at this moment after so marked an encomium on his musical tastes never, I believe, was made known, but my father felt relieved when luncheon came at last. The lunch being over, my father retired to finish his correspondence, or, more strictly speaking, to give time for the laird to make his first im-

[1] doubting.

pressions. It had been arranged that my father's absence should not extend beyond twenty minutes, and when that elapsed, he returned to the drawing-room, where, to his infinite surprise, he found the laird alone. "Where is Miss ——?" "O," said the laird, "she has been *awa a* lang time." "What do you call a long time?" "Weel, for guid fifteen *meenuts.*" "What the deuce," said my father, "does this mean? I know you could have said nothing that was rude." "Dear me, no, sir." "Tell me exactly what you said." "Weel, you know, I *swithered*, as I told you, about your leaving the room, as I am a bad hand at talking." "Now do go on, as I am quite impatient to hear what passed." "Weel, then, sir, you were scarcely *oot o'* the door, when I just said, 'Miss ——, you have come from London *ceety;*' and she said, 'Not from London *ceety*, but from London.' I wish to be quite correct." "What next?" "Weel, then I said, 'London is a large *ceety;*' and she said it was. The *niest*[1] thing was, 'It's a lang journey *frae* London to this, isn't it, Miss ——?' 'Yes,' she said, 'a very long journey.' 'Please, Miss ——,' for I *keepit* up the talk pretty weel as far as this, 'tell me *hoo lang* the old *leddy* and *yoursel* were on the journey?' And I think she said, either a fortnight or three weeks." "Well," said my father, "there was nothing wrong or that could give offence in all this." "I then *lookit* at the door, and I would *hae gien*[2] *twa* o' the best sheep I hae, if at that moment ye had come into the room, for it is as true as death, I did *na ken* what to say then." "Did you remain silent?" "Na, I just *askit anither bit* o' a question." "What was that?" "I said, 'Miss ——, *aiblins*[3] ye can tell me the price o' *cuddochs* in London?'" "What!" exclaimed my father. "Good gracious, did you ask her the price of cuddochs in London?" "Yes, I did that; I *thocht* there was *nae* harm." At this moment my father saw shipwreck

[1] next. [2] have given. [3] perhaps.

ahead to his hopes; he therefore quietly asked the laird what she said in reply. "Why, she repeated my word twice—'cuddock, cuddock!' she *couldna* get the word *weel oot*, and I just *helpit* her, and said, 'Cuddoch, Miss ——.' She then *glowered*[1] at me, got *aff* her chair as if she was *fleyed*[2] o' me, *gied*[3] a bit o' a jump and a sort o' a skip, and clean *oot* o' the room she went; that's the whole *trowth*,[4] I can assure you, sir."

Young ladies, in mercy to the laird, must not ask me if the negotiations which my father commenced, and which he thought he had begun so auspiciously, were ever resumed, otherwise I shall be obliged to tell them frankly they were not, and to remind them that with this laird, as with others, the course of true love did not run quite smooth. In this instance, the poor laird's path became thoroughly blocked up by the cuddochs. In justice to my part of Scotland, I must inform you that, although the young lady declined to travel on any road where "cuddochs" were to be met with, she discovered one where they were unknown, and there met with a clerical swain, whose happiness she cemented with her own, and further augmented it by a large and charming family.

The laird, although he promised faithfully to my father—and no doubt acted up to his promise—to renounce for the future ever mentioning in the drawing-room cuddochs, especially if young ladies were present, died a bachelor in 1850.

I should add, by way of explanation, that a cuddoch is a well-known term in Galloway for young cattle from their twelfth to their twenty-fourth month. They are "calves" till six, "*stirks*" till twelve months, and then "cuddochs" till they become two-year-olds.

[1] stared at me. [2] frightened. [3] gave. [4] truth.

76. *The Late King of Hanover.*

When he had a seat among the peers, no member of the House was more obliging in regard to the privilege of franking than the late Duke of Cumberland.

The late Mr. William Gibson, formerly of Charleston, South Carolina, a native of Ayrshire, who, for several years toward the close of life, resided in London, was in the habit, during the sitting of Parliament, of daily spending some hours in the committee-rooms. He was a tall and imposing-looking old gentleman (a septuagenarian), and had made an extensive parliamentary acquaintance. Among others was the Duke of Cumberland, who always treated him very courteously. Mr. Gibson had an aged relation in Scotland to whom he frequently wrote; and the Duke, when he met my friend, usually addressed him, "Well, Gibson, how do you do?" A profound bow, "I hope I see your Royal Highness well?" "Am I to give you a frank to-day for Mrs. McTurk, of Polquhorter, New Cumnock, Ayrshire?" Another bow, one of acquiescence, followed, and His Royal Highness was at the table writing the frank, in handing which to the old gentleman, he generally repeated, "Mrs. McTurk, of Polquhorter, New Cumnock, Ayrshire—rather a difficult address for some of us here; but you see I never forget it, do I, Gibson?"

77. *Mr. Samuel Anderson.*

There could not be a more joyous, hospitable man, than my late friend and countryman, "Sam Anderson," as he was called in "Modern Athens." The last twenty years of his life were spent in London, where he held the appointment of Registrar of Affidavits in the Court of Chancery. He possessed a rich vein of humor, and his powers were somewhat remarkable as an after-dinner *improvisa-*

tore, one of those whom the French would describe, *qui font des vers sur le champ.* Probably he approached nearer Theodore Hook in this respect than any man of his period. He could also relate a laughable occurrence admirably, and I recollect an amusing one that had taken place, and which he gave us at his own table in his happiest manner a few hours afterward. Among the party whom he delighted with the recital and imitation, were Sir Augustus D'Esté, Mr. Ferguson, of Raith, M. P., Mr. Hope-Vere, of Craigie, Mr. McCulloch, the political economist, Mr. James Stuart, of Dunearn, my father, and myself.

It was a *dies non* in the Registrar's office, and he had resolved to get rid of cobwebs in the room in which his friends were to dine, by absenting himself. He left his domicile soon after breakfast to have a walk, out and home, over Highgate Hill, and had only reached Euston Square, when it began to rain heavily. He at once said to himself, "As I have lost my twenty miles' walk, I shall have a forty miles' ride instead, for the inner man must be shaken up, and this can be done for five shillings." In those days the omnibus ran to and from Paddington Green to Bartholomew Lane, Bank of England. He seated himself in his first omnibus, on its way to the city, and found himself in some twenty-five minutes at the Bank; he paid his sixpence, and told the conductor he would return with him. "Glad hof hit, sir." On his arrival at Paddington Green, he was obligingly informed, "Now, sir, Paddington." "But I don't wish to get out, I am going to return with you." "Hobliged to you, sir, but hi dines now, hand ve changes osses: put you hinto hanother bus, sir." "All right," said the traveller. He was in due course handed out of the one into another. Within the hour, our friend had arrived for the second time at the Bank. The other passengers descended, but he remained, handing the conductor his sixpence, at the same time announcing an important fact: "I return with you, conductor." "You does, does you, sir?" "Yes, I do." "Hall right, sir." In due time our friend was for the second time at Paddington, found himself once more the sole occupant of his carriage, and with his accustomed regularity, paid his sixpence. The conductor bawls into our friend's ear, "Ve stops eere, hand hain't a going back." "Oh, then I must take another omnibus to go back to the city." "You'd better, sir."

Arrived at the Bank, our friend, who calculated that he had twenty miles of his forty to accomplish, sat still. The ten minutes before the return journey commenced was fully occupied in listening to the remarks of all kinds, from coachmen and conductors, with whom he found he had become the subject of deep speculation; the more so for having heard the conductor, in coming up Pentonville Hill, say to a colleague who was passing, "Vy, Bill, I've got the mad un this time." The worthy Registrar had two hours left to complete his day's ride, each periodical inspection becoming minuter both at the Paddington and city terminus. Just before leaving Paddington for the last time, to get down at Euston Square *en route* to Chancery Lane, he addressed the conductors and coachmen who were gazing at him, thus: "Well, I can give a very good account of you to Her Majesty's Government. You seem a steady, respectable body of men; I have heard little or no improper language from you during the six hours I have been inspecting you, nor have I seen any case of 'nursing,' which, if I had, would have been visited with my highest displeasure, and an immediate dismissal of the guilty parties would have followed: moreover, and I state it as highly creditable to you, as you did not know me, that you have paid me marked attention throughout the day; good-afternoon, put me down, conductor, at Euston Square." Instantly a most earnest conversation ensued among the brethren of the whip, which delayed the departure of the omnibus for some minutes, giving our friend the advantage of hearing some portion of it. One of them exclaimed, "Vell, crikey, here's a go; hinstead hof hourn ha vatching he, hee's been ha vatching hus. Vat luck hit vas e never seed me ha nursing hof Arry hall the vay from the city. Vell, you never can judge hof these ere coves."

Our host concluded his amusing description of his day's journeyings by omnibus, by expressing his conviction that before the evening closed, one of the conductors was congratulated by a large section of his fraternity, on having failed to carry out his threat of depositing him in St. Luke's.

78. *An Anglo-American's View of the Abyssinian Expedition.*

At the *table d'hôte* of the Railway Hotel at Glasgow I saw a Maclean, a Mackenzie, or a Macgregor—I forget which—work himself into a towering state of excitement with an American visitor, whom he described as a pervert. "*Na, na*, there's *nae* excuse for him, for it is *no* as if his *grandfaither* had emigrated to America when it was a British Colony, but this gabbler *o'* a *fallow* went there some twenty years *syne*[1] and by carrying on some mercantile trading between the United States—united indeed!!—and Great Britain, made his money and lost his nationality, if he ever had *ony*. But in regard to this man's renunciation *o'* the land *o'* his birth, *ma* opinion is, we are *weel* rid *o'* him. In the whole *coorse o' ma* experience, I never met this man's match in audacity *o'* statement, nor did I ever hear *sic*[2] a piece *o'* heartless bombast *fa' frae* the lips *o' ony* man, much less *ane* who left his *hame* a subject *o'* Queen Victoria." It was in addressing me in reply to an observation I made about the success of Sir Robert Napier's expedition to Abyssina. This 'pervert' assumed a

[1] since. [2] such.

very consequential and patronizing tone, "which," said my countryman, "I will stand from no man, especially from *ane* who would fain *mak* himself appear at the end of twenty years an American *ceetezen* of importance." "Well, so you Britishers consider this a great victory?" "Yes, we do, a great military success, which will always form a leading chapter in our military annals." "Indeed, so you look upon it as a great military exploit, do you?" "We do." "Why, sir, your English general seems to have had some difficulty in returning one officer killed, and one or two privates slightly wounded. We don't carry on war on our side the Atlantic in that way." '*Na*, by *ma* faith, you don't," exclaimed the son of Scotia. "We emancipated our slaves in the West Indies without spilling *bluid*, and only spending *aboot* twenty millions sterling in awarding a moderate compensation to the planters; whereas, you emancipated your slaves by entering into a *ceevil* war, the most cruel, the most unnatural, the most disastrous, that ever disgraced humanity; and this, mind you, in the nineteenth century. *Weel*, after this most cruel butchery, *brithers fechting* against *brithers*, probably *faithers* against their *ain* bairns, sacrificing half *o* million *o'* lives, I believe a million would be nearer the *trowth*,[1] to say *naething o'* spending six hundred millions *o' poonds* sterling, which you will *no ca* '*naething*' by-and-by when *yer* taxes *hae* to be met to cancel your greenbacks. *Ma guid*, sir, you'll *no* be seeking war wi *oursels* or ony *ither* power in Europe for a *guid wheen* years, I promise you, unless *ye* are deevilish fond *o'* taxation in America. Then because our great General of Engineers, Napier, carries an expedition into the heart *o'* Abyssinia, where he had the dangers *o'* a tropical climate to apprehend, and accomplishes the responsible duty intrusted to him by his Sovereign, in a manner to command the respect and admiration of the nations of Europe, al-

[1] truth.

though it would appear the Western world, which you seem to represent, is an exception, by securing the deliverance of the English and other prisoners immured in the dungeons of a *bluid*-thirsty tyrant. *Noo*, as the British General and the brave men whom he led not less skilfully than safely through the parched defiles and mountain-passes of a strange *kintra*, achieving success without spilling oceans of human gore as it flowed with you on the banks of the Potomac and under the walls of Richmond, you think proper to sneer at our *bluidless* victory. Why, sir, I wonder you are not ashamed to express such sentiments. Lucky, sir," continued our indignant countryman, "that you are not a Scotchman, for upon my faith, had you been *ane*, I should *hae* been inclined to *mak* the *kintra ower het* for you." He had now expended his phial of indignation, and looking to the right and left, and addressing us in a somewhat loud whisper, informed us, "that he was only, after *a*,' a hybrid Yankee, or what we should *ca* in *Scoteland* a mongrel."

79. *A Candidate for Sudbury.*

I had an esteemed friend in London who was unrivalled in his powers of descriptive narrative, accompanied by graphic truth and humor. One of his happy efforts was Mr. Dyce Sombre's candidature for Parliamentary honors, through the then *immaculate* and since disfranchised borough of Sudbury in Suffolk. A West-end friend had told the wealthy Asiatic, whose attention had been suddenly directed toward the borough in question, that the only man in London who could assist him in reaching St. Stephen's as M. P. for Sudbury was Mr. ——. Accordingly, the Eastern magnate called upon him with a note of introduction, and informed him that, *coûte que coûte*, he must make him a member of Parliament, and that he should like to represent

Sudbury, at that moment ready to receive not only the address but the embrace of any liberal-minded wooer.

My friend, finding the aspirant for Parliament, in regard to any political knowledge whatever, as "chaste as unsunned snow," informed his visitor that his safest politics—for he wished him to be not only the successful but the popular candidate—would be so-and-so. He was ready to conform to any politics. With such ductile *matériel* the honorable gentleman's address was then and there prepared, and next day it appeared in the leading journals. Mr. Dyce Sombre's agents at Sudbury were forthwith appointed.

The "Sombre" candidate was most anxious to visit Sudbury without delay, to make himself known to the electors, and render things "pleasant." This proposition met with my friend's *point blanc* opposition, as his greatest difficulty was the *point noir* of his candidate. He therefore assured him that the Sudbury people, especially at the period of an election, were difficult to transact business with, and that it would be infinitely better arranged in London than on the spot; that his (Mr. Dyce Sombre's) presence was not required until the day of election had been fixed, previous to which he would have the pleasure of accompanying him to the scene of action. The honorable candidate was specially cautioned on no account whatever to receive or be at home to any one approaching him from Sudbury, nor was he to write (in Hindostanee, I presume) a single letter on the subject of the election; at the same time he was informed that, if he followed out strictly these instructions, he might rely with full confidence on seeing himself a member of Parliament. The time had arrived, and the honorable gentleman was apprised that he and his political guide and appriser must leave London next day for Sudbury, four post-horses at each stage doing what the railway now so easily accomplishes. The journey was so arranged as to prevent a daylight ovation to the candidate on getting within the precincts of that once famous borough, where first settled the Flemings, who were brought over by Edward III. to teach the English the art of manufacturing their own wool. It was at an advanced hour of the evening when my friend introduced the honorable candidate to his proposer and seconder, who on retiring strongly advised that Mr. Sombre should not be produced next morning at the nomination. The poor gentleman had accordingly to consider himself an invalid, and confined to his room, the incarceration to be in force all the following and next day, down to the close of the poll. He was not allowed even to take a carriage-drive, and was to be invisible to all his supporters save and except his proposer and seconder; and as a further precaution, the waiters at the hotel were specially instructed as to the precise *bulletin* they were to give from hour to hour, and that they were to pay no attention whatever to idle questions. Few men under such circumstances could be more ably or happily represented on the hustings than was Mr. Sombre by my friend, an extremely skilful and effective speaker, and unrivalled in keeping an audience in good humor. The political bill of fare which he supplied on behalf of the invalid candidate was what no enlightened and independent constituency could possibly reject. My friend afterward confessed to me that he made one most appalling mistake in his speech on the day of nomination. "I was not content, as I should have been, with the vociferous and complimentary reception which Mr. Dyce Sombre's political sentiments enunciated through me as his organ had experienced, but in the effervescence of the moment I foolishly threw down the gauntlet too boldly, and said, 'If there was any elector who wished to put a question to him, acting on that hustings for my estimable friend, I would do my best to answer it.' Up started an elector and said: he 'had one question, and only one, to *axe* Maister ——.' 'I shall be happy to answer it.' 'Then, Maister ——, I *axes* you this ere simple question, is it true that the candidate you've brought us is a black un?' 'It is unnecessary for me to answer such an extraordinary question, as I fully hope I shall have the pleasure of introducing the worthy gentleman to you to-morrow, when I know before the clock strikes four you intend to return a liberal-minded man—yes, gentlemen, liberal in every sense of the word—as member of Parliament for your ancient borough.'" He did produce his friend next day shortly before four o'clock, and soon after that hour left him, to make not a speech, but his bow as member of Parliament for Sudbury, hearing on his right and left the remark: "Ah, Maister ——, you've been too much for us."

80. *Lord Castlereagh and the Rev. James Reid.*

A laughable circumstance occurred in my county in Scotland more than fifty years ago, the shaft of the Government having been directed, through Lord Castlereagh, against as good a man and as loyal a subject as King George III. had in his dominions.

The Rev. James Reid, minister of the Reformed Presbyterian Church in Newton Stewart, rented a house on my father's estate, and he had been our tenant for a series of years. In early life he had spent a short time in America, and any thing that he saw that was worthy of admiration in the institutions of the United States he always urged as deserving of being adopted in his own country. My father concluded that Lord Castlereagh, when posting through Wigtonshire in going to and returning from the North of Ireland, must have heard of Mr. Reid's political proclivities; for it was well known that the noble viscount, in changing horses, or in dining and remaining for the night at any inn *en route*, always launched extensively into conversation with landlords and waiters, so as to pick up all the local information he could, and in this way possessed himself of much provincial knowledge, the nature and extent of which often puzzled those with whom he was associated in public affairs.

My father, who occasionally corresponded with Lord Castlereagh, one morning received a letter from his lordship, making strict inquiry respecting a Rev. James Reid, of whom he had heard a very bad account (politically). In fact, my father was requested by his noble correspondent to keep a careful surveillance over the reverend gentleman, whose political opinions were so objectionable to His Majesty's Government. It so happened that Mr. Reid was that day to dine at our house, to meet two friends who also resided on my father's property, General the Honorable Sir William Stewart, formerly member for the county, and Captain (subsequently Admiral) McKerlie.

Nothing was said until the ladies had retired, when my father told his guests what a dangerous person they associated with in their reverend friend. On the Cabinet Minister's alarming communication being read, it was agreed that it was not "a privileged communication," and could be taken under review at that table without any breach of confidence, or danger to the state. My father had answered the Secretary of State's letter in the forenoon, and I, as a lad, had to transcribe it, for my father wrote a hand most difficult to decipher.

His answer to Lord Castlereagh was very amusing; he told his lordship that the worthy parson was that day to dine with him, and would meet an old parliamentary friend of his own, General Sir William Stewart, and a gallant post-captain in His Majesty's service, in addition to certain most loyal county magistrates. His lordship wrote a droll reply, assuring my father that all fears which His Majesty's Government might have entertained in regard to Mr. Reid had in consequence of his letter entirely subsided. I know

I lost a day's shooting by it, for nothing I dreaded more than my father taking up his pen to write upon a public question to a public man, for it always fell to my lot to make a copy of it.

81. *Religious Toleration.*

Although I never attended to my father's political lessons, there was one of his on another subject, namely, religious toleration, which I can never forget, and which was highly appreciated by a large section of the population in his district.

That worthy and excellent man, the late Rev. Dr. Andrew Carruthers, the Roman Catholic Bishop of Edinburgh, and who resided for some years at New Abbey in the Stewartry of Kirkcudbright, made periodical journeys to Wigtonshire to visit his clerical friends and their flocks.

Although my father and mother were excellent Protestants, they always gave Dr. Carruthers a hearty welcome at Merton Hall, which he made his home during his stay in our part of the country. Their carriage was considered solely at the disposal of the reverend gentleman during the visit, which generally lasted for a week. The worthy Bishop, in after-years, used to refer to the agreeable visits he paid to our family. The severest and most prejudiced critics my father had were two of his own ploughmen. They were afraid to speak to the laird on the subject, but were open-mouthed to our tutor, my brothers, and myself. "Ay, is it no *dreedfu'* to think that the laird should harbor in his *ain hoose* that *awsome* (terrible) Roman? He is *no* a bad man, I *dar* say, *himsel*, but he's a Roman; and it's a *wonner* (wonder) to us that yer (your) *gude mither* the leddy, would *thole* (endure) it; ay, it is sad, *vera* sad."

82. "*How these Scotchmen do play into each other's Hands!*"

This language I had applied to me some thirty-five years ago under the following circumstances, and I leave others to determine whether it was merited:

Her late Majesty Queen Adelaide had intimated her intention to the authorities of St. Paul's, of attending the anniversary of the Charity Children assembling within the Cathedral, and at the same time the Lord and Lady Mayoress were apprised that Her Majesty would afterward pay them a visit at the Mansion House, and lunch there. Accordingly, invitations were issued by the Lord and Lady Mayoress to those whom they wished to honor. Several members of my family, with myself, were honored with invitations. Her Majesty was accompanied by Prince George of Cambridge, then an affable vivacious youth, and of whom it was augured that, on reaching man's estate, he would be short and squat! Her Majesty was pleased to hold on the occasion, at the Mansion House, a limited drawing-room, which highly pleased the ladies. A grand *déjeuné* followed. Her Majesty and Prince George sat at a small circular table with the Lord and Lady Mayoress, while the Royal suite, with the visitors, occupied a large table in juxtaposition to that of Royalty. I happened to be near the Lord Mayor, and in the middle of the Royal table stood a magnificent pine-apple, the largest I had ever seen, and, unless I was wofully mistaken, this pine divided much of the attention of those visitors who threw their glances toward the Royal party.

Little did I suppose that this rare specimen of that delicious fruit was to involve me in almost a service of danger, and connect me with an illiberal remark—"How these Scotchmen do play into each other's hands!" It is nevertheless an unquestionable fact that certain guests of the

Lord Mayor, who sat at the lower end of the large table, seeing that the pine was still uncut, had made up their minds to conclude their *déjeuné* by having a substantial slice on the departure of the illustrious visitors. The Lord Mayor had anticipated some such result, for when Her Majesty rose to take leave, and had accepted the Lord Mayor's arm, he said to me, in passing, "Oblige me by saving the pine." I inferred that Her Majesty was to be the recipient of the pine, owing to its rare dimensions, at Buckingham Palace, before the day closed, otherwise I should not have fought or struggled to preserve it as I did. Although I knew I was not defending Her Majesty's colors, as I hope I should have done upon the heights of the Alma or at Inkerman, still I felt convinced that I was defending Queen Adelaide's pine-apple in the Mansion House of the City of London: I therefore waited rather nervously, as I now clearly discovered that the eyes of a section of the visitors were more directed to the spoils on the Royal table than even to departing Royalty itself; for no sooner had Her Majesty and her nephew left the banquet-hall, than a rush was made toward the circular table. The Lord Mayor's request had to be complied with; and without ceremony, I seized the vase containing the pine. My position must have resembled the huntsman holding the fox above his head from the hounds until the brush had been secured. I thought I should be worried to death in protecting, as I supposed, Royal property, and never stood more in need of assistance. I luckily recollected the line from the Poet Burns, "*Scots wham Bruce has aften led,*" and at the same time that the Lord Mayor's head butler's name was Bruce. I therefore vociferated, "Bruce, to the rescue!" Luckily, that eminent functionary had fulfilled his mission, so far as he was concerned in the departure of Her Majesty, and he instantly came to my support, when I told him in audible language, "The Lord Mayor desires that this pine shall be kept." This quelled the outbreak so far, and Bruce went off with the pine-apple. The Lord Mayor returned, and the first person to whom he directed his steps was to myself, inquiring, not altogether *sotto voce*, "Have you saved the pine?" "I have." "That I will vouch for," exclaimed a bystander who had heard the question. "All right," said the Lord Mayor. "I presume, my Lord Mayor," said one of the disappointed candidates for a slice of the redoubtable pine, "that it is to be sent to Her Majesty?" "Nothing of the kind," said the Lord Mayor, who was well known to be an outspoken man. "Why, then, my Lord, is it not to be eaten?" "It was to be eaten by the Queen, not by you," said the Lord Mayor; "but as Her Majesty declined to partake of it, I return it to whence it came" (Birch's, Cornhill); "I arranged to pay two guineas for the loan, or seven guineas if it had been eaten; and as it has not been eaten, I save five guineas."

"Well, to be sure," exclaimed another admirer of the pine, and one of the dissatisfied grumblers, "here is a specimen of Scotch economy for you: all I have now to say is, 'How these Scotchmen do play into each other's hands!'"

83. *Dining with an Ambassador.*

In London I was a guest of the late Mr. James Stuart, of Dunearn, the day after he and the late Mr. McCulloch, the political economist (a member of the Institute of France) had dined with M. Guizot, then French Ambassador at the court of St. James's." At that period, Mr. McCulloch had never crossed the Straits of Dover. They made us laugh at their description of the rapidity with which a dinner at the Embassy could be dispatched. They sat down at seven, and at nine were again from table. I asked the political economist, who never allowed his own guests to depart before eleven, what he and his friend did under the circumstances. "Well, we had nothing else for it than to go home; but before we separated, I said, 'Stuart, this is very early to be turned out on the world; still, it will impress the fact the more strongly on our minds of the honor we have had in dining with the Ex-Premier, Historian, Orator and Ambassador of France. Ah, Stuart! France—which I have yet to see—must be a great country, to produce at once a Guizot and such magnificent claret.'"

84. *Grosvenor Street* v. *Grosvenor Square.*

Many years ago I was asked by a friend residing in Grosvenor Street—Doctor W——, F. R. S.—to dine with him to meet a Scotch friend, who was paying his first visit to London. The party, numbering ten or twelve, were in the drawing-room anxiously waiting the arrival of the stranger, who was much past his time; it was agreed to give him ten minutes' law; but before this had expired he appeared. Apparently under great excitement, he attempted to stammer out an apology for being late; and somehow or other a strong feeling of curiosity prevailed to learn the cause. Dinner was now ordered up, and our host considered that the interval could not be better occupied than by asking his friend what had happened. "Happened! Why, I *hae* been grossly insulted, and you, Doctor, *cam* in for a share of it." "Indeed! how was that?" "*Weel*, you know I am quite a stranger in London, and I drove to Grosvenor Square instead of Grosvenor Street. *Weel*, I got *oot o'* the hackney-carriage, paid *ma* fare, and asked the lackey at the door if the *hoose* was number—. 'Yes, sir,' said he, 'it is;' and of *coorse* I walked in, and took *aff ma* cloak. I must say I was not a little bewildered, for there were six lackeys on one side, and six on the other, all in grand liveries." "Surely," said our host, "you did not imagine that I, as a London physician, kept twelve footmen." "No, that is very true, Doctor; but I was in a quandary, and I marched right up through the line of flunkeys until I reached a d— *manial* at the foot of the staircase who asked my name. I then said, 'Does Dr. W—— live here?' The insolent scoundrel put himself full in front of me, as if he was going to knock me down, and in the most impudent tone repeated, 'Doctor W—— live here?' and then made me back out toward the door, as if he suspected I had come to rob the *hoose*, exclaiming, so that all his brethren might hear it, 'Who ever heard of a doctor living in Grosvenor Square?' I really was thankful, Doctor, that I got back *ma* cloak." It appeared that the worthy but highly-indignant Scot had entered by mistake a certain noble lord's residence, where a grand banquet was to be given that same evening to one of the Royal dukes.

85. *The Old Glasgow Hand-loom Weaver at Greenwich Hospital.*

I once had the pleasure of aiding in the work of transforming an old Glasgow hand-loom weaver into a Greenwich pensioner. My man, Rock—as good-hearted an Irishman as ever crossed St. George's Channel—came suddenly into my room one afternoon, to tell me that a poor *ould* Scotchman, a namesake of mine, was very anxious to see me, and further, that he was "about very narely starving." I desired him to show my countryman and namesake upstairs, and then to look after some food on his behalf without delay. He was a slightly-built, short, wiry old man, apparently about sixty years of age, with a mild, intelligent countenance and pleasing manners, one of "Nature's gentlemen;" and the introduction so far was satisfactory. "I learn, my good man," said I, "that you and I are namesakes." "It is *vera* true, sir; and, in fact, that caused me to *tak* the *leeberty* to *ca'* upon you, for I am *sairly* put tillt" (put to it). "Pray, what have you been?" "I am an *auld* worn-*oot* Glasgow hand-loom weaver, sir." In the mean time Rock had brought him something substantial; but the fact that I seemed inclined to be his friend appeared to reinvigorate him as much as Rock's lunch.

The poor old fellow lisped out, "Ay, sir, a *frien* in need is a *frien* indeed." His meal finished, he went on jauntily enough with his little but eventful history:

"The *trowth* is, I *hae* been working hard for the last *thretty* (thirty) years as a hand-loom weaver in Glasgow; but we *hae* been clean *dune* (altogether superseded) by machinery; and *ye canna wonner*, for *naething* can *stap* the advance *o'* machinery; and it is quite *recht* it should be sae; and I was sure it was coming, notwithstanding *a'* (all) Mr. Gillon, the member *o'* Parliament did in the *Hoose o'* Commons to serve the hand-loom weavers, to whom he *wus* always a warm and kind *frien*. I said to *ma puir dochter*, who, with her husband—also a hand-loom weaver—has always looked after her *faither* for years, 'It *winna* do, Mary, *ony langer*. It *braks ma* heart, Mary, to see the bairns stinted *o'* their food to feed their *auld grandfaither*. *Na, na*, Mary, I can *stan* it *nae langer:* I'll find *ma* way up to London.' And here I am sir." I asked him how he came from Scotland. "Weel, sir, I got *thegither* fourteen shillings before leaving *hame*, and I *hae* walked *a'* the way, but it has *taen* me *mair* than *sax* weeks to manage it. It is a *lang* journey for an *auld* man, sir." "Or for a young one either," I added. Now the old man might have come from Glasgow to London by the third class for twenty shillings. I next asked him what object he had in coming to London. "Weel, sir, that's a *vera* reasonable question, for it has turned *oot* a fool's errand *a' thegither;* but I think, sir, you'll justify me *a wee* in the attempt, first, to relieve ma *puir dochter* and her husband *frae* a heavy burden (here the old man wept bitterly), and *niest*, sir, to be doing something for mysel. *Noo* I think it *recht* to tell you that I *fand ma* way to the Kent road, to a naval sort *o'* institution, *whare* I could learn *hoo* I was to manage to get into Greenwich Hospital, and I *wus tauld* to send in *ma* papers, which I did, and yesterday I *wus* informed they could not admit me." The old man again became much affected, but I told him to cheer up as I would be his friend. "You have, then, been a sailor?" "Oh yes, sir; I *wus* at sea at the end of last century, and the beginning *o'* the present. I was pressed *oot o'* a merchant-ship into a man-o'-war, but as I served only ten years and four months in the navy, I was not considered entitled to a pension." "Did you see much service?" "Oh yes, sir; I saw a *dale o'* service, frigate actions, and *a'* kinds *o' fechting* ashore, and in boats, cutting *oot* under the enemy's batteries, and *nae* end *o'* it." "Now, do you mean to say you have been rejected at Greenwich Hospital?" "I *hae* indeed, sir; and when I got the answer, I *didna ken* whatever to do; and I *couldna* write *ma dochter* to tell her *a'* this; it would *hae* clean *brocken* her heart, as never had a *faither* a better bairn than she *haes* been to me." "Have you got your papers with you?" "That I *hae*, sir; but I am afraid they are in an untidy state, for I *hae* had them knocking *aboot ma* bit *kist* (box) for *mair* than *thretty*-(thirty) five years." On inspecting them, I said with an expression of surprise, "I see you were at the battle of Trafalgar." "Yes, sir, I was at *Tra-falgar*." "In what ship?" "The *Sparshiette* (Spartiate), Captain Francis Laforey." It so happened that I had heard more of the "Spartiate" than any other ship at Trafalgar, in consequence of Sir Francis Laforey having been the intimate friend of my wife's family; and Admiral John M'Kerlie, the first lieutenant of the "Spartiate," had known me from boyhood. I found my namesake the hand-loom weaver, now converted into an old man-of-war's man, strictly correct in his statement; but I thought I might test his memory, *not* his veracity, with an additional question. "Who was your first lieutenant at Trafalgar?" "*Ane* by the name *o'* M'Kerlie, a Scotch gentleman, a fine-looking young man, who had lost his *recht* (right) arm under Sir Edward Pellew (Lord Exmouth) in his action *wi'* a French squadron off the *coost o'* Ireland in Bantry Bay." In every thing I found my weaver-sailor friend extremely intelligent. I now brought a most interesting *tête-à-tête* to a close, informing him that I should see he was comfortably lodged and looked after, and in the mean time his papers would be laid before the Admiralty authorities. Admiral Seymour, who was a Lord of the Admiralty, repudiated at once the idea of such claims for admission to Greenwich being rejected, and on inquiry discovered that the applicant's papers were returned to him by the messenger, never having reached the Board. A week or ten days afterward Rock came to me, "Well, sor, the Scotchman is here *agin;* and it is now *shure cartain* that it is all right *wid* him this time; for, *yer* honor, he is in a beautiful new dress, almost like an officer." Sure enough, here was my namesake in the new suit of a Greenwich pensioner. The metamorphosis was so extensive that I scarcely recognized him, for her most Gracious Majesty's uniform had added vastly to the rotundity of the last elected member of Greenwich Hospital. The poor old man, on being presented to me in his new character by Rock, held down his head and smiled, for he scarcely knew himself; and in terms of deep gratitude and loyalty to his sovereign confessed that *mony, mony* years had passed *ower* his head *sin* he had been so comfortably clothed. After I had fully inspected his uniform, and congratulated him on reëntering the navy through the palace of Greenwich, I said, "I thought I should have seen you before this." "Weel, sir, to tell you the *rale trowth,* I *didna* like to come until I got *ma new claes,* as I *thocht* ye *wud* like to see me in them."

My grateful namesake paid me a visit every six months; and I was much struck with one circumstance, rarely to be met with among the old tars at Greenwich. On the first occasion I placed five shillings in his hand, but he respectfully and firmly declined it, saying, "I am truly *thankfu'* to the Almighty for the good fortune that has now fallen to me; I *hae* as much pocket-money as I can desire, and every comfort. Besides, sir, Maister Rock has just *gien* me an excellent *denner;* and then, sir, I *coudna* be feeling comfortable in coming to see you, if I thocht I *wus* to be always receiving money." John Boyd rose to be boatswain's mate of his ward, a rating which gave him five shillings a week money allowance, and a distinctive badge. He passed the last twelve or fifteen years in much comparative comfort at Greenwich; and I believe, next to his *dochter* and her husband, he liked me better than any other person in the world. He died in 1855.

86. *Mexico in* 1827.

A friend lately described to me the first journey he made from Vera Cruz to the city of Mexico. The party consisted of several ladies and gentlemen, one of the latter being the Mexican-Spanish Attorney-General. At a particular point of the journey the ladies became terribly alarmed on learning that they were about entering a district infested by brigands. Their companion, the Attorney-General, instantly relieved the ladies and the others of all fear by informing them that the brigand-chief was his intimate friend, and was aware that he was travelling. It would be somewhat difficult to picture or realize Her Britannic Majesty's Attorney-General being congratulated next day in Westminster Hall and Lincoln's Inn for having rescued his fellow-passengers by the old Windsor stagecoach on Bagshot Heath from robbery, in consequence of his intimacy with the chief highwayman. Such, however, was the state of Mexico in 1827. Forty-three years have in the mean time passed away, and the question may now be asked, Has the empire which Montezuma ceased to rule in 1520 really improved in three centuries and a half?

87. *Captain Nolan, of the 15th Hussars.*

Poor Lewis Edward Nolan, who was the first to fall in commencing the ride into the Valley of Death at Balaclava, was my intimate friend; and some little history of him may be interesting to those who have entered the service since the Crimean War, and since Tennyson wrote the "Charge of the Light Brigade."

"Half a league, half a league,
Half a league onward,
All in the valley of death
Rode the six hundred.
'Forward the Light Brigade!
Charge for the guns!' he said.
Into the valley of death
Rode the six hundred."

In the present day of competitive examination, when a knowledge of modern languages is so indispensable, I may mention that Captain Nolan and his brothers had a remarkable facility in their acquisition; and I presume that to his correct musical ear—for he was an accomplished flautist, pianist, and violinist, as well as a sweet singer—may, to some considerable extent, be ascribed the purity with which he spoke different languages. His father, the late Major Nolan, told me of an instance where his son's extreme proficiency elicited the praise and a marked encomium very flattering to the young soldier from the brother of the late Emperor of Austria, then Viceroy of the Austro-Italian States. Nolan originally was an officer in an Austrian hussar regiment, and was orderly officer to his colonel on the occasion of the Grand Duke reviewing the troops at Milan. The colonel mentioned to His Imperial Highness that he had a young officer in his regiment with whom he was desirous he should converse, being a great linguist himself, as he wished His Imperial Highness afterward to say to what country he belonged. The Grand Duke smiled, and desired the colonel to present to him this young master of languages. His Imperial Highness first addressed Nolan in Hungarian, who replied with fluency and correctness. He then went to Polish (Nolan's regiment had been stationed on the borders of Poland), and here he was equally at home; Italian and German followed with the same result. Next came English, and lastly French. The Duke then said: "Colonel, all you told me of this young officer is true; and it is only from his light hair and mustache that I see he is German." "No, sir, he is an Englishman;" at which he expressed extreme surprise, looking upon it as something marvellous to find so accomplished a modern linguist in one of my countrymen. A melancholy and striking incident was related to me by a Crimean officer in connection with poor Nolan's death. His friend Morris, of the 17th Lancers (Colonel W. Morris, C. B., who died a few years since at Bombay, when Assistant Adjutant-General), and himself had exchanged letters, Nolan's addressed to his mother, and Morris's to a member of his family. Morris was severely wounded in the charge, and, being unhorsed, was staggering back bleeding from his wounds. At last, from exhaustion, he fell down alongside a dead soldier. That soldier proved to be Lewis Nolan, in whose pocket was found Morris's letter, and in Morris's pocket was that of Nolan.

88. *General Lord Lynedoch and his Trees.*

The late Mr. Robert Cockburn, brother of Lord Cockburn, an eminent Scotch judge, told me an anecdote of the brave old general in his capacity as a Perthshire landowner. Mr. Cockburn was on a visit to the hero of Barossa, either at Balgowan or Lynedoch, and just as the visitors, who were on horseback, were about to close their afternoon ride, the old general said: "I must show you some trees in which I take more than a common interest, for this is their birthday." The party having reached the trees in question, he told his friends: "It is eighty years to-day since they were planted by my brothers and myself; they look all well and healthy, and I don't think *I* have any thing to complain of in that respect."

I once met Lord Lynedoch in London on an exciting occasion. I think it was after General Sir de Lacy Evans's return from the command of the British legion sent to Spain in 1835. We were giving a public dinner in the Freemasons' Tavern to General Mina, the famous guerrilla chief, whose desultory mode of warfare, by harassing the French armies with constant attacks on different points by independent bands acting in a mountainous country, was adopted with varying success in the north of Spain during the Peninsular War. Lord Lynedoch took the chair; he was then in his 85th or 86th year. Next to General Mina sat Señor Arguelles, known in the Spanish Cortes as the "divine Arguelles." Our venerable chairman, in spite of his great age, painted in glowing colors a few of the more prominent features of the guerrilla general's military career, some of which were highly amusing. Lord Lynedoch subsequently proposed the health of Señor Arguelles, beginning his speech by reminding us that during the French invasion the Cortes were convoked at Cadiz, where the affairs of the Spanish nation were conducted during the war of independence. Lord Lynedoch, as we know, commanded the division of the Duke of Wellington's army in and around Cadiz, near which is the battle-field of Barossa, which I visited in 1839. His Lordship now proceeded with his toast: "One day I was absolutely pestered by officers coming to me asking for leave, and the very natural conclusion I arrived at was that a bull-fight was coming off; I was rapidly losing all patience, but not my temper, which was as rapidly increasing as the former was diminishing, when in walked a steady, middle-aged officer to ask for the day's leave. I stared at him with astonishment. 'Are you going with that pack of youngsters to a bull-fight?' 'Oh no, general, we are hurrying off to the Cortes, as the divine Arguelles is expected to speak.' Through a misconception I had nearly prevented them from going, but I shall not deprive you any longer now of listening to the illustrious statesman, not, however, in the Cortes, but in the Freemasons' Tavern." Although Señor Arguelles is said to be an accomplished English scholar, I endeavored to "dwell on the melting music of his tongue," but the reference to the Cortes had carried him back to the language of the Cortes, so that the magic influence of that eloquence which had almost emptied Lord Lynedoch's camp of its officers was in a great measure lost on those who were not Spanish scholars; still, it was gratifying even to have spent a few hours in the society of a man of whom the world had heard so much, and from whose lips "resistless streams of oratory rolled." To those who were not born until long after General Sir Thomas Graham had fought the battle of Barossa (March 5, 1811), or who are only commencing a military career, it may interest them to know that Thomas Graham, of Lynedoch—created in 1814 Lord Lynedoch—did not enter the army until he was forty-five years of age, at which time of life Wellington had nearly closed his active career at Waterloo. He was suffering under severe domestic affliction in the loss of a young wife, a daughter of Charles, ninth Lord Cathcart, and in consequence he sought occupation in an active profession. He had commanded a regiment of militia in Scotland, and had the rank of lieutenant-colonel confirmed to him on entering the service, by bringing with him a body of kilted Highlanders.

He died in December, 1843, in his ninety-third year, and was succeeded in the command of the First (the Royal) Regiment by General the Right Hon. Sir George Murray.

89. *The Major* (*par Excellence*).

A wealthy but most unostentatious friend of mine possessed an estate of a few hundred acres in one of the metropolitan counties, about twenty miles from London, and he had a neighbor whom he could not endure, called the major. The gallant individual in question, my friend alleged, by "toadying" the lord-lieutenant of some Scotch county, had attained the lofty position of major in His Majesty's —— Regiment of North British Militia. But there was a mystery as to the particular Scotch county which had given him birth. I was consulted once on the point, and as one Scotchman can generally detect another's county accent, I declared in favor of the county of ——, especially when I found that the major, on learning that I was a Scotchman, began instanter to anglicise his Scotch. A lucky thought struck the major, that he would migrate from the banks of the Tweed, Clyde, or Tay, to those of the Thames, where the militia field-officer's rank might possibly be turned into available capital. The major was evidently born under a lucky star, for after some inquiries, he determined to take up his residence in the district of So-and-so, in ——shire, where he gave out in strict confidence, to all whom he came across, "that he *wud* never rest *sa*-tisfied until he had *ma-ried* into a *coonty fa-mily*, for he liked the *coonty.*" The light of the major's military rank was not allowed to be placed under a bushel, as he was to be found constantly hovering about all county meetings, Boards of Guardians, etc., most desirous, as he wished it to be understook, "to *mak* himself *ga-nerally* useful." It soon became rumored that the major's attentions, followed at some distance by his affections, had suddenly settled upon a poor invalid lady, who had an excellent fortune, and belonged to a *coonty fa-mily.* The malady under which she suffered might have been a difficulty to most men, but my countryman viewed it differently. The afflicted lady required a protector; and who so well suited for the position as the major? My friend declared that it was a scandal to our Church to have permitted the union, but I may here observe that I always heard that the major took great care of her. She resided throughout her seclusion in her own house, the major regulating the household and the banker's account. She predeceased him a very few years. Her means added to his own soon secured for the major the position of an English *coonty* magistrate, and his honors did not stop until he was made deputy-lieutenant, thereby giving him the military precedence of a lieutenant-colonel in the army.

The major was a sportsman, and wished very much to gratify his tastes in the covers of my friend; but when the usual annual request on this subject was submitted, it met with the uniform response, that although he never himself shot, he kept his shooting invariably for his London friends, two of whom were my brother and myself. Nothing daunted, every season the major "renewed his motion," but during all the years he brought it forward, it never even passed a first reading. After dinner, among the first questions we asked our friend was, "How is the dear major?" "Oh, confound the major!" We knew this would bring out something in which the major had been making himself the hero. "How that man can be so mean-spirited when he must see I wish to avoid him! I have never been, as you know, in Scotland; but surely you have not another man in it like the major—now—have you?" "Well," I said, "it is just possible we may have another." "You cannot, indeed; the major is not to be matched in any clime or society. He bores me to death; in fact, had he resided here before me, I should not have purchased the property. I cannot shake him off, do what I will; only last Sunday in our church, he saw I had a few friends, and that our pew would be full. He was out of his into the aisle in an instant, '*Maister* ——, there's plenty o' room in *ma sate.*' Fortunately, a friend of mine had opened the door of his pew, and I got my party the seats they required. But did I tell you the story of him and our fishmonger in the village? for there is the man all over." We requested our friend to proceed in his second charge against the major. "It appears that he went to the fishmonger, and in his detestable Scotch twang, 'Fishmonger, I wish to speak with you *sa-riously.*' 'Well, sir.' 'You charge me a deevil o' a price for your fish.' 'I am sorry you think so, sir.' 'You do indeed; *noo* understand me, I *donn't* mean to say, fishmonger, your fish is not *guid*—far from it. It's very *guid* fish. It is excellent, but it is *awsomely*[1] dear. *Noo*, fishmonger, I want to *mak* an arrangement with you, as I *donn't* wish to go by you, or bring *ma* fish from London. It may answer your purpose, and it will answer mine, for I was always through life fond o' fish; but I will not go on paying the price you charge. *Noo*, what I want to propose to you is this, that as I *donn't* object to eating second day's fish, provided you *mak* a corresponding reduction o' price, you'll find me a steady and constant customer.' Now, I ask you what you think of your countryman?" "But, my good friend, do not be too severe, for Scotchmen are not exceptional; de gustibus non est disputandum."

[1] terribly.

My friend, who was extremely hospitable, had his town-house; and it was impossible for the conversation to close after dinner without some one asking for his friend the major, and if there was any thing new in that quarter. Our host was a peculiarly quiet, gentlemanly man, one who could command every luxury of this world; but whether in the arrangements of his table, his stable, or his household, he showed in the retirement of private life the same good taste that characterized him in his intercourse with the busy world. Had the major made him his model when he entered the *coonty* of——, and laid aside all his "blaw and blether,"[1] he might have had a popular passage through life; but his little failings, among which pomposity stood prominent, made him the laughing-stock of those with whom he was brought into contact. My friend generally wound up his observations thus: "I know nothing of Scotland, but I know what a gentleman is." "Well, for my part," I said, "I think you would be very dull without the major, for he is the cause of more good stories than any man I know."

The major received one day a terrible blow, which nearly killed him, and confined him to his bed for a whole week. I had gone to dine with my friend (the major's *neebor*) at his town-house, and on reaching the drawing-room, found that the major was the subject of a very serious conversation connected with an affair that had that day exploded and created a general panic on 'Change, and throughout London. About a week or ten days previously, the major met our friend in the country. "*Maister*," said he, "as I always wish to be on *frienly* terms, and as I know you to be a *vera* rich man, with always a large *amoont* o' spare capital at command, I wished to call your attention to some *Exchaquer* bills that yield a half per cent. higher interest than the others do. There has *onnly* been a quarter o' a

[1] inflation and nonsense.

million o' them issued, and as a great favor to myself, and as a half per cent. is a half per cent. *noo* a days, they have kindly let me have £14,000 o' them, and I *thocht* it *onnly frienly* and *neeborly* to call your *nottice* to them." The poor major soon afterward discovered that he had invested his £14,000 in some spurious Exchequer bills which had been abstracted, altered, and countersigned by a delinquent government clerk. He subsequently received his money—not however, until he had undergone months of mental torture and deep anxiety, during which he was sorely tried by some of his *neebors*, telling him that an additional half per cent. on *Exchaquer* bills was not *always* a half per cent. in *banco.*

90. *The Late Miss Anne Sutton.*

I was formerly on terms of friendship with the late Miss Anne Sutton, who was an excellent person, and had made herself somewhat remarkable through life by strictly confining her charities within one channel, namely, in support of the societies for the suppression of cruelty to animals. On my first introduction to her, she became most favorably impressed toward me on discovering that I had formerly known one whom she had never seen, but whose name she revered beyond any other, Mr. Richard Martin, M. P. for the county of Galway, so well known in the Irish House of Commons previous to the Union, as "Dicky Martin," and subsequently in the Parliament of the United Kingdom as "Humanity Martin." I do not know what the consequences might have been—as Mr. Martin was an excellent husband and father—had he been alive, and I had been the medium of introduction between Miss Sutton and the Lord of Connemara—the head of one of Galway's most "ancient tribes;" they must inevitably have run in the same groove for the rest of their lives, for she perfectly idolized the name of Richard Martin of Ballinahinch Castle. Their sympathies flowed from the same source, and I am convinced from personal observation they must have blended and united to any imaginable extent in the suppression of horsewhips and spurs, and not improbably in the use of butcher's-meat itself. Miss Sutton was at all times prepared to subscribe her £100, or more if required, for a monument in Westminster Abbey, and another £100 for the erection of a pillar on the highest mountain in Ireland, "To the Memory of Richard Martin, the Friend and Protector of the Poor Dumb Animal." I recollect calling to her notice one peculiarity of Mr. Martin which appeared to me at variance with his principles of conduct toward the brute creation, as I considered they might also have been extended with advantage to the human family. I described to Miss Sutton the famous Donnybrook Fair, and told her that in a conversation I had with Mr. Martin, and alluding to the broken heads that usually resulted from that annual gathering, I had said to him, "You would, of course, not recommend me, were I ever to attend that or any similar fair in Ireland, to carry my shillelagh, or knotted thorn-stick, with me?" "All I can tell you," said he, "you would be a big fool if you went without it, for a crack over the *showlder* or *aven* the head does Paddy not a *haporth* of harm." She listened with marked attention to my little divergence on the use of the shillelagh, or thorn-stick, at an Irish fair; but fearing that I might even unintentionally lower her *beau ideal* of a statesman and a man of feeling one step of the pedestal he occupied in her estimation, she parried my question by saying that she had never been in Ireland, and therefore could not offer an opinion. I left this questionable ground to inform her that Mr. Martin had mentioned to me that his bill for the suppression of cruelty to animals was introduced by him in the fewest possible words ever previously known. "That interesting fact," Miss Sutton declared, "I was not aware of; but this I know

—it is the best Act of Parliament ever passed by the Legislature."

She was a placid, silent, and retiring person—the personification of mildness; and I can say in all sincerity that, until the scene occurred which I am about to describe within my knowledge and observation, "her passion ne'er brake into the extremity of rage." I was somewhat busily engaged in my private room when Miss Sutton was announced, and, on rising to receive her, I felt that I was greeting one who had raised herself by her actions very high not only in my estimation, but of all those who could understand and appreciate her. As the poor lady could scarcely address me in her excitement, I took the initiative, at the same time begging her to be seated and to be tranquil. She clasped my hand with more than her usual cordiality, and then told me that, on going to the Bank of England to receive her half-yearly dividends, a man there —"no, not a man," she exclaimed, "a brute "(I immediately thought of the Society for the Suppression of Cruelty to Animals), "told me, 'Why, madam, you are dead!' 'Dead! What do you mean? I am addressing you.' 'Well, madam, I cannot help that; you are made dead here, and I cannot pay you any dividend.' I demanded what right he had to make me dead when at that moment I was speaking to him?" By this short and pungent recital of her wrongs, I was attacked with a violent and irresistible fit of laughing even on so grave a subject. This, I observed, caused my amiable friend much surprise; but as soon as my own power of articulation returned, I assured her she should be restored to life at the Bank of England in a very few minutes. I then accompanied her to the great national establishment. Hanging firmly on my arm, walking with a strong step, and with a decisive expression of countenance, which I can still recall, she placed herself in front of the official who had told her that she had "been made dead."

My risible faculties were once more aroused, so as to be entirely beyond my control. She instantly opened upon one of the mildest and most obliging of men. "Do you mean, sir, still to say I am dead?" "Why, madam, you are made dead in our books." She then turned round hurriedly to me. "I am glad *you* have heard him apply the word *dead* to me." The attack was now resumed on her gentlemanly and urbane opponent, by declaring most emphatically that he should be ashamed of himself. The gordian knot was soon untied. My friend was described in the books of the Bank of England as "Anne Sutton of Cheltenham, Spinster;" but there was another Anne Sutton, a stockholder, and moreover a spinster, who had actually departed this life, whose death had been duly announced in the obituary of the *Times*, and in registering the probate of her will the mistake arose—to wit, the dead Anne Sutton was kept alive by the Bank, and the live Anne Sutton was made dead. My friend was now speedily calmed by seeing her namesake made dead instead of herself. I now told her that I had a matter to arrange with her in connection with this affair, as she must not overlook the fact that she had used rather violent language toward a meek and courteous man, so much so, that could I have anticipated the event of that day, I should have persuaded my friend, Mr. Richard Martin, in applying to Parliament for an act for the suppression of cruelty to animals to have inserted a special clause for the protection of the gentlemen of the Bank of England. My appeal to her was at once responded to; the *amende* being made to the gentleman in question; but Miss Sutton maintained that she was fully justified in the protest she had offered against being made dead before her time.

91. *The Melancholy Death of a Highland Chief.*

The following incident was related to me with much feeling and pathos by a Highland gentleman, himself a chieftain, and very conversant with Celtic history.

The chief of the Mackinnons died at Leith in 1808, in great pecuniary distress: he wrote as follows to Coll Macdonald of Dalness, a writer to the *Signet* in Edinburgh:

"My dear Sir: Not to perish from want, I have resolved to put a period to my existence.

"For particular reasons, I do not shoot myself in a mortal place; and if you will come quickly, you will be still in time to see the last of the unfortunate

"Mackinnon."

Mr. Macdonald started immediately, but on his arrival at the poor chief's lodgings in Leith found that he was dead, having, in ignorance of anatomy, shot himself in a place, as it turned out, peculiarly mortal—namely, in the thigh, causing hæmorrhage which proved in a few minutes fatal.

I sent a copy of the above melancholy epistle to the present Mr. Mackinnon of Corry, in the Isle of Skye, who replied, saying: "I think it must have been the last Laird John, who died in 1808, who wrote that touching letter of which you send me a copy." Mr. Mackinnon adds that the deceased chief "was a highly-cultivated man."

The letter is truly Johnsonian, and verifies the remark of Mr. Mackinnon.

92. *How B. B. managed to be present in Westminster Abbey at the Coronation of Queen Victoria.*

The late Mr. Thomas Young, when a bachelor, lived in the Albany, Piccadilly, where I frequently dined with him. His dinners were very attractive, not so much from their *recherché* character, as from the delightful circle of political and literary friends who met at his hospitable table.

On the occasion to which I am about to refer I was not present, so I am obliged to tell my tale at second-hand.

The chief topic of conversation was Her Majesty's coronation, which was to take place in a few days. It appeared that eleven out of the twelve at dinner had secured tickets of admission for the ceremony in Westminster Abbey, my brother being the only exception. Mr. Young, in addition to an official appointment under Government, the duties of which were not onerous, was private secretary to Lord Melbourne during his premiership, and from the kind acts he performed in lending a helping hand where he was satisfied the candidate was an efficient person, he was familiarly styled in the social circle, by way of sobriquet, the Deputy Premier.

He had the private room of almost every banking and mercantile house in the City open to him at all times, and during the sitting of Parliament he usually came Eastward between three and four o'clock in the afternoon to pick up news, so that at the meeting of the House, the first Lord of the Treasury was made *au courant* as to whether the Bank of England had raised or lowered the rate of interest; in what position the cotton, sugar, corn, and wool markets stood; whether matters were buoyant or depressed in Mincing and Mark Lanes; the state of credit in Lombard Street, and on the Exchange; what was doing in stocks, etc. Whatever changes of importance had occurred from the previous day, the Prime Minister had his synopsis furnished him by his very able and accomplished private secretary, who was also, to some extent, a member of the Commercial Community, as an original, or at all events a very early director of the London and Northwestern Railway, and on the board of more than one of our Joint Stock and Colonial Banks, Insurance Companies, etc.

The conversation becoming almost entirely absorbed in the pageant that was to come off, my brother expressed his regret that he alone of the party should be under the salt in regard to a ticket, and appealed to his host, as Deputy Prime Minister, to procure him one. The request caused a laugh around the table—the bare idea of obtaining a ticket for the great ceremonial within four or five days of its taking place was deemed something utterly absurd. My brother, seeing that Whitehall influence would not avail him, closed his part of the conversation on coronation matters by simply observing, "I must manage to be there."

Whether the Royal portal through which he subsequently entered the Abbey had struck him at the moment, I am not aware; at all events he kept it to himself; but next day he thought he might succeed through the Duke of Sussex, and accordingly in the afternoon he found his way to Kensington Palace. He had had the honor of occasionally meeting his Royal Highness at the dinners of the Highland Society of London; he therefore added to his card, "Member of the Court of the Highland Society of London," and was at once ushered into His Royal Highness's presence, who graciously recognized him and gave him a hearty reception. He broke the ice with his Royal Highness by alluding to diffidence not being a very prominent feature with Scotchmen, and then expressed his great desire to witness the coronation in Westminster Abbey, to which the Duke at once replied, "And so you shall." His Royal Highness even went into the question of attire, and which was settled should be the dress uniform of the Royal Yacht Club, my brother being a member of that squadron. A Royal command to an early breakfast at Kensington Palace, with a seat in a Royal carriage to Westminster Abbey, followed.

"What was my astonishment," said Mr. Young, in telling me the story on my return from the Continent, "I leave you to conceive, on entering the Abbey and taking my seat, to observe your brother in the Royal circle, in full conversation with the Duke of Sussex, who was laughing very heartily at, no doubt, some good Scotch anecdote.

"My friends who had dined with me a few days before, were equally surprised to see your brother so comfortably located in juxtaposition with Royalty. The puzzle to their minds and my own was a most difficult one, how it had been accomplished; and your brother, although we pressed him hard, allowed the fever of the coronation partially to subside, before he gratified our curiosity."

93. *The Late Mr. Richard Jones, the Comedian, or, as he was called, "Gentleman Jones."*

I had occasionally to speak in public, and having certain Scotticisms from which I wished to be freed, I made up my mind to apply to Richard Jones, the ex-comedian, as an elocutionary instructor. Aware how much he must be occupied with his pupils, and as best suiting my own arrangements, I found myself one afternoon between five and six o'clock pacing up and down Chapel Street, Grosvenor Place, where he resided, so as to watch the first exit of an elocution pupil. There was a groom riding up and down, leading his master's horse; and just as the clock struck six, out issued Sir William Molesworth from Mr. Jones's house, mounted his horse and rode off. The rising young statesman was one of Jones's greatest admirers, as well as one of his boldest pupils, for he never minced matters, nor was in the least reticent on the subject of reading with Richard Jones. He was constantly asked in the House of Commons by one facetious friend or other, especially before bringing on one of his motions on Colonial Reform, "Well, Molesworth, and how is Jones? Have you been up in the pulpit to-day?" Jones had a raised desk or rostrum from which the student delivered his prepared speech. "Yes, I have," replied the future Colonial Minister. "Ah, so I thought; for I observed the nags taking their usual exercise in Chapel Street."

During my course of reading with Mr. Jones, I never heard the name of one of his pupils mentioned, Sir William Molesworth excepted. His plan was not only to correct pronunciation and modulate emphasis, but also, to prevent a recurrence of mistakes, we had to put down his corrections in a little pocket companion, or *vade mecum*, to be referred to at leisure. I have a distinct recollection of my instructor asking me at the end of the first fortnight to read over my *errata* to him; and in doing so, and making up the list, a fearful total of 180 delinquencies was brought out against me in pronunciation and quantity. "Ah," he used to say, "they can teach Greek and Latin in Scotland, but not English." However, by way of encouragement for me to persevere, he brought forward himself as an instance to show what a provincial might overcome. He was a native of Manchester, and a *nut* with him in youth was a *noot*. He came to London with a strong letter of introduction to the manager of one of the theatres, and had scarcely spoken a dozen words when the manager told him that he much feared that he had mistaken his calling, but that if, by studying under ——, he could get rid of his deeply-rooted Lancashire dialect in six months, he would give him a fair trial when the theatre reopened. Jones followed this advice, and made good his position with the manager, having thoroughly overcome the provincial dialect, and afterward rose high in his profession.

His dinner-parties, which were frequent, and always delightful, never exceeded eight, including Mrs. Jones and himself. A constant guest was the late Honorable Edmund Byng, one of the Commissioners of Colonial Audit, and long connected with the household of the Duchess of

Kent. He had nursed the infancy and watched the girlhood of her who now rules an empire on one portion or other of which the sun never sets. Mr. Byng, when a boy, was a page to the Prince of Wales, and on obtaining his commission in the Guards, he told me he could not write the simplest note without half the words being incorrectly spelled. He joined his battalion at Gibraltar, where he had to commence his education, the educational standard for the army in 1780 not being quite so high as in 1870. He always spoke in language of deep affection of the illustrious inmates of Kensington Palace. He had some peculiarities, one of which he described to me very minutely, that he had jocularly forewarned the illustrious Princess that when Providence removed the then Sovereign, and Kensington Palace was exchanged for St. James's, he would not be found *ever* presenting himself at court. He was told he was "very naughty," but he acted up to it. "Well, as you will not come to see me, it shall not prevent my coming to see you."

The late Rev. Doctor Croly frequently dined with Mr. and Mrs. Jones. The Doctor was an agreeable companion, though on one occasion he placed me, as the youngest man at table, in a position of embarrassment, for, being a giant in conversation, he was entitled to say, "When I ope my lips let no dog bark." The reverend gentleman was telling an excellent story which he had evidently only recently heard, but I had known it for years; and at one point of the recital his memory failed him; he hesitated and got among the shoals, when the word wanted to give him the key and again make him "master of the situation," I unfortunately supplied. He stopped abruptly, and requested I should continue the story. All the party saw that my interruption was the slightest possible; still, the Doctor, in rather a patronizing and satirical tone begged me to conclude it, as he had nothing further to say. To this I replied that I should never presume to attempt to follow out a description so ably commenced by Doctor Croly, but if the party chose—having long known the amusing circumstances—I should be happy to relate them, as I had often done before, in my own way, *ab initio.* I did so, and Jones made us all laugh by turning the tables against the Doctor, at the same time making things worse for me, by an allusion to the Scotch Thistle, and calling out, "*Nemo me impunè lacessit.*" He then told his reverend guest, in that quaint and grave style in which he was so happy, that his loss of memory, which he was sorry to observe in regard to an important word, was a fortunate circumstance, as it had saved an excellent story in his (the Doctor's) hands from shipwreck. The impeachment was acknowledged.

Among other agreeable people I have met at Mr. and Mrs. Jones's table were the late Sir William Chatterton and the charming and accomplished Lady Chatterton. Sir William and his brother, now General Sir James Chatterton, as youths had been pupils of Mr. Jones, and the greatest mutual regard existed between them. He often alluded to the younger brother, when a young officer of Dragoons, finding time on the evening of June 18, 1815, on the field of Waterloo, to write him a note on horseback (in pencil, I believe) to tell him the great fight was over, showing him that his young friend, even amid the confusion and excitement following upon the events of that ever-memorable day, had a spare thought for his tutor.

Few men knew personally more of the political and literary characters of the period than Jones, and his anecdotes, which I have ofter regretted I had not at the moment noted, were not only numerous and instructive, but most interesting.

There was one that now occurs to me: the circumstances under which he was unexpectedly presented with a testimonial, in the shape of a check on a London banker for three hundred guineas (£315). He was sitting in his drawing-room with Mrs. Jones, when the servant announced Lord and Lady ——. He had long had the honor of knowing his Lordship, who informed him he had come to see him on a matter of importance to Lady —— and himself. "Jones, I am sorry to tell you our son is disappointing us very much in Parliament; he is so idle, and seems to take no interest whatever in politics; and possessing as he does first-rate abilities, we looked for a very different result. He says he wants pluck, and cannot get up to address the House, and a great deal more trash of the same kind, but I ascribe it to sheer idleness. However, if it be shyness or *mauvaise honte*, I wish you, Jones, to remove it. The dog, next week, is to have a petition from his constituents to present, and he threatens to shirk the duty, and ask a friend to take charge of it; this has put me so much out of temper that I have come to talk to you. Now, I am going to send him to you, to show him that to present a petition is not a very alarming affair; and if you once take him in hand, it will be all right." "I was not," said Jones, "to reveal having received any parental injunctions, nor even a parental visit. The youthful senator, whom I had never previously seen, called upon me with his father's card, and described to me the nervous political ailments under which he suffered, and the dilemma and fix he was in with a confounded petition he was expected to present in a few days. 'Well,' said I, 'let us tackle this ghost at once; and in order to do so I shall now make you Speaker of the House of Commons, by requesting you to get into my pulpit.' The election of Speaker being completed, I took up a bundle of papers, and soon convinced the youthful member that his 'present fears and horrible imaginings,' in regard to the presentation of a petition, had no reality. 'Now, we must change places; I must constitute myself the first commoner in England, by taking the Speaker's chair, and call upon you to present your petition.' Another rehearsal followed, and the operation was complete. He told his father he liked me very much, and described to him minutely the pulpit scene, and that he was going to read with me." The petition proper was presented, laid on the table of the House of Commons in due form, etc., Jones witnessing from under the gallery (of the former House) how his *protégé* played his part. The noble lord wrote Jones a private note, giving him a hint that he wished his son very much to speak on Mr. M——'s motion, to come off in about ten days. Jones and his pupil had become, on their second or third meeting, great friends. The question to be debated Jones brought judiciously on the *tapis*, asking him his opinions on different heads of the subject, and having elicited these, he suggested that, as he appeared so well up in it, he could not have a better exercise, and would suggest his writing out what he would say, supposing he had occasion to speak upon it at a county meeting or elsewhere. This advice was followed, and at their next meeting in Jones's studio, after the paper had been carefully read by its author, Jones then ordered his pupil to mount the rostrum. "Well," said Jones, when he came down, "as a first rehearsal, I like your speech very much, but I never give my opinion until after the second, and I shall hope to see you to-morrow afternoon. In the mean time, I have to beg that you will read over your notes once or twice, so as to impress your arguments and statistics firmly on the memory."

The second rehearsal was perfection; "I was," said Jones, "in ecstasies with my brilliant pupil; but my work was not yet complete, for I had now before me a task that required very difficult, or, at all events, delicate handling, i. e, to move the 'venue' from my sanctum to the floor of the House of Commons. 'Well,' addressing the embryo statesman, 'do you mean to say that with such a mastery of facts and details you would allow Mr. ——'s motion to come forward without taking part in the debate?' 'Indeed, I would.' 'Well, all I shall say is this, that if you lose such an opportunity of breaking ground within St. Stephen's, I must apply to you a trite, but not the less valuable, adage: "You are not worth salt to your porridge;" and further, may I ask you, did your constituents send you to Parliament to be their silent member? Every thing must have a beginning, and if there ever was a question in which you seem at home it is this.' My departing pupil laughed heartily, and said we should talk over this branch of the question at the next reading." Jones's persuasion carried the day; a brilliant speech in Parliament followed, and Jones listened to it with peculiar attention, as may be easily conceived. Lord and Lady —— called upon him next day to congratulate him upon breaking the Parliamentary egg for their son, on which occasion they pressed his acceptance of the draft on the London banker to which I have alluded. "That son," said Jones, "within a few years became a Cabinet Minister and one of our ablest debaters."

Jones never lost an opportunity, or hesitated, if he could secure a joke, to share its responsibility. He encouraged me in a trick I played on a friend in London—a young Scotch laird whose politics were of an extremely indefinite stamp. He had a mania for public speaking, and so long as the *cacoëthes loquendi* could be gratified, he would lose sight of the precise political principles which he was supposed to hold, and nothing pleased him more than that the party replying to him should acknowledge that he had a difficulty in following the honorable gentleman in his statement. But one great question with him was paramount to all others; and on this, and this only, was he consistent. The Corn Laws, he felt, must be retained in their pristine integrity, and their repeal would be fraught with utter ruin to the best interests of Great Britain; these laws, therefore, throughout the last few years of their existence formed his great staple or stock speech. One afternoon, about five o'clock, he called upon my brother to tell him confidentially that the following Friday evening he was to address a meeting at Exeter Hall on the subject of the Corn Laws; and as the occasion was an important one, and as he had satisfied himself that Parliament would never sanction their repeal, he was desirous that my brother should hear what he firmly believed to be the correct bearings of the whole question. I happened to be in the next room, and for one hour had listened to a long speech from my friend, of which even a closed door did not deprive me of a single word. As it was hopeless to proceed with my own correspondence, I occupied myself in transferring to paper as much of the Corn Law speech as I could condense. I was reading with Jones at the time, told him the story, and showed him the digest or summary of what I had taken down. He laughed heartily, and declared I should subject myself to his greatest displeasure if I did not at once prepare a speech for Exeter Hall to confute and upset, to the best of my ability, the arguments of my friend and countryman. Nothing was thus left me but to obey instructions; and with the aid of Adam Smith, David Ricardo, and Mr. McCulloch, I got up a speech, in the preparation of which I burned largely of the midnight oil. The evening before the meeting Jones called upon me to deliver it before him from his rostrum. He encouraged me by stating that I had been a diligent pupil, and if I acquitted myself as well in Exeter Hall as I had done in his pulpit, I should receive his unqualified praise. "Then, if that is your command, which I am bound to obey, you must give me your able advice, as I have never yet spoken in public." "That I shall do," said Jones; "but first let me tell you, in case you don't already know it, that there are tricks in all trades, and public speaking is no exception."

I hope the secret into which the most gifted of professors of elecution let me, and which I am about to disclose, may be found useful to the oratorical *débutant* or *débutante*, for now that the political claims of the fairer portion of creation are being advocated, and their right to enter the learned professions freely canvassed, we may henceforward look to public discussions in which the ladies shall hold their own. Under such circumstances, it would be most gratifying to me to know that Mr. Jones's hints proved of value to them practically. "To give effect to your speech, you must make a point of rising the moment your friend sits down; and to secure this priority you should take some paper in size and appearance to resemble your manuscript as nearly as possible, and, moreover, you must go to the meeting in good time, so as to occupy a prominent place in front of the chairman, or as close to him as you can manage to be. You should likewise have your own pen and ink, and whenever your friend rises to address the meeting, you must have your blank paper at once out, and begin scrawling away, as if you were taking down the speaker's remarks. Your friend will be pleased to observe this, and consider it complimentary to himself. Then, when he is near his peroration you will quietly exchange the papers on which you have been scrawling for your own manuscript, and as you were seen by the meeting to be busily engaged writing during the speaker's address, you can, should your memory fail you, refer to your papers from time to time. If this is done judiciously, you will never be suspected of delivering a prepared speech. You may even very effectively state a something which your honorable opponent did not say, adding: 'If I am wrong the honorable gentleman will correct me;' of course the honorable gentleman will do so forthwith. A little digression or by-play of this kind often tells well in a speech, and acts as a partial antinarcotic on the audience. But on this head I must offer you an additional suggestion, as it is not at all unlikely to happen about nine o'clock in the evening. If, on looking round, you observe a state of somnolency in some, and an evident near approach to it in others, all you have to do is to pronounce the last word of the sentence loud, and then suddenly stop, keeping your eye fixed on the chairman, otherwise he might suppose you had closed your observations. By this course, you will instantly rouse the sleepers in obedience to the doctrine of acoustics, and probably secure their attention for another short period, after which, if they should again appear to be dropping off, you must make them wake up in the way I have explained."

I was able next day to tell my elocutionary instructor that my speech came off very well, as the speaker by whom I was followed stated that I had exhausted the subject and, most probably, the audience also. A day or two afterward I acquainted my friend whom I had victimized, and who was praising me as a debater, with the joke which Mr. Jones and I had practised upon him, and he enjoyed it immensely.

The late Bishop of London (Dr. Blomfield) was one of Jones's warmest supporters, as a professor of elocution. If a curate called upon the Bishop, the curate being about to undertake duty in the London diocese, and was found defective as a reader, the bishop sent him immediately to Jones; the thoughtful prelate at the same time telling the young clergyman that he had arranged with Mr. Jones a clerical tariff that would not alarm him—one-fourth the ordinary charge.

Dr. Croly used to twit Jones for assuming a dictatorship in the English language. "How do we know, Jones, that you are right?" "This is very true," said Jones, "for I am probably to blame in not seeking out my authorities on the banks of the Liffey"—then giving me a sly look—"or even the Tweed. I confine myself at present to the banks of the Thames, leaving them when the famous river enters the land of Cockayne." "We are mightily obliged to you, Jones, for letting us so far into your secret," said the Doctor, "but I presume there are authorities whom you do deign to consult. You cannot, my dear Jones, be always right." "Well, then," said Jones, "as you do not ask me to go to Dublin, you shall know the three authorities on whom I at this moment rely, but keep it to yourselves, for if my clients know what market to go to, Othello's occupation's gone. I listen to the sermons of Blomfield, Bishop of London, to the legal judgments of Copley, Lord Lyndhurst, and to speeches of Law, Earl of Ellenborough. They are my models for speaking the English language purely, not only in regard to pronunciation, and the construction of sentences, but also to the arrrangement of arguments." Jones maintained that he could cure the most perverse cockney, particularly if he had a musical ear, of dropping the *h*, or misplacing it, or of exchanging the *w* for *v*, in one week. "How many men," he said, "have had themselves laughed at, and thus shipwrecked, in the House of Commons and elsewhere, from their obstinacy in not having such errors corrected, which the least care could accomplish!"

Jones used to say that he had more difficulty in driving into the head of a Scotchman the correct way of pronouncing *was* than any other word. "I *wuz* just going to say, Mr. Johnnes." "*Wuz* you, indeed," replied the great authority? "But let me tell you that you would greatly please me for the future by saying *was* and not *wuz*, and calling me by my correct name, Jones, and not *Johnnes*." He was most amusing when he got upon the Scotch-English of two of our distinguished Lord-Advocates, who entered Parliament and have passed from us since Lord Grey's Reform Bill. How two such accomplished men should have been all their lives (Jones knew Edinburgh well) engaged in a contraband trade in passing spurious English among their friends and clients, was a matter of much surprise to him, as no one, even the merest tyro, could have failed to detect the supreme affectation in their mode of addressing the House of Commons or the Lord Chancellor in Scotch Appeals, and had, in consequence, drawn down upon themselves through a long professional career the most laughable criticism. "Na, na," said Jones, "*gie* me *Harry* Dundas's broadest Scotch in preference to the mongrel attempts of the two learned Scotch Lords to be considered purists in the English language."

Jones would suddenly break off when he had made us laugh, as he thought sufficiently, and look to one of the visitors for some anecdote or story. "We have been talking enough Scotch and English; let us now have something French;" then, turning to me, "Pray do give us your countryman's antiquarian researches at Bayonne." The story was this: A gallant Scotch officer who had fought and bled in the cause of freedom in Portugal, and subsequently in Spain, in General de Lacy Evans's army, then stationed in and around St. Sebastian, with a party of brother officers, had obtained a few days' leave to visit Bayonne. My countryman devoted the first day, from breakfast to dinner, in a minute exploration of this ancient city and seaport of the Lower Pyrenees alone, rejoining the party in the evening at dinner. He gave his friends an interesting account of his rambles, and that he had discovered Bayonne must have been at one time a Scotch colony, as he found the prevailing name in almost every street was Bains. After the important announcement on Bayonnese archæology a strong hope was expressed by Colonel Sir —— and all present that the War Office would take an early opportunity of submitting to the sovereign the name of the gallant discoverer for the knighthood of the Bath.

Jones could describe with infinite *naïveté* the characteristics of the three classes of his pupils. The young English clergyman and barrister came to him for one object, and avowed it—to have errors in pronunciation corrected, and the modulation of the voice and emphasis in reading and speaking improved. The young Irishman, usually a hearty, joyous fellow, came and declared that he wished to be put into shape as a *spaker*, and when detected in a bull, laughed as heartily in having it pointed out to him as Jones himself did; but when the Scotchman came, Jones said: "I was prepared for circumlocution; he approached me with some hesitation, and an apology for coming at all usually followed. 'The fact is, Mr. *Johnnes*, *ma frien* Mr.——, of the Temple, mentioned your name to me, as he *thocht* it *wud* be as *weel*, as I had come to London to read for the Bar, that I went through a *coorse* with you. How *mony* lessons, Mr. *Johnnes*, do you consider a *coorse?*' 'Why, many of my pupils—at least, those who choose to fag—do not require to take more than ten lessons.' 'I should read very hard, Mr. *Johnnes*. I believe *yer* terms are a *gueenea* a lesson?' 'Yes, ten guineas for a course of ten lessons.'" (This was always paid in advance.) "'Vera weel, Mr. *Johnnes*'" (Jones spoke Scotch admirably), "'I'll *tak* a *coorse* with you, although the fact is, I did not think I *wud* require to read with you; however, *ma frien*, whose *cairde* I *brocht*, says there are several words which we *pronoonce* somewhat differently in *Scoteland*, and that it *wud* be as *weel* that I saw you.' 'I am much obliged to your friend for mentioning my name to you, and I hope you will prove an exception to most of your countrymen, for, I assure you, instead of several words only being pronounced differently in Scotland to what they are in England, their number is legion, and although you do not become my pupil until Monday, when we shall commence in earnest, I think it right to apprise you that I have already detected in our short conversation at least a dozen solecisms.' 'Indeed, Mr. *Johnnes*, you perfectly surprise me, as I *wuz* always rather complimented at home in the way I *spok*. May I ask you, Mr. *Johnnes*, where ye find me wrong?' 'Why, you have just told me that you *leeve* in PALL MALL. Now a Londoner would say —and I hope *you will* next week—I live in Pell Mell, not pronounced as it is spelt, Pall Mall. Then, in regard to my own name, Scotchmen, you of the number, generally call me *Johnnes*, instead of Jones. You also told me you had been *makin' a tower* on the Continent; we may build a *tower*, but we make a *tour*.'"

Jones considered his Scotch pupils, as a rule, peculiarly thin-skinned, always in the greatest dread lest it should be known that they required elocutionary instruction, but if an unfortunate Englishman blundered in a French word or an Italian termination, my countryman, he alleged, was most critical and severe:

"Slow to their own defects, but quick to spy
Another's failings with the eagle's eye."

Richard Jones survived his excellent wife a few years. He was universally respected and beloved; he was in every sense of the word "Gentleman Jones;" he was kind and charitable, liberal and hospitable. Nevertheless, he left a moderate fortune to his relatives, having no family of his own. The late Sir William Chatterton, Mr. Crofton Croker, and myself, were his executors.

94. *Shooting at Midnight.*

I have pleasant reminiscences of the late Lord Saye and Sele (William, the twelfth lord), and of his hospitality at Belvidere, in Kent. One evening, when I was there on a visit, his old keeper, Croker, looked into the dining-room at eleven o'clock at night, and called out to our host, who was sitting with his guests, "My lord, the guns be hall ready." "All right, Croker, come up here and have a glass of wine." The old man immediately made his way to the head of the table, to drink his half tumbler of port. "Have you got many rabbits for us, Croker?" "Vy, my lord, hi netted honly two dozen, thinking has ow hit vas has many has yer lordship hand tother gents voud care habout. My lord, please mind the moon's hall right, hand the sooner veere hat hour vork, the better." "Whenever you are ready, Croker, we shall be." "Hi his ready, my lord." Croker and his assistants had placed a white paper collar round the neck of each rabbit, and when he had given us each our gun, his difficulties as quartermaster-general arose. Bacchus had no warmer admirer than Croker when his official duties did not interfere, but when they were to be performed he was as sober as a vegetarian. However, being a good judge in such matters, he ran his eye over the party, much as a detective would do, and at once saw he had heavy responsibilities on hand. He therefore addressed us in the following pithy, although somewhat disquieting terms: "Gemmon, hi vishes to see my rabbits killed, hi does, hand 'is lordship knows hit, but hi vishes hat same time to *preswarve* 'uman life—that his, that you don't a shoot none on yourselves, for hi tells you plain, that hif you moves ha morsel from the *pints* hi puts you hat, hi von't hanswer by no manner o' means, for you'll be a firing hon heach hother; you vill hindeed. Don't larf, dear gemmon; pray, my lord, do speak *seerus* to 'em." We promised Croker to profit by his warning, and pledged ourselves to follow out his instructions most carefully. In a few minutes we were in the places in front of the mansion which Croker had arranged for us, and at such a distance as to satisfy us that the noble proprietor's windows were appreciated by him. He had also looked to the safety of number one, as rabbit No. 1 was placed in a pigeon-trap, to which a very long cord was attached; this Croker and colleagues manipulated and controlled in perfect safety to themselves at the rear of the midnight sportsmen. "My lord, ven you says pull, hi pulls." "Pull," and a discharge of ten or a dozen barrels followed. The same precautions being observed in respect to rabbit No. 2, the guns were reloaded, and as each was handed back, Croker had a compliment to pay us. "You keeps your place, sir, beautiful, you does, hand no mistake." The operation of single rabbits becoming rather tedious, and twelve o'clock having struck, Croker gave his trap a duplicate until his number was exhausted. Notwithstanding the heavy firing, which we afterward learned had created a good deal of sensation among the crews of the vessels passing up and down the Thames, not more than six rabbits were killed.

Next day Croker was congratulated on the able manner in which he had carried out the night's sport. "Vell, hi haint ave nothink to say hon that 'ed, but this hi vill say, that hi never vas so thankful to see 'is lordship's friends a going hall right to their beds, for some hon yar gemmon—hi means no hoffence—voud a been better hin hit afore you comed to shoot." This was assented to *nem. con.;* and now those friends of mine, or readers, who may not have shot rabbits with white paper collars on at midnight, by taking a hint from Croker, may learn how to do so, and *safely* too.

95. *Lieutenant Thomas Waghorn, R. N., the Hero of the Overland Route.*

I knew the indomitable, persevering, and courageous Waghorn intimately. He was a good-hearted man, whose only failing was an excessive love of stimulants. "You have made for yourself a great name," I would say to him, "and I wish to see you enjoy your honors for another quarter of a century; you have been blessed with a magnificent constitution, but it will soon break down unless you leave off." The poor fellow's only reply was: "'Tis too true, my good sir, but I cannot help it." I have often said to him: "Why, Waghorn, I have never met a man to be compared with you in point of energy and determination of purpose, and had you lived thirty-five or forty years earlier and been the associate of Lord Nelson and Lord Cochrane, you would not have allowed the former of those great men to have boarded the San Nicholas and San Josef, or the latter l'Esmeralda in Callao Roads without being one of the party." "I would not, you may rely upon it."

He often lunched with me, and it was a treat for any of my country friends to meet so great a lion, and if his time, theirs, and my own permitted, I generally led him into a little sketch of his own career for the information, and not improbably the amusement also, of my visitors, for I knew the precise chord to touch. He was born in 1800, and had been a midshipman in the navy from 1812 to 1817; but being without interest he sought employment in another branch of the service, and went out to Calcutta as third mate of a merchantman, where he obtained an appointment in the Bengal Marine in the pilot service of the East India Company.

The practicability of the Overland Route had long occupied his attention, and as he sailed up and down the Red Sea, he settled in his own mind that it could easily be accomplished. At last the thought occurred to him that he would solicit an interview from Lord William Bentinck, then Governor-General of India. This was granted, and so much struck was his Excellency with the man, and his world-important project of an overland route from Europe to Asia by the Red Sea, that he suggested his going home forthwith to lay his plans before the East India Company and the Board of Control. In accordance with Lord William Bentinck's views, he made arrangements to proceed to Europe, the Governor-General furnishing him with a letter of introduction to the Chairman of the Company, and one to Sir John Cam Hobhouse, the President of the Board of Control. Waghorn worked his way home from Bombay up the Red Sea, making himself master of many important details. At this point of his narrative Waghorn's pulse always rose, his countenance became rubicund, and the table never failed to receive a tremendous blow from his fist. "Gentlemen," looking round at each of my guests, "*you* shall hear—Mr. Boyd knows it well—how I was treated for bringing Bombay within twenty-six days and eight hours of the capital of England. I went to the India House, and asked if the Chairman was in his room. He was. I sent my name and was received. I handed my letter of introduction from the Governor-General to the Chairman. He read it, placed it on the table, and was about to resume his writing, but *thought* better of it. I waited patiently, when the Chairman addressed me as follows: 'Mr. Waghorn.' 'Yes, sir.' 'You are, I find, in our service in India.' 'I am, sir. I am one of the Honorable Company's pilots.' 'Are you in bad health, Mr. Waghorn?' 'I am in perfect health, sir.' 'Well, then,' said this Chairman of the East India Company, 'Mr. Waghorn, take my advice, and return to your duties in India, for I have to inform you that I, as Chairman of the Honorable Court of Directors, am quite satisfied, as heretofore, with sending our letters and dispatches to India by the Cape of Good Hope, and receiving our replies by the same route.' He then resumed his pen, telling me his time was much occupied, and that he had given his decision. I then said, 'I assure you, sir, the Governor-General looks upon the plan I had the honor of submitting to him most favorably, and the last words, on my taking leave, which his Excellency was pleased to address to me after my full explanations, were, that he was convinced the Overland Route could be carried out.' What answer did I get from this enlightened Chairman? 'I take a different view, as representing the Court of Directors (pronounced with great emphasis), leaving Lord William Bentinck to entertain what opinion he chooses; for, as I have already said, our postal communication, as conducted *viâ* the Cape of Good Hope, is all that the authorities in Leadenhall Street require. I must now request that our interview ends.'

"I left the Chairman's room instantly, and, not forgetting the reception I had met with on my entrance, I was determined my departure should not be forgotten, for I gave his door such a precious slam (a stronger word was used) as to be distinctly heard through the corridors of the building. I hurried to one of the hall-porters, and asked for a sheet of paper and a corner from which the poor *tabooed* Bengal pilot might address a few lines to the mighty lord of Leadenhall Street. My letter was short and as follows:

"'*To John Harvey Astell, Esq., M. P., Chairman of the Hon. East India Company.*

"'Sir,—I this day resign my employment as a pilot in the Hon. East India Company's Bengal Marine Service, and have the honor to remain,

"'Your obedient servant,

(Signed) "'THOMAS WAGHORN.'

"Without even asking the porter for an envelope, and the ink still wet, I rushed back to the chairman with my letter. "There, sir, is my resignation of my position in the Company's service; and I tell you, John Harvey Astell, esquire, member of Parliament, and chairman of the Hon. East India Company, that I shall stuff the overland route down your throat before you are two years older." I then dashed out of his room, slamming the door even more violently than I had done five minutes previously. That is the way, gentlemen, a poor devil is served who has the good of his country at heart.

"I have still something to tell you; for, after the treatment I received at the India House, I should immediately have presented myself at the Board of Control; but my feelings were so exasperated, that I required a couple of days to calm them down. I then repaired to Cannon Row, where I soon discovered that an arrow had been sped from the quiver in Leadenhall Street which had reached the Board of Control before me, as, from the whispering and staring that went on in the outer chamber, I much doubted whether I should ever see the inner, where sat the Minister for India. However, after deep consideration, I was told that Sir John Hobhouse could see me. What a piece of condescension in a well-paid minister of the Crown! I was received with extreme frigidity. The key-note, sounded in Leadenhall Street, had obviously been reëchoed in Cannon Row, for if Harvey Astell was rude and offensive, Sir John Hobhouse was doubly so. After handing in my letter of introduction from the Governor-General, I recapitulated all that had passed between Lord William and myself, as well as communicating my own observations as concisely as possible on the general question of the overland route, but without making any impression on the Right Hon. Baronet, who seemed to view its unimportance as Mr. Astell had done. In his remarks, Hobhouse so grossly insulted me, that the only return I could make in hurriedly leaving his presence, was striking my own body in a manner which I was informed afterward was extremely distasteful to the President of the Board of Control, affording me, with not a few others I can assure you, intense satisfaction and great amusement, and I hope I may now include you in the number. My revenge, gentlemen, on these men was seeing my plans carried out, and in being enabled to say, '*There, be-*

hold another route to India besides the Cape of Good Hope.'"

Shortly after this, Waghorn became hard run at his banker's, and a member of the House of Peers, a sailor lord—either the Earl of Hardwicke, Earl Talbot, or Lord Colchester—promised to speak to Lord Melbourne, then Prime Minister, on his behalf. Accordingly, his lordship was asked to interest himself with Sir John Hobhouse, as President of the Board of Control, to make a grant of £500 to Waghorn in order to relieve him from his difficulties, which were very pressing at that moment. On hearing Waghorn's name in conjunction with Hobhouse, Lord Melbourne started to his legs, and was seen convulsed with laughter. "Mention Waghorn to Hobhouse!" said Lord Melbourne. "No, not for the world! You evidently don't know the story;" and taking his noble friend to one side of the House, he described the whole affair, at the same time suiting the word to the action, and the action to the word. "Oh no," said the facetious premier, "that cock will never fight, but you may tell his friends at the Bar, that I shall go to-morrow to the Treasury and get him £500, and without troubling my friend Hobhouse." At this time he was made a lieutenant in the navy.

Lord Palmerston, when Minister of Foreign Affairs, saw a good deal of Waghorn, and was always most kind to him. This attention of the great statesman was highly appreciated, and Waghorn never lost an opportunity of contrasting it with the code of manners he had encountered at the India House and Board of Control. One afternoon Waghorn asked me to go with him to the Foreign Office to see his lordship in reference to a postal communication from Pointe de Galle to our Australian and New Zealand Colonies, a subject in which I was much engaged at the time. I hesitated, as it was late. However, he felt anxious that I should accompany him; but it was five o'clock before we reached Downing Street. Lord Palmerston, who it was well understood did a great portion of his hard work at home (he then lived in Carlton Terrace), had not come, and there were several people already waiting to see him. When his lordship arrived, one of the gentlemen of the department remarked to those waiting, "I shall take up your names to his lordship; but I think it as well to apprise you," smiling at Waghorn, "that the overland route, or rather its author, always takes precedence at the Foreign Office." The parties waiting appeared quite reconciled to this, by having an opportunity of seeing a man of whom they had heard so much. I had just time, and no more, to take Waghorn in hand. "Now," I said, "recollect you must, at such a late hour, strictly confine yourself to receiving the letters for the Austrian Government promised you by his lordship, *but on no account whatever* enter upon the Australian question, for if you do, you may convert Lord Palmerston from being your firm friend and patron into a chairman of the India Company, or a President of the Board of Control." As he was to start that night for Vienna and Trieste, he followed my advice, and the interview was over in two minutes. In the act of leaving the Foreign Office, he looked into the room where we had left those waiting to see his lordship, and made them laugh heartily. "The course is clear, gentlemen, now go ahead." Waghorn occasionally spent a day or two at Vienna on postal arrangements, and was always kindly received (thanks to Lord Palmerston) by Prince Metternich the Prime Minister, who asked him to dinner and paid him other attentions. "I recollect," said Waghorn, "firing into the Prince and making him laugh at the humbugging delays which I had several times met with on my different journeys through Austria; and I was determined now to speak out. 'Surely,' I said, 'your Highness, when your Government have to write to your consular agents in the

East, must be anxious to have the letters delivered as quickly as the British Government; and how the deuce, your Highness, is this to be done, if I am to be constantly hauled up and stopped in the middle of the night to undergo some foolish police inspection, and compelled to fumble about in my pockets, when I am half asleep and more than half perished with cold, to produce the authority your Highness some time ago furnished me with? and then when I call out to the driver, "Go ahead, go ahead," "push on," one of your confounded officials says, "Sprechen sie deutsch," holding on like grim death at the carriage-door. "Sprechen sie fiddle-strings!" I exclaim. I tell you, Prince, it won't do; your empire is dreadfully behind the rest of Europe; and if I am to take charge and expedite the British and Continental correspondence to the East, you must remove those absurd interruptions I complain of, and that pretty sharply.' The Prince promised me that he would do so, and like a good man kept his promise, as I never had any thing to complain of afterward. I can tell you the post-horse fellows in Austria were wide awake alter this when Tom Waghorn was on the road. This plain speaking of mine to the famous Metternich, it seems, caused a good joke; for on my return to London from the East some three months afterward, I went to the Foreign Office to pay my respects to Lord Palmerston, and on my name being announced his lordship laughed heartily. 'Come along, Waghorn, and tell me all about the Vienna affair,' making me relate the whole story. 'Well, Waghorn, you have said more to the head of the Austrian Government than I ever dared to do.'"

No man felt a kindness shown him more than Waghorn, although he evinced his sense of it in a manner peculiar to himself. In 1846 I had suggested to some gentlemen deeply interested in the question, the expediency of calling a public meeting to be held in the City of London to promote steam communication with Australia; and as Europe and America owed to Waghorn the opening up of the Red Sea as the channel of postal communication with India and China, I considered it only just, that if we succeeded in extending the line from Pointe de Galle to Australia and New Zealand, Waghorn's name should not be overlooked in the movement. I therefore sent for him to communicate to him my own view, in which I felt satisfied I should be supported by others. The tears ran down his cheeks, and he said, "Ah, my kind sir, you never allow my candle to be hid: I am greatly obliged to you." "Now, Waghorn," said I, "come and dine with us to day, and you will meet some friends who are to take a part with me in this matter, and we shall talk it over after dinner." I suggested that the advertisement convening the meet ing should be headed "Waghorn's Australian Meeting," and we drew out some half-dozen copies of the advertisement. These Waghorn put in his pocket, and with the aid of a hansom cab—it was midnight when he left me—he drove round to the newspaper-offices, for next morning the Waghorn advertisement appeared in the papers. This was a slight specimen of the "go-ahead" principle with which he wished to indoctrinate the Austrian Government.

He always declared that I had done him one of the best turns possible in the City by suggesting that the meeting at the London Tavern (April, 1846) to promote a postal steam communication with Australia should be called the Waghorn Australian Steam Meeting. One day I was much amused by his bringing with him an old friend from India to be introduced to me as the gentleman who had said the year before all those kind things of him at the public meeting in question. Waghorn had this part of my speech by heart, and I am convinced that had he died a millionnaire he would have left me a very handsome diamond ring, a kohinor at least, as a memento. But he could not allow his friend to leave *me* until he heard from *myself* the remarks I had made. "Mr. Boyd, in seconding the resolution moved by his honorable friend, Mr. Scott, said, he must congratulate Mr. Waghorn on this large and influential meeting; and when he recollected that it was only a few days ago that a near relative of his own, prevented by indisposition from being now present, in conjunction with his friend Mr. Browning and himself, consulted Mr. Waghorn on the important subject for which they had met, he felt satisfied whatever Mr. Waghorn undertook he would see carried out, and that the great object for which they had assembled would be achieved, namely, a steam communication with the colony of Australia *viâ* India. For some time past, in consequence of the urgent entreaties of friends in Australia, this most important matter had occupied the serious attention of Mr. Scott and Mr. Browning, a gentleman intimately acquainted with Australia and her coasts, as well as with the different islands in the Indian Archipelago. We all knew from experience that Mr. Scott (M. P. for Berwickshire) would urge the claim of Australia for this great commercial boon with the Government with his usual energy and attention; but it appeared to us that the initiative must be taken in the city of London, and that the Government would wait for this step: our eyes were therefore at once directed to the man who having 'brought Bombay within twenty-six days and eight hours of London,' might likewise bring Sydney, New South Wales, within fifty-six days and eight hours of the British metropolis. Mr. Waghorn was of all men the one to be consulted, the one to whom all classes, commercial and otherwise, owed so heavy a debt of gratitude. Palmam qui meruit ferat."

Waghorn died in 1849, and no one more heartily rejoices than I do that Monsieur de Lesseps, as a distinguished Frenchman, has added to his own well earned and imperishable honors by raising in Egypt a bust to Thomas Waghorn. At the same time, this should remind the English nation that they have likewise a duty to perform toward the memory of one who in the face of an opposition that would have daunted and dismayed most men carried his point. I have recently seen it stated in the public prints that the practical inception of the enterprise is due to another; but I presume he was one who would not have the courage of a Thomas Waghorn to meet the scowl of a chairman of the East India Company, by at once sacrificing his commission in the service as Waghorn did.

I contend that this brave and persevering man, aided by Lord William Bentinck and encouraged by Lord Palmerston, gave us the overland route from five to ten years earlier than we otherwise should have had it. In all probability the question, so far as the all-powerful influence of Leadenhall Street could prevail, would have been shelved until the expiry of the company's charter; therefore, even the opinions I see adduced of two most distinguished men with whom I had the honor of being acquainted, the Hon. Mountstuart Elphinstone and General Sir John Malcolm, in favor of the Red Sea route, were as dust in the balance against the autocrats who then ruled the destinies of our Indian empire.

96. *The Late Joseph Hume, M. P.*

I originally met Mr. Hume at the hospitable table of my late esteemed friend, General Nicholas Smith, of the Bengal Army. The General had commanded in India the regiment to which Mr. Hume was attached as assistant surgeon, though subsequently he became Persian interpreter to the army during the Mahratta war, and received the thanks of General Lord Lake and the other high functionaries for the efficient manner in which he discharged his public duties.

The old General resided in Harley Street: the custom still obtained to drink wine with your friends at table; and he rather amused me on the first occasion, when he called out, "Joe, a glass of wine?" I observed that he scarcely ever replied to the General without preluding or concluding with "Sir." He once caught my eye, and saw that the "sir" attracted my attention. Stretching his head slightly across to me, he said, "Recollect"—pointing to the top of the table—"he was my chief in India, I must not forget that." The aged General was much attached to Mr. Hume, and this feeling was fully reciprocated.

The honorable member discovered from some observations which I made, that I took an interest in the navigation laws, particularly in the jurisdiction of the Vice-Admiralty Court in New South Wales. Finding the opportunity favorable, I entered at some length into the anomalous provisions and mischievous workings of the Act 2 William IV. c. 51, which professed to regulate the practice and the fees in the vice-admiralty courts abroad; and I showed the pernicious consequences of the system, which had been so forcibly denounced by my brother at Sydney, in the detention of the "Margaret" whaler, under the provisions of the Act in question.[1] This discussion led to intimate relations

[1] Extract of letter from B. Boyd, of Sydney, New South Wales, dated July 11, 1846, to M. Boyd, London:

"They (the navigation laws), as at present administered in the colonies, are ruinously expensive, and by the detention of vessels alike disastrous to the shipowner and to the shipper—leaving not only the ship but her valuable cargo completely at the mercy of a refractory crew who, abetted by designing long-shore attorneys, are ready to allege the omission of performances on the part of the captain of some condition in their articles of agreement; and the time generally selected is that when it is most vexatious, namely, the moment of the ship's intended departure. On the other hand, the captain possesses no *practical* means of enforcing redress for non-performance on the part of the crew of any portion of the articles of agreement. The exemption from the effects of the above constitutes one of the greatest advantages the foreign owner possesses over the British, consequently a repeal of the British navigation laws must be simultaneously accompanied by an approximation of our admiralty laws to those of other maritime nations," etc.

between Mr. Hume and myself, on the subject of the repeal of the navigation laws: and I here take leave to mention, for those who supposed that his only qualification as a member of Parliament was the rigid economy which he urged, that had Mr. Hume possessed debating powers commensurate with the labor and industry which he used in his closet to master details, he must have attained a very high position as a public man. The question of the repeal of the navigation laws was one which I frequently discussed with the honorable gentleman. I had written him (23d January, 1847) a note expressive of the satisfaction which I experienced in reading his remarks in the House of Commons on the previous Thursday on an alteration of those laws, at the same time enclosing to him a lengthened extract from a letter that had reached me from my brother in New South Wales, in which the writer expressed (11th July, 1846) his satisfaction that Sir Robert Peel had carried the repeal of the corn laws, predicting that it would initiate a general system of free trade, in which the navigation laws must go by the board, etc.

That Mr. Hume well considered and probed deeply into every subject on which he addressed the House I soon became fully persuaded; and I cannot bring an instance more strongly corroborative of this fact than the following:

My letter with its enclosure was dispatched to him on the morning of the 23d January, 1847, and his reply, which I now transcribe, was dated the same day.

"Bryanston Square, *January* 23, 1847.

"My dear Sir: I have your note of this morning, with an extract of a letter from your brother in Sydney, regarding the mischievous effects of the navigation and admiralty laws on the trade and commerce of that part of the country; and it is somewhat singular (but marks the universality of the evil) that your brother should have expressed himself to the same purport as I felt it my duty to do in the House of Commons on those points. I have been attacking these laws for the past three years, as good opportunities offered, in and out of the House. But I have been left alone, scarcely one M. P. has ventured to support me, and many have objected entirely to meddling with them. My chief opponents have been and are the shipowners, who of *all the community are the sufferers the most;* and they, *from ignorance of the working of these laws*, have always objected to relaxation or abolition; but having obtained the recognition of Free Trade principles by both parties in the House, I have taken my course *to force the abolition of these laws*, and commenced with the first move in the House; and as the Government have agreed to a committee of inquiry *into the navigation laws, and other laws affecting our commercial shipping*, I shall now follow it out, with a view to a total abolition of these restrictive laws; and then of the complex and oppressive admiralty laws. If you can contribute any thing to point out *where* and to *what* extent the existing duties on ship materials, the rules and regulations of shipping, etc., and you may be able to find in the city some well-informed men to collect information, and so expose the abuses and burdens of the present system, I shall be glad to hear. Your brother, and all who think with him, should call public meetings in every colony and place, embodying all their complaints in petitions to Parliament, and forward them for presentation. Such proceedings will forward my objects against the prejudices of the shipowners chiefly. I shall be pleased to receive any further information from you on the subject, and remain, etc.,

"JOSEPH HUME.

"M. BOYD, Esq."

When Mr. Hume wrote me this off-handed letter he was in his seventieth year. Shortly after this I received from the honorable member a notice that I must consider myself retained by him as a witness to appear before the committee moved for by Mr. J. L. Ricardo on the subject of the navigation laws. I had, therefore, at once to go to him to assure him that my views were crude and undigested on the vexatious operation of the navigation laws, as well as in respect to the antiquated, expensive, and cumbrous machinery of the Admiralty laws, which in the colonies were almost as dilatory as proceedings in our Court of Chancery. I had further to apprise the veteran statesman that I had never visited a British colony, that my voyages had not extended beyond the Bay of Biscay, the Mediterranean, and the Baltic; that during those short experiences of marine life, so far from thinking of the navigation laws or any other laws, I was unceasingly occupied in casting up accounts altogether distinct from those with which *he* had been battling for so long a series of years for the advantage of the nation. At this he smiled, but I added, "Mr. Hume, I pledge myself to produce a substitute whose evidence shall do good service in your committee-room." With the earnestness of a man thirty years younger, he asked me to whom I referred, "as *we must*," he said, "only bring forward witnesses of undeniable experience." Seeing how anxious he was on the point, I informed him I must now submit to him what I considered to be the qualifications of the gentleman to whom I alluded, Mr. Samuel Browning, who, while engaged in commercial pursuits, had resided in France, Holland, Germany, and Portugal, had passed two or three years in the United States, during which time he was an attentive observer of every thing connected with shipping and ship-building there, and in our North American colonies; moreover, that he knew our Australian colonies from Swan River to Sydney, had visited in the course of his trading the chief ports of China, and in mercantile circles was looked upon as a man of extensive information. "Now," said Mr. Hume, "you have satisfied me that he will be a valuable witness; and we must go to work at once, for every day is of consequence; the committee will commence its sittings within a fortnight, and I should very much wish to have some meetings with Mr. Browning and you previously; but the only time I have at command is from ten to twelve in the morning." It was then arranged that our first conference on the repeal of the navigation laws should take place next day in Bryanston Square, at Mr. Hume's house. Mr. Browning and I were so much astonished at the wonderful vigor and energy which a man of threescore and ten could evince, that I made the following memorandum at the time: "Mr. Browning and myself, for a fortnight before the committee met, spent two hours every other morning with Mr. Hume, from ten to twelve, at his house in Bryanston Square, in discussing the question of the navigation laws. The honorable member impressed us as being one of the most painstaking and methodical men of business we had ever met. He had his Parliamentary reports and references in such order, that he could at once direct his secretary to look up any question since the period of his first taking his seat in the House of Commons (1811), and in those debates where he took part, or in the evidence before committees of which he was a member, would be found his own marginal notes and comments in the Blue Books. He mentioned that he had found these notanda invaluable during his long Parliamentary career in abridging labor."

We were particularly struck with the systematic manner in which the old gentleman proceeded to elucidate the question; and I well recollect his calling for all the Blue Books in which the reports of different committees of the House of Commons on the combination laws appeared, as he was desirous Mr. Browning should make himself acquainted with the bearings of this branch of the subject on the main issue. He adduced an instance somewhere between 1816 and 1820—which he seemed to recollect as if it had happened but a few months previously—of the ship-builders at Dublin being compelled in consequence of the exactions to which they were exposed from their workmen, in addition to the mutinous and turbulent spirit existing among this body—to invite Scotch ship-carpenters from Greenock, Leith, and other places in the north. The result was an outbreak, in which two of the Scotchmen were killed and several severely injured, and the others, under threats of being murdered, were only too happy to get back to Scotland without delay. I mention these particulars to show the great care and assiduity with which Mr. Hume collected every fact that bore directly or even remotely on the inquiry he was conducting. At twelve o'clock he always mounted his horse to ride down to the House, where he had committees to attend, or other business occupying him until the House met. I believe during the sitting of Parliament, with the exceptions of the Wednesday and Saturday, he rarely was ever able to dine with his family. There was something peculiarly agreeable in sitting, as I may term it, in council with the ex-member for Weymouth, Middlesex, and Kilkenny, and the *de facto* member for Montrose. My own responsibility in having introduced a witness who was to bear the brunt of examination before a committee of the House of Commons was at once relieved by Mr. Hume calling me back at the conclusion of our first day's sittings in Bryanston Square and telling me in a whisper, "I like your friend very much; he is a sound, clear-headed man. Don't forget Thursday, *at ten sharp*."

At last the day arrived when Mr. Browning's examination was to begin; it occupied three meetings of the committee. On the first day the late Sir Robert Peel was unable to attend as a member of it until two o'clock, but he appeared at a fortunate moment, as one of the committee who seemed quite at sea on the subject of the navigation laws was asking the witness a question which neither he nor any one else understood. I distinctly saw Mr. Hume, who was as much of an economist of the time as he was of the money of the public, biting his lip and lisping out, "Tit tit," in other words, "What trash! what nonsense!" when the great and lucid Sir Robert asked permission to put the question differently, and subsequently for the rest of the sitting took upon himself the examination of Mr. Browning.

When the committee rose, Mr. Hume came to me evidently much satisfied, and said, "Don't our cock fight well? Do you see how Sir Robert listens to his replies; and I tell you further, he will lose no more of Mr. Browning's evidence." Mr Hume was right, as Sir Robert came into the committee-room on the next occasion at eleven, and remained throughout the day.

The following week Mr. Browning had his last examination, when Sir Robert again attended.

There was another instance that came under my own observation, showing the astonishing perseverance and actual labor which the aged member would undergo in order to detect and stop an abuse. He wrote me a note to say that he hoped he would find me at home the following day at three, as he wished to talk to me on a subject he had serious thoughts of calling forthwith to the attention of Parliament—to wit, the salvage awarded to Her Majesty's ships for assistance rendered to merchant-ships in distress. He asked me my opinion on the subject. I merely answered in general terms, that I considered Her Majesty's fleet the police of the sea, and bound to render all and immediate assistance in their power to ships under the British flag; and I presumed the Admiralty would expect their officers to do the same for the ships of an alien flag; and in case of actual salvage, the sum awarded to be as a matter of course regulated according to the risk incurred. Sometimes, I said, underwriters complained, and with good reason, that the demands made by British ships-of-war on account of salvage were exorbitant. I mentioned an instance of the kind that occurred on that part of the coast of Scotland with which I was connected. A large trading-schooner in the Irish Channel had in a gale of wind lost her captain, mate, and all the crew, with the exception of the cook and cabin-boy, in a gallant attempt to rescue the crew of a sinking vessel. The cook knew the Isle of Whithorn, and with the assistance of the boy got the vessel before the wind, and ran her safely into port. When the vessel had got into smooth water, and all danger of being wrecked at an end, she was boarded by the officer and boat's crew of one of Her Majesty's revenue cutters who assisted in mooring her. Lloyd's agent summoned a jury of county gentlemen to take evidence and award compensation. I, as a lad, was present. The captain of the revenue cutter claimed £1,000 salvage. My father, who had been formerly an extensive underwriter, and fully understanding the question, but with no personal interest in it whatever, pointed to the cook and cabin-boy as the real salvors. It ended by the revenue cutter receiving £100 for their services, and the cook and boy being recommended to the liberal consideration of the underwriters. "But," said Mr. Hume, "I can put my finger on a case where a British merchant-captain on the coast of South America found his ship, owing to a strong current, drifting on shore, although still some miles from it. He applied to the captain of a British man-of-war for assistance, but as the vessel was not in immediate danger, the gallant naval captain withheld his aid until the merchantman was in a position of danger. *Then* the assistance was rendered, and the ship was worked out to sea, for which a large claim for salvage followed." Mr. Hume considered the case most flagrant and wished to expose it; and had he done so, I very much fear the captain's commission would have been cancelled. His opinion was, that a British man-of-war was paid by the country to protect its ships and commerce, and had no legal claim to salvage. This was the view he held twenty-five years ago. I have quoted these facts in regard to Mr. Hume at greater length than I intended, as coming within my own knowledge; but they may be interesting to those who knew that excellent man only by report; and from such examples they may form a pretty correct estimate of the value of a Parliamentary career which commenced in 1811 and closed only in 1855.

97. *St. Thomas in the West Indies, and St. Thomas in the City of Oxford.*

I never hear our former West India possession of St. Thomas mentioned without mentally connecting it with the parish of St. Thomas in Oxford. I was passing a week in the learned city at the time that Mr. Maclean, one of the members for Oxford, was visiting his constituents. Mr. Alderman Tawney was then Mayor; and, at his residence in St. Thomas's in the suburbs, all the friends of the honorable and learned member received great kindness and hospitality. Among other visitors was the worthy M. P.'s father, General Sir Fitzroy Maclean, Bart. I came in for a full share of the hospitality of the week; and I partook of it *without prejudice*, as my politics were not exactly in accord with the "Macleanites."

At the conclusion of one of the dinners in the city at which the Mayor was not present, and sitting next to Sir Fitzroy, I said to him in rising, "I know you will support me in the toast I am about to propose—the health of our kind friends at St. Thomas's." It was received with a round of applause, when to my utter surprise uprose the vigorous old general who had braved more years in the

West Indies than probably any other officer in the British army, and addressed the company in an animated speech. The following is an outline of what he said: "Gentlemen, I thank you sincerely for the manner in which you have received the toast proposed by my excellent young friend—(putting his hand on my shoulder)—I consider the enthusiasm with which you have accepted the toast a great personal compliment. It has brought back the recollection of events that occurred nearly thirty years ago" (a masonic sign now passed round the table directed to me not to undeceive the worthy baronet). "Gentlemen," exclaimed Sir Fitzroy in clear and emphatic language, "I hoisted my flag as governor of the island of St. Thomas on September 8, 1808, and that flag was not lowered until April 15, 1815, when that island and the island of St. John—of both I was governor—were restored to the Danish Government. I was also sole Commissioner for the Dutch and Danish loans. Gentlemen, during that eventful period I maintained untarnished the honor of the flag of England. I protected the commerce of our merchants, and, by holding the scales of justice impartially, I reaped my reward, on retiring from the responsible duties I held, by being pronounced a painstaking and popular governor." In fact, the gallant ex-governor of St. Thomas made an admirable speech, the only portions of which that alarmed me and placed me on the horns of a dilemma were, when he turned to me to repeat his thanks for referring to that colony in which his most important public services had been fulfilled—of which fact, until that evening, I was as ignorant as the rest of the company, the members of his own family present excepted, but who were equally anxious the secret should not ooze out. We had to attend a public ball the same night, and although this post-prandial *plaisanterie* had created vast amusement and Sir Fitzroy was the happiest of all, I felt miserable, for, as I knew the world to be at times censorious,

I was convinced that before the evening was over, some kind friend would let out the joke, and that the gallant old Highland chieftain would come down upon me with his claymore for not being ingenuous toward the representative of *Gillian-ni-Tuiodh.* Each time the old baronet found I was not dancing, he stuck his arm into mine, I receiving a repetition of praise for so thoughtfully and appropriately connecting him with the island of St. Thomas, which he remarked his son's supporters in Oxford never would have known had it not been for me, and I, in return, telling him, what was strictly true, that his speech was the best and most interesting delivered that evening. "All's well that ends well." Still, in promenading the ballroom, knowing as I did that even the mothers and daughters had heard of my short speech and Sir Fitzroy's long one, I found myself walking on glass, terrified lest some cruel wag might peach, for the General was commonly reported by those who served with him in the army to be as "jealous in honor, as he was sudden and quick in quarrel." For myself I never saw any thing that even augured a tendency to the latter. Be that as it may, I was delighted to see "the Maclean" inside the stage-coach for London next forenoon; and from him I received as hearty "a grip of the louf (shake of the hand)" as any Scotchman ever gave another. After this, in occasionally meeting Sir Fitzroy on his way to his club, his greeting was always of the kindest description, and our conversation rarely failed to include some reference to St. Thomas in the West Indies, which with equal certainty brought vividly before *me* St. Thomas in the city of Oxford.

98. *General Sir Fitzroy Maclean, Bart., and the Horse Guards.*

Like many other distinguished officers whose services had been confined to the capture and defence of our West

India islands, not having shared in the glories of the Peninsular campaign, Sir Fitzroy felt acutely being overlooked from time to time at the Horse Guards. But, as he himself told me, that, having battled a West Indian climate for so many years, and been actively engaged at the reduction of various islands, wearing a medal for Guadaloupe, etc., seeing how patronage ran after Waterloo in one channel, he early made up his mind to keep his own claims before the authorities at the Horse Guards, where His Royal Highness the Duke of York candidly confessed to him, when a regiment became vacant, that it had been secured for so and so, who, as Sir Fitzroy said, was almost invariably a Peninsular or Waterloo officer. Levee after levee without fail found the General wending his steps to pay his respects to the Commander-in-Chief, frequently not meeting with the most courteous reception either from His Royal Highness or Sir Herbert Taylor. Still, his resolution to present himself on the appointed day was, like the laws of the Medes and Persians, unchangeable. One day while in the waiting-room, the door of the Duke's sanctum being open, he heard His Royal Highness ask Sir Herbert what officers had arrived for the levee. "Maclean, as usual," was the reply. On which the Duke, in language, if not altogether refined was most consoling to the ears of the Highland chieftain: "I tell you what it is, Taylor, I may offend Wellington, but I cannot help it, as I am resolved that Maclean shall have the first regiment that becomes vacant."

After this burst of royal indignation had somewhat calmed down, out came Sir Herbert, and said, "Maclean, don't wait to see the Duke to-day, His Royal Highness has had a good deal to worry him; but I may tell you matters look very well for you." "My walk," said Sir Fitzroy, "on my return from the Horse Guards, was the most agreeable I had had since I first obtained my commission. A few weeks only passed when my next visit to the Horse

Guards was to thank His Royal Highness for having appointed me to the command of the 84th Regiment, to which I was gazetted on July 28, 1823, being subsequently transferred, December 30, 1840, to the 45th Regiment. Ah, you young men should keep impressed on your minds through life, as I have done ever since I left school, those words, 'nil desperandum,' and 'persevero.'"

99. *Mr. Simon Cock of the City of London, and Colonel Wilson of the* Ceety *of York, M. P.*

My friend, the late Mr. Simon Cock, was a man of high mental capacity, so much so, in fact, as to have attracted, when a youth, the notice of William Pitt. In after-years, from his great commercial and financial abilities, he was on different occasions employed by the Government of the day in negotiating with foreign powers on commercial matters, such as the removal and modification of restrictive duties, and had his career been in Parliament and his party been in power, he must have attained to the Chancellorship of the Exchequer or the Presidency of the Board of Trade.

He was a man of benign and intellectual aspect, reminding me both in height and appearance of a former prime minister, Earl Grey. In latter years he was a sad martyr to asthma, but when relieved for a time of his sufferings was one of the most delightful and cheerful companions at the head of his own table or at the table of a friend. I remember a very laughable incident, in which Mr. Cock was the chief actor and exponent.

We had met at the table of a most hospitable countryman of mine in Portland Place, where there was a fairly-balanced proportion of the English, Irish, and Scotch element, represented respectively by Sir John Lowther, the late Lord Keane, and Colin Campbell (afterward Lord

Clyde). One of the party, a Scotchman, and acknowledged on all sides to be one of the strangest specimens of the Caledonian to be met with, had gone out to the West Indies from the village of Moffat some forty years previously, and evidently long before he had finished his education. Fortune, however, had favored him, as he was enabled to return to England with a handsome fortune a little over middle life, and the first investment he made of a portion of it was in the purchase of a castle and estate in Yorkshire, becoming very shortly afterward one of the representatives for York in Parliament. Finding that I was from Scotland, he communicated to me the fact that he also was from that part of the world, and imparted to me the high senatorial position he held, as well as his former military rank, a colonel of West India militia. He then touched upon the important annual motion approaching in Parliament for the repeal of the Corn Laws, on which subject he considered it incumbent that he should lay his opinions, through the medium of the House of Commons, before the country. "You must keep in mind the position I hold, as one of the two members for the second *ceety* in England. It is absolutely *requeered o'* me that I should speak; *ma* constituents will expect it, and I would not like to disappoint them. I should further tell you, Mr. Boyd, that I am an auld Tory, what they *ca noo* a Conservative, and that the Harewoods, and in fact *a'* the Lascelles family, and the Lowthers there"—Sir John Lowther was sitting opposite—"will look *oot* for me speaking on the motion; but I should just tell you that I am *vera* far *frae* being *weel* up on the subject." "Then, colonel, as you have made up your mind to join in the debate, the very ablest man you could consult on so important a matter is our friend there, Mr. Simon Cock." "That's a *vera* good suggestion, Mr. Boyd." Although it was our first time of meeting each other, he was by no means reticent on the important political attitude he was about to assume in the *Hoose*, therefore, so soon after dinner as the opportunity offered, he at my suggestion addressed Mr. Cock, or rather Mr. *Koke*, the name he gave him throughout the evening. "Mr. *Koke*, you are aware that the annual motion for the repeal *o'* the Corn Laws, which is *a' nonesense*, is coming on, and I think as I am member for the second *ceety* in the kingdom, and never yet having *spokken* in the *Hoose*, I must do so *noo*. But, Mr. *Koke*, I should tell you that I *hae* never *thocht ower* (over) the subject, and therefore should feel greatly *obleeged* to you if you would kindly write *oot* a bit *o'* a speech for me." All eyes were directed to Mr. Cock, whose gravity and dry humor were now to be tested. "Well, colonel, you must first inform me what your precise views are." "*Noo*, Mr. *Koke*, there's exactly where you might assist me, for I tell you candidly, I ken (know) far *mair aboot* West India sugar than English corn." "Then am I to understand that you will oppose Mr. Villiers's views on corn-law repeal?" "Oh, certainly, and I should like to speak early in the debate." This we all highly approved of. "*Noo*, Mr. *Koke*, understand me, when I tell you that I am for the *maintenance o'* the Corn Laws, I *tak'* the same view with Lord Harewood, and *a'* the Lascelles clique, and with *ma frien'* there, Sir John Lowther." "Well, colonel, you have made it quite clear what I have to do for you, but as you hold the prominent position of member of Parliament for the ancient and historical city of York—" "Quite true, Mr. *Koke*." "Would you not like to bring forward, which you could introduce in the course of your argument, a scale of protective duties of your own—something different from the present scale—an original idea and suggestion coming from yourself?" "That's excellent, Mr. *Koke*, it would be the *vera makin' o'* me as a politician, and there's no man that would be better pleased than *ma frien'* Sir John Lowther, for there's *nae* jealousy between us." "Colonel, I shall be delighted." It may easily be conceived the amusement all this afforded, with the accompaniment of Mr. Cock's humorous remarks. "*Noo*, Mr. *Koke*, ye *maun mak* (must make) the *hale o'* the speech for me, and I promise you to get *mysel weel* up *in't*."

Accordingly Mr. Cock a day or two afterward fulfilled his promise *verbatim et literatim*, for he wrote out in plain and distinct language a most excellent speech for the honorable member for the *ceety o' York* or for any other honorable member advocating non-repeal principles. Unfortunately for the colonel, the speech was written on half sheets of paper on one side only, to which he had not been accustomed. But the great misfortune to which he was exposed, was an omission on Mr. Cock's part in not numbering his leaves. Hence the catastrophe that ensued, otherwise the colonel might have gone down to posterity as famous as "Single-speech Hamilton." The night of debate arrived, but I had been unsuccessful in getting my name on the Speaker's list, or an admission to the gallery. I was told that a fair muster of the gallant colonel's political admirers were in their places, as he was to speak early, who were much amused to witness the assiduity with which he was perusing his lesson and turning over the half-dozen sheets of manuscript. That he had got the speech by heart *in cumulo* there is no reason to doubt, as he delivered the first page of the *exordium* with great fluency, and in a vernacular so pure as to bring back to the House of Commons, in the recollection of one or two members who still survived, the days of Pitt's famous minister, Dundas. Had the leaves of his brief only been paged, so excellent was the colonel's memory, that those who heard him, and were in the secret, felt convinced that although "they came to laugh, they would have stayed to praise;" but as he delivered the contents of page 4 where 2 should have come, and 5 instead of 3, etc., he produced a medley such as seldom had been served up in the House of Commons.

I dined with Mr. Cock the day after the speech was reported in the papers, and the first thing he said was, "I am the luckiest man in London, for it was ten to one, when the member for the *ceety o' York* found he was interrupted in the delivery of his oration, he had not informed the House that the views he held on the subject were those of Mr. Simon Cock. If this had happened," continued my facetious friend, "I should have passed under the *sobriquet* of the ex-member for the *ceety o' York* for the rest of my life."

100. *Ballooning.*

Aërostation was one of the hobbies with which my brother was at one time greatly enamoured, and he repeatedly ascended with Green in his balloon from Vauxhall. To this my father was *insurmountably* opposed, as dangerous and expensive too.

My father did all in his power to alter his son's taste for ballooning, and the result of a recent descent pleased him immensely, for one evening Mr. Green and his friends made their descent with difficulty, and were sadly knocked about in landing, my brother reaching his home black and blue; indeed, how they escaped with their lives puzzled many. The events connected with this ascent and descent had quite an opposite effect to what my father anticipated. They only whetted his son's appetite for ballooning. One beautiful summer evening, a clear and serene sky, not a breath of wind, Vauxhall was in all her crowded glory, and it was announced that Green's balloon would ascend at half-past six. The grappling-iron was all right this time; no apprehensions felt by those about to enter the car of being bumped on returning to mother earth, as on the last occasion. I heard my brother describe this ascent to his father as one of ineffable stillness, for, as he wittily remarked, even while floating slowly over the Houses of Lords and Commons he could discover no "sensible motion." In the present case, what little wind there was shifted, and at the end of an hour and a half after leaving Vauxhall, Mr. Green espied an inviting spot to cast anchor, which he thought to be Osterley Park, the Earl of Jersey's, and as there was a party chiefly of the fairer portion of creation gazing most anxiously at the balloon, they were unanimous in their desire for a descent among the ladies. This the skilled aëronaut readily accomplished, for in a few minutes he had his party blending, as he supposed, with the visitors of the Earl and Countess of Jersey. It, however, proved not to be Osterley Park, and the names of the host and hostess were not distinctly heard. The reception was of the heartiest description, indeed extremely flattering to the intrepid *voyageurs*, and the ladies collected round the balloon to witness the process of its being emptied of its gas, in which Green was assisted by the servants of the establishment. When this was complete, and the machine ready for a land journey to London, the party were invited to the hall, where they found the hospitable board already provided with every thing in the shape of fruit and wines the most fastidious could desire. The lady whom my brother handed to table, immediately on being seated, touched him confidentially on the arm, at the same time bringing her lips as close to his as propriety could sanction, addressed him in a whisper—"Pray don't tell Sir Henry, but I am going to London to-night with you in the balloon." My brother began to puzzle his brain who Sir Henry could be, and this lady's strange conversation increased his perplexity. At last Sir Henry said, "I hope, Lady Ellis, you are attending to your friends at your end of the table." The problem that had been working in my brother's mind was instantly solved. The *Bal-loonatics*, as my father called them (the first time it was alleged he had ever been suspected of approaching any thing bordering on a *bon mot*) were the inmates of Sir Henry Ellis's asylum for insane patients, and where, as a witty friend remarked, they had been most hospitably treated, as their strait waistcoats testified.

My father declared that had he been a commissioner of lunacy or a magistrate for that county, he would have sentenced one and all of Mr. Green's party to the custody of Sir Henry Ellis for the period of one month, paying their own costs. Such a sentence, he confidently stated, would do more to *put down* ballooning than any thing else.

101. *Another Balloon Adventure.*

The comparative cheapness of coal gas and a feat which Mr. Robert Holland, then M. P. for Hastings, in conjunction with two friends, achieved under the guardianship of the veteran Green, made this recreation *highly* fashionable. In a stupendous balloon carrying a ton of ballast they ascended from Vauxhall in November, 1836, crossed the Channel, and after a flight of eighteen hours descended safely in Germany in the territory of Nassau. This revived the hope that balloons might be rendered available for useful purposes. Mr. Green was open to any reasonable proposition, and was of opinion—the wish being father to the thought—that, if the wind blew steadily from the south, the balloon would go direct through the heart of England and Scotland, and land its cargo in Sutherlandshire.

Important arrangements were now going forward vigorously in the Green cabinet, and brilliant anticipations of some great achievement were discussed, as Green and his friends projected an all-important aërial experiment. The party numbered six, including the veteran pilot. He had issued his instructions, on perceiving the wind to be coming round to the point desired, that the five *savants* should hold themselves in readiness to join him at Vauxhall within half an hour of receiving his message. Two days' provisions, with a moderate quantity of wine and brandy, were already on board the balloon, now swinging at anchor within the "Royal Property," as Vauxhall was called; and as Mr. Holland's party had carried up a ton of ballast, Green authorized each to have a small carpet-bag, in addition to a warm overcoat, in case, through some unforeseen contingency, they reached nearer Greenland or Nova Zembla than contemplated in their programme. The writs of summons were at last issued by the aëronaut, and within an hour the *savants* were afloat, with the choicest wind, to all appearance, that could blow for Scotland. Shortly afterward they found themselves amid strata of dense clouds, and, to their infinite chagrin, the wind was blowing strongly from an opposite quarter to what it was when they left Vauxhall. Green was sanguine of meeting with a different current; at all events, he must give his passengers an airing, and therefore allowed the balloon to pursue its own course, which proved to be a most rapid one, for on clearing the clouds through which they had been passing for an hour and a half, they discovered, to their utter confusion and consternation, the Bill of Portland, and the wide expanse of the Channel before them, so that, instead of crossing the Grampians during the night, as they had calculated upon doing, they had an immediate prospect of spending it in the Bay of Biscay. An instant descent followed, but, on nearing the earth, Green found it impossible to effect a landing, and having unfortunately let off more of his hydrogen-gas power than he should, he was forced to lighten his ship by discharging cargo, so overboard went carpet-bags, great-coats, and even provisions, knives and forks, port, sherry, and brandy. Having again reached a sufficient altitude, he was able to select a spot where he landed his living freight safely, one or two of the party having lost their carpet-bags, and all of them their dinner, as well as their great-coats.

The only advantage I ever heard the scientific world was to gain by this ascent and descent was in being afforded an opportunity of inspecting on our sideboard a wine-glass that had been thrown out of the balloon at some fabulous height, and had fallen in a ploughed field without breaking. This was considered so very remarkable that the glass was encased in silver, on which the full inscription of the great height it had fallen from Green's balloon was stated.

After this there was a gradual subsidence with my relative in his balloon mania, as he ascended only once afterward with Mr. Green. Mr. MacCulloch, the eminent political economist, in dining with us a few days afterward, was most anxious to learn where he had landed on this occasion. The answer was, "Among the flats of Essex." "A most appropriate locality," exclaimed my distinguished countryman, "and one which shows how true it is that 'birds of a feather flock together.'"

102. *A Friend outside the Foreign Office.*

I wrote the following, after reading an admirable notice of the deceased lady in a leading journal:

My late friend, Mr. William Watson, a most intelligent merchant at Liverpool, who had spent many years in Mexico, arrived in town late in the day to solicit an interview with Lord Palmerston at the Foreign Office; but as it was after office-hours, he accompanied me to my residence in Kent, to spend the night, hoping to be able next day to explain to his lordship the grievance under which he and others connected with the trade of Mexico suffered. I advised my friend to be at the Foreign Office next day about three o'clock, where he was informed that his lordship had not arrived. As time pressed, he was recommended to wait upon his lordship at his private residence in Carlton Gardens, but he was not at home. Mr. Watson had just said to the servant, "How unlucky!" when Lady Palmerston, who was passing at the moment to get into her carriage, heard this, and immediately said, "I know Lord Palmerston will return in a few minutes; pray do come to the drawing-room," her ladyship leading the way.

Mr. Watson was a man of exceedingly good and winning address, and possessed of more than a common share of *bonhomie;* he was made *à son aise* by Lady Palmerston, who said, "I find you are very anxious to see my husband; pray tell me all about it." Mr. Watson began by explaining that the mail for Mexico would leave in a few days, and that he was most solicitous to be able to report what impression he had made on Lord Palmerston, for whom, he assured her ladyship, the parties complained against stood in very wholesome dread. He then explained the whole affair to Lady Palmerston; the recital occupied some twenty minutes, and interested her much, when Lord Palmerston entered, and found himself introduced to Mr. Watson by his wife, who, in rising to retire, shook Mr. Watson cordially by the hand; then, turning to Lord Palmerston, said, "Oh, it is a very cruel case. I hope, Mr. Watson, you will succeed in making Lord Palmerston view it as I do." At this Lord Palmerston laughed heartily. Mr. Watson returned to my house to dinner, and, I may add, highly satisfied with the result of his interview with the head of the Foreign Office, as well as greatly pleased with the circumstances that had preceded it.

103. *Mr. William Watson, of Liverpool, and Sir Astley Cooper.*

My friend Mr. Watson related to us, after dinner, the following anecdote:

"Twenty-five years ago I was sent home from Mexico, by my medical man, in what he considered a precarious state of health. On my arrival at Liverpool, my doctor there told me I must go to London and see Sir Astley Cooper forthwith. I followed orders, and met a large party in the distinguished surgeon's anteroom. At last I was admitted, and explained my case as concisely as possible, referring to my long residence in Mexico. It appeared to me that his mind at once began to run infinitely more upon Mexico, her native Spaniards, Creoles, and Mulattoes, with her mines of gold, silver, copper, etc., than upon any bodily ailment I might be supposed to suffer from. As to the ten or a dozen unfortunate patients waiting—now probably doubled—they seemed entirely forgotten, and probably were growing impatient. He wrote me a prescription, which I was to begin that day; it was a Tuesday. 'Now,' said he, 'as it is most important that I should have ocular proof as to the state of your appetite after taking my medicine for three days, you will come here on Friday, precisely at six o'clock, and dine with me. I shall then be able to judge how you are; although it may be satisfactory for you to hear that I consider there is very little the matter with you.' I rose to make my bow and pay the fee I had been instructed to give by my Liverpool doctor, namely, two guineas for a first, and, of necessity, a long consultation; but before there was time for this, while my right hand was in my pocket to elicit the fee, my left hand had received a fee from the world-known surgeon. I was puzzled. 'Do you know,' said he, 'I have been searching everywhere for the information you have furnished me with in regard to Mexico, which is very much more valuable than my professional service? But as I never wish to press money upon any one, I shall put the fee I intended for you again in my pocket, and you will put the fee you intended for me again in your pocket.' Sir Astley kept me three weeks in London, cured me, gave me a dinner three days a week, but never would take a fee."

104. *Was not that better than* slaping?

Very nearly thirty years ago, in the end of May, I had a charming view of the Russian summer fleet cruising in the Baltic. I was a passenger to St. Petersburg, on board the steamer "Sirius," the first vessel under steam that had ever crossed the Atlantic to America, notwithstanding Dr. Lardner's opinion that for a steamer to cross the ocean was an impossibility. She was commanded by a very pleasant, accomplished, kind-hearted, and rollicking Irish half-pay lieutenant in the navy, of the name of Waters. At three o'clock one morning he opened the door of my cabin, and soon aroused me from a profound sleep, by asking what was the use of *paple laving* home to travel, if they hadn't their eyes open at three o'clock on such a beautiful morning as that. "But it is very early, captain," I said. "Early, do you say? Why, you shouldn't have lost a moment of the *whoule* night, but have been with me on the poop. Why, sir, I saw you *rading* the smallest print at twelve o'clock last night on deck, and you may *rade* still smaller print in this part of the world at three o'clock in the morning, but that's not what I called you for. You *most* get up this very *moument.*" "Oh, be merciful, captain!" "I'll be nothing of the kind; here's the *whoule Rossian sommer flate* on the starboard tack; *bedad, jost* as if the Emperor Nicholas knew you were coming, and sent it down here for you to *sae.*" The appeal was irresistible. I was immediately on deck, being richly rewarded for severing myself from that "best friend of frail humanity," by witnessing a magnificent sight. The Baltic was so calm a lake "that not a wrinkle ruffled her smooth face." There was just breeze enough to fill the sails of twenty men-of-war. Lieutenant Waters endeavored to explain to me the evolutions of the squadron, and, seeing that I was highly interested, said to me, "Now, I'll tell you what I am going to do with you, but you *nade* not be talking of it at headquarters when you get back to London, and it won't after all inter*fare* a *marcel* with our arrival at Cronstadt. I'll give you a run right up through the *flate*, and then back down through the *flate*." In the mean time I suggested that our fellow-passengers should be apprised of what was going on.

I observed, as we passed near some of the ships, that ours was warmly greeted, and I asked our commander to explain. "Why, bless you *sor*, Dominic Creagh Waters and the *Sarius* are as well known at Cronstadt as the biggest fort there." We had now said good-by to the Russian fleet, and were assembled at breakfast, when our lieutenant-commander entered, and, addressing me, said, "Was not that better than *slaping?*"

Waters, whose attention to his duties, and to the comfort of his passengers, was unremitting, made our week's voyage from the English to the Russian capital one of rapturous delight. He would not even allow me to be seasick; he had always something to *stap soch hombog*. "Now you drink that while I tell you an anecdote, and attend to me and not to the other thing, for if this were *ounely* followed, there would be a *dale* less *sae*-sickness." It was quite impossible to ask him a single question without his answer securing for you a hearty laugh. I recollect, just as we were starting for the Thames, opposite the Tower, I said, "Captain Waters, when shall we be at St. Petersburg?" "Well, we shall be at Cronstadt *forst*, but I suppose you are not particular to an hour." "Not in the least." "I promise you that if you don't *ate* your dinner at the latter place next Wednesday, you shall drink your *tay*, but at same time it is *ounely* right to tell you that it's a *dale* farther than *aither* Windsor or Richmond. Now look at that clock, it's on the strike of eight, and this is Wednesday morning, and if the *ould* "Sarious" and myself *doun't* quarrel by the road on Wednesday *avening* next, she and I will have you 1,650 miles away from Billingsgate Market, and *mourover*, in the *intervaning pariod*, we shall give you the best inside of a day in Norway, and the same in Denmark, to yourself; say, eight hours in one, and twelve in the other. You have, of course, heard *spake* of a Norway fiord." "Oh, yes." "Well then, you will have into the bargain a sail up one to Christiansand, and after you have *sane* it, all you have to do is to apply a magnifying-glass, and you will be able to make it as big as any fiord in Norway. Joking apart, in going up and coming down you will be able to *jodge* right well of the *fatures* of the *contry*, and I am only sorry I can't give you time for a little salmon-fishing. There is a great advantage and economy of time for the tourist in this northern latitude," said our Irish captain, "as there's daylight during the night at this *saison*."

The morning after leaving Christiansand, at a very early hour, Lieutenant Dominic Creagh Waters shook me rather sharply in my berth, holding in his other hand a book, and exclaiming, "Shake *aff* this downy *slape*." "What is it, captain?" "I was *tould* in London to be mighty civil to you, and it shall be your *owne* fault if I am not; now, wake *op*, for I have brought you 'Hamlet,' which I wish you once more to *rade*, and that mighty sharp, for in an hour we shall be *aff* Elsinore, and you will be able, when you get back, to show your *larning*, and talk with any of them about Claudius, King of Denmark, Hamlet, *Ophalia*, Rosencrantz, and the *whoule* boiling of them. Now wake up, for, upon my *soule*, you can stand a *dale* of *slape*, more than any Scotchman I ever met with, for, generally *spaking*—you are an exception—they are wide *enoff* awake when it is to benefit them.—Steward, bring a wet towel here and *rob* Mr. Boyd's eyes until you get the *slape* out of them."

Never had Shakespeare before sunk in my estimation, but at finding myself suddenly withdrawn from the warm embrace of "our foster-nurse of Nature," a feeling of deep regret crossed my mind that our illustrious dramatist had ever written "Hamlet."

At six o'clock A.M. we were at Copenhagen, our captain exclaiming, "Well done, *ould Sarius.*" It being Sunday morning, and the weather most charming, the passengers were all on *deck* and *decked* in their best. Our incomparable captain thus addressed us: "Ladies and *gintilmen*, I am now going to give you twelve hours' *lave* of absence to do your *chorch*, the city of Copenhagen, and the kingdom of Denmark. Remember me kindly to Thorwaldsen, and don't be complimenting Lord Nelson too highly to the Danes."

105. *How soon a Man may become a Lion.*

I had visited the grave of our great novelist, Fielding, in the English cemetery at Lisbon, had steamed up the Guadalquiver to pay my devotion at the shrine of Columbus in the Cathedral of Seville, had inspected her Alcazar, her "Murillos," her churches, palaces, hospitals, manufactures of silk and tobacco—in fact, had examined, as minutely as time would admit, the famed capital of Andalusia. I had told a learned friend of mine, a Q. C., that if I lived another year, I hoped to spare him for the future dunning into my ears what I believed to be his only Spanish quotation, "Quien no ha visto Sevilla, no ha visto maravilla."

I found myself, after a delicious ride on horseback from Gibraltar, at Malaga, on my way to the Vega and Alhambra of Granada.

I had a most valuable pocket companion, not then always obtainable, namely, a passport from Lord Palmerston, with letters of recommendation to secure me protection—rather important at that moment in Spain—and attention from H. B. Majesty's Consuls, among others to the Consul at Malaga. He kindly invited me to place myself next day under his escort, to inspect the lions of this city and seaport of Upper Andalusia; but I little anticipated I was myself to become for the nonce one of the most prominent of the lion tribe.

On leaving the Consulate, to commence our walk, I observed a collection of people near the door, which kept increasing, all staring at me in a manner to which, as an humble subject of Queen Victoria, I had been unaccustomed; yet, there was a benignity of expression in every countenance that made the microscopic view of which I found myself the object, the reverse of disagreeable. "Ah, I see that, to become a great man, all we have to do is to be a traveller." My facetious friend the Consul—as I discovered—said I might as well occasionally raise my hat to the majesty of the people—an injunction I carefully followed out. Up to this point I was chiefly a source of attraction to the *hoi polloi*, when I observed little knots of well-dressed people, as we passed through the Alameda, viewing me with an expression of respect and deep interest extremely puzzling. My more numerous and more humble beholders, on one or two occasions, appeared anxious to cheer me. This, probably, the presence of some police authorities alone prevented, but with the others there was a disposition to melancholy imprinted on their countenances, and an evident desire to avoid every thing like obtrusiveness toward one whose thoughts they concluded at that moment to be steeped in painful reflection. I said, "Consul, what does all this mean? The kingdom or province of Granada seems to have very few tourists, for I have never met, in either Austria or Russia, where travellers are minutely scanned, any curiosity, or whatever you choose to designate it, in the least to be compared with what has occurred during the last two hours." This elicited a smile from the Consul, who said he would explain all to me when we got round the next corner. I was naturally impatient for the elucidation. It appeared that my passport the previous evening had been extensively read and keenly inspected by the Spanish authorities, and an immediate conclusion arrived at that I was a brother of poor Robert Boyd, who, in 1831, threw himself into the political scale with General Torrigos, in opposition to Ferdinand, and whose party were betrayed, forty-nine in number, and shot on Sunday morning, December 11, 1831.

As my visit to Malaga was limited to another day, the Consul thought it best to allow matters to remain as they were. I said: "Consul, I have no objection, as I was quite unprepared for such an ovation on Spanish soil, thanks to the *manes* of my unfortunate namesake; still, I should prefer the British flag over me while in life to its being placed as it was by you over the murdered body of Robert Boyd; for I cannot be blind to the fact that the Carlist and Christino war is at this moment raging throughout Spain." The Consul admitted that my reasoning was sound, and promised I should be well taken care of *while* within his consular jurisdiction, but beyond that he would not be answerable.

To those who have entered life since that bloody morning in 1831, some particulars in connection with the murder of Robert Boyd may be interesting. I may prelude them by stating that the victim of Moreno's treachery was a member of an ancient family in the north of Ireland; he had one brother not less eminent and distinguished as a lawyer and king's counsel than another is, who still survives, as a divine. A younger brother, who, had he been now alive, would have had his flag (Captain McNeill Boyd, R. N.), was drowned when in command of the port ship in

Kingstown harbor, in a gallant attempt to save human life. Robert Boyd, it is said, made large personal sacrifices (as much as £5,000) in the fitting out and equipment of the ill-fated expedition which fixed its rendezvous for a short time on neutral ground at Gibraltar. General Moreno was the confidental agent of King Ferdinand, and was looked upon as the perpetrator of his most barbarous cruelties. It is beyond all doubt that he decoyed Torrigos and Boyd, with their companions, to the Spanish shore, by forwarding to them letters at Gibraltar, stating that the district of country around Malaga was ready to rise. A letter of Moreno's was known to be in possession of a respected gentleman in London, in which letter he went so far as to point out the spot for landing, and the precise ground which his future victims should occupy on reaching the shore. The party consisted of forty-nine persons, General Torrigos, Mr. Boyd, and several ex-ministers and members of Cortes and officers of rank. Moreno lost not a moment after their capture in dispatching to Madrid, in the most private manner (in order to prevent the interference of the British Consul) an express bribed to extraordinary alacrity by the promise of a great reward. Moreno, who resolved on the destruction of Boyd, said nothing of any foreigner being among the prisoners, though he had in his hand the list with the name and designation of Mr. Boyd. The dispatch had not been a moment sent off from the farm-house where the party were surrounded and taken, when Moreno had the individuals of which it consisted huddled together in the refectory of an old convent, loaded with chains, and tortured. No trial of any description took place. On the Saturday evening after the capture, which took place on a Tuesday in December, 1831, Moreno received a warrant from Ferdinand, for the execution of the whole of the individuals so inhumanly kidnapped; and next morning he had them all shot under his own eye. Food was refused them for the eighteen hours after the warrant was received which preceded the execution. They were brought out in a fainting state. The first party, consisting of twenty-five persons, including General Torrigos and Mr. Boyd and the most eminent persons, were forty-five minutes under the hands of the soldiers: after the first volley was fired, the second party, consisting of twenty-four persons, were fifty-nine minutes under their hands. The bodies had been previously stripped by convicts, and after the execution with the exception of Mr. Boyd's (which was claimed by the spirited British Consul, who placed with his own hands the flag of England over it), they were cast into the scavenger's cart, and carried to the Campo Santo and thrown into a ditch, within two hours of this terrible butchery. Moreno gave a splendid public breakfast to the hell-hounds by whom he had been assisted. For this savage exploit, Ferdinand promoted Moreno to the rank of Lieutenant-General and made him Captain-General. He continued a favorite at court until the Queen became regent, during Ferdinand's life, when she, greatly to her honor, immediately after assuming the reins of Government, forbade him her presence, and also prohibited his appearance at Madrid. He was placed for months under the surveillance of the police at Seville, but, after the death of the King, he made his escape on horseback and joined Don Carlos in Portugal. He afterward came to a merited end, having been shot by his own men.

Robert Boyd met his fate like a brave man. The last words that passed his lips were, "Life's fitful fever will soon be o'er."

106. *My Visit to Granada.*

Having no desire for a repetition of the marked attentions I had received the day previous from the Malagueños, I desired my Spanish groom to have the horses at the door at three o'clock in the morning, and we were soon ascending the winding heights above the flourishing city of Malaga, whose imports of broadcloths, cotton, hardware, and cutlery, were only counterbalanced by its exports of wine, brandy, fresh grapes, raisins, figs, almonds, oranges, lemons, oil, etc., the yearly annual value of which when I was there, thirty years ago, was about £1,000,000 sterling.

The excitement I had passed through having partially subsided, I called a halt, so that I might look down calmly from the elevated position we had then reached on our way to Granada, upon the famous city of Malaga, which Ferdinand and Isabella had wrested from the Moors after an obstinate siege of three months. I never enjoyed a more charming view. It was a splendid morning in the beginning of May. I was gazing upon the harbor of Malaga in the light of a bay of the Mediterranean, spacious enough to accommodate a large fleet; and at that moment, as a solitary traveller in a country where a civil war prevailed *à l'outrance*, I observed with satisfaction, floating on its bosom, two vessels-of-war belonging to Her Britannic Majesty. My faithful Spaniard, but not more faithful than he was intelligent, called my attention, aided by my pocket telescope, to the Moorish buildings, and although last, not least, to the grand boast of Malaga, its famed Moorish castle, erected six centuries before. At this period of the morning, after being two hours in the saddle, I was, as usual, a prey to that "universal wolf, appetite," and had to mention this to my guide. We pushed on for a cool spring and shade, and dismounting, looked first after our horses and adjusted their nose-bags, as we carried their corn as well as our own breakfasts. The latter always consisted of a loaf of excellent bread, hard-boiled eggs, a piece of fat bacon, and a bottle of Malaga. During this equestrian tour I thought nothing half so good a beverage as Malaga and the limpid spring.

I should mention that while at Gibraltar I had expected to be accompanied by a party of friends, but the political state of Spain deterred them, and in lieu of their companionship, they gave me a farewell dinner, declaring it would be the last I ever ate under the British flag, and that I must be a descendant of Don Quixote to undertake a riding tour in a country heaving with internal revolution. Under this threatening aspect of affairs, and being in no way covetous of the honors of knight-errantry, I consulted two British merchants, Mr. Glover and Mr. Leach. The former had resided on "the Rock" for thirty years; and as I was then a bachelor, he assured me if I placed myself under the entire guidance of a Spaniard whom he would select, and who would supply the horses, a man whom he had often trusted with confidential dispatches, I should be quite safe; but that I must enter Spain as a non-militant, leave my pistols behind me, wear no rings on my non-wedded fingers, nor any tempting brooch in my neckcloth; and that I must have £5 in silver coin in the saddle-bags, a portion of which I was from time to time to dole out to my Spaniard for daily or nightly disbursement. This fund, which was always to be kept up at this amount, I presumed, Mr. Glover considered would be the highest ransom the brigands or banditti would require for my release. How very different from that recently demanded from our unfortunate countrymen on the plains of Marathon! I was told by Mr. Glover to look upon this fund of specie as belonging to my miscellaneous or secret-service estimates, as in case of capture it was my best *corps de reserve* at once to bring up, and that I should very soon have ocular proof of its efficacy. A journey of a few miles, after entering Spanish territory, showed me how excellent Mr. Glover's advice was, and gave me a clear insight as to the manner in which the silver was to be used. An armed man stopped us, when my courier told him, in all good humor, that I was making a tour for my health, etc., at the same time handing him a coin (about half a dollar) to drink my health with. He thanked me most courteously, and throughout a journey that otherwise might have been perilous, owing to the war, I escaped all further annoyance. When we reached the road-side venta at mid-day, where we had to rest ourselves and horses for some hours until the sun had partially declined, my initiatory step, while my man "Friday" was stabling the horses, was to enter the cocina and be hale-fellow-well-met with the male loungers, following out implicitly my escort's admonition, and in these cases I found that "ignorance was bliss," as I knew nothing of the language.

A military friend once told me that he discovered the words "buono" and "non è buono" were quite enough to travel with in Turkey, and I found "vino, vino" sufficient in Spain. By the time that my Spaniard had completed his stable arrangements he saw I had formed an alliance with "Tom, Dick, and Harry," and that we had finished a couple of bottles of wine. I now left the management of my new acquaintances entirely in his hands, and if he thought more wine desirable it was ordered; but he was prudent, and knowing his countrymen, it was "the cup which not inebriates." I especially noted the fact that, whenever we settled for the night, the landlady of the posada or albergo took great care of me, seeing that, when I retired to my sleeping-room, I had every thing she thought I might require during the silent watches, and then locked me up; but previous to this operation my attentive Spaniard came to me to see that I was safe and comfortable. I was reconciled to the imprisonment on beholding the wretched state of the country from civil war and its accompaniments—suspicion, revenge, and poverty: at the same time I was reminded of the Spanish proverb that "the open door tempts the saint" ("*Puerta abierta al santo tienta*"), so I consented without a murmur to the key being turned.

As usual, we were in our saddles at three o'clock next morning, and in two hours more at breakfast, winding up our repast with our bottle of Malaga. We were not again to draw rein until we entered the famed Vega of Granada, thirty leagues in circumference. Our ascent was gradual, but for some time I had been feasting my eyes on the Sierra Nevada; and, although the perspiration flowed at every pore, I had in perspective a region where the "cold snow melts not with the sun's hot beams." As for those of my countrymen who have not travelled in Spain, may I recommend them to visit the ancient city built by the Saracens, which was the last bulwark of the Moslems, and whose walls and fortresses, though defended by 100,000 men against Christian Spain, fell before the arms of Ferdinand and Isabella, in 1492? To those who travel but have seen only so much of the Alhambra as may be viewed at the Crystal Palace, I advise them to see the Alhambra of Granada, and view from its balcony the Vega and the Sierra Nevada. If I should be the means of inducing them to do this, I know they will thank me on their return.

107. *Spectacles* versus "*Preserves.*"

My English friends may be unaware that spectacles are frequently in Scotland called "preserves." As a boy I witnessed a ludicrous scene between an aged grand-aunt of mine and an English visitor at my father's. The old lady was born in 1738, twenty-two years before George III. ascended the throne, when, I believe, "preserves" was the universal term, in my part of Scotland, for spectacles. My aged relative, who was an accomplished woman, never gave them any other designation. "Pray give me my preserves." "Take care, boys, that you do not break my preserves." Our English friend was chatting with the interesting old lady (one who well recollected the Pretender and the execution on Tower Hill of those Scotch Peers who had supported his cause in 1745), when she asked him if he used "preserves." "I never eat them, madam." "Good gracious! eat your preserves!" "Madam, I assure you I never do." The old lady, who was on the verge of ninety, thought she was talking to a crazy person, and turning to her nephew, my father, said, in an audible whisper, "Is he right in his head?" "Oh, quite right." With this assurance she resumed the conversation by stating, "My good sir, I never thought that you would eat your preserves." He, in his turn, considered the old lady to be in her dotage, and by way, as he thought, of keeping up the joke, reminded her that she had asked him if he ever *used* preserves. "Yes, I did," at the same time becoming somewhat animated in her utterance; "and you told me you never *ate* them, as if I thought you would do any thing so absurd." My father's English friend now discovered that the nonagenarian lady could hold her own in debate, for he was completely puzzled; but as the parties present at this passage of arms had had their hearty laugh, my father, fearing further results, explained the synonyme to his friend, who instantly confessed his own stupidity to his aged combatant, and the *entente cordiale*, which at one time appeared endangered, was immediately resumed.

108. *The Late Governor Wall.*

Some forty-five years ago I had accompanied my father, who had never previously crossed the Channel, on a few weeks' excursion to France: we found ourselves, on an extremely wet and unusually cold evening for the season of the year, confined to the table-d'hôte room of the Hôtel du Nord, Boulogne, with a party of twenty or more English tourists unable to move outside the threshold. The consequence was, that as many of us settled round or as near the large stove as was practicable; the vin ordinaire, when finished, being replaced—owing to the temperature having suddenly become Norwegian—by Cognac and Schiedam. In that circle were to be found representatives of the senatorial, clerical, legal, military, naval, and mercantile professions. My father was a "grave and reverend seignior," born in 1770, of considerable conversational powers, with a retentive memory, and an experience of London extending over an eventful period in British history. He recollected the death of William Pitt's father, the famous Earl of Chatham, in 1778. He had seen a woman brought out to be burnt in front of Newgate for coining: the pile having been prepared during the night, was ignited about half an hour before the wretched creature appeared, and after going through the form of having first her right hand and then her left thrust into the flames, she was raised to the scaffold and hanged. He remembered the *éclat* which Prince William Henry, the third son of King George III., received as the first prince of the blood-royal who had ever landed in North America, etc.

The conversation flitted from Lord Ellenborough and the Court of King's Bench, to Lord Stowell and the Court of Admiralty; from Colonel Picton (Sir Thomas, who fell at Waterloo) and his alleged cruelty in the West Indies, to Governor Wall, who, while Governor of Goree in Africa, had ordered Benjamin Armstrong, a soldier, for some act of disobedience which he considered brought him within the powers of the Mutiny Act, to be tied to a gun to receive 800 lashes, under which he died. A peculiar feature attending the case was, that the punishment on the unfortunate man was inflicted on June 17, 1782, and on January 28, 1802, ex-Governor Wall was executed for it at Newgate. The circumstances led to the severest comments of the press, and public indignation was roused to such a point against Wall, that on reaching the British Channel on his return from Goree, he received a caution from his friends not to land, and escaped to Belgium, taking up his abode for the next twenty years at Ostend. At the end of this period, his friends and family connections in England deemed his expatriation no longer necessary. He had in the mean time married the Honorable Miss Mackenzie, a daughter of Lord Seaforth, by whom he had an only son. Mrs. Wall's sister was married to an English peer, and the relatives in England unfortunately believing that the affair at Goree, which had happened a fifth of a century before, was blotted out from the memories of the last generation, and could scarcely interest the rising one, persuaded the ex-Governor to put his foot on board an Ostend packet, and come to London, where, as my father informed us, he had not arrived many hours when he was arrested under the Home Secretary's warrant, brought before a magistrate, and committed to Newgate.

Several of the party had never heard of Governor Wall, and my father was requested to enter upon the subject at greater length than he intended, first exposing the cruelty of that article of war which authorized a sentence of 800 lashes, nay, even 900, so that it was kept under the legal maximum of 1,000. My father contended that Governor Wall had not exceeded the authority of the Draconic article of war under which he acted. He at the same time admitted that, if the witnesses gave their evidence free from prejudice and correctly, after an interval of twenty years, there were features in the case that militated against the ex-Governor in the public mind. The fate awaiting him was greatly accelerated and forced on the authorities by the excitement prevailing among the masses in London and through the great towns of the kingdom, who had been imbibing deeply the revolutionary doctrines of the day, dominant in France. Governor Wall's blood was called for, and the appetite of the populace for it was the more sharpened from the circumstance of the accused having been Governor of a British colony, and the son-in-law of one noble lord and the brother-in-law of another. The view my father took, as an impartial observer, and cognizant of the facts as derived at the time from the most reliable sources, was, that after the lapse of twenty years, which must have been a period of painful remorse and repentance if the conscience of the unhappy accused told him he had erred on the side of cruelty, the extreme penalty of the law should not have been carried out. There was one of our circle who took up my father's opinions strongly, and seemed to me as an attentive listener, even more familiar with the details than my relative; at the same time evidently on terms of intimacy with, or at least possessed of a full knowledge of, Wall's family connections. My father related an anecdote which this gentleman had never heard. It would appear that Mrs. Wall had come to London from Ostend, accompanied by her infant and its nurse, to see her family and spend a few weeks with an aunt of my mother's. One day, the old lady with my mother, then a girl, took Mrs. Wall's child with the nurse out in the carriage for a drive, during which she paid a visit to Lady Anne M——y, one not more distinguished by wealth and position than by the prominent part she took in all that was religious and charitable. On entering the drawing-room, the nurse and child following the old lady and her niece, the former said, "Lady Anne, I have brought Mrs. Wall's sweet little boy for you to see." "Take it away," exclaimed this Christian-minded lady, "I will never look upon the child of a murderer." "Oh, Lady Anne," said my aged relative, "not look upon this innocent child! What has this sweet infant to do with its father's offence?" But the appeal was of no avail. "Take it away, nurse, I will not look upon the child of a murderer." My father went on to say that he never could tolerate Lady

Anne's name afterward. The time had arrived for bedroom candles, the party dropping off one by one, until my father and this gentleman, who had taken so much interest in all that had been said about Governor Wall, with myself, were left a trio. The instant the last stranger had retired, the gentleman in question started to his feet, and addressing my father under the strongest feelings, said, "Sir, is this young gentleman your son?" "He is." "Then let me tell you that I am the child of the murderer. I have known who you were, sir, for the last hour. I have often heard my dear mother talk of you and your amiable wife, who I hope is still alive." "She is," my father said, almost unable to make the reply. Then followed a scene which Edmund Kean, whom I have beheld in the deepest tragedy, never surpassed, never equalled, for what I witnessed was reality. Here was the only child of Governor Wall, a captain of one of our Highland regiments, bursting into a paroxysm of grief, the tears rolling down his face, and almost throwing himself into my father's arms, his utterance nearly choked, exclaiming, "Ah, my revered and respected friend—if such you will permit me henceforth to consider you—your fair and impartial criticism of my unfortunate father's case has made me to-night the happiest of men."

Captain Wall for the following fifteen years was the cherished friend of the members of my family, when the tomb closed on the only descendant of Governor Wall.

109. *Mr. Samuel Anderson and the Siege of Seringapatam.*

Mr. Anderson, whose name is already familiar to my readers in the inside of a London omnibus, was a prodigious favorite with the late Mr. Charles Mathews, who frequently on his professional tours would sup with Mr. Anderson, who then resided in Edinburgh.

Sydney Smith, we are told, declared that it required a surgical operation to get a joke into a Scotchman's understanding. If it is so, I once witnessed a practical illustration of the fact. At a dinner-party in London, where Mr. Anderson was a guest, there was a general officer present (a Scotchman), and in some allusion to the siege of Seringapatam (1799) it transpired that he was there as a lieutenant in an infantry regiment. Anderson made capital of that fact at once, for my friend, as master of impromptu, and always anxious to oblige, knew he would be called upon. After the usual verse to the host and hostess and one or two other guests, he proceeded to open a most complimentary battery on the gallant General, attributing to him the whole success of the siege, and ultimate fall and capture of Seringapatam. When he had finished, up rose the General to thank Mr. Anderson for his verses and the company for their cheers, as well as to explain that he was the last man in the British army to claim a merit to which he was not justly entitled; he therefore wished it to be clearly understood that Mr. Anderson was entirely in error in attributing the successful termination of the assault to himself; that he was simply a lieutenant of His Majesty's — regiment of foot; that it was only fair and proper for him to explain that the officers entitled to the praise which Mr. Anderson had lavished on him were General Lord Harris, Major-General Sir David Baird, Lieutenant-Colonel James Dunlop (afterward General Dunlop, and many years M. P. for the Stewartry of Kirkcudbright), Lieutenant-Colonel the Hon. Arthur Wellesley, and Lieutenant-Colonel (afterward General Sir John) Sherbrook. "Ah, then," said the gifted maker of extemporaneous song, "I must, I find, add a few additional verses." He then complimented the general on his extreme modesty, told us that all the circumstances connected with the celebrated siege now flashed before him, that he could assure us he had not exaggerated the general's services in that brilliant action in the least, and that he could therefore allow no diminution to be made from the estimate he had formed and submitted to them of those services, etc. The poor General was again on his legs to offer further explanations, but they were of no avail, as he stood that evening proclaimed as the Hero of Seringapatam.

110. *The Scotch Laird and the French Language.*

The Laird of ——, a few years after the battle of Waterloo, took his family to France for economy and education. A former neighbor of his in Scotland, who had never been on the Continent, resolved about 1832 to visit his friend, who had taken up his abode at Tours or Dijon. The day after his arrival, he and his host (as cicerone) were strolling through the streets of the old town, the Laird explaining every thing minutely to the new-comer. At last they came to something which even puzzled the Laird, and greatly interested his visitor, who said, "Do ask this person to explain and tell us all about it." "*Na, na, naething o'* the kind," said the Laird, "for I *maun* (must) tell you that I hate the people and I hate their language, and *hae* I not *hauden weel aff* (have I not managed well) not to *hae pickt ony o'* it up in fourteen years?" "Well," said his visitor, "as you have considered France a country good enough to live in for the last fourteen years, I should not have turned my back so much upon the language as you appear so successfully to have done." The Laird made no reply.

111. *Taking Time by the Forelock.*

My grandmother once awoke my grandfather in the middle of the night, and told him that she much feared their son Willie, who slept next room to them, had become deranged, as she had been listening to him for some time speaking loudly and rapidly to himself. Her husband listened, and came to the same conclusion; and they forthwith hurried into their boy's bedroom to know what was the matter. Willie's explanation was, that as they were going to the seaside next day, he wished to save time, and was saying his prayers over and over to last him during the holidays.

This reminds me of our cook in Scotland, whom I found one night after twelve o'clock sipping her tea. "Hallo, cook! how late you are in drinking your tea." "Na, na, sir, I am *no* at my tea, I am at my breakfast, as I *thocht* it best to *tak* mine *afore ganging* to bed, as you and the *ither* young gentlemen *hae* ordered yours to be ready at five, that *ye mae* get aff in *guid* time to the *muirs.*"

112. *A Singular and Depressing Incident at the Close of a Public Meeting.*

The executive members of the Society for the Promotion of Australian Emigration and Colonization had been invited by the authorities at Brighton to hold a public meeting in the Town Hall, where we met a party of Chartists, who had assembled in considerable force to put the speakers down, and it was found no easy task to stem the torrent of fierce abuse by which we were assailed. After much time had been wasted, we at last succeeded in convincing the majority of the meeting, not only of the purity of our motives, but of the wisdom of our plans. We had to disabuse the minds of a certain section of our auditory of errors and prejudices, which might have done much to counteract the benevolent designs of the society. Our leading objects were—first, to afford the latest, fullest, and most authentic information regarding the Australian colonies; and next, by enlisting the rich in the cause, to help those who had not the entire means themselves, but were otherwise eligible, to reach our possessions in the southern hemisphere, whose prosperity was advancing at a rate to which history affords no parallel, and was limited only by the scanty supply of labor from the mother country.

Our meeting took place at eight o'clock in the evening, so that all classes might have the opportunity of attending. Some foolish exclamations, uttered in the body of the hall by persons who called themselves Chartists, demanded to be promptly corrected, as their example, it was feared, might lead to similar obstruction in the towns to which the society proposed to proceed in their tour of enlightenment and of assistance, in a matter of great interest to all classes, but vital to the laboring-classes of the Kingdom. The remarks I had intended to make in regard to Australia had to be postponed that I might assist in quelling the uproar that had so unexpectedly broken out. One of the Chartist speakers was a man of unquestionable talent and of great fluency, with a command of varied language seldom to be met with. He was a tall, intelligent-looking person, wearing a shabby-genteel blue military frock-coat, buttoned up to the throat; and apparently he was about thirty-six or thirty-eight years of age. Having made his own speech, he seemed determined that its effect should not be neutralized by any reply I could offer, for ever and anon he kept crying out, "Stay at home; there is plenty for all of us here." "*That,*" I exclaimed, in as loud a pitch of voice as I could command, "I very much doubt." My opponent, who was close in front of the platform, began, I suspect, to discover, that I, like himself, had a pretty loud and powerful voice, and although I did not presume, like a Stentor, to be able to silence the voices of fifty men together, I now decided to enter the lists with my troublesome adversary, and addressed him as follows: "I beg to assure my opponent that our interest alone, if no loftier feeling is conceded to us, is to see the emigrant comfortably embarked, well fed during the voyage, safely landed, and happily settled in that great possession of the British Crown. Really one would suppose, from what has been said in opposition, that no working-man in the United Kingdom finds it difficult on the Saturday night to provide what every one engaged in pastoral and agricultural labor in Australia receives as his weekly ration, namely, ten pounds of butcher's meat, ten pounds of flour, two pounds of sugar, and a quarter of a pound of tea. If this occasions you no difficulty—if you can lay your heads on your pillows and say to yourselves, 'Well, if death overtakes me, I leave my wife and children, if not in affluence, at least independent, with no poorhouse staring them in the face;' if this be your position, working-men of Brighton, I shall not ask you to emigrate against your inclination; but if your wives and children are not guarded against such a contingency, I consider that a heavy responsibility attaches to any man in this assembly who dissuades you from listening to the advice we tender you."

My turbulent opponent with his colleagues had early in the evening enlisted a party of sailors to aid him in his attempt to interrupt our proceedings; and I thought that, if I could by some means conciliate them, as the Chartist orator had considerately allowed me to deliver the foregoing lengthy sentence without a single interruption, we might still hope to get into smooth water. Looking toward the nautical section of the crowded assembly, as I was "in possession of the house"—or rather wished to be—I said: "I can tell you the loaves and fishes are in Australia, and I wish you to have your share of them.[1] Yes, my friends, and when I say fishes, let me tell those honest-hearted and hardy-looking blue-jackets I see before me, that the fisheries

[1] Whale-fishing was at that time a very profitable source of commerce on the Australian coasts, and highly popular with sailors, who were paid by certain lays or shares on the profits of the voyage, in addition to monthly wages.

of Australia present a splendid field for the enterprise of the men of the Sussex coast; I can tell you that there is an inexhaustible field for your industry on the coasts of Australia." Jack had now become an attentive listener, and the Chartist element had also subsided, but I thought I might farther ingratiate myself by still spinning a short yarn with Jack, so on I went. "Moreover, I tell you, that the shipowner, in consequence of the want of hands, is entirely at the mercy of those he has there, who are so petted and spoiled by high wages and the luxuries of that brilliant climate, that they have almost lost the character of British tars." The only interruption I now received from the sailors, who had given up their allegiance to the Chartist leader, was a round of cheers. I then proceeded: "Now, here is an instance of my meaning. A relation of mine has a large steamer running from Sydney to Adelaide in South Australia, calling at the intermediate ports. On a late occasion, mentioned to me in my last letters, the steam was up, the bell ringing for the start, the passengers assembled on deck (we may fancy ourselves at the end of the chain-pier witnessing the occurrence), when my brother went on board, and found his captain, mate, and engineer in dismay. The captain informed him that the crew had gone to drink at a public-house close by, saying he must wait *their* pleasure. My brother had a party of South-Sea Islanders working for him at his wharf—for such is the scarcity of sailors that a large portion of every crew consists of New-Zealanders, and every day the South-Sea Islander is becoming a more and more valuable addition to our mercantile marine in that part of the world. The captain was asked if with twenty picked men of those at the wharf the steamer could put to sea. He said 'Yes,' and in the course of a few minutes the owner was seen at the head of a band of fine athletic South-Sea Islanders, hurrying to the vessel. This was too personal for Jack" (the Brighton blue-jackets enjoyed the story very much), "as the movement had been observed from the public-house, and the party there started off at last, only just beating their wild competitors, and the steamer went out of harbor with her proper but over-indulged crew. This, my friends, is no exaggerated picture of the want of labor."

My speech, which was entirely different to the one I had intended to make, and had commenced so inauspiciously, was well received, and the resolution I had to propose was passed by acclamation.

The meeting did not break up until midnight, and while pushing through the crowd with the mayor and other members of the Brighton Corporation and of our own deputation, I found myself jostling against the man who had opposed me so vehemently in the commencement of my speech. I said, "Hallo! how is it that a man of your ability should have such mistaken views on the subject of emigration and colonization?" He pressed my hand, and, in a subdued tone, or rather whisper, said, "Mr. Boyd, I am starving." I was so much taken by surprise as to be unable to make a reply for the moment, so many contending thoughts flashed through my mind. "What do you mean?" He shook his head, and again in a whisper declared it was too true, he was starving. "Let me speak to you," I said, "when we get outside the building." Accordingly I walked with him to the back of the Town-Hall, while my party went to our hotel, when he burst into a flood of tears and repeated not only that he himself was starving, but all at home were—a wife, two children, and an aged mother. His little history was, that he was a North of Ireland man, had received a good education, and had served his apprenticeship as a tailor; had then enlisted in one of our Hussar regiments, in which he became one of the tailors, and the regiment having been stationed at Brighton, where he had several friends, he was recommended, when he got his discharge, to settle there as a journeyman; but, instead of finding full employment, he was sometimes five days in the week without any work. Having given him some temporary relief for his poor family and himself, I then asked him if he would like to emigrate to Australia; his reply was, that he should like nothing better. I therefore gave him my card for our secretary, whom he called upon next day, and for months I supposed he had sailed for the colony; but it appeared that, when all the poor man's arrangements were complete, a difficulty arose, of which I as a member of committee was not informed, about his aged mother (from whom he would not separate) accompanying the family; in consequence his plan to emigrate through the assistance of our Colonial fund was upset; whereas, had I been aware of the obstacle, a few pounds would have removed it. However, his noisy eloquence at our meeting made him somewhat prominent at Brighton, and secured him, as I was happy to learn, what he so much needed, full and continuous employment. This was fortunate, for, in the state of mind of that man with which I was made familiar inside, and subsequently outside, the Town-Hall of Brighton, he was then only fit "for treasons, stratagems, and spoils."

113. *The Three Clerks at Cambridge.*

Among many excellent anecdotes I have heard my friend the Rev. Arthur Hubbard relate, was the following: He was on a visit to his father, a rector, near Lewes, in Sussex, and met at dinner Dr. Carr, the Bishop of Chichester, to whom he was introduced for the first time. In the course of the evening the bishop asked him whether he had been at Oxford or at Cambridge. "The latter, my lord." "Then you can enable me to answer a question I was recently asked by His Majesty (George IV.), with whom I am to have the honor of dining to-morrow at the Pavilion. Were there three professors at Cambridge at the same time of the name of Clerk?" "There were, my lord; Stone Clerk, Professor of Mineralogy; Tone Clerk, Professor of Music; and Bone Clerk, Professor of Anatomy."

The bishop thanked Mr. Hubbard, and said he had enabled him to give His Majesty the information he required.

Mr. Hubbard on that occasion related an anecdote which the bishop had not before heard, and probably it was repeated the following day at the royal table after the three Clerks, Stone, Tone, and Bone, had been served up. A clergyman had commenced an able discourse, when one of the hearers, an accomplished but eccentric man, exclaimed, "That's Tillotson!" This was allowed to pass, but very soon another exclamation followed: "That's Paley!" The preacher then addressed the disturber: "I tell you, sir, if there is to be a repetition of such conduct, I shall call on the churchwarden to have you removed from the church." "That's your own!" was the ready reply.

114. *Dr. Blomfield, Bishop of Chester, afterward Bishop of London.*

The Rev. Mr. Hubbard was dining with his friend and neighbor, Mr. Conyers, at Copthall in Essex. One of the guests was Lord Raglan, who was on the eve of his departure to take command of the British Army destined for the Crimea.

The conversation took a clerical turn, in the course of which Mr. Hubbard repeated the lines epitomizing part of a charge addressed, as it was alleged, by Dr. Blomfield to his clergy in the course of his primary visitation of the Diocese of Chester.

Hunt not, dance not,
Fiddle not, flute not,
Avoid every evening party,
Especially never play at écarté—
Interfere not with the Whigs,
But stay at home and mind your pigs,
But it is my particular desire
That, once in the week at least, you dine with the Squire.

Lord Raglan was so much amused with the lines that, on reaching the drawing-room, he requested Mr. Hubbard to write them out for him, which he did, little supposing at the moment that the noble lord, who had already run so eventful a soldier's career in the Peninsula, closing it, as might reasonably have been expected, on the plains of Waterloo in 1815, was about to reopen it in 1854, to fight the battles of the Alma and Inkermann, but never again to meet the festive circle at Copthall.

Lord Raglan's calm death in camp, after braving the battle-fields of Fuentes d'Onore, Badajoz, Salamanca, Vittoria, Pyrenees, Nivelle, Orthes, Toulouse, and Waterloo (where he lost an arm), Alma and Inkermann, reminds me of the epitaph I have read in Westminster Abbey to a General of a former century—Sir Francis Vere:[1]

When Vere sought death, armed with his sword and shield,
Death was afraid to meet him in the field;
But when his weapons he had laid aside,
Death, like a coward, struck him, and he die l

115. *The Post-Office.*

I have an agreeable recollection of a very pleasant dinner I had at the General Post-office with the late Sir Henry Freeling. I was the escort to a party of friends from the country, to witness, on the royal birthday, an

[1] A distinguished General of Queen Elizabeth, born in 1554, died in 1608, and buried in Westminster Abbey.

interesting sight—which railways have superseded—the departure, at eight o'clock, of nineteen mail-coaches out of the twenty-five which then left London every evening. The guards and coachmen on such occasions were in their new liveries, and the horses also frequently had new harness. Sir Henry, from his long intercourse with society in every phase, from royal princes down to letter-carriers, was full of anecdotes, and no one could relate them better. Among others, he mentioned the extraordinary change for the better that had suddenly taken place in the habits of the mail-guard and coachman; as, when he first entered the department, under his father, Sir Francis, one of his duties in the morning was to inspect all the way-bills, containing the postmaster's and guard's logs of the journeys of each mail-coach throughout the kingdom, and it was quite frightful in those days to look through the recital of accidents. A day without some such misfortune was of rare and exceptional occurrence. Sir Henry said that four of the accidents out of six were occasioned through the drunkenness of the coachman, and too frequently the guard was a participator in the offence; and at the root of the evil were the passengers themselves. "Well, coachman, it is a cold night, what will you have to drink?" But for this mistaken kindness, the coachman and the guard would have been, comparatively speaking, sober men, as they could not afford to be otherwise. A fresh light unexpectedly broke upon the fraternity, and an important diminution of the drunkenness existing ensued. Two mail-guards had been appointed on the London journey who were men of steady and sober habits, whose social position was somewhat superior to their colleagues, and who never went beyond a glass of sherry.

"Vy, Bill, can't ve drink sherry wine ven ve hare haxed, has vell has the two nobs?" "But, Bob, you must recollect, they von't drink hale neither; that's a stickler, ain't hit?"

Such was a conversation heard in the Post-Office yard one evening before the mails started, and reported to Sir Henry, who, although amused, was deeply interested as to the result. He assured me no revolution was so instantly carried out among mail-guards and coachmen throughout England, and at the period of this conversation taking place between him and myself, he declared he would almost make a bet that if I, travelling by one of the mails from the London Post-Office yard, offered a guard or coachman a glass of gin he would refuse it, and if I put the question in another shape, the answer would be, "Thank you, sir, a glass hof sherry vine, or a glass hof port, hif hit his hall the same." The emphasis, as Sir Henry added, "halvays hon vine." The blessed results of the change were that our sovereign's loyal subjects henceforth travelled, comparatively speaking, in safety by mail-coach, casualties diminishing in number as sobriety kept increasing.

After assuring him that I had listened with deep attention to the valuable statistical information he had given me, I had to request him to enlighten me on another point, as he appeared to me to inflict on delinquent mail-guards, in some cases, an extraordinary class of punishment. He smiled, and inquired to what I alluded. "Well, I shall tell you, but it must be without prejudice—I hope with advantage to the party." This being promised, I mentioned that I had been shooting grouse the previous autumn in the far north—Caithnesshire—and that, in travelling by the Thurso and Inverness mail, in walking up one of the hills with the other passangers and talking to the guard (we were not far from John O'Groat's at the time), I discovered he was a Cockney. "How comes it, guard, that you are in this part of the world?" "You may vell say that, sir, the fact being, that hi ham han hexile hof Siberia." "An exile of Siberia, what do you mean?" "Vy, sir, hi vas hon the Hexeter Road vonce, hi vas hindeed, hand hi vas halso hon the good hold Bath Road; hin fact, hon the best roads hout hof London, hand now, sir, hi ham on the werry vorst. Please, sir, jump hin hand hi'll tell you the rest hat next 'ill." At next 'ill I was made master of the affair, which, in brief, was, that "vicked people habout the 'ead hoffice 'ad told the secretary that hi, has mail-guard hon duty, vas hin liquor ven hi 'anded hin the letter-bags vone morning—hit vas a preshus cold morning—hand hi 'ad honly a drop o' rum-hand-milk hon han hempty stomach."

Sir Henry recollected the circumstance of the guard in question being sent to Siberia, as he described it; and he authorized me on my next vist to the northern Scotch county to tell him that when he, Sir Henry, learned that he had not transferred his taste from English gin to Scotch whiskey, he might expect to be recalled from Siberia, but not till then.

I promised to note this; at the same time I recommended Sir Henry to enter upon his own agenda-sheet the fact that the natives of the counties of Caithness and Sutherland had as much dislike to having their necks broken through the agency of a banished, drunken, English mail-coach guard, as the inhabitants of Middlesex or Berkshire. He promised duly to register in the archives of the Post-Office the view I had propounded, as he held the county of Caithness, and all members of the clan Sinclair, and especially the conservative section of it, in high respect.

116. *The Cutty-Stool, or Scotch Stool of Repentance.*

I find I have the advantage of Dean Ramsay, if it can be called so, in having witnessed in early life, at least half a dozen times, one of the most painful exhibitions that could possibly be witnessed under any circumstances, more particularly in the house of God.

The Very Reverend Dean observes: "A circumstance

connected with Scottish church discipline has undergone a great change in my time. I mean the public censure from the pulpit, in the time of divine service, of offenders previously convicted before the minister and his Kirk session. This was performed by the guilty person standing up before the congregation on a raised platform, called the *cutty-stool*, and receiving a rebuke. I never saw it done," says the Dean, "but have heard in my part of the country of the discipline being enforced occasionally." The Dean then proceeds: "Indeed, I recollect an instance where the rebuke was thus administered, and received, under circumstances of a touching character, and which made it partake of the 'moral sublime.'"

The case I am about to give, and which I witnessed in our parish church, partook, to a large extent, of the "moral ridiculous." We shall all agree with the Dean, as the most distinguished delineator of Scottish character, that such public censures "were more honored in the breach than the observance." I must preface the instance I am about to describe by stating that my father had for a lengthened period used all *legitimate* means to see abrogated and annulled what he considered a most *illegitimate* method of inflicting Church censure, and contended that if the Church of Scotland, in its wisdom, believed such a mode of public exposure was the only proper course of stopping one *crying* evil—which my father ventured to declare it never would have the effect of doing—the least that the heads of families in the parish had a right to expect was to be previously apprised when the miserable exhibition of a poor erring creature on the cutty-stool was to come off, so that the female branches of their families might have the opportunity of staying at home. I think my father even threatened to raise a fund to meet the fines from time to time, which, if paid to the Kirk session, saved the wretched exposure. He declared that the enormity should be bracketed with whiskey-drinking as the great scandal of Scotland. The pecuniary fine to supersede the necessity of standing, not in a white sheet, but in a long blue-headed woollen cloak, averaged from three to five pounds, the receipt of which, by the Kirk session, my relative pronounced to be the very sublimation of the mammon of unrighteousness. "Condonation," he exclaimed, "can be purchased in my parish at from sixty to one hundred shillings for each offence." He lived before his time, for, with all deference to clerical authority, he held that if "the rebuke" (the term used) in accordance with the ecclesiastical canon, could not be dispensed with, it should be administered within the closed doors of the sacred edifice; in fact, as executions now take place *inside* not *outside* the walls of Newgate. The worthy clergyman of our parish, a Doctor of Divinity, and one of the most amiable men in the Church of Scotland, had been in early life my father's tutor, and he therefore conceived he might reasonably endeavor to exercise some wholesome influence with his reverend friend to stop such obnoxious and revolting proceedings, which he designated a public scandal and disgrace in a civilized country. However, I presume, as a clergyman, he could not procure the consent of his presbytery. My father, in his indignation, declared it to be an item of Church revenue, easily raised from the affluent offender, whereas, not so in regard to her who should have been admonished privately, and counselled in soothing language by her pastor "to go and sin no more," but not through the channel of a public exposure. In "Hamlet," we are told, "For 'tis the sport to have the engineer hoist with his own petard."

Many of us know, from bitter experience, how often the pioneer of improvements and reforms has to be sacrificed himself before the goal he aimed at is reached. These words will apply to my father, who contributed in no small degree to the removal of a most offensive custom, as the following incident proved the death-knell to the solemn mockery of the *cutty-stool* in my parish :

Before the abolition of the slave-trade, there was, from my district, in Scotland, an excellent young man who was surgeon of one of the ships carrying slaves from the African to the American coast. He had returned to London after one of his voyages, and had come into Surrey, where my father and mother resided, to pass the Saturday and Sunday with them. He was accompanied by a little black boy, the hero of this tale, and through whom an important reform was effected. The child was too delicate to be landed in South Carolina; and the kind-hearted doctor brought the poor little fellow with him home. My mother said to the young doctor, "You have acted your part by this child, and I should now desire to act mine, and bring him up." The youthful surgeon was delighted to hear this. She then said that, as her own infant (my eldest brother) was to be baptized in a few days, it was her intention her little African charge should at the same time be received within the bosom of the Church, and that, when the day was fixed, she would apprise him (the doctor), as she wished that he should be present. The day arrived, and the party was assembled in the church; my mother's infant had received his baptismal name, and now came his little African colleague to receive his. My father and mother had not thought of a name when the clergyman made the inquiry. It had of course to be fixed instanter. "Well," said my father, "what shall it be?" "Don't you think, my dear," said my mother, "you had better give him your own name?" "A very good idea, and my name he shall have," and forthwith received it. Young Africanus was to all appearance between eleven and twelve years of age. He began his lessons, the first being to get rid of a habit of swearing which the sailors had taught him. For other literature he showed no particular taste; but his immense affection for the baby had no bounds: he was always volunteering his services as nurse; in fact, ever since the baptismal ceremony, Dick—the name the servants gave him, and by which he was known for the next thirty-eight years (Edward Boyd was the name the parson gave him)—claimed a joint proprietorship in my mother's infant, and jealously did he insist on his rights, to an extent that sometimes was troublesome. Next to baby, his affections centred on horses, and nothing did he relish so much as being put on the back of one; but he had so many falls my father told him he should not again mount a horse until he had learned to ride—on the principle of learning to swim before going into the water. My father, finding his instructions on this head so little attended to by Dick, saw that the sooner he commenced his equestrian studies the better, and the plan he adopted to teach him was this: He desired the youngster to be dressed in his Sunday suit, with the addition of his upper coat, and his riding-horse, which was extremely fresh, to be brought out. Dick was firmly strapped on, and the strapping being concealed under the upper coat, the groom led the horse to the edge of Clapham Common, and let him loose, my father and a few visitors being present. Both horse and rider seemed to enjoy the fun. Dick grinned with intense delight, showing his brilliant set of teeth to all who came near him and his Bucephalus. Mr. Boyd's little black lad was immortalized that day on Clapham Common as one of the most fearless riders whom the residents had ever seen, as no straps were visible. The horse kicked, leaped, pranced, and galloped about the Common for two hours, at the end of which, Tom, the horse, thinking that he had had enough of it, trotted leisurely back to his stable.

One day my father, at his country residence, recollected that he had omitted an important message to the captain of one of his ships, to sail that night from Gravesend.

There were no steamboats or railways in those days, but twenty-five miles to be accomplished by turnpike-road, and his groom and coachman were both absent. Dick had been up and down to Ramsgate during the summer, and had the bump of locality largely developed. He heard my father expressing to himself his anxiety as to how a communication could reach the captain of the ship "Wheatfield" at Gravesend. "Massa, me go to Gravesend." "You go to Gravesend!" said my father, "you don't know the way." "Me do, massa; me go Blackheath, Dartford, den Gravesend." "Well, Dick, that is quite right, but you can't ride Tom." "O massa, me ride Tom every day you in London." This my father long suspected. "Now, Dick, if I send you with an important letter for Captain Young of the ship 'Wheatfield,' what will you do?" "Massa, me go to Gravesend, me put up Tom at de stable, den me go down to de sea and take de boat, and me say, 'Take me to de ship "Wheatfield,"' and me go on board, and Captain Young know Dick, and me say, 'Captain, me have letter from massa in my pocket, and you, Captain, take it out, and you write massa letter,' and me bring back letter to you, massa." "That will do very well, Dick—now go and dress yourself, and tell a man from the garden to saddle Tom and bring him round." In a quarter of an hour Dick was off to Gravesend with the letter sewn in his coat, and ten shillings in his pocket to pay his expenses.

My father's mind was quite relieved, and he was much pleased with Dick's precocity and readiness. Within an hour Tom came galloping back without his rider. Dick, of course, was supposed to be somewhere having his wounds dressed, and the opportunity lost for dispatching this important letter. While my father was puzzling what was to be done, up drove a coach with Dick in or on it, uninjured, and the letter equally safe; but Dick was mortified in the extreme to learn that Tom had reached home first.

There was no time for Dick's vivid description as to the manner in which Tom had dislodged him from his back, for in ten minutes my father was himself on it, reached Gravesend in a marvellously short time, and delivered his dispatch in person.

Dick's first step of promotion in our family was to that position now termed "buttons," but in this capacity he was at times inconveniently ingenuous. On one occasion, during a dinner-party, there was something asked for out of the common way, upon which he announced to the whole room that there was none in the house. My mother next day said, "Dick, you must not in future be at a loss, nor must you speak so loud." Shortly after this, my mother having gone on a visit for the day, my father had for a guest his old friend, Sir James Shaw, who used to tell the following anecdote of Dick: Tea was ordered, and Dick was desired to pour it out. Sir James and my father discovered it was only hot water and milk. "Dick," exclaimed my father, "there is no tea!" "No, massa, no tea. Missy take away the keys." "Then why did you give us hot water?" "Cause, massa, missy always say to me, 'Dick, never be at a loss.'"

I must now carry Dick down to Scotland, where he spent the next twenty-five years—the horse Tom about fifteen of that number, half of which he carried that glorious old soldier on his back, General the Hon. Sir William Stewart, to whom my father presented him—hero and horse having now both gone on the retired list.

Dick was pronounced, whether in the capacity of footman or butler, one of the best servants to be met with. He was honest, obliging, and affectionate. Probably he had too much of the last quality. The dinner was served up one Saturday, when suddenly our cook resigned the seals of office which she had held for years with the highest of characters, and retired to her relations in our village.

Next day being Sunday, when tittle-tattle rules round the kirk-door, before and after service, to any conceivable extent, a dreadful rumor was floated to the effect that a "little stranger" had appeared, of somewhat an African hue. Dick's uneasy manner and chop-fallen look soon showed that he knew the secret of the rumor, and that he did not dispute the honors of paternity. My father's distress was acute, for he mourned bitterly over the loss of his excellent cook. My poor mother viewed the case from a more serious point. She feared there had been something terribly defective on her part, although she was always exhorting Dick to be sober-minded, and endeavoring to mould him as much as possible after the character of Joseph.

A few weeks had passed over, and the subject was dying gradually away. We were all at Church—the sermon was over, the last hymn sung, when the clergyman announced, with the usual solemnity, that we were to keep our seats, as a most painful and needful duty had to be performed, *videlicet* to "administer a rebuke." There was nothing which so instantaneously or so magically riveted the attention of His Majesty's liege subjects in a Scotch kirk as these words.

There stood a tall woman, dressed and hooded in a long blue cloak. My father's countenance was now mantling with indignation to find that he was still no more successful "in putting down" this enormity than the sagacious alderman who was bent on "putting down suicide." But he was utterly unprepared for what was now to be enacted in the presence of a large and respectable congregation, including his own wife and family. "There you stand," said the clergyman, adding the name of my father's late cook; and after the two awful words, "heinous crime," etc., followed the name proper of his black man Dick, who, it will be recollected, was christened after his master, Edward Boyd. "What's in a name?" A great deal more than is agreeable, thought my father at that moment, as he sat in the front seat of the gallery overhanging the pulpit, and was forced to listen to the administration of the rebuke.

Sydney Smith, the witty Dean of St. Paul's, said that we should never have safety in railway travelling, until a bishop was burnt in one of the carriages; and here was my father, one of the most active magistrates of his county, if not *burnt*, at least thoroughly *roasted*, for no one would admit that black "Dick" was recognized by any other name, and it was not very easy for my father to persuade people in Wigtonshire that Dick was not really Dick, but Edward.

"Well," said my father, "I acknowledge I am hoisted with my own petard, but my execution shall be the grave of the cutty-stool in this parish." And so it was.

117. *A Lincolnshire Parson and his Diocesan.*

My late friend the Rev. Dr. W. Wright, a tithe of whose anecdotes I wish I could bring to my recollection, told an excellent one that occurred within his diocese, Lincoln. A brother clergyman, a character in his way, and a favorite with his bishop and every one else, had a parish in an extremely fenny district. The bishop, taking the position into consideration, authorized the incumbent to perform duty only every alternate Sunday during the winter. But a complaint having reached his lordship that the reverend gentleman had not had the doors of his church open for the previous six weeks, he was obliged to administer a sharp letter of rebuke. To this the parson replied, "My lord, I have had the honor to receive your lordship's letter, and all I have, in explanation to your lordship, to say is, that the devil himself cannot get at my parishioners during the winter, and I promise your lordship to be before him in the spring."

The doctor used to describe the manner in which an auctioneer was interfered with in the sale of the next presentation to a living. He was expatiating, in the usual eloquent strain, on the prospect of an early succession. The incumbent was present as a matter of curiosity. "Why, gentlemen," said the auctioneer, "the holder of the living is seventy-four years of age, with one foot in the grave." At this announcement up started the reverend gentleman, a stout, hale man, stamped loudly on one foot and then on the other, when he requested the knight of the hammer to tell him which foot was interred.

Dr. Wright's story of the Lincolnshire parson and his bishop, reminds me of a story I have met somewhere of the poor minister in a far north parish in Scotland, who was called over the *coals* for describing the lower regions as a cold and bleak abode, very different to what we are taught to believe them to be. He acknowledged the charge brought against him, for which he had only one observation to make, that his parish was about the most frigid, wretched, and miserable in point of climate of any in Scotland, and had he described Satan's kingdom as being a warm region, his parishioners would have been off to it in a body long since!

118. *The Chiltern Hundreds.*

Our nearest neighbor in Scotland was the Hon. Montgomery Stewart, fourth son of John, seventh Earl of Galloway. He represented the county of Kirkcudbright in Parliament from 1804 to 1812, and died in 1860. There was a story in connection with the Chiltern Hundreds which I often heard at Mr. Stewart's and my father's table, and which I hope I may relate with as much piquancy as it deserves. "Ah," he would say, "the acceptance of the Chilterns usually brings something good, but it was not so in my case." After a tremendous contest, in which almost more money was spent and more bitter feeling generated, than ever was witnessed at any county election in Scotland, Mr. Stewart was elected M. P. for the stewartry of Kirkcudbright. After the election, the noble earl, his father, said to him, "Monty, I wish you to sign this letter." The young and obedient senator acceded to this as a matter of course, especially as he had been desired to do so by one who had just helped to raise him to his proud position. He entered the House of Commons as the supporter of the politics of his family, which were those of the Government then in power (that of Mr. Pitt); the Earl of Galloway, I should add, was a knight of the Thistle, and one of the lords of the bedchamber to George the Third, and, a few years previously, had been created an English baron. I think it not improbable that his father, in taking this letter, had some misgivings in regard to his son's political creed.

A struggle subsequently arose between two rival and competitive statesmen, Viscount Castlereagh and George Canning. The member for Kirkcudbrightshire became the friend and ardent admirer of Canning, and so long as he restricted himself to admiration of the man, and of his eloquence, no injury could be inflicted on those family interests and political prospects that might be looming in the future. But a hostile vote in favor of Mr. Canning and against the noble lord who was the all-powerful member of a strong Government—this was an act of heresy and disobedience not to be easily forgiven.

It would appear that Mr. Canning had moved, in a speech of unrivalled eloquence, an amendment to a motion introduced by Lord Castlereagh, and divided the House against the noble lord. The division list, next morning, to the surprise and indignation of Lord Galloway, gave his son's name as a supporter of Canning. Although highly incensed, he did not send for his mutineer son, but took another course. He went to his escritoir and took out the letter which his then dutiful and submissive son Monty had signed at his election. That letter, which required only the date to be inserted, was a very important document. It was an application addressed to the Speaker of the House of Commons for the Stewardship of the Chiltern Hundreds. The Earl placed the letter in the hands of a member who, on the House meeting, moved that a new writ be issued for the county of Kirkcudbright, vacant by the acceptance of the Stewardship of the Chiltern Hundreds by the Honorable Montgomery Stewart, who, quite unconscious that his father had made himself so busy that day to obtain an office under the Crown for him, sauntered down to the House some hour or two after his political extinction. A respectful bow as he was about to enter the House from the door-keeper rather surprised him, as the latter stood in front of the doorway. "Why, sir, I beg pardon, but you are not now in the House." "I know that, but I shall be in a minute." While exchanging words with the door-keeper, out came a member, who, I suppose, in the parlance of the present day, said, "Why, Stewart, what's up? A Lordship of the Treasury or Admiralty, no doubt. Ah, you Scotchmen, another job!" "What do you mean?" "Why, my dear fellow, you have taken the Chilterns." "Not I." "Well, all I can tell you is, that ——, two hours ago, moved for a fresh writ for your county." "All I can say is I know nothing of it." As the House of Commons had closed its doors against him for that night at least, a visit to the parental roof suggested itself, where, it may be supposed, a tolerable explosion followed. We must presume that the matter got well ventilated throughout the House, that the recently-appointed youthful Steward of the Chiltern Hundreds repudiated his appointment, and the Earl, having time to reflect on the bill of costs which his son's seat for Kirkcudbrightshire had already brought upon him, began to repent of his hasty act. His influence, however, was sufficient to have the letter withdrawn, as Mr. Stewart remained M. P. for the stewartry of Kirkcudbright until 1812. But I have been told on excellent authority, that even after the death of his father, which occurred in 1806, he was much too honest a politician to allow himself to be dictated to regarding his votes during the six remaining years of his Parliamentary life, and that this feeling of independence on his part frequently led to family differences which had better have been avoided.

119. *The Two Sir James Grahams of Netherby.*

Sir James Graham of Netherby was not distinguished as a politician, like his eminent son and successor James Robert George, who, it was said, inherited his great and varied talents from his mother, Lady Catherine Stewart, eldest daughter of John, seventh Earl of Galloway, to whom I have already referred; but he was an excellent man in all domestic relations—a kind and good landlord, and held in estimation by his tenantry and dependants. He was fond of a *bon mot*, and not unfrequently perpetrated one successfully. He was attending a county meeting at Carlisle, accompanied by his son, the embryo statesman, who had arrived a day or two before from Sicily, where he held a diplomatic appointment. An old friend of the house of Netherby came up to him in the street, when Sir James introduced him to his son, one of the handsomest young men of his day, upward of six feet in height, athletic and strongly built, whereas papa was a slight little man, of about five feet six inches. The introduction over, his friend remarked, "Why, Netherby, your son could put you in his pocket." "That may be, but all I can tell you is, he is never out of mine."

I at this moment recollect a rather singular occurrence

in connection with the future emminent statesman. His mother, Lady Catherine Graham, as a widow, resided with the then unmarried members of her family for a few years on Clapham Common in Surrey, and dining one day with an aunt of mine, accompanied by her son, Commander Charles Graham, R. N., when, talking over different matters with my father after dinner, connected with his profession, she remarked, "Ah, my brother James, with his extreme politics, has completely blasted my prospects in the service," etc. Within six months of that dinner-party, Sir James Graham was First Lord of the Admiralty.

Captain Graham, dining with my brother and myself shortly after the accession of Earl Grey to office, referred with a smile to the conversation he had had with my father as to the ruin of his prospects through the whiggery of his eldest brother! He was a witty and hospitable man on board his ship, and a good story is told of him on leaving Spithead for the Pacific, sending for his steward, and desiring him to keep every cork that was drawn for his *own* cabin. This order was strictly observed, for on his return at the end of three years such a collection or accumulation of corks was never before issued from any captain of a man-of-war's mess. Sir James laughed heartily when he heard of the extensive importation of corks from the South Seas, and asked his facetious sailor brother what he meant by it? "Well, James, you know you *speak* for the family, and I *drink* for it." "Charles, you are incorrigible." He died a vice-admiral.

120. *The Marquis of Blandford.*

One day Mr. Stewart called upon my father with his handsome and agreeable nephew, the Marquis of Blandford, afterward George, fifth Duke of Marlborough, who had got himself into a double scrape. It appeared that, on the previous Sunday, in posting across the country from Glasgow, his man had let the dogs down to have a run: they soon found game. His lordship forgot the day, and his servant forgot to remind him of it, nor was the proprietorship of the land inquired into. His gun was in instant requisition, and a brace of grouse bagged, but, unfortunately, on the property of a laird who was on the reverse of friendly terms with the noble family of Galloway. The report soon spread that the son-in-law of an exemplary peer was seen shooting on the Sabbath, and committing a trespass on another man's estate, in addition to the offence against the "Sabbath." "What is to be done, Boyd?" "Well," said my father, "my opinion is founded upon the answer the German innkeeper gave to a former Duke of Brunswick, who, while travelling, had stopped with his suite to breakfast at his auberge. When the duke called for his bill, he observed an enormous charge for eggs, and sent for the landlord, holding the bill in his hand. 'Why, eggs must be very scarce in this country?' 'Oh, no your Serene Highness, eggs are not at all scarce, but grand-dukes are!' Therefore," said my father, addressing Mr. Stewart, "you and I must not interfere; but as young and handsome marquises are scarce in this country, the ladies of the offended laird's family must be consulted; and my advice is" (addressing the marquis) "that you drive over to the laird without delay, confess your fault, and apologize to the ladies for having overlooked the sanctity of the day, and, if I mistake not, you will return to your uncle's with a verdict of acquittal." The advice was forthwith followed, and next day the marquis came to see my father, to thank him for his sound counsel, which had been more than realized, for, in addition to the hospitality he met with, the laird gave him *carte blanche* to shoot over his lands then and in all times to come. How the marquis settled his offence with the clergy I forget; but I assume that the clergyman and elders of the parish in which the brace of grouse were slain either passed a bill of indemnity or granted the young lord of Blenheim a free pardon.

121. *Admiral M'Kerlie and Sir James Graham.*

My late gallant friend Admiral John M'Kerlie, then a post-captain, had been invited to join at Mr. Stewart's a party of distinguished sportsmen, one of whom was the First Lord of the Admiralty, his own nephew, the late Sir James R. G. Graham. It was arranged that they were to shoot in pairs. "M'Kerlie," said Mr. Stewart, "you had better shoot with the First Lord, and *make your game!*" The post-captain had lost his right arm in action under Sir Edward Pellew (Lord Exmouth), but was an excellent shot. During the day Sir James asked him if he ever intended again to go afloat. "That, sir, entirely rests with the First Lord of the Admiralty." "Oh, I am very glad," said the First Lord, "that I asked the question, as we are bringing forward two frigates for commission, the 'Vernon,' and the 'President,' and you shall have one of them;" and at the same time he made a memorandum in his pocket-book. The promise was kept, and my esteemed and gallant friend—a Trafalgar officer—served his full time on the active list, and died a rear-admiral, highly respected in life and deeply regretted at its close.

122. *How to get rid of Tramps.*

I was lately dining with a gallant and hospitable friend of mine in a suburban county, and a discussion after dinner arose on different country annoyances to which a resident proprietor was exposed, particularly within a certain radius of London. Among our party there was a very agreeable member, who had passed many years in the Life Guards, and knew the environs of the great metropolis, and its social grievances and their remedies, better than any of us. "Well," said our host, "there is one I would thank you immensely to cure for me: as I am pestered and overrun daily with tramps." "Yes," answered the veteran ex-officer, "that I can easily do. I will give you a leaf out of my elder brother's book; and if your servants will act strictly up to it, I promise a speedy and effectual remedy. The year after my brother was High-Sheriff of Berkshire, he was annoyed, beyond measure, by tramps, and after pondering for some time for a preventive, he bethought himself of the following: He told his butler to apprise him of the first tramp that appeared; and, in accordance with routine, there was an early arrival, the bearer of the usual tale—'Starving, sir, hi hassure you; not a ha'porth o' bread, hor a morsel o' wittals, 'as passed down my throat since yesterday morning.' He had therefore a formidably thick slice of dry bread cut and handed to the starving tramp; and he waited until he saw him eat it. There was a glass of water in addition at the tramp's command; but this was optional, whereas eating the bread was compulsory. If he ate his slice of bread, he was then asked to say the Lord's Prayer, after which, if he was perfect in it, he was presented with one penny and desired to depart. Frequently the tramp, in telling his woful tale, had overlooked the fact of having previously breakfasted, and when the butler or other domestic presented him with his thick slice of bread, the dimensions of which were strictly adhered to, he found himself in a fix. He had then to move his ground. ''E 'adn't a-paid for 'is last night's lodging hin the willage vich 'e vished to do, hand a few coppers to make up jist has much has vould carry him hon to 'is hown parish.' Nothing would satisfy the ex-Sheriff. 'You said you had tasted no food since yesterday, and that you were starving; eat that bread and then I shall see what I can do for you.'

As the tramp's inner man was already full, this was impossible, and there was no alternative but to take himself off. Tramps, like other select bodies, meet at times in convocation for the discussion of important matters affecting the interests of their body. The High-Sheriff was declared in one of these convocations to be 'no good vatsomedever.' 'Vy, he stuffs vun vith dry bread, *jist* hafter *peraps* you've 'ad yer hown 'earty meal: then you must be hable to say the Lord's Prayer, hand hif you does this right, he pitches you a single copper; but hif you can't say no Lord's Prayer, you gets no copper. No, 'e hain't no good, that 'ere 'Igh-Sheriff, hand hif you takes my hadwice' (addressing a brother tramp about to start on a journey) 'you von't bother wid 'im, for hit's a no good.' In this way my brother relieved himself from tramps in Berkshire, and you may do the same in Surrey."

123. *Matrimony.*

Some twenty years ago, a middle-aged spinster lady told me I should rank among the greatest discoverers of my period, and that, although the present generation might delay weaving my chaplet, a future one would not fail to deck my tomb. I felt overwhelmed, as well I might, with the astounding announcement, and I begged her to explain. She assured me that those of her own sex with whom she had conversed on the subject, declared that I had discovered the philosopher's stone, and solved a problem which the immortal Newton had never even attempted. Moreover, she added, that had she known me twenty years earlier, and listened to the wisdom that had fallen from my lips, she would have followed implicitly the advice I then gave.

I was so overcome by the announcement that I scarcely dared to ask what I had achieved in mathematics to have my name connected with that of Sir Isaac Newton; I consequently confined myself to one inquiry. "Pray, madam, is it in pure or mixed mathematics that my elevation has been gained?" "Oh, in mixed." I hurried over in my mind what I deemed a simple task, i. e., every problem from the *pons asinorum* to the last I ever attempted to solve; and I still failed to discover the source of my mental pre-eminence. She at once referred me to a speech that I had delivered in the Town-Hall of Birmingham on December 14, 1848, when engaged in "the heroic work of colonization." I had been expatiating at some length on the manifold advantages which Australia offered, my anxiety being to divert some portion of the huge current of emigration from the United States and the Canadas to the vast island continent of Australia. Among other topics on which I enlarged, was that of a wife and family being a source of capital and strength to a man in our southern colonies, instead of being, as is too often the case at home, of encumbrance and poverty. Then turning my eyes to the galleries occupied by the ladies, I called attention to the fact of the arrival of the ship "William Stewart" at Melbourne in the previous July with an interesting list of passengers, among whom there were twenty young spinsters, eight of whom were married next day.

In reference to this statement, in a short article under the title of "The Land for the Lasses," Mr. Punch declares that, *if any young woman wishes to know when she will be married, she may satisfy her curiosity by a very easy process. Let her take her passage for Australia, calculate the length of the voyage, and add to it twenty-four hours. Within that time she will be a wife or a voluntary spinster.*

124. *An Excursion to Orkney and Shetland in* 1839.

My esteemed friend the late Mr. Anderson, M. P. for Orkney and Shetland, said one day to me in London, "I wish you would talk up our Islands among your friends, and induce them, when they go to Scotland, to include Orkney and Shetland in their tour: a visit will amply repay them." "Well," I said, "I am as anxious as any one to see that part of the world; so I promise you next time I go to Scotland to carry out your wishes in regard to myself." When I returned to town, I called upon my friend and told him I had been delighted with the excursion he had planned for me. "Then do oblige me by making a sketch of your visit, and send it to our 'London and Shetland Journal.'" This I did in a letter to the editor. It ran as follows:

"Having recently returned from Scotland, after a month's grouse-shooting and salmon-fishing, or rather attempting the latter, as I never landed a single fish, I should be ungrateful did I not acknowledge the obligation I am under to you for having added much to the pleasure of my excursion, in calling my attention to a tour I had often wished to make, and the fear of its occupying too much time. I allude to Orkney and Shetland. Your advertisement, 'Pleasure Trips to the Orkney and Shetland Islands,' attracted my attention when in Aberdeen. I learned with no little satisfaction that I could leave Aberdeen on the Friday evening, visit Wick in Caithness, Kirkwall in Orkney, and Lerwick in Shetland, with two days to see the lions in the last-mentioned isles; in fact, explore *Ultima Thule*, and be in Modern Athens on the following Wednesday afternoon. So much for steam. Within half an hour I was at the wharf waiting the arrival from Leith of the steamer 'Sovereign.' I had mistaken the hour of sailing, having at least two hours to spare. These, however, were very pleasantly spent. It happened to be the fishermen's fête-night at the conclusion of the herring-fishing season on the Aberdeen coast, and they were giving their families and friends the annual ball at the tavern close to my place of embarkation. I therefore betook myself to the scene of gayety, secured an apartment adjoining the ballroom, taking care to leave my door open; and I must say I never saw a happier party: as to the fair sex, they were a galaxy of healthful beauty.

"I had been thrashing the river Ythan in the earlier part of the day for salmon, with my usual want of skill and success. Had the fates been only propitious, I should have sent in my card and claim for admission to the ballroom as a brother professional. The steamer's arrival called me from the contemplation of this piscatorial Almacks, and I soon found myself seated in the cabin at supper with a pleasant set of passengers. As I felt anxious to find out the characters of some of my companions, who were all bound, or the greater number, for the same point as myself, I cast my eyes around, and beheld, seated next to me, a rotund person of bilious look and excited expression, that plainly bespoke him a non-amphibious. Another also in juxtaposition to me, and about to curl himself up for the night, had such a fixed melancholy in the face as was sufficient to satisfy me that he was calling number one to account for having trusted himself upon the faithless bosom of the ocean. In both cases I was convinced they had read your tempting advertisement.

"One of our party was a French gentleman of very lively manners, whose volubility could gain nothing but monosyllabic growls from this couple, being a sorry return for *la politesse française* which he eminently possessed. Close to us sat a young Oxonian or Cantab, who seemed quite occupied in discussing a small basket of evidently choice provisions, as he appeared in no way desirous for any thing political or literary. Another, of nautical exterior, according to the last slop-shop pattern, was describing to his neighbor some extraordinary points of sailing, which he solemnly averred he had achieved in his own yacht, and they appeared to be believed, judging from the attention of the listener and the high state of gratification of the narrator.

"We started at twelve, and at daylight were crossing the Moray Firth, shortly coming in sight of the Caithness coast, and those singular-looking hills, the Paps of Caithness. The coast appears to be unusually studded with ancient castles—among those we saw were Berriedale, Dunbeath, etc. At mid-day we reached Wick, and spent two hours there. I was much interested during our short stay in observing the process of herring and codfish curing, but my gastronomical tastes and London ideas were shocked to see the beautiful cods' heads carried off for manure. Can your intelligent correspondent Peter Peregrine not suggest some mode by which this seeming waste of the treasures of the deep may be obviated? If he cannot, is there no 'Peregrine Pickle' who can? After leaving Wick, we rapidly passed along the coasts, parts of which were bold and imposing, with different castles rearing their heads: among them old Wick, Grinigoe, and Bucholly. On rounding Duncansby Head, the far-famed John o' Groats appeared, and the Pentland Skerries. We then crossed the Pentland Firth, coasted along the Islands of South Ronaldsa, Barra, Shafsina, and reached Kirkwall about 5 P. M. We landed, spent an hour looking at the town and its ancient Cathedral of St. Magnus, in which is laid the honored dust of Scotland's historian, Laing. We reëmbarked, and during the night were much interested with that singular phenomenon, the Northern Lights or Aurora Borealis. At daylight we were passing Sunburgh, and in the distance saw the Fitful Head. At 7 A. M. we reached Lerwick, and on landing were somewhat alarmed to hear that there were no hotels or taverns. We were recommended to a boarding-house, where, though we did not find the luxuries to be met with at like establishments in Bath or Cheltenham, still, we experienced much attention, and were made very comfortable. Most of our party had a letter of introduction to Mr. ——, from whom and his family we met with great kindness and hospitality. It being Sunday, the first thing we did (in the language of the North) was to make ourselves decent and attend the kirk.

"After service we agreed to cross the island to Scalloway, and accordingly issued orders for a troop of shelties (*alias* ponies) to be put in requisition. None appearing, our patience became exhausted, and we inquired the cause of delay, when we were told by the shelty proprietor that we should have bespoken them the day before. We called his attention to the fact that we had arrived only that morning, which we thought he knew. He good-humoredly admitted the impossibility under such circumstances of giving the shelty order, adding, 'Gentlemen, *ye* shall *no* be disappointed, for we'll *gang* to the hill and catch the shelties.' It may be interesting for some of our Brighton friends who follow the harriers or hired nags to know —in case my meagre description may induce them to think of a 'tallyho' across Shetland—that our Nimrodian party were mounted at an expense of 1*s.* 6*d.* each. Our French companion, a compact, well-built little fellow, 5 ft. 6 in. in height, and about five times that in years, proved to be a very intelligent and agreeable person, and a great acquisition to us. He had travelled much, spoke English tolerably, but was far from *au fait* in Scotch. He, however, gathered sufficient from our conversation to know what our plans were. 'Vat,' said he, 'are vė to catch de vild oss on de montagne?' On learning this was resolved upon, he began to jump and skip about in the street like a Merry Andrew, to the no small astonishment of Her Majesty's quiet and orderly lieges. 'Oh, capital! excellent! le diable! catch de vild chevaux, de vild oss—I mean de vild *h*oss.' 'No,' I said, 'ponies.' 'Oui, certain, vild ponneys,

I meaned all de time vild ponneys.' After we had somewhat tamed our French friend, our next object was to scale the *montagne*, to ascertain the tameness of the ponies. For this purpose we got some youngsters to assist in forming a cordon, and we soon captured as many as our party required. When the bridling and saddling had commenced, I observed at this particular juncture that our French friend was no longer so vivacious and active as the residents of Lerwick had so recently witnessed, but was absorbed in reflection, and altogether lost to the otherwise animated scene around him. I felt anxious to know the cause of this sudden change from gay to grave. I therefore roused my friend from his reverie by calling out, 'Monsieur, montez, montez.' 'Oui, oui, monsieur,' at the same time approaching me with the expression on his countenance of one who, heavy at heart, was suddenly relieved by the opportunity afforded of disburdening his mind of a heavy load, he thus addressed me: 'C'est de fait is mon cher friend, I vas nevare à cheval in tout mon life; dat is, I nevare have ride de oss or de ponny, nevare.' 'This, indeed,' said I, 'is an important discovery, and we must therefore ride at a moderate pace, and select a quiet animal for you.' As I had been made a *confidant* in his dilemma, he asked me if I did not think, as he was active and excelled in gymnastics, that in case of the little Shetlander proving obstreperous and likely to make a field-officer of him, he might not be able to throw himself off and secure a safe retreat from the heels of his Bucephalus; and before mounting, by way of giving me the opportunity of judging of his gymnastic qualifications, he made several hand-over-head turns or somersaults on the rugged hill, during which I feared he would perpetrate on himself infinitely more injury than the poor pony would inflict, even if so inclined. We got our friend mounted, and with the aid of the mane, the pommel of the saddle, and his legs, which alternately touched the ground and thus restored the equilibrium, he managed his steed wonderfully well, so long as we kept to the mountain-road; indeed, he became gradually so bold as to be able occasionally to get abreast of the party, lisp out an observation, and venture a squint to the right and left in search of the picturesque. We were now approaching Scalloway Bay, with its ancient castle, when we were met by a party of eight or ten men, whose appearance created some little hesitation among us. One had a musket, and the others had knives *à l'Espagnol.* Our guide was more at a loss than ourselves. I recollect, speaking for myself, that I experienced for the moment some heart-twinges and awkward misgivings, forgetting I was at home, in meeting these peaceful brigands as they proved to be, as a few months before I had been an equestrian tourist in the south of Spain during the Christina and Carlist War. They were the crew of a Spanish vessel lying in Scalloway Bay, taking in a cargo of fish, and evidently themselves alarmists from the mere fact of exhibiting their weapons to Her Majesty's most quiet and docile subjects of the Islands of Zetland, who are unaccustomed to such warlike displays amid their tranquil homes.

"Our guide now inquired whether we should prefer returning to Lerwick by the same route, or across the moor. The latter was adopted, and by no one more heartily supported than our by French friend, who had entirely overlooked one circumstance, that a fresh set of equestrian tactics would be required, for we were to have a new sample, and, as it turned out, a most amusing one of a steeple-chase, with this exception, that we were about to exchange fences and gates for ditches and moss-hags. Monsieur, who had so warmly sanctioned the new route, had not bargained for leaps, and never shall I forget the scene of merriment which his first Meltonian essay created. The guide was anxious to get us across the moor before a dense fog reached us, which he discovered fast approaching, and, therefore, had to request *mounseer* to take his leaps more expeditiously than he exactly relished. Monsieur retained his temper tolerably, although rarely his seat, until his little gallant steed had cleared the ditch, when he instantly opened a battery, half French, half English, upon the unfortunate guide for his apparently uncalled-for haste, and had it not been for our interposition we should have had the attractions of the hunting-field merged in the horrors of the prize-ring between the Gaul and the Shetlander. I only wish I had the descriptive pen of Scott, or the pencil of Cruikshank or A. Crowquill, to set before you a representation of what passed. The guide pleaded the necessity of dispatch, on account of the fog, and the danger that threatened us if we were overtaken by it, as well as the distance we had still to accomplish; he likewise pleaded the dinner-hour, keeping the rest of the party waiting, etc. All these were trifling reasons to urge in monsieur's opinion. He d——d 'de fog, de guide, de distance from home, de dinner-hour, and de bagatelle nonsens of de keeping de partie vaiting.' We at last reached Lerwick, in pretty fair time for dinner, and after many a hearty laugh, in which monsieur joined, and—

> " Riding our steeple-chase o'er again,
> Retired, fatigued and soberly, at ten."

The following morning we were up betimes, made our purchases of Shetland hosiery, visited a Greenlander just arrived from the Northern seas, found her a full ship, and inspected her minutely—this by way of making up for our disappointment in missing the sea-fight two days previous at Orkney, when the capture of a large number of young whales took place.

"After a substantial Scotch breakfast, we resolved to visit Brassey and the far-famed Noss. The Holme of Noss and the celebrated cradle are well worthy the attention of the Northern traveller. The distance across the strait appeared to be about sixty yards; the perpendicular height of the cliffs on either side from 400 to 500 feet. The cradle, by which the adventurous fowler crosses the terrific gulf, works on parallel ropes. It is, at first sight, most trying to the nerves, and requires no little persuasion ere you rally courage sufficient to intrust yourself to such an apparently crazy machine. Great caution must be observed while getting in and out of the cradle, and that it is held steady. One of the party (the writer) had, during the excursion across from Lerwick, mentioned a rather hazardous adventure in which he and a friend had been engaged in Italy the previous year. On reaching the cradle it was quietly agreed that the Anglo-Italian traveller, who was a short distance behind, should now have the post of honor assigned to him. This by way of testing his tale. Luckily for him, he overheard the conversation, bit his lip, screwed up his courage, and rejoined the party. 'Do you intend to cross?' said one. 'I don't,' said another. 'Nor do I,' said a third, and so on; and most probably I should, as the narrator of the Italian incident, have been among the noes, but for the observations that had reached my ears a few minutes before. The cradle floating in ether, at the height of St. Paul's, if not of St. Peter's, was far from encouraging; but the *Rubicon* had been crossed, and the *Noss* had to be crossed. The boatmen were, therefore, instructed to prepare the cradle, while I prepared myself for the honor of taking my seat. I am quite sure, if there was as much trepidation in taking a seat in St. Stephen's, there would be fewer candidates for Parliamentary distinction. You are obliged to crawl to the brink of the precipice, and let yourself drop into the cradle amid the innumerable fear-creating cautions of the boatmen, such as, 'Noo, sir, turn your back; noo your face; hauld firm. You had better shut you een. Are you weel seated? Be ready, as we are aboot to let you off,' and so forth. To increase the awe and sublimity of the scene, you have the waves dashing against the rocks in the gulf beneath, the wind howling through the strait, the sea-fowl screeching, and a wide expanse of ocean before you. All this, added to the appearance of your humble servant, their Anglo-Italian companion, dangling midway, had lulled into calm the noisy facetiousness of the party. Three out of twelve only ventured to cross, but no persuasion could prevail upon our Gallic friend to try this second mode of Shetland travelling. He expressed himself by no means alarmed, *but his stomac vas so delicat, and he had already, oh yase, crossed vone suspension bridge at Bristole, six weeks before, yase at Bristole, vich vas veri terrible, still he moch preferred it to the cradle of Noss.*

"We returned to Lerwick delighted with this and our former day's excursion, partook again of our kind friend's hospitality, and at 7 P. M. we were off on our return to Orkney and Leith."

P. S.—In his "Statistical Account of the British Empire," Mr. M'Culloch states that the stock of shelties bred in Shetland is estimated at ten or twelve thousand. They are never housed, nor receive any food except what they gather for themselves. Some of them are exceedingly well-proportioned, active, and strong of their age. The horses of Orkney are held in inferior estimation.

125. *Colonel Sir Thomas Mitchell's First Visit to Granada.*

There are some features of the journey from Malaga to Granada now avoided by the railway traveller, but which, in my case, as a tourist by public highway, created feelings not of the most comfortable or encouraging character in commencing an otherwise most interesting ride of two days from the coast.

I observed by the road, at a short distance from Malaga, a wayside cross. On my asking my guide for an explanation of its erection, he reluctantly confessed it was the spot where a robbery and murder had taken place. My eyes, henceforth, were on the alert for crosses; and, before we had reached the City of the Moors, I had counted sixteen, which my Spaniard was obliged to acknowledge were spots where some unfortunate traveller or travellers had been assassinated.

My friend, Colonel Sir Thomas Mitchell, the Surveyor-General of Australia, had arrived in London from the colony on leave, and I had asked some friends to meet him at our house at dinner. He knew Spain well, with the exception of Granada, having served under the Great Duke during the Peninsular War. Subsequently, at the Duke of Wellington's suggestion, being an able draughtsman, he visited the different battle-fields of the Peninsula, and made sketches. In the course of conversation, and without alluding to the crosses, I mentioned having visited the ancient Mussulman city of Granada; and he jocularly remarked, that as at that time he had penetrated farther into the interior of New Holland than any other man, it was a shame to have neglected to reach the Sierra Nevada when he had formerly visited Spain. As private affairs required his going out to Portugal next month, he added that he would take that opportunity of making a hurried excursion to Granada. This intention he carried out, and, on his return, when dining with us, he said to my wife, "Your husband let me into a good thing by his description of the Alhambra and Vega of Granada when I last dined with you." I begged the great explorer to explain what he meant. "I was a passenger by the diligence on my way back to Malaga from Granada, when the other passengers, with myself, were hurriedly aroused about midnight by finding our carriage stopped and surrounded by armed men, who ordered us all to alight. Being a Spanish scholar, I demanded to know what it all meant. The only answer I got was a pistol being pointed at my breast, and a command instantly to lie down on my face. I" (continued the gallant knight) "who never turned my back on an enemy in Spain, or anywhere else, to be told by a —— bandit to lie down with my face toward a confounded dusty Spanish road, was beyond all bearing. I was on the point of telling the scoundrel that I would see him first in the regions of Pluto, when a fellow-traveller most earnestly implored me to do what I was desired, as otherwise my brains would be blown out in a moment. I had, therefore, no time to make a protest with such a villain, and down I went with my face in the ignoble dust."

The distinguished Surveyor-General's last remark made all my friends laugh heartily. "Thank goodness, my circular notes so far saved me, as all the rascals got out of me was eight pounds and a few shillings, and which" (addressing me) "I think you should recoup, for, had it not been for your florid description of the Moorish city, the money would now be in my pocket." The gallant knight would not let me alone: "Why, sir, you must be a descendant of Don Quixote, to have gone upon your travels in Spain with a civil war raging. I heard the story of you at Valencia." It was simply that I delivered a letter of introduction I had from the Foreign Office to Colonel (afterward General) Lacy, the British Commissioner in the South of Spain. I had partaken of the most delicious breakfast I had seen in Spain or anywhere else, with the Colonel, in the palatial residence of some distinguished absentee Spanish *notable*, and afterward accompanied him to visit the citadel and public buildings. I promised to dine with the British Commissioner, when I recollected that I had engaged a carriage to carry me out to the headquarters of the Army of the South, to deliver a letter of introduction to General Borso.

The Commissioner laughed heartily at this, and the first thing he did was to take me to the top of one of the churches. "There," he said, "is General Borso, and between him and Valencia are 7,000 Carlists" (pointing out the camp), "so that in twenty minutes after leaving the gate of the city, you are a prisoner, and it may occupy me six months in negotiation before you are released. Boyd is," he continued, "a name—after what occurred some years back at Malaga—the most dangerous a man can travel with in Spain." General Lacy, in after-years, often laughed at my narrow escape.

126. *Who is a Good Absentee Landlord? El Señor Duca de Ciudad Rodrigo, etc., etc.*

I very much regretted that, while in Granada, I lost the opportunity offered me of spending a long day on the great estate of the Duke of Ciudad Rodrigo, but was obliged to be content with a bird's-eye view of it. At the hotel there I met a gentleman who wished me to accompany him to Molino del Rey, to be introduced to the Duke's agent, at that time a retired British officer. I believe the agent or agents of the estate are still English.

The Duke of Wellington, as we know, at the conclusion of the Peninsular War, was created Duke of Ciudad Rodrigo, and had presented to him by the Spanish nation the royal estate of Soto de Roma and Molino del Rey, said to be 8,000 or 9,000 acres in extent. The income at the time I speak of (1839) was stated to me not to exceed £3,000 to £4,000 a year, but the estate possessed capabilities that might, at no distant day, bring it up to four times that amount. Its position is one of the most beautiful that can be conceived in the province of Granada, as from it can be seen the Alhambra, with the churches and high buildings of the city. The view of the ridge of the Sierra Nevada is magnificent. I was altogether unprepared to find that at the end of May many of the peaks and chasms of the Sierra were still clad in snow.

Between the two divisions of the estate—that is, from La Torre and La Casa Real—the distance is not less than five miles. A writer thus describes it: "Of the situation of La Torre it is impossible to speak with sufficient rapture. Granada is, in point of beauty, the most precious jewel in the Spanish diadem, and La Torre is, perhaps, the very spot in the whole region from which the unequalled loveliness of mountain and plain can best be taken in at one glance. Granada, the Alhambra, and the Sierra, rise almost due east before us across the plain like a mirror. Close in our rear is the bare and bleak ridge of Parapanda, screening us from the north and east; and all around, in sublime undulation, spread the broad acres of the Duke's domain, old groves and new vineyards sloping down to the rich alluvial flats of the Vega."

This estate had passed through the hands of Richard Wall, the Irish minister of Charles III. of Spain, of Godoy (the Prince of Peace), and of King Joseph Bonaparte. Since 1864, under the auspices of Don Horacio, an English gentleman, dwelling and farm houses have been erected, and, under the authority of the present Duke, report says a wilderness is being converted which is capable of producing £10,000 a year. The duke has authorized Don Horacio to repair the house and premises of Molino del Rey, as well as the mansion of Casa Real and other buildings, and is about to erect at La Torre a villa which may yet become a ducal residence, should His Grace visit his Spanish estates.

It is said that a bodega or wine-cellar is being planned, capable of containing 1,200 butts; the largest, at Jerez, only contains 3,000 butts. Don Horacio has imported vines from Montilla, from Moriles, from Johannisberg, from Pauillac, near Bordeaux, from even Hebron, in the valley of

Eschol in Palestine. The writer in question says, that the Duke's wine, only two years old, which he tasted, proved to be exquisite in flavor, and is kept thoroughly free from alcoholic admixture.

Round the hill of La Torre is now being carried a vineyard which, when complete, will cover a large space of ground. Soto de Roma is situated in the plain, and is a large cornfield. It is believed that the duke takes much interest in his Spanish possessions, and is desirous of improving them, chiefly with a view to ameliorate the condition of the people by affording them well-remunerated employment. It was with this view that Don Horacio was authorized four years ago to plant vineyards on an estate not hitherto made to yield a single bunch of grapes. Extensive works, both as a builder and an agriculturist, I am told, now afford evidence that the noble owner of Strathfeldsaye, although an absentee proprietor of Granada, is working out a great problem in that province. It is said that, under the Duke's instructions, the agent, during a recent winter, when famine ravaged Andalusia, took starving people into his employ, occupying them in vine-planting, road-making, land-clearing, building, etc. Therefore, I presume, all will agree with me that Su Excelencia el Señor Duca de Ciudad Rodrigo is a good landlord, albeit an absentee.

127. *A Sheep-Stealer astonished.*

We had a hearty laugh after dinner at a ludicrous scene that had been witnessed that day on the Oxford Circuit. Mr. Donald Maclean, M. P. for the city of Oxford, was defending a prisoner for sheep-stealing. The learned gentleman had a very difficult case to conduct, inasmuch as the prisoner, who watched the evidence with peculiar attention, on hearing some strong fact brought against him, stretched his head toward his counsel, and, in an unmistakably audible whisper, said, "There they goes, sir; I knoed they would kotch me." Mr. Maclean waved his hand to him to be quiet, but the very next reply of the witness produced a repetition of the whisper, "There's no use, sir; I knoed they would kotch me." The prisoner's attorney then stationed a clerk as near him as possible to keep him silent; but what he was prevented doing in the way of loud whispering, he made up in contortions of the countenance, expressive grimaces, shaking the head, looking up and then down, every movement conveying the impression to the Court that his own patience was exhausted, and that it was all nonsense wasting more time in the business. The judge summed up, and the jury, after a short consultation brought in a verdict of "Not guilty." The prisoner did not hear this distinctly, and asked one of the officers of the Court what the verdict was. He was told that he was acquitted. "Not guilty, does you mean to say?" "Yes, not guilty." "Vell, hif ever!" On leaving the court, he was most desirous to shake hands with Mr. Maclean, but that favor was not granted. He then proceeded to the nearest public-house, and declared to some of his friends that Mr. Maclean "vas the werry cleverest lawrer hin the ole hof Hengland, hand advised Jim, Bob, hand Sam. never to hemploy any other, hif they vished to get hoff."

128. *It's an ill Wind that blows Nobody Good.*

As a youth I held thunder-storms in high appreciation: possibly because the good couple with whom another youngster and myself boarded were frightened by them almost into fits, and the husband on such occasions made a point of going down to the cellar for a bottle of his old port, and one of his equally good sherry, which he placed on the tables with those glorious accompaniments in the eyes of a schoolboy—Scotch shortbread and bun, sponge cake, and biscuits. If we arrived from our classes after the storm commenced—and we never allowed ourselves to be long absentees—we endeavored to look awfully grave on entering the dining-room; our host shaking us by the hand very earnestly, and desiring us, *sotto voce*, to help ourselves to a glass of wine. After that, we were always helping ourselves, as we returned to no classes that day.

My old friend, while on a visit to England, had purchased a large and elegant upright hand-organ. It had four barrels, each throwing off ten tunes, so that the moment the lightning flashed, and before "Heaven's artillery thundered in the skies," he hurried to the organ and kept grinding with all the impetuosity and courage he could command, till the storm was over. My old friends were an excellent couple, and, moreover, serious people, although it may appear somewhat paradoxical to mention that they never went to church. Their *illeeberal neebors* asserted that their alarm at thunder was "only a *joodgement* on them for no' *ganging* to the kirk."

I lived three years with the worthy couple, and had I, as I have often since regretted, kept a daily journal, I should now be able to furnish, as a matter of statistics, the precise number of "red-letter" days annually which I enjoyed in connection with electrical atmospheric disturbance, and probably some other rather singular phenomena. One fact is fixed indelibly on my memory, even at this distant day, that we never by any chance—unless it was furnished by our own friends—saw a glass of wine on the table or side-table, unless it was to counteract the effects of a thunder-storm.

129. *Beware of an Auld Wife.*

The late Mr. Ker, Secretary to the General Post-Office at Edinburgh, a man equally respected in public and private life, found he had been twitted by an English friend for having allowed himself to be knocked down by "an auld wife," and so severely injured that it was feared at first his skull was fractured.

"I feel exceedingly," exclaimed the Londoner, "for my friend Ker; but how, in the name of wonder, he could allow any old woman to knock him down is to me surprising; for when he discovered that the antiquated Amazon was an overmatch for him, he surely could call for assistance. That would have been infinitely wiser than allowing the old harridan to maul and injure him as she has done. Why, I sat with him to-day for half an hour, and am happy to say he is rapidly recovering, but his head and part of his face appeared one mass of bandages. I asked him how it happened, as I did not believe what I had heard. He confessed to me that he had been knocked down by 'an auld wife,' as he called her. I did not like to say any thing to him, but before he leaves his room I shall give him a hint to keep the affair to himself, as it does not impress one with a very high estimate of either Ker's powers or his personal courage, to be vanquished in single combat by an old Scotch woman in the streets of the Modern Athens."

The remarks of the Englishman, which he was allowed to close without interruption, created vast amusement at the dinner-party where they were made, as "an auld wife" in Edinburgh is also a chimney-pot, one of which during a storm alighted on the head of the respected Secretary to His Majesty's Post-Office in Scotland, and nearly killed him. Thus much by way of a solution for my readers south of the Tweed.

130. *A Useful Flash of Lightning.*

Some twenty years ago I had some friends occupying the last house of Kensington Gardens Terrace, immediately opposite the end of the Serpentine.

I was one day praising the charming view which they had from their drawing-room windows. "Yes, the view would be perfect, if the branch of that large tree," to which they drew my attention, "did not interrupt it." "Well," I remarked, "it is somewhat singular that I walked to your door with the nearest relative in London of the Chief Commissioner of Woods and Forests (the Right Honorable Mr. Milne), and I shall ask him to inquire whether the branch can be removed without injury to the royal tree." I accordingly wrote to my friend in the evening (Tuesday), and on Thursday morning my friends discovered to their infinite satisfaction, that the obstructive branch had disappeared; and, as a natural sequence, I came in for a warm benediction, and the Woods and Forests for their full share of praise as an exceptional department of the State, where red tape was not used, and circumlocution unknown.

The Chief Commissioner, on reading my note to his relative, gave orders on the Wednesday to the superintendent of Kensington Gardens to look at the tree, and if the branch could be taken off without serious prejudice it was to be done. The superintendent reported at headquarters on the Thursday that on visiting the tree at an early hour that morning he found the branch in question lying on the ground, having been struck off by lightning during the heavy storm of the previous night.

The Chief Commissioner wrote an amusing letter on the occasion, alleging that I really must be one "who *could call* spirits from the vasty deep," and had evidently transferred my powers to Kensington Gardens, acting on the suggestion given in Richard the Third, "With lightning strike the murderer dead."

The same day I visited the tree, which appeared, saving the amputation of the large branch, to have escaped all other injury. Had other trees not suffered severely in

Kensington Gardens that night, it might have led to a special inquiry or inquest to ascertain whether it was lightning or a saw that *I* had employed in obliging my friends. I told them they owed every thing to the lightning, as I was much inclined to think that the Chief Commissioner, with every desire to meet their wishes, might possibly have deemed it his duty to postpone the consideration of the removal of so large and umbrageous a branch from the royal demesne to the "Greek Calends."

131. *Scotch Hospitality.*—"*Ex uno disce omnes.*"

An English friend who had never been in Scotland, asked me if it really was the case that so much hospitality ruled there, as he had observed nothing remarkable in that respect among my countrymen on this side the Tweed. I told him that I must decline entering upon the discussion of the question how far the Scotch character degenerated in regard to hospitality after blending with the natives of the south, but that, as he asked for information on a characteristic on which my nation justly prided itself, I was prepared to answer him. He was aware, I presumed, that Washington Irving referred to Scotland when he defined hospitality as "breaking through the chills of ceremony and selfishness, and thawing every heart into a flow." He might have also heard that diffidence was a striking feature with Scotchmen, which I felt at that moment, as the illustration I was about to give had occurred to myself, and from it I should leave him to draw his own conclusions.

At the period to which I am about to refer, I had been a resident in London for ten years, when the directors of one of our oldest and most powerful Scotch insurance companies consulted my late brother and myself as to forming a board of directors and branch of the company in London.

The preliminary arrangements called me down to Edinburgh, and occupied me there some weeks. When the London branch of the company was formed, a deputation of directors went from Scotland to London to inaugurate the new establishment, and considering that a good dinner was the best mode of commencing business, they invited the chairman, deputy-chairman, and directors of several of the London insurance companies to a banquet at the Albion, covers being laid for 110 guests. During the evening my health was proposed by the chairman, as the member of the London Board who had gone to Scotland to mature the arrangements. In the course of his speech, he expressed his regret that my visit should have taken place at the season of the year when they had little opportunity in the northern capital of showing me the hospitality they could have otherwise wished to do. In my reply, after disposing of the business points, I came to the charge brought by the chairman against himself and colleagues, and which I hoped to prove satisfactorily, before I sat down, was entirely erroneous. One of our directors extraordinary of the insurance company was that late gallant and excellent man, William, eighth Lord Napier, who was present, and who was just about to proceed to China. I said that, for the information of my English friends, I would address myself to his lordship on the question of Scotch hospitality. I then proceeded to state that on the occasion in question I had remained in Edinburgh forty-nine days, on forty-eight of which I went to dinner-parties, to say nothing of invitations which I received and accepted to other kinds of entertainment for which Scotland is so famous, namely, her breakfasts and her suppers. I therefore left the company to say whether they considered that I had been neglected. Moreover, I was prepared to prove my case by exhibiting my hotel bill, which, had I been in the least aware such an issue was to be raised that evening, I should have put in my pocket, for by it it would be seen that I had dined at my hotel only once, namely, on the day of my arrival. Next day the Scotch hotel bill was placed in Lord Napier's hands. He was a gallant sailor, and at that time a lord-in-waiting to our Sailor King, and whether it was exhibited to His Majesty to show that he had one of his loyal subjects who could attend forty-eight dinner-parties on forty-eight consecutive days I know not, but I recollect the lord mayor, two of the aldermen, and one of the sheriffs were present, who declared that no members of the Corporation of London could show front with me as a diner-out.

132. *Not bad.*

I recollect a humorous M.P. pointing out to me a retired West India judge not very remarkable for sagacity on the bench. There was a ball at Government House, and the judge began to criticise the waltzing of a witty member of the West India Bar. "Ah, my friend, you are a bad waltzer!" "Ah, but you are a bad judge."

133. *One of the "Forty-twa."*

When I first came to London I met at the house of a friend, at dinner, a countryman of my own, who had spent thirty years or more in the West Indies. Our host described him as one of the *forty-twa.* It appeared that about the beginning of the century forty-two young Scotchman embarked at Greenock for the West Indies. The ship discharged her cargo and loaded with sugar, which detained her about six weeks, and returned to Greenock, bringing back the trunks, *alias* the *kists*, of twenty-seven of the young men, who had within that short time fallen victims to yellow fever. Mentioning this circumstance to the late General Frederick Maitland, of Berkeley Square, who had served many years in the West Indies, he told me that one

Saturday he and seven brother officers sat down to mess, and the following Saturday he was the only survivor of the party.

134. *The Bombay Sermon.*

One 31st of March my brother and myself found our eyes directed to a pamphlet in a London publisher's window, "An Address to Young People." Then came a long and appropriate text, followed by the author's name, "William Boyd." Now, as we had a brother William in India, and as next day was the 1st of April, we bethought ourselves of practising an innocent hoax on some friends of ours in the neighborhood of London, with whom we were to pass the following Sunday. Accordingly, we purchased the 'Address," and got our printer to add our brother's designation at full length:

"William S. Boyd,

"Political Commissioner for Guzerat, and Resident at the Court of the Guivocar of Baroda."

A polite note had next to be written from the Chapter Coffee-House to the excellent lady with whom and whose family we were to spend the Sunday, as if from a Bombay chaplain, just arrived from India, who had great pleasure in sending her an early copy of the able and instructive "Address," which he deemed it his duty to have printed immediately on his arrival in London, and it was added that the reverend gentleman on his return from Devonshire would call to pay his respects.

We were accompanied to our friend's house by my father, whom we had not let into the secret. One of the first questions on our arrival was, "You have, of course, heard from Bombay?" "No." "Nor from the Reverend Mr. ——?" "No." "All in good time." "Ah," said our hostess, addressing my father, "your son is coming out just now in a manner that will delight you as a parent." As we were to remain all night, nothing more was said until the domestics had assembled in the drawing-room to hear a sermon as usual, when one of the family circle said, "Let us have William Boyd's 'Address' or, more properly speaking, sermon read." "What!" exclaimed my father, "my son's sermon?" "Yes, indeed." He instantly put on his spectacles under evidently strong feelings of excitement, and to his horror read aloud, "An Address to Young People, by William S. Boyd, Political Commissioner for Guzerat, and Resident at the Court of the Guivocar of Baroda." "Too true," adding, with a deep sigh, "he must be mad." "Oh, Mr. Boyd, when you have heard the sermon you will change your opinion." All this, though in a subdued tone, was audible throughout the room. "My son write a sermon: what nonsense it must be!" This was the precise estimate at which my brother and myself, after perusal, had arrived. My father's was a foregone conclusion, for however high his opinion might be of his son as an Eastern diplomatist, he had never discovered the celestial fire, that *mens divinior* in him as a youth, which the lady in whose house we were then guests declared burned brilliantly. After some persuasion my father agreed to listen to his son's sermon. Unluckily for us all, it was twenty pages in length, and although beautifully read by one of the yonng ladies of the family, my father declared to those on his right and left, in whispers sufficiently audible for all, that greater trash and rubbish he had never listened to, and, to the infinite surprise of the household, he added that his son in India must have become a madman.

The "Address" being concluded, some one referred to the beautiful text which was frequently quoted in it. "Yes," said my father, "it is the context, not the text, that is the production of an imbecile; and as to that ass of a Bombay chaplain, to have published such a tissue of nonsense, he deserves to have his nose pulled; and to-morrow before twelve o'clock he shall know my opinion of him. But how my son, living at Baroda, a remote station, and distant from Bombay, could find young people to address is at present inexplicable." The ladies, by way of tranquillizing my father's mind, said that all no doubt would be satisfactorily explained by next mail. To this he observed that he fully expected to find that his unfortunate son would arrive by next steamer at Southampton in charge of keepers. He then hurriedly wished the family group good-night, and went to his room in a most unhappy condition of mind. My brother and myself, fearing results, followed him and explained the authorship of the Bombay sermon; and he joined his friends at breakfast next morning in spirits very different from what he had left them the previous night.

135. *The Siege of Antwerp, and Colonel Colin Campbell (Lord Clyde).*

The affecting incident recorded in these pages of Mr. Fitzgerald's journey from Brussels to Waterloo, accompanied by his aunt, to search among the slain for the body of her husband, reminds me of a melancholy and exciting journey I made with a friend to the siege of Antwerp. Within five miles of the Brussels gate we first heard the boom of artillery, and throughout the journey, which is under thirty miles, we were constantly meeting military ambulances with wounded soldiers.

To one who was witnessing for the first time the horrid results of the "rough frown of war," nothing could be more impressive or more painful. Every portion of the Brussels road from Vilvorde was a scene not to be easily forgotten —straggling soldiers, provision-carts, ammunition-wagons, groups of cavalry billeted in every village, spring wagons *en route* to Brussels with four or five wounded men in each, and regiments of infantry moving to the scene, etc.

We were too late for the fall of Fort St. Laurent, but not for that of Fort Kiel, which was blown up the night of our arrival. My old friend Colonel Colin Campbell, who had been in Antwerp from the commencement of the siege, received my friend and myself most kindly. It was interesting for us, as non-combatants, to hear so distinguished and intelligent an officer who had won his spurs nineteen years before (in 1813) under the walls of St. Sebastian, where he was twice wounded, talking over, with other members of his profession, the prospects of the siege in a manner not at all unlike what some of us had been accustomed to on the London Exchange when a Baring might be discussing the prospects of the produce-market, or a Rothschild those of the stock-market. I recollect the future field-marshal telling us, in language clear and full of energy, "The work will soon be done; the siege is becoming more and more interesting every hour, and you have arrived just at the right time." My gallant friend having now discovered that my companion, who—though, like myself, a civilian—was possessed of strong military tastes, went on to describe to us as if we had been young officers of artillery that "the workings from the distant parallels were necessarily less precise than from the third parallel (where the French then were, the attacking party), and that the batteries against Fort de Sécours would open next day, which could be safely done, now that Fort St. Laurent had been silenced; that General Gerard (the French commander-in-chief) had determined to take the citadel without using any other works near the town other than Montobello, so that Antwerp was perfectly safe, except from stray shot and shell." I recollect the morning after our arrival his pointing out to me le Duc d'Orleans and his brother le Duc de Nemours, who daily went into the trenches for several hours. Their case appeared to me one of great hardship, as they seemed to be expected to look cannon-balls in the face more frequently than any other soldiers in King Louis Philippe's army. The conduct and devotion of those royal youths secured much admiration on all hands throughout the progress of the siege. King Leopold arrived from Brussels one afternoon, and next morning when I saw him I should have much liked to know how His Majesty slept, for the Dutch and French batteries kept up such a fire during the night that I could not close my eyes, and the king was in our street; therefore, unless royalty is exempted under such circumstances, his slumbers must have been greatly disturbed.

Having for years been in the habit of meeting Colin Campbell at the dinner-table in town, and of listening to his interesting details of the Napoleonic war in Spain and Portugal, in which he shared, my feelings are not easily described in finding myself within forty-eight hours of leaving home the companion of that brilliant soldier, and listening to his minute explanations of siege operations; with reference to which he would say, "Mind you, we have been at peace for seventeen years, and the advance of science in the mean time has put artillery on a very different footing from what it was in my early days at Badajoz, Ciudad Rodrigo, and St. Sebastian."

My friend and myself devoted one afternoon to a visit to the camp of the 7th Regiment of French Infantry, in which there was an officer, a friend of my father's, who had been a prisoner of war in Scotland prior to Waterloo. The camp was posted in the park of an Antwerp merchant, whose forefather had amassed wealth when his city, like Bruges, was one of the depots of the commerce of the world. The entrance to it was the road-way of what had been a splendid avenue, with Gothic temples and verandas, but its sylvan beauty was gone, its fine timber cut down for firewood for the troops, and scarcely a tree left: never was such desolation, giving one more than a faint idea of the horrors of war. We found the gallant French veteran who had commenced his military career at Austerlitz. He had many questions to ask me on family matters, after which he alluded to what appeared to him inexplicable, that two sane Englishmen, unconnected with military life, should come as amateurs to witness the sorrowful realities of war.

Colonel Campbell, who was *au courant* as to what was passing at the French headquarters, being in the same hotel, came to our room in the evening to inform us that next day the largest mortar ever cast, a 108-pounder, would be fired against the citadel. What would they say now at Shoeburyness to a 108-lb. shot?

The colonel seemed to me to have his doubts as to so large a gun being successful. I think only eight shots were fired from this, the famous "monstre mortier d'Anvers." My companion's military appetite having been, with my own, sharpened to a high point, we made up our minds to visit the trenches, and the breaching battery, now in full operation, at the distance of forty-five yards, against the citadel in which the brave Chassé and his devoted garrison had been defending themselves for six weeks. As this could not be done unless we appeared in uniform, we applied to our friend the colonel, who rated us both well for our stupidity in not bringing a military dress of some sort, even, as he said, had we gone to Seven Dials or Houndsditch for it. Then, addressing me, "Why did you not bring your Scotch dress with you? It would have done as well to be shot in as any thing else." My friend, though a lawyer, was too young to have belonged to the "Devil's Own," that famous corps so felicitously described by Lord-Chancellor Campbell, and which, when formed at the commencement of the century, struck such terror into the breast of even the great Napoleon. The obliging colonel procured us uniforms, and after his servant had brought them, he paid us a visit and said, "Here they are for you, but recollect I take no further responsibility." Next morning, the breach being practicable, Chassé gave in, so as to save the bombardment and assault. It was about seven o'clock (Christmas morning, I think) when Colin Campbell rushed into our room and announced the fact. He found me in my red coat, the first I had ever worn. "Your incipient heroism," said he, "is checked; and now to breakfast with what appetite you have."

We devoted the whole of that day to passing and repassing through the labyrinth of parallels, examining the different French batteries up to the breach in the wall of the citadel, where we found the fascines placed across the ditch all ready for the grand rush of the French, had Chassé offered further resistance. Such a scene of wreck and devastation as that which presented itself was difficult to realize; cannon-shot, exploded and non-exploded shells, lying in all directions, and the beautiful suburban villa residences of Antwerp merchants and citizens, within the radius of the Dutch batteries, either wholly or partially destroyed.

Could all this not have been averted by skilful negotiations? I presume we must wait until the leading powers of the world agree upon a general system of disarmament before the millennium of peace shall have commenced.

To compel the King of Holland to give up the citadel of Antwerp, King Louis Philippe brought against it an army of 66,450 men, 14,300 horses, and 222 guns; and the French lost during the siege 108 killed and 695 wounded; total 803. The Dutch had 4,937 men in the garrison, of whom they lost 122 killed, 369 wounded, and 70 missing; total 561. But how small a reckoning is this to set against that of the present terrific struggle between France and Prussia!

136. *The Casting Vote of the Speaker of the House of Commons.*

I had often heard my father allude to this vote in reference to the charge brought against Henry Dundas, first Viscount Melville, better known during the twenty-five concluding years of the past century as Harry Dundas, who was charged, as Treasurer of the Navy, with official misconduct. The gravamen of his impeachment by the House of Commons was laxity of supervision in the department; but beyond this his personal honor and integrity stood unquestioned. I had so frequently listened to my father's recital of the sensation which the affair produced in Parliament and throughout the country, that I was glad to meet with it in one of Mr. Reginald Palgrave's "Illustrations of the History and Practice of the House of Commons;" but it bears on the death of Mr. Pitt so differently from any thing which I have heard from other sources that I here transcribe the extract. Mr. Palgrave says: "A Speaker once was driven into the corner; he found that 'ay' or 'no,' guilty or not guilty, must be settled by his casting vote. For the question he had to decide was, whether or no Lord Melville, as Treasurer to the Navy, had been guilty of official misconduct. It was in the year 1806 (the impeachment was in 1805) that this accusation was brought before the Commons, and it provoked, you may suppose, the utmost zeal and heat. Much was proved against Lord Melville; much, however, of the desire to prove his guilt sprang from party hate. His accusers may have loved justice, but they certainly also loved to plague an antagonist. Mr. Pitt, the Prime Minister, was strong on Lord Melville's side, his friend and colleague, but the opposing party was zealous and powerful. The fierce debate ended with an even vote—216 members declared for Lord Melville; 216 voted for his guilt. Lord Melville's fate was thus placed in the Speaker's hands, to be decided by that one vote. Yet it was long before the Speaker could give his vote; agitation overcame him: his face grew white as a sheet. Terrible as was the distress to all who awaited the decision from the chair, not less terrible was the Speaker's distress. This suspense lasted ten long minutes. There the Speaker sat in silence: all were silent. At length his voice was heard; he gave his vote, and he condemned Lord Melville. One man at least that evening was overcome. Mr. Pitt was overcome: his friend was ruined. At the sound of the Speaker's voice, the Prime Minister crushed his hat over his brows to hide the streaming tears that poured over his cheeks; he pushed in haste out of the House. Some of his opponents, I am ashamed to say, thrust themselves near 'to see how Billy looked.' His friends gathered in defence around, and screened him from rude glances. During a quarter of a century, almost ever since he had been a boy, Mr. Pitt had battled it in Parliament. His experience there was not victory only, but often defeat. This defeat, however, he sank under: it was his last; he died ere many months had passed. The death of that great man was hastened by Speaker Abbot's casting vote."

Lord Melville was afterward tried by his Peers, and acquitted. Mr. Palgrave says that Mr. Pitt sank under this defeat. I am more inclined to think that the victory gained by the French against the Austrians and Russians at Austerlitz on December 2, 1805, had much more to do with the death of William Pitt than the casting vote of Speaker Abbot.

137. *A Lady's Description (in After-life) of the Event that caused her, at the Time, the Greatest Mental Agony.*

At a Christmas-party where I was present, after the solution of the usual quantity of conundrums, the question was asked, "What particular event in our experience had caused us at the time the deepest pain?" I was to lead off, and I recollect being sent to Coventry for my answer. I had been placed by one of Lord Breadalbane's keepers, at Taymouth, in a most favorable sheltered position for a shot, when a majestic red deer actually stopped and stared me in the face at the distance of twenty yards. My gun had ball in one barrel and buck-shot in the other. I took, as I vainly thought, a choice aim at the choice quarry (of which we know nothing in my part of Scotland), fired both shots, and missed. A lady of the party at once said, "I know what caused me the bitterest feeling, and although many years have since passed away, I cannot forget it; it is much too deeply impressed on my memory." They begged her to relate the circumstance, which they trusted would be something more interesting than what they had just heard from me.

"I had returned home for the holidays from my boarding-school," she said, "and my brother David from his, when a day or two afterward mamma received an invitation for us to spend a week or ten days with some rather exclusive relatives of ours, at their country-seat. My brother felt, as I did, delighted. My dress-maker was immediately sent for, and my brother was off to his tailor to be refitted. The following Saturday we arrived at the hall. On Sunday evening, at nine o'clock, a larger retinue of servants than I had ever previously seen in a private family entered the drawing-room to listen, with the large circle of visitors, to a sermon read by the family tutor and chaplain, followed by the usual prayer. All had left their recumbent positions, my brother excepted, which being observed by the lady of the mansion, she beckoned to the butler and the others to remain, and in a whisper to her guests intimated that my brother was still in prayer. I well knew the contrary. What were my feelings at that moment! 'Oh!'

I exclaimed within myself, 'oh! Davy, Davy, how you are exposing me and yourself! What will mamma say when she hears it?' There we all stood in silence. The agony of my feelings at that moment I cannot describe; and the worst had still to come, for my brother, wishing to change the position of his head, in the act of doing so gave unmistakable nasal proof that he had apportioned at least a moiety of the previous ten minutes to something besides prayer. The lady of the mansion, with a dignity of countenance vividly impressed on my memory, said to her domestics, 'You may now retire.' There was not even the relief of a smile permitted in that house on a Sunday evening, which only increased the embittered feelings under which, on that distressingly trying night, I retired to my room. As for my brother, to whom I had no opportunity of communicating the nature and extent of his offence against decorum, he provoked me by making himself as much at home and at ease as if nothing dreadful had happened."

I had so utterly failed in interesting the family circle by my description of missing a double shot at a red deer in a Scotch forest, that I was called upon—in fact, was to have another chance given me of relating something that presented to my mind at the time it occurred feelings of horror and distress. I had Kremlin-ized, lion-ized, opera-ized the ancient and original capital of the Russian Empire, looked at and from as many of the 600 church and other towers as any other previous English tourist, and in a couple of days was to retrace my steps to St. Petersburg, when the landlord and landlady of the English hotel, Mr. and Mrs. Howard, a good and worthy old couple from Staffordshire, who recollected the Emperor Paul, told me I must not take my departure until I had visited the Siberian prison in the suburbs of Moscow. A permission having been obtained, I drove there next forenoon, but altogether unprepared for the melancholy spectacle that awaited me. The kingdom of Poland was at this period convulsed throughout the length and breadth of the land in another of her many but futile struggles to throw off the dominion of Russia. I was to see, and gloat an idle curiosity with the inspection of, one of those weekly batches of political prisoners whose rendezvous was Moscow, before being dispatched on a fearful journey of some thousands of miles to Siberia, occupying many months in being accomplished. The prisoners I saw appeared to me to belong to the higher classes, and I understood afterward that they did so. Never shall I forget what I suffered for seeking to gratify a prurient desire to see the unfortunate Polish prisoners—my only palliation being that I was a member of the Polish Association of London, of which Lord Dudley Stuart was president; this fact, however, was not alluded to in my passport. I think it was a Saturday, and on the following Monday morning, at an early hour, the solemn cavalcade was to commence its melancholy journey. Could I in the least have anticipated what I was to behold, no persuasion could have induced me to visit such chambers of horrors.

In the first to which I was taken, there was a family of distinction and of great personal attractions: the husband a remarkably handsome, military-looking man, apparently about forty years of age; his wife, a few years younger, a beautiful and attractive woman, tall and of commanding appearance, with a mildness of expression and a resignation in her demeanor not to be forgotten. They had three sweet-looking girls, the eldest probably eighteen. The warder by whom I was accompanied had entered the apartment rather abruptly, and before the devoted family had time to rise, being clasped in each other's embrace, and, as it appeared to me, engaged in prayer, and bathed in tears. At that moment I should have sacrificed any thing to have been outside this prison. Something was said by the warder to this unfortunate and interesting group, as they were all instantly on their feet, because, forsooth, an idle English tourist was present. The afflicted prisoner whom I had so unintentionally disturbed, at once assumed a military attitude, and his countenance a firm but pleasing expression. I had now witnessed more than my feelings could support, and burst into tears, at the same time imploring the warder to hurry me from the scene. I made a solemn bow to the family whose privacy I had so innocently broken in upon, in their communion with him from whom in a few hours in all human probability they were to be severed forever in this world. In leaving the chamber I placed my hand on my heart, and I hope I conveyed to that unhappy family the distress I at that moment experienced in having so reluctantly violated their privacy. On the Monday morning I was invited to witness—"last scene of all"—the departure of the exiles to Siberia, but I had too recently left their presence with a bitter heart to witness a renewal of those mental struggles, which we only witness under a different phase when the hearse drives from the door.

138. *Respectability in Guernsey.*

The upper classes of this island are always suspected of being extremely exclusive; and I remember, many years ago, when making a short tour among the Channel Islands, to have heard that the people of Guernsey rather looked down upon their neighbors in Jersey.

A clerical friend of mine recently told me that I was misinformed on this head, as it was not so; and I begged him to explain the foundation of the popular error which he, as a native of Guernsey, no doubt could do; at the same time the origin of the three grades of society in his island—the 60's, the 40's, and the 20's. It would appear that somewhere at the end of last century a club of gentlemen, heads of families, who accidentally numbered 60, joined in the erection of a ballroom, which my reverend friend contended they had as much right to establish as the leaders of Almacks' or the *élite* of Bath. "Well," I said, "I must, I presume, accept your explanation of the non-exclusiveness of the Guernseyites; still, it is inconsistent with what I have invariably observed in you Guernsey people, that if one alludes to the Jerseyites, you are sure to say you know little or nothing of them, and seem desirous to leave the impression on the mind of the hearer that the only pure and unalloyed 60's can be met with in Her Majesty's Island of Guernsey." I suppose that, if this sliding scale of respectability is really current and recognized in Guernsey, the world has a specimen of that kind of constitution which Aristotle or Plato—I forget which—is in the habit of terming a "Timocracy" or "Plutocracy."

139. *Mr. Missing, the Barrister.*

An eminent judge used to say that, in his opinion, the very best thing ever said by a witness to a counsel was the reply given to Missing, the barrister, at the time leader of his circuit. He was defending a prisoner charged with stealing a donkey. The prosecutor had left the animal tied up to a gate, and when he returned it was gone.

Missing was very severe in his examination of the witness. "Do you mean to say, witness, the donkey was stolen from that gate?" "I mean to say, sir," giving the judge, and then the jury, a sly look, at the same time pointing to the counsel, "the ass was Missing!"

140. "*Then, John, I shall not dine with you to-day, you may depend upon it.*"

At the end of the last and beginning of the present century few of the great London merchants had their private residences in the West End. They lived chiefly in the City, or in the suburbs.

There was, however, an exception, one whose exercise for six days in the week was his walk into and out of the City. Moreover, he dined in the City, immediately on 'Change closing, returning for an hour afterward to his counting-house to sign his letters, and see the transactions of the day complete. He was a stately and methodical personage in all he said and did. He had for years dined at a coffee-house in St. Paul's, and his habit was in the morning, on his way eastward, to enter the coffee-room, and address the head-waiter thus, from which he was only once known to make a deviation: "Well, John, and what have you got for dinner to-day?" "A nice slice of Thames salmon, sir; soup as always, and haunch o' mutton, sir." "Then, John, I shall dine with you to-day, you may depend upon it." These questions and the answers were almost as well known to the frequenters of the coffee-house as the establishment itself. One July morning, under a broiling sun, the great merchant entered as usual. "Well, John, and what have you got for dinner to-day?" "Werry nice dinner indeed, sir, to-day; ain't it vonderful hot, sir?" the perspiration pouring down John's face. "Sir, there's a beautiful salmon, sir, two kinds of soup, sirloin o' beef, turkey and sassages; the burial-people, sir, dines vith us to-day." "The burial-people, John?" "Yes, sir, the poor gemman vat died in the room over this of putrid fever on Tuesday is to be buried to-day, as we fears e von't keep no longer."

"Then" (hurrying to the door), "John, I shall *not* dine with you to-day, you may depend upon it."

141. *Simpson's Tombstone.*

A Scotch neighbor of mine in England, who tells his anecdotes admirably, mentioned to me the following, which I understood him to say he had sent to Dean Ramsay, but as it did not appear in the Very Reverend the Dean's charming work, "Reminiscences of Scottish Life and Character," I have availed myself of it without any felonious intention:

John Simpson, or John Simson, had prepared in life the epitaph which he wished to appear over him in death, and kept it in his house. His executors, in a few days after his interment, carried out his instructions, and the parishioners next Sabbath were reading in the churchyard—

"TYRANNIC KINGS,
GRASPING PRIESTS,
AND
ABJECT SLAVES, MUST ALL LIE WITH ME,
JOHN SIMSON,"

(or Simpson). The clergyman of the parish, after consultation with his elders, raised a legal question for the removal of the obnoxious tombstone, but before the matter was decided he himself died. It was suggested to the parson who succeeded, to revive the issue, which his predecessor had commenced, but he demurred to this, and being asked for his grounds of objection, "Well," said he, "it is quite clear to me that the deceased was not very particular during life in his associates, and I should recommend our letting him alone in death to rest quietly in his grave."

142. *A Grumbling Widow cured.*

A friend of mine used to relate an instance of a lucky expedient he adopted to cure a perverse, obstinate, discontented, and ill-tempered ward, for whom he had been appointed trustee on the death of the best and most indulgent of husbands. He and others had observed that their deceased friend's mucous membrane had been for years out of order: this they attributed to the constant worry and irritation to which he was exposed in the home circle. He at last died, and the only act of unkindness, said my friend, "I ever experienced at the hand of the deceased was when he took up his pen and signed his name appointing me under his will his acting executor, thus involving me in the guardianship and protection of his widow. Unfortunately, there was no family. My late poor friend"—he proceeded to tell me—"was somewhat of a wag; and, therefore, instead of leaving me a ring or some slight memento, he devised to me a living legacy, so that I, who had gone through years of uninterrupted happiness at home, should not be allowed to pass to my rest without a taste—and it proved a very bitter one—of that experience he had acquired in wedlock. If there was a woman under *her* bereavement who should have been comfortable and happy, it was this person. Her home was charming, even luxurious. She had a circle of friends anxious to be kind to her—if not on her own merits, at least on those of the husband whom she had lost. She had the expenditure of a jointure of £3,000 a year; but nothing pleased her. One day it would be that her coachman had neglected to remind her of a call she should have made during the drive of the previous afternoon, although she had told him particularly to attend to this. As a matter of course, the executor must look into the grievous act of omission forthwith, and advise whether the coachman should not be at once discharged. At another time the gardener had neglected some little hot-house arrangement, a matter which, as involving the question of heat, it may be conceived with her took precedence of all other complaints. Then, so as to keep her pulse as near to fever-point as possible, and prevent the previous growling-fit to subside, some answer that her maid had given her was deemed insolent, and she conceived that the duties of an executor compelled him to demand an apology from the bedchamber offender, or mistress of the robes.

The old man-servant of her late husband was the only person below-stairs whom she feared. She had made the trial once to put him down, but only once, for he showered upon her such a torrent of family reminiscences that she thought it wiser, with one whose memory was so clear and retentive, to let *him* alone for the future.

The woman could not exist without having a weekly grievance to report to her husband's executor. On one occasion there was a little difficulty between the joint and the cook, and the executor was summoned next forenoon. He had the head of the culinary department under examination for some minutes in the drawing-room, and was on the point of declaring, in the presence and hearing of mistress and cook, that he considered the charge, in parliamentary language, against the accused "both frivolous and vexatious," but the former, who was extremely astute, saw that a hostile decision was coming, and desired cook to withdraw. My friend, in telling his story, said: "I now found my own mucous membrane and digestive powers rapidly succumbing under my executorial annoyances. I had sacrificed much valuable time for this woman, and my patience had now reached the last stage of exhaustion. During the poor cook's cool and calm explanation, my blood had been simmering, but was now rapidly approaching the boiling-point; my interesting ward observed this, and just at the moment my vessel of wrath and indignation was going to flow over, bethought herself she would adopt with me without a moment's delay the soothing system: 'My dear sir, you see exactly how I am treated by my servants; what would you recommend me to do?' I instantly rose from my seat, seized my hat, gave her a look which she never forgot. '*Do*, madam,' I exclaimed, 'why, *die*, or I must;' and left her to her own meditations, with the word *die* echoing in her ears and throughout her corridor." The following week my friend discovered that his own domestics had been talking to his wife of the great reform that had taken place in the widow's household. "Vathever, ma'am, as hour master been a doing vith Mrs. ——, has er servants his now so appy? They says, ma'am, master as made her turn hover a new leaf. Vat a vonderful leaf, ma'am, hit must a been!"

143. "*Now, my dear Duke.*"

When residing in one of the metropolitan counties, before railways existed, or even the first Reform Bill had passed, the passengers of our four-horse stage-coach had frequently, as a fellow-traveller, a London alderman and ex-Lord Mayor, who was one of the members of Parliament for the City. One daily traveller, a joyous-hearted man and fond of a joke, if he found any new faces to amuse, could never resist throwing out his hook for the alderman, who at once rose to it. A year or two previous to this, as Lord Mayor, he had been connected with the extensive City improvements, commenced soon after the erection of New London Bridge, in which, as is well known, the Duke of Wellington took a great interest, occasionally riding on horseback into the City as early as six o'clock in the morning to inspect their progress. The alderman was a very good-looking, gentlemanly man, with much *bonhommie* superadded to great volubility, with this peculiarity, that once Lord Mayor, always Lord Mayor; for to the stranger who met him for the first time, and whose fortune or fate it was to have a two-hours' stage-coach drive with him, he was chief magistrate of London *in præsenti*, and once touch on the City improvements you had him instantly, within the walls of Apsley House, in familiar *tête-à-tête* with the Great Duke, and himself Lord Mayor. If the City architects had suggested any alteration, my Lord Mayor, or my ex-Lord Mayor, deemed it incumbent upon himself to communicate in person the fact to the Duke as Premier, or as Governor of the Tower. The interviews, as described for the enlightenment of the outside or inside passengers of the coach in question, as the case might be, and in accordance with the state of the weather, consisted chiefly of emphatic expressions, such as, "Now, my dear duke, I do assure your Grace," etc.; to which the noble Duke was made to reply, "Now, my Lord Mayor, I have such confidence in your sound judgment in regard to the city improvements, and my time at present is so fully occupied, that I leave every thing in your hands." "All this" (as the alderman felicitously expressed himself) "was, of course, extremely flattering and gratifying to me, coming, as it did, from such a man as the Duke of Wellington." A good deal more on the same exalted topic followed, as may be supposed.

Another weakness of the alderman was to have his name ventilated at this time as the intended purchaser of a large estate in the County of Kent, then in the market. The alderman's dimensions as a millionnaire, be it observed, were in an inverse ratio to his own estimate of his personal qualifications as a senator and high city functionary. A county newspaper had announced that Mr. Alderman —— had spent a couple of days in minutely examining the splendid estate of Somerhill, and it was currently reported that negotiations had already proceeded so far that they, as journalists, might almost announce authoritatively that the purchase was on the eve of completion. A copy of the county journal had reached our facetious friend, the passenger to and fro by the stage-coach, and a cruel surmise was floated that it had been posted, though not addressed, by the alderman. "Ah, Alderman ——, how sly you have been! but every thing oozes out where great men are concerned. Still, I do think you might have taken us into your confidence, instead of leaving us to find out that you had purchased that magnificent estate. Far from kind, Mr. Alderman, and, I tell you frankly, I feel your want of ingenuousness extremely." "I assure you, my good sir, the negotiations are all at an end—I could not entertain the timber question for a moment. Only think of their valuing the timber on the property at £25,000!" "Ah, then," said his friend, "as the matter is generally spoken of in the city and elsewhere, may I consider myself authorized to say that you split on the timber?" "Entirely, for, had this outrageously high valuation not been put on the timber, I had seriously considered the question of making myself a land-owner in Kent." "Alderman, I now understand you perfectly. Your bankers won't be sorry to hear that your proposed large investment in land is at an end, for you would have drawn your balance pretty close. It is not all of us, alderman, who can command £180,000, with or without timber."

It was a lucky matter for the alderman's coach companions, that a great capitalist actually became the purchaser of the estate and the timber upon it; for, so long as it remained unsold, unless there was something important to discuss politically—and we had no London morning papers so early in those days—the invariable question cropped up, "How fares it, alderman, with the Somerhill Estate?" Which was usually followed by a Scotchman who travelled daily by this coach quietly remarking to his fellow-passengers, "What a *puir blethering* silly *crettur* this alderman is, not to see that we make a laughing-stock of him!"

In closing these remarks on this London city magnate, I may mention another little instance of his vanity, which I also witnessed. The Lord Mayor *de facto* was entertaining some members of the Cabinet in the Mansion House, at which I was present. The evening closed with one of London's densest fogs. The time had arrived for the party to break up, and accidentally meeting the alderman in the drawing-room, some one said he feared his (the alderman's) coachman would find it impossible to take him into the country that night. "Oh, dear, quite impossible; I remain at the Mansion House; in fact, the state bed has been ordered." We had never heard of the "state bed;" but the alderman was communicative, and informed us that "there was a state bed in the Mansion House, which was occupied only by a member of the Royal Family or of the Court of Aldermen."

144. *Were you ever at a Lap-dog Soirée?*

I was lately asked the above question. "A lap-dog *soirée!*" I exclaimed. "I do not wonder at your surprise," said the lady; "I went to one, but shall never go to a second." I begged her to describe it. It would appear that a rich old bachelor at Brighton, where my friend had been staying, wrote to her, inviting her to come to his lap-dog *soirée*, and bring her dear little Bella, making her look very smart. In accordance with the request, Bella was festooned all over, in addition to an ornamental cord. That the interesting little darlings might get home early, the hour fixed was five, when carriages and little dogs, to the number of about thirty, inclusive, reached the door of the entertainer. On entering the drawing-room, it became manifest to my friend that the controlling power was deficient, as violent altercations sprang up on all sides of the room, whether from fits of jealousy, or from what cause, was never clearly ascertained, but a general fight soon ensued, at the very moment the alarmed ladies were preparing to withdraw themselves and their pets, and the combatants were separated only by a strong force of footmen entering, but not until wounds had been inflicted, many so serious as in some cases to require weeks to heal.

My friend's interesting little creature, possessing, unfortunately, great personal beauty, and whose sex, one might have anticipated, would have protected her, was cruelly mawled, and her mistress's own feelings deeply lacerated; otherwise, as the mildest and most gentle of women—"one who loses all sense of *self* in the sentiment of kindness, tenderness, and devotion to another"—she never would have been betrayed into using such strong language toward the host of the entertainment as the following: "What a fool a man must be to give a lap-dog *soirée!*"

145. *How a West-end Party can be managed.*

I heard a humorous English country clergyman make a large party laugh very heartily, by describing his own and his wife's astonishment, as a young couple, at their first peep into London society. They had come up to town to pass a few weeks during the gay season, and calling upon the Countess of ——, one of their parishioners, her ladyship said she was glad to see them, as she had a nice party for them the following Friday, and, going to her secrétaire, filled up a card for Mrs. ——'s assembly. As a quiet couple from the provinces, they found themselves on the night in question amid *la crême de la crême* of the West End, and in a mighty crush. In the course of the evening they were next to a lady whose amiable countenance gave encouragement to address her. "Pray, madam, could you point out to us Mrs. ——?" "Oh, I am Mrs. ——" (the lady giving the party). "I beg pardon, madam, as we are comparatively speaking strangers in London; and it was through the kindness of the Countess of —— that we had the honor of receiving your invitation." Finding that the hostess was apparently glad to talk to my wife and myself, and being anxious to have some of the lions and lionesses pointed out, I asked her which was the Russian ambassador. "Really, I cannot tell you, as I fear I know very few more in the room than you do, for my very dear and kind friend, the Countess, undertook the charge of the whole affair, and I did not, at her request, issue a single invitation."

146. *A Bet on a Sermon.*

Admiral —— told me he once heard in the churchyard of his county parish, within ten minutes of the service commencing, a parishioner betting with the parish clerk a pot of beer that he knew what the sermon would be. "I'll bet you a pot of beer you don't." "Vell, hit vill be the 'sounding brass and tinkling cymbal' sermon; hi thinks this his *jist* habout the times o' year hit comes round." The bet being made, the clerk hurried off to the parson to ask him what his sermon was to be. "Why do you ask such a question?" "'Cause, sir, —— as betted me a pot of beer that it is the 'sounding brass and tinkling cymbal' sermon." His reverence, finding he was a party implicated in the bet, desired the clerk to go up to his room and bring down the first sermon from the top, and put this one at the bottom. The clerk afterward bragged at the public-house of the way in which he won his pot of beer.

147. *A Countryman of Mine on the Ignorance to be met with in England.*

A well-known London actuary used to tell a story of his having gone into the country on purpose to look at the house of his favorite poet, Dryden. Meeting a rural policeman, he asked him where the house was. "Do you mean, sir, the ouse vere the man his vot as got ahind vith is rent?" was the intelligent answer. Another anecdote of the same actuary was to the effect that in passing up Regent Street he saw a vase in a window, or some choice article of vertu, that attracted his attention, and went into the shop to express his admiration of it. In the course of his observations he exclaimed, "How much Benvenuto Cellini would have enjoyed this!" "Well, sir, if you will tell the gentleman to call, I shall be happy to show it to him."

A Scotchman who was present, and who never changed a feature, or manifested any thing in the least approaching a smile, said, "*Weel*, gentlemen, I *donn't* at all object to the anecdotes themselves, but I beg to say that such a thing could not have happened in Scotland; *naething o'* the sort; and it is *onnly anither* instance—and I *hae* met *wi' mony o'* late—*o'* the *fearfu'* ignorance that prevails in England. But at the same time I am ready to admit—and I do it with extreme reluctance—that the Scotch character *fa's aff* sadly in England. I recollect I was forcibly struck with this some years ago. I had come to London for a few weeks, and had been engaged one Saturday forenoon in the *ceety*, and after I had got through *ma* business I got into an omnibus at the Mansion House to carry me to Pall Mall. I found myself sitting *niest* to *ane o'* your big merchants, a Scotchman. I had known him for years, not intimately, but still *weel eneuch* to shake hands and get into general conversation. After this, I *couldna* exactly *mak oot* what he was *havering* and *jabbering* to me *aboot* his carriage. At last I discovered what he meant, which was, that I was to know that he always drove into and out *o'* the *ceety* in his carriage as far as Southwark Bridge, but his *cotchman* had that day made a mistake and had not come for him. *Weel*, then, just before we got to the Duke *o'* Northumberland's *hoose* at Charing Cross, he said to me, 'Do you know the fare from the *ceety?*' I was *deevilish* angry at this piece *o'* upstart pride, and I answered him somewhat sharply, 'You should know the omnibus fare better than I do, a stranger in London; but it was *saxpence* when I was last here.' I wonder what his poor *faither* or his *grandfaither*, had he been alive, would have said had I *tauld* him this on getting back to Scotland. His *grandfaither* was a very *wee* body in his time, and had to look on *baith* (both) sides *o'* a *saxpence* before he parted with it. I was *tauld* that this great London merchant, who had a country *sate* some miles from London, imitated what royalty, or the lord-lieutenant *o'* the *coonty*, as representing the sovereign, is only entitled to do, but certainly not a *ceety* merchant—namely, to have a flag hoisted on his arrival and lowered on his departure, as if the public cared a jot whether he had his pen *ahint* his *lug* (behind his ear) in the *ceety*, or was digging up gowans (dandelion) *oot o'* his bit *o'* a park in the country. *Ma* (my) opinion is, that a man is a great fool for this sort *o'* display, for if he has not got some *o'* 'the *bluid o'* the Howards' in his veins, the hoisting the flag is sure to call up his antecedents, which otherwise would have been allowed to remain quiet."

148. *A Matter of Choice.*

Among the numerous anecdotes of my late Lincolnshire clerical friend, the Rev. W. Wright, of Brattleby, was the following:

The clergyman of a mountainous district in Yorkshire, whose parsonage was under repair, arrived at the public-house of the village to attend to his duties on the Sunday morning. The rain was descending in torrents, and, when the time had arrived for going into church, he sent the clerk to see what sort of congregation there was, who returned and reported that it consisted of Smith and Davies, the two shepherds. On hearing this the clergyman said, "You had better go and ask them whether they would prefer a sermon or a pot of beer." He came back immediately to inform him that they would much prefer the pot of beer. The pot was sent for and discussed accordingly; and the sermon put by for a "more convenient season."

149. *The Late Robert Crichton Wyllie, Minister of Foreign Affairs to the King of the Sandwich Islands.*

A few months before my poor brother lost his life on the island of Guadalcanar, in the South Seas, he wrote me an interesting letter from Honolulu, and by the same ship sent me a piece of the rock on which Captain Cook, the famous navigator, was killed, in 1779. In this letter he mentioned having renewed his acquaintance with Mr. R. C. Wyllie, the Prime Minister, or Minister of Foreign Relations, to the King of the Sandwich Islands. Some of my readers may feel a desire to know how Foreign-Office affairs are conducted at Honolulu, and, as I possess a letter from the department addressed to my late brother, the following is a copy:

"Department of Foreign Relations,
"Honolulu, February 21, 1850.

"SIR: By order of the King, I have the honor to convey to you His Majesty's thanks, for your humanity in rescuing from a situation of great danger, during the late severe gales, on the coast of Maui, a boat containing seven subjects of His Majesty, of which act of kindness information has been received through His Excellency the Governor of that Island.

"And I am further commanded to acquaint you that it pleased His Majesty, in Council, this day, to order that no port charges whatever be levied on the yacht Wanderer, or any other yacht navigated for purposes of pleasure or service, and not for those of trade.

"For myself, I have to add that it pleases me much to be the organ of this communication to a friend for whom I entertain so much personal esteem, and to assure you of the high respect with which I have the honor to be, Sir,

"Your most obedient servant,
(Signed) "R. C. WYLLIE.

"Benjamin Boyd, Esq.,
"The Wanderer, Royal Yacht Squadron, Honolulu Roads."

As it is somewhat remarkable to meet with one who begins life as a medical man, then becomes a merchant, subsequently a London West-end Club man, and lastly Minister to the King of the Sandwich Islands, I had prepared a little sketch of my deceased friend's career, but, having had handed to me an extract from one of our leading Scotch journals, the *Ayr Advertiser*, I adopt it, as very much better than any data I possessed:

"An Adventurous Life.

"The mournful intelligence has this week reached us of the death of Robert Crichton Wyllie, Minister of Foreign Affairs, etc., to the King of Hawaii—a gentleman who raised himself by his indomitable perseverance and talents to a high position of honor and fame. He was born at Hazelbank, in the parish of Dunlop, on October 13, 1798. He was the second son of the late Alexander Wyllie, Esq., of Hazelbank, and Janet Crichton, of Culstraw, Stewarton. Those who knew him in boyhood can well remember that from his earliest years he gave every indication of being possessed of talents above mediocrity. He received the first elements of education under the late Mr. Bryce, parish teacher, Dunlop, and afterward for some time attended the late Dr. Barr, of Glasgow, while he taught a number of families in the district of Broadlie, in this parish. Thereafter, Mr. Wyllie left for Glasgow College, and received his medical diploma before he was twenty years of age. He soon after left as surgeon in a vessel bound for the North Seas, and endured hardships and braved dangers like a true Scotchman. He was thrice shipwrecked, and returned to Liverpool, but not to home, having left with his firm resolution to do so only after he had earned a fame worthy of his name. Through the instrumentality of his late teacher, Dr. Barr, who was then in Liverpool, he reëmbarked in a vessel bound for South America, where for a short time he practised as a surgeon, but soon turned his attention to mercantile affairs, for which, in tact and talent, he was in every respect adapted.

"After a sojourn of fourteen years there, he revisited his native land, and, as one of the first fruits of his success, built a mansion-house for his parents on the lands of Hazelbank. He proved truly a devoted son, and those who were acquainted with his aged parents can well remember the feelings of pride and gratitude they ever cherished for him till their dying day. He then, feeling time hanging heavily on his hands, left for London, and was soon again engaged in mercantile transactions. But, acting on an idea which seemed to have actuated him, he went to the Sandwich Islands, where for the last twenty years he occupied an important field of usefulness, with great benefit to the natives there and much honor to himself. It is gratifying to find that, from the highest to the lowest in that land of his adoption, all are at one in testifying to his many virtues, and recording his death as truly a national calamity."

My late friend was brimful of Scotch anecdotes, which he related admirably. There was one he scarcely ever avoided repeating to me when we met, be it in the street, the drawing-room, or the Club. He had it from his father, who knew "daft Sandy." Poor Sandy was a half-witted creature, with an admixture of sly, humorous cunning, what we call (Scottice) an *auld farrant haverel*, who wandered about his district, receiving food and shelter from one or other. He was quite harmless, and generally a welcome visitor, for he was famous for rhyming to any thing that was said to him. One day Lord Boyd and his neighbor, Laird Crawford, saw Sandy coming, and Crawford said to his friend that he would puzzle Sandy. Lord Boyd said he would not, and a small bet followed. Crawford the Laird was not the most moral man in the county, and daft Sandy knew this. As Sandy approached, Crawford put down his head to butt Sandy, at the same time making a noise as like a bull as he could—boo, boo, boo! To this Sandy gave an instant rejoinder:

"The worthless Crawford and Lord Boyd,
Of grace and manners baith are void,
Wha like twa bulls amang the kye,
Ye boo at folks as they gang bye."

It was alleged that Laird Crawford was never colloquial with daft Sandy after this.

150. *An Intended Scotch Breakfast at Greenwich.*

The late Mr. James Stuart, of Dunearn, Fifeshire, so well known in Scotland fifty years ago as a leader in Whig politics, but who, for the last twenty years of his life, resided in London, was one of the kindest and most hospitable of men. On the occasion of a holiday early in the parliamentary session he had invited a party of his political and non-political friends to meet him at the Trafalgar Hotel, Greenwich, the following Friday morning, at ten, not to eat whitebait, but to partake of what he emphatically called, in his note of invitation, "a first-rate Scotch breakfast." He added that he expected two or three English friends to be present who were strangers to such an entertainment. He had written to the landlord to provide a "Scotch breakfast" for twelve at 10 A. M., and a dinner for the same number at 6 P. M. We were likewise told that our Caledonian breakfast was to be succeeded by a comprehensive pedestrian excursion over Blackheath and Woolwich Common to the summit of Shooter's Hill, so that we might do justice to our English dinner.

The party arrived at the hour fixed, with appetites well attuned by a sharp March frost for the good things that awaited them. The landlord, Sharp by name and sharp by nature—in regard to punctuality at least—announced that breakfast was ready. Never was an intimation more joyously received by hungry men who had been for some minutes painting in their minds the scene that was awaiting a realization in the adjoining apartment—*videlicet*, tea, coffee, chocolate, with those envied exotics in the eyes of a Londoner, fresh or new-laid eggs, in abundance, broiled and cold ham, Findon haddock, of course, possibly salmon steaks, in addition to that splendid garniture of a Scotch breakfast table, Dundee marmalade, with heather honey, strawberry, that queen of jams, raspberry and currant jelly, etc.

What was our surprise on entering the room to observe a large tureen at the top and an equally large one at the bottom of the table! Nothing else on it—not even a tea-cup visible. The giver of the breakfast was almost speechless, his famished guests appalled; but they were much too hungry and prudent to allow their indignant host's orders to remove the obnoxious tureens to take effect—a slight inspection having convinced us that they were tenanted with excellent mutton broth of a most substantial character—the crowded nuggets afloat of well-cooked meat attracting peculiar attention.

The landlord was called upon by our excited entertainer for an explanation; he stated that, never having before prepared a Scotch breakfast, he had consulted a friend, who told him that if they were Scotch gentlemen the correct dish was broth. This explanation, if possible, rather added to the excitement of our friend. An order, and a very peremptory one, was now given for tea, coffee, with et ceteras; but before they arrived, the contents of both tureens had disappeared—an operation in which our English colleagues ably assisted. Our inability to do more in the way of breakfast now became manifest.

We proceeded on our walk, and whenever our attention was for a time withdrawn from the sylvan attractions of Greenwich Park, or from settling the question of the rival claims of Blackheath and Woolwich in the matter of landscape, we had to listen to a violent anathema hurled by our host against the unfortunate landlord of the Trafalgar.

Our English friends assured him they had never breakfasted more satisfactorily, and one of the party declared to us that he had heard one of the waiters say quietly at the side-table: "Vat vonderful happetites these Scotch gents as, hand so hearly hin the day, too!"

We endeavored to calm our friend by suggesting that his well-meant attempt at a Scotch breakfast at Greenwich should now be looked upon as a thing of the past, but, as his English visitors had still to be indoctrinated in its mysteries, we should hold ourselves disengaged for another morning, when, should his instructions be clearly defined—which, in justice to the landlord, we pronounced to have been extremely vague—we had no misgivings that a very excellent breakfast *de more Scottorum* might be produced at the Trafalgar.

151. "*Please, Sir, will you kindly give me a little Salt?*"

Talking of a Scotch breakfast—or an attempted one—at Greenwich reminds me of an anecdote the late Mr. Coates used to tell. He had, he said, never known a request so ably or so judiciously put, inasmuch as it was complied with fourfold. A boy, on a hot summer morning, was passing down St. James's Street, or along Pall Mall, when he observed two gentlemen agreeably occupied at breakfast at their Club window, which was open. Adopting as rapidly as possible a supplicatory attitude and tone, he addressed one of the gentlemen thus: "Please, sir, will you kindly give me a little salt?" "A little salt, boy; what do you want with a little salt?" "Oh, sir, please do; for, if you give me a little salt, perhaps this gentleman will give me an egg." Not only was an egg forthcoming and salt,.but a good-sized cup of coffee, in addition to a muffin.

Another of Mr. Coates's anecdotes, which he liked to address to me as a Scotchman, was the difference between the London-Irish bootmaker and the London-Scotch bootmaker. An Irish gentleman entered the shop of a countryman of his own in the West End, and was measured for a pair of boots. A few days afterward he came to try them on, but was highly displeased with them, and called upon the Hibernian bootmaker to explain. "*Bedad, sor*, it is mighty *aisey* to explain. You've got, *sor*, a large foot, and a very *clomsy* foot into the bargain." After this plain matter-of-fact statement and the explosion that followed, the offended gentleman, indignantly rejecting the boots, sought solace and relief at a Scotch bootmaker's close by, and, while his measure was being taken, he explained to the more cautious-spoken Scot how the impudent fellow, whose shop he had just left, had served him and at the same time insulted him very grossly by telling him that he had a large foot and a very clumsy foot. "*Weel*, sir," said the Scotchman, who was taking his measure with much care, "I will not say that you have *aither* a large *fut* or a very clumsy *fut*, but I will say this, that it will *tak* a *dale* of leather to cover it." The story of "Please, sir, kindly give me a little salt," reminds me of the story of a gentleman being politely asked, when driving on the high-road, by a respectable-looking man, if he would have the kindness to give a lift to his great-coat to the next town: he told him he had no objection, on which the pedestrian stepped up in all speed into the carriage and took his seat. "Why, sir, you asked me to take your great-coat?" "Yes, sir, I did; but I am inside my great-coat, and I know, sir, you are much too polite to separate us."

152. *Lord Stowell and Dr. Johnson.*

Lord Stowell, it is said, felt much hurt that John Wilson Croker had not consulted him while writing the "Life of Johnson," as he was the only surviving public man who had really known the doctor, and could have furnished many most interesting anecdotes of the celebrated lexicographer, which, unfortunately, went to the tomb with the great judge of the Court of Admiralty.

Lord Stowell, then William Scott, of University College, Oxford, entertained Johnson. In those days the dinner was at two; the party sat till five, after having imbibed a fair quantity of port, eight years in bottle, and fruity. This was the port the Brothers Scott liked; and it is said that it was supplied by their relative Mr. Surtees, of Newcastle-on-Tyne. The party adjourned to the College garden, and Johnson observed Scott pitching snails which had come out after rain on the walks into his neighbor's garden, "Hallo, Scott," exclaimed Johnson, "do unto thy neighbor as you would be done by." "But, my dear doctor," said Scott, "he is a Dissenter." "A Dissenter!" ejaculated Johnson; "then pitch away."

Lord Stowell used to refer with a smile to Dr. Johnson and his promising pupil, Sir John Ladd, the future four-in-hand celebrity, to whom he was for a time private tutor. The young baronet, when he reached his majority, succeeded to an unencumbered property of £40,000 a year and £100,000 in cash. One day a friend asked Dr. Johnson how his pupil got on. "Why, sir, he is as wild as the wind, as light as a feather, and does not know that twenty shillings are equal to a pound."

The youthful baronet went to Oxford, and was shown a set of rooms that had been prepared for him. "What! are these to be my rooms?" "Yes, sir; nothing better in the College." "Nothing better?" "No, sir." "Then," turning to his servant, "order four posters, as I shall return to London forthwith;" and here ended Sir John Ladd's University career. He frequently became the associate of royalty, living a good deal at Oatlands with the Duke of York, and ultimately became a pensionary of the Regent. He is said to have been in the days of his adversity a successful negotiator in making up marriages, drawing a commission for his services. With this calling he united that of touter for fasionable coach-builders, who paid him handsomely for any orders he procured. My reverend friend, to whom I am indebted for these anecdotes of Lord Stowell, Doctor Johnson, and Sir John Ladd, recollected, as a young man, the charioteer Baronet visiting his father from the Duke of York's, at Oatlands, and on each occasion his great desire seemed to be to induce his worthy parent, the rector of his parish and lord of the neighboring manor, to drive with him. He at last succeeded, and from the moment the worthy divine mounted and occupied the box-seat of the drag Ladd's ambition appeared to be to dart into every kind of danger, and court, if possible, an upset. I think I understood my reverend friend to say that he at last secured a "a spill," but nothing serious was the result—quite enough, however, to make his father resolve for the future to abstain from intrusting himself to the coachmanship of Sir John Ladd.

William Scott and John Scott—the future Lord Stowell and Earl of Eldon—were much attached to each other, and in early life always devoted at least one day in each year to a lark together in the country. On one occasion they had dropped upon a country inn where, to their excessive delight and satisfaction, the port-wine was excellent—in fact, first rate. This attraction soon determined the learned brothers to cast anchor, dine, and pass the night. Next day—we must assume it was the evening—they found themselves charged for eight bottles of port. Lord Stowell used to say, "Whether we drank them I can't exactly say; but we paid for them."

An aged friend of mine told me within the last few months that he had been dining, as a young man, at the Pitt Club, the late Lord Harrowby in the chair, and that as the party were breaking up he found Lord Eldon, after his usual potation of port, at the top of the staircase, looking anxiously down it, evidently weighing in his legal mind the question of descent, at the same time measuring it by the eye! "My Lord Chancellor," said my friend, "can I be of any assistance to your lordship?" "Of the greatest, at this moment," seizing my friend by the arm. It was now, comparatively speaking, a *facilis descensus*, and the keeper of the King's conscience was safely seated in his carriage.

My friend who had acted as the Lord Chancellor's prop mentioned another anecdote. Lord Stowell had told his brother that he had made a certain purchase which he had been some time contemplating, and that he was to pay the money into So-and-so's credit at his banker's that day. "Don't make the payment to-day, William." "But I must, John." "Oblige me by not making it to-day." The fact was, the Lord Chancellor had that day signed a fiat of bankruptcy against the firm.

153. *The Buono Mano.*

When I was in Italy, a quarter of a century back, it used to be alleged that, pay an Italian post-boy as liberally as you liked, he would still ask you for a "buono mano."

An English nobleman, who was travelling with his family, resolved to test this statement. Accordingly, the *postiglione*, at the end of the post or day's journey, was desired to wait upon his lordship, who gave him double what he was entitled to. The recipient made his bow, returned thanks, and retired; but just as he had reached the door he turned round, and attiring his countenance in that beseeching expression at which the Italians are adepts, exclaimed, "Oh, signore, buono mano."

The Irish Dublin carman is said to belong to the Italian school in this respect. The peculiarity came on the tapis at a dinner-party at Morrison's Hotel in Dublin, when one of the party present defended Paddy from what he considered an unjust imputation—a member of a hard-working, facetious, and obliging branch of the community—and, in support of his opinion, offered to bet his friends £10 that he would drive from their hotel to the Rotunda at the top of Sackville Street and back without any such importunity, one of the party to accompany him as a guarantee that nothing *ex curia* was said to Paddy *en route.* Accordingly, an outside car was sent for, and started for the Rotunda, the rest of the party awaiting its return outside the hotel. Paddy set down his two passengers and was presented with three half-crowns, being more than three times his fare. He turned them over in his hand and then said, "Och, yer honor, can't you *jist* make it the *nate* half sovereign?"

154. *Whist.*

I was rather interested, last summer, while looking over the hand of a septuagenarian friend of mine, a member of the Portland (since deceased), and one of our most excellent whist-players, in listening to the advice which from time to time he offered a young man who was his partner, and who overrated his ability as a whist-player. My friend had evidently formed a very different estimate of his knowledge of the game, and consequently was led to tender him some useful hints: "Never, if you take my advice, go beyond ten shilling points, and at this rate you may lose £14 in an hour; for, through a long course of whist-playing, I made it a rule, as far as I could adjust it, to rise when I had lost this sum. Moreover, I was satisfied, under such circumstances, with an hour at the game. By adhering to this as closely as I could manage to do, and having at the same time the satisfaction of sitting down at my Club with some of the best players in London, my losses have never averaged more than £60 to £70 in any one season, nor have my gains been different. Another rule I acted upon was this—and I should recommend it for your adoption—that, if I lost £14 at the beginning of the week, no inducement would make me play until the following Monday. In this way, I can confidently assert that no man in a long life has enjoyed greater pleasure in his rubber than I have." He mentioned that one season he had accompanied a young friend to Wiesbaden, and afterward to Baden-Baden, who had a penchant for play. "I said to him, 'Will you take my advice?' He said he would. 'Well, then, if you do so, you may make money; at all events, you won't ruin yourself. Never risk more than two pounds or fifty francs in *one* night; when that is gone, you go home to your hotel.'"

Turning to me—I had a book in my hand with rather small print—"You require advice, also, which I heard the late Sir Henry Halford give: 'If you wish to preserve your eyes, never read by candle-light any thing smaller than the ace of clubs.'"

155. *Sydney Smith and the Bishop of London* (*Dr. Blomfield*).

It was always suspected that a sly passage of arms was constantly going on between the Canon and his diocesan. His lordship being asked by one of his clergy connected with St. Paul's for leave of absence for a few months on urgent private business, the Bishop said, "I have no objection whatever, provided Sydney Smith will allow me."

The Bishop had accepted an invitation to dinner at a house where Sydney Smith was also to be present. The non-arrival of his lordship delayed the dinner, when at last a note reached the host to say that the Bishop, as he was entering London House, had been bitten by a dog, so that he must be excused. The note was read to the assembled guests, when the Dean remarked that he should much like to hear the dog's account of the affair.

When the question of putting down wooden pavement around St. Paul's was first mooted, the Bishop summoned the authorities of the Cathedral to meet him. Sydney Smith arrived early, but when some little impatience was expressed at the non-arrival of the prelate and other dignitaries, the witty Dean remarked that, as the question of blockheads had to be discussed, they had no other course left them than to wait.

The late Lord Lansdowne used to declare that Sydney Smith was essential to his existence; but whether the reverend Canon stood in a similar important relation to his diocesan, I am not informed.

156. *Parliamentary Corruption.*

The following anecdote should be told only after the close of a general election, not before; but, as we hope shortly to enter the millennium of purity in such matters, my relating it will now be innocuous.

The late Mr. ——, the eminent solicitor, contended, speaking of parliamentary corruption, that nothing was easier to carry out, if common prudence were only observed. He described a case where he was professionally employed to administer a *solatium* of £2,000 to an important election agent. He was desired to be looking in at a print-shop window in the Strand *precisely* at twelve o'clock, when a party behind would tap him on the shoulder, and repeat a line of Shakespeare; that at five minutes past twelve he would receive another tap, and have a second line from the same illustrious author repeated in his ear; that a further interval of five minutes would ensue—his watch to be consulted—when the immortal Shakespeare, already made a *particeps criminis*, was again to be a subsidiary—"to what vile uses do we come at last"—and a third line from his divine page administered with the indispensable tap on the shoulder. "Then to some foul corrupting hand, their craving lusts with fatal bounty feed, they fall a willing, undefended prize."

After this, the learned gentleman handed from his pocket to his poetical but mythical friend behind a packet containing the bank-notes. When the disputed election came to be investigated before a parliamentary committee, he was able to swear that the person produced was one whom he had never seen in his life.

157. *A Channel of Promotion open to Question.*

My father used to joke an excellent and religious woman, my grandaunt, for the manner in which she obtained a step of well-merited promotion in the Navy for a brave young officer who shortly afterward married her niece.

The lieutenant had come to London to pass a few weeks, after years of varied and most distinguished service afloat. On the Saturday she said to the lieutenant, "You must not go to Windsor to-morrow, as you intended, but accompany us to church, as we have a friend to whom we give a seat in our pew, who generally lunches with us afterward, and whom we particularly wish you should know."

The visit to Windsor Castle was postponed, and Lieutenant Pringle Stoddart, R. N., went to church with his friends. After service he had given his arm to my mother, and was walking close behind my two relatives and their friend, when he was called to the front, and, to his enormous surprise, was introduced to Lord Barham, the First Lord of the Admiralty, who succeeded the first Viscount Melville in 1705. "The better day the better deed," for the first Lord, after lunch, desired the lieutenant to come to him next day at the Admiralty, and a commander's commission followed in due course.

It has often puzzled me why the cheap honors of the Crown are scattered with so sparing a hand to the brave men of the two gallant professions.

As Admiral Pringle Stoddart, who was as modest as he was brave, has been dead for more than twenty years, I quote him as an instance, and I say it is inexplicable to me that such a man, after so brilliant a career, should pass away without the C. B. even attaching to his name.

He was, no doubt, but one of many other brave men similarly overlooked, but few can boast of seeing so much service as Stoddart.

It may appear somewhat inconsistent and singular that my worthy relation did not apprise her dear young friend Pringle Stoddart, in whom she took so deep an interest, that he was to meet in her pew at church the First Lord of the Admiralty. Her explanation on this point when I first heard the circumstance was quite conclusive—that she acted for the best—although she may have laid herself open to the charge my father brought against her of something bordering on spiritual jobbery. The reason she assigned for her reticence was this: that the young sailor, who, although he had "dared the battle and the breeze" for years, and had spilt his blood on more occasions than one, was of so diffident and retiring a disposition, that, had she prepared him for sitting alongside the great official who then presided at the Admiralty, one of two things must have resulted—either that he would have carried out his first intention of spending the day at Windsor, or have had his mind so distracted, never having been before in proximity to the man who stood at the helm of naval affairs in Whitehall, that one of the famous Dr. Newton's evangelical discourses would have been entirely lost upon him.

Those of my readers who may read the subjoined note must agree with me that Rear-Admiral Pringle Stoddart should not have passed to the tomb undecorated by his sovereign.[1]

158. *A Son of Mars taking Office.*

This explanation reminds me of a case somewhat analogous, where a son of Mars, not of Neptune, showed great perturbation of mind, although he had twice shed his blood

[1] Pringle Stoddart entered the Navy in 1783, and the same year was in Sir Edward Hughes's action with Admiral de Suffrein. As a lieutenant in the Russian Navy—a service in which British officers were at that period allowed to enter—he was present, in 1788–9, in two actions with the Turkish fleet, and in a desperate battle, fought July 9, 1790, between the Russians and the Swedes. On the first and last occasions Stoddart was wounded. On returning to the British Navy, after a variety of service, he next joined the "Valiant," one of Lord Howe's fleet, in the action of June 1, 1794. He also shared in Lord Bridport's *rencontre* with the French fleet in 1795. In the "Tremendous" he witnessed the capture of the Dutch squadron in Saldanha Bay, August 17, 1796. In the "Trusty" he accompanied the expedition to the Helder, in 1799; and in the "Kent" assisted in 1801 in expelling the French from Egypt, where he received the "most unequivocal praise of Sir Ralph Abercromby" for his exertions while serving with the Army on the memorable 8th of March, and was highly commended by Sir Sidney Smith for his zealous and gallant conduct in the battles of the 15th and 21st. In acknowledgment of his efforts during the campaign he was presented with a gold medal by the Turkish Government. As a commander in the "Cruizer" he took on January 6 and 26, 1807, "Le Jena" and "Le Brave," privateers of sixteen guns each. He was in the attack upon Copenhagen, and received the praise of Admiral Gambier for the bravery and energy he displayed in a long and heavy contest with a powerful flotilla. He subsequently distinguished himself on the coast of Norway in the capture of two Danish privateers, etc. He was advanced to his flag rank in 1841.

on the battle-field. A public establishment in the City of London which had just been formed, and has since attained a position of great eminence, required a secretary, and my ex-military friend, who had retired from the Army, having, in early life, been brought up in one of our great similar Scotch establishments, had his name and qualifications submitted by my brother to his co-directors. His testimonials being approved, he had merely to go through the simple form of being introduced to the directors. That day, at twelve o'clock, he was to meet them for the first time in their board-room. My brother had taken him there some half-hour previously, to show him where he would sit. It seemed that the twelve empty chairs frightened the embryo secretary as much as "when spirits walk, and ghosts break up their graves," for, at twelve o'clock, to my brother's utter dismay, no secretary appeared to be presented to the Court of Directors.

Their newly-appointed official entered no appearance that day. My brother was puzzled beyond measure, so was I. Hours rolled on, and the dinner-hour came. No Prime Minister had ever defended a colleague who got himself into a mess more earnestly than my brother did the new secretary. However, the bottom of the Thames was not required to be dragged, nor Shooter's Hill to be searched, for the absentee, whose disappearance had caused so much anxiety, as he was again present in the flesh at our dinner-table.

My brother, addressing him seriously, asked him what it all meant. "Well," he said, "to be perfectly candid, when I saw those formidable chairs in the board-room, and reflected that each was to be occupied by a director, who would all fire a shot into me, I knew I could not stand it." "Then," said my brother, "why did you not tell me this?" "I did not like to do so." "What became of you, as we searched and inquired far and near for you?" "Well, I walked right away into the country, knowing that I could explain matters to you." "What part of the country?" "The place I got into was Hackney Kirk-yard, and I spent the day reading the inscriptions on the tombstones." "Well," said my brother, "I thought you were entombed somewhere; but surely you did not gain your spurs as a Knight of the Tower and Sword of Portugal and of San Fernando of Spain" (both of which he was) "by seeking refuge in a church-yard when you were wanted?"

We had a hearty laugh, and next day he commenced his secretarial duties without any formal introduction to the directors or to their chairs, and very efficiently discharged those duties for the next twenty years.

159. *St. Petersburg.*

As a school-boy I had read "The Travels of Dr. Clarke," who declares that "the united magnificence of all the cities of Europe can but equal St. Petersburg." I never forgot this passage in his works, for I immediately set down in my *memoria technica* "City of the Czar, and said to myself, D. V., I must see the modern and ancient capitals of the Russian Empire.

The first thing that puzzles one in going up the Neva by steamboat from Cronstadt is, why Peter the Great founded his city on a low, marshy island; and, as I knew that this most remarkable man in all he did had some great object in view, I felt anxious to have the reason of this fact explained. He had conquered the spot from the Swedes, and he required a fortified sea-port to keep them in check at the mouth of the Neva, as he at once saw that, through this channel, he was to establish, uphold, and develop the resources of his empire, and thus connect himself with civilized Europe. The first great attraction I met with, even before landing from the steamer, was one of the passengers calling my attention to a remarkably handsome man looking over the granite quay, from among the *hoi polloi*, at the passengers landing. My astonishment was unbounded when I was informed that it was the Emperor Nicholas. There was no cheering or any demonstration whatever. He was there simply as a private citizen. Within a week, I witnessed His Majesty in another capacity—commanding a division of his army, amounting to 45,000 men, in a sham-fight against one of his marshals, who commanded a moiety of the force. Englishmen, especially travellers, in Russia, meet with so much courtesy and attention, that during the battle, which lasted from eight or nine in the morning until three in the afternoon, I had myself moved from one mound to another of the field—Zarskoje-Selo—so that every movement and evolution of the troops could be watched. I recollect being told I was about to see something I should not meet with at Wormwood Scrubs, namely, a charge of 10,000 cavalry. The Emperor was defeated, after which there was a muster of marshals, generals, and staff, in the centre of whom, mounted on a magnificent charger, was his Imperial Majesty. At that moment I thought the two handsomest men I had ever seen were the Emperor Nicholas and the late Sir William Maxwell, of Monreith, M. P. for Wigtonshire, who lost his arm at the battle of Corunna. One of the novelties of that day was seeing the evolutions in a supposed battle of 3,000 Cossacks. I had now to devote every day I could command to the inspection of palaces, churches, bazaars, universities, and academies; institutions for army, navy, and gymnastics; an Oriental institution here, a mining academy there; female schools and foundling hospitals; collections of all sorts, zoological and antiquarian; imperial and other libraries, cabinets of coins, etc.

No man, since Peter the Great laid the first stone or pile of his future beautiful city, in 1703, was ever a better customer to the drosky-driver than I was. I was also fortunate in securing the services of a countryman of my own, of the name of Sharp, as a valet-de-place, in calling to my attention every thing that was interesting. The day was fixed for my long land journey to Moscow—no railway at that time existed—when Sharp told me I should be obliged to attend at one of the public departments respecting my passport. I was introduced to a very gentlemanly young man, who asked me my object in visiting Russia, and, finding that the Imperial Government had nothing to apprehend, he said he would see that instructions were transmitted to Moscow to facilitate my seeing the "lions" there, etc., all of which was fully realized. He had made himself so agreeable, and gave me so much valuable information during our interview, that I ventured to make one remark before leaving, which was, that I had had that day in our agreeable and lengthened conversation an opportunity of judging for myself of the extreme facility with which Russian gentlemen acquired a foreign language, as I had never heard the English language more beautifully or purely spoken. He thanked me for what I had stated of his proficiency as an English linguist, and then, laughing very heartily, told me he was an Englishman. I presume I was in a star-chamber of some sort, to have a crucial test applied to me before I was permitted to commence my six hundred miles' journey to Moscow.

160. *The Sensational.*

My brother was a great collector of autographs, and I have never been able to satisfy myself what has become of his collection. The tocsin had been sounded inside the House of Commons by Mr. Robert Wallace, M. P. for Greenock, and outside by Mr. Rowland Hill, that there must ere long be a penny postage, when, of course, the privilege of franking would cease and determine. In consequence, my brother, seeing that the days for franks were now numbered, wrote a note to the Right Hon. Mr. Stewart Mackenzie, M.P., then a member of the India Board, accompanied by a formidable packet of two dozen covers, each containing a sheet of paper, so as to be within the prescribed weight, and begging his Right Hon. friend to use his own time in obtaining the franks of statesmen who *were* or *had been* Cabinet Ministers. To have the verification of the post-office the franks were to be addressed to our residence in Scotland. One day, in the parliamentary committee-rooms, Mr. Stewart Mackenzie ran against the Duke of Wellington and other great statesmen, for he posted in the evening eight letters addressed to my brother by the Duke, Sir Robert Peel, Mr. Goulburn, and others. The arrival of such a batch of letters, and superscribed by statesmen so eminent, created in our little town of Newtonstewart an immense sensation, and during the forenoon the privileged classes were allowed to inspect them. "Whatever can Mr. Boyd be *aboot?* There must be something *vera* important on hand, to *hae a'* those great people writing him and *a'* at *ae* time." As the postmaster had received no instructions to retain the letters, they were readdressed to my brother at the Exchange Rooms in London. Well do I recollect, on going to receive our letters, to find an actual crowd of the members of our Exchange round the letter-bar inspecting the franks, and surmises of all kinds being floated as to what it meant. But the secret was far too profound to be divulged, and for a long period my brother's friends on 'Change looked anxiously for the public affair with which his name was to be connected. The other franks from eminent Whig statesmen, and an occasional one from a conservative ex-Cabinet Minister, came dropping in periodically; thus keeping up the sensational interest—but the solution of the conundrum we kept to ourselves; and I think we were wise in so doing, for nothing is more true than the old saying, "*Omne ignotum pro mirifico.*"

161. *George IV. on the Field of Waterloo.*

I was accompanying my father over the field of Waterloo, when our guide, an old British soldier who had been in the battle, stopped us rather abruptly at what I should say was the northeast corner of Hougomont. "Here, sirs, his the werry spot vere Is Majesty King George IV. said the werry cleverest thing that vas hever said afore hor since by hany king, hi doesn't care a morsel vere ye picks im. Vell, sirs, ven King George vas hon is journey to 'Annover, he pay Waterloo a wisit, hand vas haccompanied by Is Royal Ighness the Duke o' Clarence hand Is Grace the Duke o' Wellington. Just hon this ere spot the Duke o' Wellington's oss slipped hup hon the dry tuff hand a throwed the Duke. Is Majesty vas for ha moment hafeared, so vas the Duke o' Clarence; but the Duke o' Wellington vas hon is feet hin ha moment, hall right. Ven the King sees that, he says to is brother: 'Vell, Clarence, ve can say vat tothers can't, that ve seed Wellington a floored hat Waterloo.'"

162. *Fra (from) Bor-doax, in France, to Lisbon, in Porten-gale (Portugal), or the Difference between Writing and Pronunciation.*

I recollect, many years ago, being introduced to a merchant at Liverpool, a countryman of mine, and a member of a very important firm, who, although he had been an absentee from the "land o' cakes" for half a century, retained his Scotch in as genuine purity as on the day he left it. There was one staple anecdote in reference to a long walk he had been compelled to take in early life, which a witty member of the Club had trotted him out upon for many years, without his ever suspecting that it was so. If there was a stranger who had never heard the anecdote, and every one wished to hear it, the process was very simple, by a slight previous arrangement. "Ah, how do you do? Where were you yesterday?" "Why, taking a confoundedly long walk of nearly twenty miles, from which I have scarcely yet recovered." "You must not call that a long walk before my friend here; he can tell you of something like a walk." "Weel, it's *vera* true, it *wus* (was) the *langest* walk I ever had, and it *wus* in a deevil o' a hurry, too." "Pray, where was it?" "It *wus frae* Bor-doax, in France, to Lisbon, in Porten-gale." "What induced you to take so long a walk?" "*Ye wud hae dune* the same *yersel gin* ye had had a parcel o' French *bag-gonets ahint* ye."

163. *A Useful Book.*

I had made an appointment with the late Mr. Clason, a Writer to His Majesty's Signet, to be with him the following forenoon, at eleven, in Queen Street, Edinburgh, on a matter of business. On my arrival at his house at the hour fixed, the weather being Scottice, "*raal saft*," Anglice, "raining in torrents," I found my learned friend unable to attend to me for the next two hours. In giving me the newspaper, he at the same time handed to me a very dirty-looking volume—awfully thumbed—telling me when I had finished with the former I should find the latter, notwithstanding its uninviting external appearance, amusing and interesting. I soon discovered this description to be extremely meagre, for I had only read a few pages when my attention became absorbed—I may say riveted—so much so, that Mr. Clason and the affair that brought me from London to consult him upon were—to use a term not unfrequently heard at Epsom and Ascot—"nowhere." It was the history of a delinquent clergyman of the Kirk of Scotland who had fought and defended himself for years against his presbytery, as well as in the Scotch courts, without his clerical superiors being able to remove him from his parish. I believe the litigation only closed with the man's death, but as I am without the advantage of possessing the volume, and Mr. Clason not being alive, I cannot speak with certainty as to this.

At the end of an hour my friend, whose humorous face I think I have now before me, looked in at the door, and said, "How do you get on?" "Oh, pray, don't hurry yourself; I cannot lay this book down at present." "How far have you got in it?" "Quite far enough to satisfy me that before I finish it I shall find the reverend gentleman had broken all the commandments that came to us from Mount Sinai." "Not exactly," said my learned friend, "for he avoided the committal of murder."

We had a hearty laugh at lunch over the contents of the volume, which Mr. Clason confessed to me was the most valuable work in his library, inasmuch as no cooling draught administered to a feverish patient by his medical adviser was ever more efficacious in mitigating and assuaging the impatience of a waiting client.

164. *The Weather in Scotland is a Delicate Subject for a Visitor to criticise with a Native.*

"Well, John, this is a very wet day." "No ava (not at all), sir," replied John, rather sternly. "It's a wee saft (somewhat moist), but it's no a *wat* day. *Raley*, sir, it *provoks* me at times to hear the remarks *o'* some *o'* the Englishers. I recollect an English leddy who *cam* here a few years *syne* (since), and she *wrot* to her *friens* that she had been a week in *Scoteland*, and had never seen a dry day nor a smiling face, and would remain *nae langer*. Noo, sir, you *maun* (must) admit it's *vera wrang* for any wooman, leddy or no leddy, to write in that *mainer aboot ony kintra, mair speeciallie Scoteland*, the *kintra aboon a' ithers* (above all others) that every *ane o'* them, gentle or simple (high or low), be they English or American, ay, or French or Spanish—the bonnie Empress *o'* the French *o'* the number—are *sae* proud to *brag o'* (boast of), for *gin* (if) they hae a *drap o'* Scotia's bluid in their veins, *they're shure* to tell you *o't* (of it), let them *alane* for that; and then to talk *o'* the *wather* (weather) as if Providence *didna* (did not) *ken* (know) *hoo* (how) to regulate the elements. Na, na, I'm no the man to say that Scotch folks *haena* their *fauts* (have not their faults) as weel as English, but I will say this, they get *awsomely* (terribly) spoilt and contaminated after they *gang amang* the *Southrons* (among the English); they are *a' recht eneuch* (all right enough) while they're at hame. Ma faither *ance wus* sairly tried *wi'* his ain brother in the *Wast* Indies as to the *mainer* in which he received ma brither oot there, for it showed *raal* clear *hoo* Scotchmen get altered from what they *wur* afore they left their ain *chimla-lug* (fireside). Ma faither said to ma brither, 'Willie, there's *naething* for you, my dear lad, to do at *hame;* you'd better *gang oot* to your uncle in the *Wast* Indies,' which Willie vera properly at *ance* said he *waud* do, or *ony* thing else, puir fallow, his faither wished *o'* him. Accordingly, ma faither fitted oot Willie, and ma mither pack't his *kist* (box) fu (full) *o'* sarks (shirts) and *nice claes* (good clothes), and sent him *ower* the sea to Liverpool, and got a frien there to *tak* a passage for him in a ship for the *Wast* Indies, to the place *whar* his uncle *wus. Noo*, the fact is, ma uncle had become a great man *oot* there, although when he first went to a distant land, I *hae hard* ma faither *aften* say, he *wus onnly* a bit *o'* a *clark* or an *owerseer* to the *blaiks* (blacks). Weel, on his landing *frae* the ship he *gaed* strecht (went straight) to his uncle, wha (who) *recaived* him *vera cauldly*, which *wus eneuch* to *dumfoonder* ony *puir* lad. 'Who are you?' said his uncle. 'I'm *yur* ain *brither's* son, sir, and of a consequence *yure nevy*'—a vera discreet and proper answer for ma brither to *mak*. 'Hoo (how) am I to know that?' and he said it in a vera angry tone o' voice. Wasn't it *eneuch* (enough) to *brak doon ony* lad's *speerit?* 'Where's your letter o' introduction to me?' said his uncle. 'Ma faither, sir, didna think there *wus* ony need for me to bring a bit o' a note to you.' 'The deuce he didn't!' *wus* the answer ma brither got to this. 'Hoo (how) am I to ken (know) that you are not a young scamp?' Wasn't that an *awfu* remark to *drap frae* his lips? But ma brither's bluid *wus* a *wee* up at this, and he said—for he *tellt* me the *hale* (whole) story in his letter—'Oh, sir, I was always vera respectable, and I never *gied ma friens* (gave my friends) ony trouble or vexation except that they *cou'dna fin* (could not find) ony employment for me *aboot* the farm, which is the cause o' ma coming oot to the *Wast* Indies.' His uncle then *lookit* him recht through and *a' ower*, and *tellt* him he cou'd see nae family likeness, to which ma brither *doucely* (prudently) made answer—for he *wus* always a vera *respectfu* lad, *wi'* (with) nice *mainers* o' his ain—'I assure you, sir, *yur ain* brither is ma faither.' To this his uncle vera unkindly remarked, 'I fear a strange bull then must *hae* strayed into the pastures, as *ma* brither could never be *sae* fool-like a man as to send a son o' his *oot* to the *Wast* Indies without a letter o' introduction.' 'But he did *sae*, I assure you, sir, and I'm speaking *naething* but the *trowth*.' 'Weel,' said ma uncle, who *aifter a' wus* a *vera guid*-hairted man, 'I thocht, when I left Scoteland, there was mair (more) common-sense in *ma* family there than appears to be the case.' That remark, when ma faither read it in ma brither's letter, stuck into him *awfu*. He then took *anither awsom* keen *glowr* (look) at Willie, and then handed him a bit piece o' paper and a quill (a pen), at the same time pushing the inkstand *afore* him, 'as he wished,' he said, 'to see what kind *o'* hand *o'* write his was.' Weel, when he saw it, he *tellt* Willie it was a *confoondedly* bad stick; but ma brither, who had been sairly tried that day by his uncle, never *ance* lost *himsel* the least in his replies, for he *wus* a shrewd *Scoatch callan* (lad, boy), and but for that he would hae been *druven* (driven) *distrackit* (distracted); he juist met it candidly by telling his uncle that he had been *waur* (worse) at the writing at school than *ony* thing else, and that it *wus* a *la-mentable* fact. *Hooever*, ma uncle began at last to take to *ma brither*, and behaved *vera* cleverly (very kindly) to him, and vera soon, by my faith, made a man *o'* him. Ma faither, *aifter* being weel *blawn* (blown) up by his *brither*, began to be *o'* opinion that it would hae been the better *coorse* to *hae gien* (have given) Willie a bit *o'* a line *o'* introduction at first to his uncle, but *ma faither* never *liket* to be thocht *wrang*, and nae Scotchman does, for it's unco (very) seldom they are wrang."

165. *Colonel James Alexander Farquharson, of the 25th (Borderers).*

"Jemmy Farquharson," as he was known in the service, was a choice specimen of the fine old soldier. He possessed those attributes which endeared him to his officers and gained him the respect and confidence of his men. He was imbued in an eminent degree with strong common-sense—a combination of firmness and decision, of kindness and impartiality. Like Admiral Pakenham of the end of the last century, Jemmy had not studied the parliamentary language of the present day, and was at times somewhat foul-mouthed; nevertheless he had the gift of being able "to win the soldier's heart," and they, in return, were proud of their captain and loved him.

My gallant and esteemed friend, Colonel Paschal, a

survivor of the Peninsula and Waterloo, had served under Farquharson in the Borderers, and has made me laugh heartily in his recital of some of his *memorabilia* of my countrymen. On one occasion the master-tailor of the regiment was brought up for misappropriating five-and-twenty shell jackets, and the charge being proved he was sentenced to be reduced, with an addition of 150 lashes. Before the latter part of the sentence was carried out he ordered all the tailors in the regiment to be paraded, and then addressed them: "I have always been given to understand that it took nine tailors to make a man, but I can safely say that every tailor in this regiment gives me more trouble than any nine men.—Drum-major, make those drummers do their duty!" The colonel was ever ready with an answer, always appropriate, and generally accompanied with some of the spice of Theodore Hook. One of the captains had arranged with a young officer to assist him in keeping the companies' accounts; he wrote a beautiful hand, but so small that he could put on one side of a sheet of paper as much as would have fairly filled four. The general (Gordon Forbes) was making one of his half-yearly inspections, and in looking over the accounts, was puzzled with the quantity of matter crammed into so small a space, and asked the colonel the meaning of it, saying, "There is no fault to be found in the manner this ledger is kept; it is like copper-plate; but why crowd so much in so small a space?" "Economy, general, economy; we are a Scotch regiment."

A Roman Catholic soldier had given the regiment a great deal of trouble by deserting; the colonel sent for the man: the sentence of corporal punishment, it was thought, was about to take place; but he had made up his mind to remit it. He questioned the culprit as to what was his religion; to which he replied, "I ought, *sor*, to be of the Roman Catholic." "So I would have sworn.—Sergeant-major, fetch me that little cross I have had made for the purpose of trying to make men of that creed true to their colors." The Sergeant-major returned with the cross, a very large black one. He now desired the culprit to go down on his knees and hold up the cross; and then pronounced the oath, which the delinquent had to repeat word by word, which was to the effect that, if he ever again committed a like offence, he hoped to suffer the flames and horrors of a certain region to an extent "worse than fables yet have feigned or fear conceived." The gallant colonel is said to have told him, if not in the precise words of Dryden, at least in substance, what he would suffer elsewhere —"Eternal torments, baths of boiling sulphur, vicissitudes of fires," etc. In dismissing the man, he added, "But I have something more still to tell you, which is, that if you desert again, may I be hanged if I should like to stand in your shoes."

Upon another occasion, on the general inspecting asking the men if they had any thing to complain of, one of them stepped out and made a charge against his colonel, which, being investigated, proved to be groundless. Some time afterward this man was sentenced for drunkenness, or some other offence, to fifty or one hundred lashes, and was brought up to the triangles, but Farquharson said, "Take him down," and, addressing the prisoner, "*You know* why I don't punish you."

The 25th and the 42d Highlanders were in Dublin together, and, at the relief of guards, an officer of the 25th was expatiating to the Highland officer, in the hearing of the men of both corps, that his colonel (Farquharson) was the stingiest man in the British Army; that even the uniform coat he wore had been turned. One of the men, who heard this and was annoyed, told Farquharson, and at the next parade he addressed the regiment, formed in square for the purpose and faced inward, officers in front: "I understand there is an officer in my regiment who knows my domestic arrangements so intimately as to be able to inform you that I have even had my uniform coat turned, which is quite true, and (holding up his arm) an excellent turn it makes; but it is far from candid—indeed, it is very unfair—that this officer, who studies my domestic economy so minutely, should not have told you, while discussing the subject of my old coat with you, that I had just received a spick and span new coat from Buckmaster, which I have never yet had on." The officer who had been so communicative regarding his colonel's parsimony dropped his sword and came up to Farquharson, who at once met him. "Fall in, Mr. K.; I have mentioned no names." Farquharson was in the West Indies when the governorship of the Island of Trinidad suddenly became vacant, and being the senior officer at the time in command of the troops, immediately left the island he was at for Trinidad, to take upon himself the duties of Governor *pro tem.* On his arrival he was surprised to find that Sir Charles Smith, of the Engineers, had assumed this position, and refused to acknowledge Farquharson's right to supersede him. However, the claimant for the vice-royalty of His Majesty's Island of Trinidad was the last man in the British Army to tolerate for an instant a glaring case of usurpation. He demanded formally his colonial crown from Smith, who, after—we must assume—consulting the attorney-general and the other authorities of the island, yielded, telling Colonel Farquharson that he would complain to the Colonial Office. "So shall I," said Jemmy. On the affair being finally closed, Farquharson wrote an amusing letter, which my friend Colonel Paschal saw, to Bob Terry, a captain in the Borderers, giving a graphic account of the proceedings, in which he explained that Sir Charles Smith had deprived him of the command the precise number of days that Jonah was in the whale's belly.

In reply to Farquharson's letter, the Colonial Secretary wrote: "You, as the senior officer in the command, were right in assuming the government of Trinidad;" and then Farquharson writes, in continuation to Terry, "and I leave you to guess what the knight got."

166. *The* Meets *outside, and the* Meats *inside, the Oatlands Park Hotel.*

A laughable scene was witnessed at Oatlands—where I wrote my first anecdote, and now write this (I hope not) my last—at the beginning of the present hunting-season.

A smart four-in-hand drove up, and its owner was met at the portico of this most delightful of all English country hotels by a German waiter, who was asked, "What meets have you in this neighborhood?" "Vat meats, *mi Lor;* vy *kalt* roast beef, *mi Lor*, *kalt* roast lamb, *kalt shicken vith am, und kalt* tongue." Roars of laughter from the outside and inside passengers of the drag. "My good fellow, I mean meets." "Yase, *mi Lor*, hi knows you does." At this juncture, the head-waiter, himself a wag, arrived on the scene; having got a hint from one of his colleagues as to what was passing, and believing that a rehearsal would not be unpalatable—as several of the hotel visitors had already reached the portico—looked gravely at the poor disconcerted German, and asked for an explanation. "Vy, Robert, I did tell *mi Lor* that ve ad *kalt* roast beef—" going through the list to his *chef de salon* most carefully, amid peals of laughter. After this, Robert explained the *meets* outside the hotel; but the German had been so lucid to the dragsmen that they resolved to become at once acquainted with the *meats* inside, leaving those outside for another day.

APPENDIX.

As I hope that my "Reminiscences" may meet with readers in both Australia and New Zealand, though I am no longer personally interested in either colony, beyond entertaining a sincere desire for their continued prosperity and rapid development, I trust I shall be allowed to say something beyond what has appeared in my Dedication, without incurring the charge of egotism.

To the generation that has sprung up since the period to which I refer, I can state as a fact that I devoted much time and money to the practical advancement of the cause of emigration, in the hope of promoting the best interests of Australia, the fifth quarter of the globe. Now that the question of emigration has become so prominent, for we find the leading members of successive administrations viewing it with a far deeper interest than I ever previously recollect, I can look with satisfaction to the evidence I hold that the share which I took in furtherance of Australian emigration was not wholly in vain. I devoted my labors to that point, because I knew the vital importance of diverting to our own colonies some portion of the stream which was then flowing, exclusively or nearly so, in the direction of the Great Republic of the West. I may, perhaps, be further excused if I allude with a feeling of pride to the large proportions assumed to our Australian movement in the inauguration of which I took so great a share. I have now before me the letter of a very able man, Mr. J. A. Jackson, formerly Colonial Secretary in South Australia, who thus addressed me after perusing a pamphlet which I wrote in connection with our public efforts on behalf of

Australian affairs in London and throughout the United Kingdom:

"Paris, February 16, 1864.

"My dear Mr. Boyd—I have read through your pamphlet, which, while it reaches many of the details of your services, was not necessary to remind *me* of what I have often felt pleasure in testifying to—your great, untiring, and well-directed exertions on behalf of Australian interests.

"To the mass of people, however, the pamphlet would be indispensable to give them any *idea* of the part you played ten years ago: but no pamphlet can make the generality of people understand the amount of patient labor and the tact required to set in motion that outward agitation which admits of being narrated in the public prints.

"I am, my dear Mr. Boyd,
"Very faithfully yours,
"J. A. Jackson.

"M. Boyd, Esq.,
"Merton Hall, Newton Stewart, N. B."

I was no less gratified by the expressed opinion of the Hon. Francis Scott (M. P. for Roxburghshire, and afterward for Berwickshire), who labored unceasingly during a series of years to advance Australian interests, the honorable member being at that time the recognized organ of the colony in the House of Commons. In writing to me on June 6, 1857, he thus expresses himself, and the pleasure of his communication was greatly enhanced by the manner in which he recognizes the efforts of one who had passed away five years previously:

"I have no hesitation in saying that many, indeed most, of the measures adopted by the Government for the promotion of the material interests of the colony, as regards the disposition of land and supply and employment of labor, had either been suggested in the first instance, or powerfully urged upon the Government by your brother and those who took the same view of advancing the prosperity of the colony; and that those measures were in no small degree promoted by your exertions in this country, the fact, therefore, being that Government adopted the measures recommended, and that those measures proved beneficial to the colony, is no small evidence of the foresight of the original promoters. I am likewise of opinion that no small portion of the disasters which overtook the colonies during the period referred to, was owing to the delay of the Government in adopting those measures."

It may, perhaps, appear by writing this statement, which I only wish my colonial friends to peruse, that (to use the word recently coined by a distinguished writer) I have reached my "anec-dotage," but the fact is, I suffered some chagrin a few years since, by others endeavoring to appropriate to themselves merits to which they were scarcely entitled, for having kept Australian questions alive in this country. As Mr. Disraeli once felicitously observed of the Whigs: "They caught us bathing, and ran away with our clothes." I felt then called upon to defend our position, and with the following extract I close the subject, and hope my readers have found something more interesting in my "Reminiscences" than in my "Appendix."

It may appear somewhat out of place to bring forward the following extract from Francis's "Chronicles and Characters of 'Change;" but considering myself called upon to give an outline of the nature and extent of the efforts made by my late brother and myself to promote Australian interests, I am entitled to produce any testimony in my possession to prove that in what we did, in conjunction with others, the welfare of all classes of the Australian community was strictly and conscientiously in view. The author, in allusion to emigration and to my brother, says:

"The efforts of Mr. Benjamin Boyd will form an important chapter in some future history of our Australian colonies, as from his determined energy an impulse has been given to emigration which no future official supineness can eradicate," etc.

I also extract from a review of Mr. Francis's work the following:

"Preceding gazettes will show the interest we have taken in this important movement" (emigration), "with which the name of the Hon. Francis Scott must ever be associated, and also the labors of Mr. Boyd's brothers and friends in England, whose unflagging zeal contributed so much to the formation of the Colonization Society and the commencement of the colonization crusade now in progress."

THE END.

POPULAR WORKS OF FICTION

PUBLISHED BY

D. APPLETON & CO.,

549 & 551 Broadway, New York.

APPLETONS'

ILLUSTRATED LIBRARY OF ROMANCE.

In uniform octavo volumes,

Handsomely illustrated, and bound either in paper covers, or in muslin.

Price, in Paper, $1.00; in Cloth, $1.50.

*** In this series of Romances are included the famous novels of LOUISA MUHLBACH. Since the time when Sir Walter Scott produced so profound a sensation in the reading-world, no historical novels have achieved a success so great as those from the pen of Miss MUHLBACH.

1. **TOO STRANGE NOT TO BE TRUE.** A Novel. By Lady Georgiana Fullerton.
2. **THE CLEVER WOMAN OF THE FAMILY.** By Miss Yonge, author of "The Heir of Redclyffe," "Heartsease," etc.
3. **JOSEPH II. AND HIS COURT.** By Louisa Muhlbach.
4. **FREDERICK THE GREAT AND HIS COURT.** By Louisa Muhlbach.
5. **BERLIN AND SANS-SOUCI; or, FREDERICK THE GREAT AND HIS FRIENDS.** By Louisa Muhlbach.
6. **THE MERCHANT OF BERLIN.** By Louisa Muhlbach.
7. **FREDERICK THE GREAT AND HIS FAMILY.** By Louisa Muhlbach.
8. **HENRY VIII. AND CATHARINE PARR.** By Louisa Muhlbach.
9. **LOUISA OF PRUSSIA AND HER TIMES.** By Louisa Muhlbach.
10. **MARIE ANTOINETTE AND HER SON.** By Louisa Muhlbach.

11. **THE DAUGHTER OF AN EMPRESS.** By Louisa Muhlbach.
12. **NAPOLEON AND THE QUEEN OF PRUSSIA.** By Louisa Muhlbach.
13. **THE EMPRESS JOSEPHINE.** By Louisa Muhlbach.
14. **NAPOLEON AND BLUCHER.** An Historical Romance. By Louisa Muhlbach.
15. **COUNT MIRABEAU.** An Historical Novel. By Theodor Mundt.
16. **A STORMY LIFE.** A Novel. By Lady Georgiana Fullerton, author of "Too Strange not to be True."
17. **OLD FRITZ AND THE NEW ERA.** By Louisa Muhlbach.
18. **ANDREAS HOFER.** By Louisa Muhlbach.
19. **DORA.** By Julia Kavanagh.
20. **JOHN MILTON AND HIS TIMES.** By Max Ring.
21. **BEAUMARCHAIS.** An Historical Tale. By A E. Brachvogel.
22. **GOETHE AND SCHILLER.** By Louisa Muhlbach.
23. **A CHAPLET OF PEARLS.** By Miss Yonge.

Grace Aguilar.

HOME INFLUENCE. 12mo. Cloth. $1.00.

MOTHER'S RECOMPENSE. 12mo. Cloth. $1.00.

HOME SCENES AND HEART STUDIES. 12mo. Cloth. $1.00.

DAYS OF BRUCE. 2 vols. 12mo. Cloth. $2.00.

WOMAN'S FRIENDSHIP. 12mo. Cloth. $1.00.

WOMEN OF ISRAEL. 2 vols., 12mo. Cloth. $2.00.

VALE OF CEDARS. 12mo. Cloth. $1.00.

"Grace Aguilar's works possess attractions which will always place them among the standard writings which no library can be without. 'Mother's Recompense' and 'Woman's Friendship' should be read by both young and old."

W. Arthur.

THE SUCCESSFUL MERCHANT. 1 vol., 12mo. Cloth. $1.

J. B. Bouton.

ROUND THE BLOCK. A new American Novel. Illustrated. 1 vol., 12mo. Cloth. $1.50.

"Unlike most novels that now appear, it has no 'mission,' the author being neither a politician nor a reformer, but a story-teller, according to the old pattern; and a capital story he has produced, written in the happiest style."

F. Caballero.

ELIA; or, Spain Fifty Years Ago. A Novel. 1 vol., 12mo. Cloth. $1.

Mary Cowden Clarke.

THE IRON COUSIN. A Tale. 1 vol., 12mo. Cloth. $1.50.

"The story is too deeply interesting to allow the reader to lay it down till he has read it to the end."

Charles Dickens.

The Cheap Popular Edition of the Works of Chas. Dickens. Clear type, handsomely printed, and of convenient size. 18 vols., 8vo. Paper.

	Pages.	Cts.
OLIVER TWIST	172	25
AMERICAN NOTES	104	15
DOMBEY & SON	356	35
MARTIN CHUZZLEWIT	342	35
OUR MUTUAL FRIEND	330	35
CHRISTMAS STORIES	162	25
TALE OF TWO CITIES	144	20
HARD TIMES, and ADDITIONAL CHRISTMAS STORIES	200	25
BLEAK HOUSE	340	35
NICHOLAS NICKLEBY	340	35
LITTLE DORRIT	330	35
PICKWICK PAPERS	326	35
DAVID COPPERFIELD	351	35
BARNABY RUDGE	257	30
OLD CURIOSITY SHOP	221	30
SKETCHES	196	25
GREAT EXPECTATIONS	184	25
UNCOMMERCIAL TRAVELLER, PICTURES FROM ITALY, etc.	300	35

THE COMPLETE POPULAR LIBRARY EDITION. Handsomely printed in good, clear type. Illustrated with 32 Engravings, and a Steel-plate Portrait of the Author. 6 vols., small 8vo. Cloth, extra. $10.50.

OUR MUTUAL FRIEND. With Illustrations by Marcus Stoue. London edition. 2 vols., 12mo. Scarlet Cloth, $5.00; Half Calf, $9.

Mrs. Ellis.

HEARTS AND HOMES; or, Social Distinctions. A Story. 1 vol., 8vo. Cloth. $2.

"There is a charm about this lady's productions that is extremely fascinating. For grace and ease of narrative, she is unsurpassed; her fictions always breathe a healthy moral."

Margaret Field.

BERTHA PERCY; or, L'Esperance. 1 vol., 12mo. Cloth. $1.

"A book of great power and fascination. . . . . . In its pictures of home life, it reminds one of Fredrika Bremer's earlier and better novels, but it possesses much more than Fredrika Bremer's descriptive power."

Julia Kavanagh.

ADELE. A Tale. 1 thick vol. 12mo. Cloth. $1.50.

BEATRICE. 12mo. Cloth. $1.50.

DAISY BURNS. 12mo. Cloth. $1.50.

GRACE LEE. 12mo. Cloth. $1.50.

MADELINE. 12mo. Cloth. $1.

NATHALIE. A Tale. 12mo. Cloth. $1.50.

RACHEL GRAY. 12mo. Cloth. $1.

QUEEN MAB. 12mo. Cloth. $1.50.

SEVEN YEARS, and Other Tales. 12mo. Cloth. $1.

SYBIL'S SECOND LOVE. 12mo. Cloth. $1.50.

WOMEN OF CHRISTIANITY, Exemplary for Piety and Charity. 12mo. Cloth. $1.

DORA. Illustrated by Gaston Fay. 1 vol., 8vo. Paper, $1.00. Cloth. $1.50.

"There is a quiet power in the writings of this gifted author, which is as far removed from the sensational school as any of the modern novels can be."

Margaret Lee.

DR. WILMER'S LOVE; or A Question of Conscience. A Novel. 1 vol., 12mo. Cloth. $1.25.

Olive Logan.

CHATEAU FRISSAC; or, Home Scenes in France. Authoress of "Photographs of Paris Life." 1 vol., 12mo. Cloth. $1.25.

Maria J. Macintosh.

AUNT KITTY'S TALES. 12mo. Cloth. $1.

CHARMS AND COUNTER CHARMS. 12mo. Cloth. $1.25.

TWO PICTURES; or, How We See Ourselves, and How the World Sees Us. 1 vol., 12mo. Cloth. $1.50.

EVENINGS AT DONALDSON MANOR. 1 vol., 12mo. Cloth. $1.

TWO LIVES; or, To Seem and To Be. 12mo. Cloth. $1.

THE LOFTY AND LOWLY. 2 vols, 12mo. Cloth. $1.50.

"Miss Macintosh is one of the best of the female writers of the day. Her stories are always full of lessons of truth, and purity, and goodness, of that serene and gentle wisdom which comes from no source so fitly as from a refined and Christian woman."

Alice B. Haven.

The COOPERS; or Getting Under Way. A Tale of Real Life. 1 vol., 12mo. Cloth. $1.

LOSS AND GAIN; or, Margaret's Home. 1 vol., 12mo. Cloth. $1.

The lamented Cousin Alice, better known as the author of numerous juvenile works of a popular character, only wrote two works of fiction, which evidence that she could have met with equal success in that walk of literature. They both bear the impress of a mind whose purity of heart was proverbial.

Helen Modet.

LIGHT. A Novel. 1 vol., 12mo. Cloth. $1.

Miss Warner.

THE HILLS OF THE SHATEMUC. 1 vol., 12mo. Cloth. $1.25.

MY BROTHER'S KEEPER. 1 vol., 12mo. Cloth. $1.25.

Sarah A. Wentz.

SMILES AND FROWNS. A Novel. 1 vol., 12mo. Cloth. $1.25.

Anonymous.

COMETH UP AS A FLOWER. An Autobiography. 1 vol., 8vo. Paper covers. 60 cents.

NOT WISELY, BUT TOO WELL. By the Author of "Cometh up as a Flower." 1 vol., 8vo. Paper covers. 60 cents.

The name of the author of the above is still buried in obscurity. The sensation which was created by the publication of "Cometh up as a Flower" remains unabated, as the daily increasing demand abundantly testifies. No work, since the appearance of "Jane Eyre," has met with greater success.

LADY ALICE; or, The New Una. A Novel. New edition. Paper. 60 cents.

MADGE; or, Night and Morning. A Novel. 1 vol., 12mo. Cloth. $1.25.

SHERBROOKE. By H. B. G., author of "Madge." 1 vol., 12mo. Cloth. $1.25.

MARY STAUNTON: or, The Pupils of Marvel Hall. By the Author of "Portraits of My Married Friends." 1 vol., 12mo. Cloth. $1.

MINISTRY OF LIFE. By the Author of "Ministering Children." Illustrated. 1 vol., 12mo. Cloth. $1.25.

THE VIRGINIA COMEDIANS; or, Old Days in the Old Dominion. 2 vols., 12mo. Cloth. $2.50.

WIFE'S STRATAGEM. A Story for Fireside and Wayside. By Aunt Fanny. Illustrated. 1 vol., 12mo. Cloth. $1.

www.ingramcontent.com/pod-product-compliance
Lightning Source LLC
LaVergne TN
LVHW020116110826
845151LV00001B/179

* 9 7 8 1 4 2 5 5 4 2 6 4 1 *